C0-BPF-397

Woman in America

AMERICAN STUDIES INFORMATION GUIDE SERIES

Series Editor: Donald Koster, Professor of English Emeritus, Adelphi University, Garden City, New York

Also in this series:

AFRO-AMERICAN LITERATURE AND CULTURE SINCE WORLD WAR II—*Edited by Charles D. Peavy*

AMERICAN ARCHITECTURE AND ART—*Edited by David M. Sokol*

AMERICAN HUMOR AND HUMORISTS—*Edited by M. Thomas Inge**

AMERICAN LANGUAGE AND LITERATURE—*Edited by Henry Wasser**

AMERICAN POPULAR CULTURE—*Edited by Larry Landrum**

THE AMERICAN PRESIDENCY—*Edited by Kenneth E. Davison**

AMERICAN RELIGION AND PHILOSOPHY—*Edited by Ernest R. Sandeen and Frederick Hale*

AMERICAN STUDIES—*Edited by David W. Marcell**

ANTHROPOLOGY OF THE AMERICAS—*Edited by Thomas C. Greaves**

EDUCATION IN AMERICA—*Edited by Richard G. Durnin**

HISTORY OF THE UNITED STATES OF AMERICA—*Edited by Ernest Cassara*

NORTH AMERICAN JEWISH LITERATURE—*Edited by Ira Bruce Nadel**

SOCIOLOGY OF AMERICA—*Edited by Charles Mark*

THE RELATIONSHIP OF PAINTING AND LITERATURE—*Edited by Eugene L. Huddleston and Douglas A. Noverr*

TECHNOLOGY AND HUMAN VALUES IN AMERICAN CIVILIZATION—*Edited by Stephen Cutliff, Judith A. Mistichelli, and Christine M. Roysdon**

*in preparation

The above series is part of the
GALE INFORMATION GUIDE LIBRARY

The Library consists of a number of separate series of guides covering major areas in the social sciences, humanities, and current affairs.

General Editor: Paul Wasserman, Professor and former Dean, School of Library and Information Services, University of Maryland

Managing Editor: Denise Allard Adzigian, Gale Research Company

Woman in America

A GUIDE TO INFORMATION SOURCES

Volume 7 in the American Studies Information Guide Series

Virginia R. Terris

Associate Professor
Department of English
Adelphi University
Garden City, New York

Gale Research Company
Book Tower, Detroit, Michigan 48226

Library of Congress Cataloging in Publication Data

Terris, Virginia R
Woman in America.

(American studies information guide series ; v. 7)
(Gale information guide library)
Includes indexes.
1. Women—United States—Bibliography. 2. Women's studies—United States—Bibliography. 3. Women—Information services—United States. I. Title.
Z7964.U49T45 [HQ1426] 016.30141'2'0973
ISBN 0-8103-1268-9 73-17564

Copyright © 1980 by
Virginia R. Terris

No part of this book may be reproduced in any form without permission in writing from the publisher, except by a reviewer who wishes to quote brief passages or entries in connection with a review written for inclusion in a magazine or newspaper. Manufactured in the United States of America.

APR 2 6 1982

Reference
Z
7964
.U49
T45

RESEARCHING

all that life women were noting down
falls in through my eyes
    women preparing food
    women bearing children
    women weeping
    women keeping silent

falls into me. . .

VITA

Virginia R. Terris is an associate professor of English at Adelphi University. She has been chairperson of Committee W of Adelphi University American Association of University Professors and a member of the state Committee W of that organization. She has organized and taught courses on women in literature at Adelphi as well as written on Muriel Rukeyser in the AMERICAN POETRY REVIEW and taped lectures on Emily Dickinson and Muriel Rukeyser. She has reviewed books and periodicals for the AMERICAN QUARTERLY and coedited THE MANY WORLDS OF POETRY, an anthology published by Alfred A. Knopf. TRACKING, a volume of poems, has been published by the University of Illinois Press. She received her B.A. from Douglass College (formerly New Jersey College for Women), her M.A. from Adelphi University, and Ph.D. from New York University.

CONTENTS

Contents

FOREWORD

When this series of information guides to research in American Studies was being planned, I was quite certain that a volume should be devoted to the history and role of woman in American society, a field of scholarly interest growing at a rapid pace. To get the right person to do the job would not, however, be easy. The talents required appeared to me to be tenacity of purpose, experience in scholarship, skill in tracking down innumerable sources in a field so relatively new as to be still chaotic, and an unswerving devotion to the subject.

Fortunately for me and for the series, I found the right person just across the hall from my office. She is my colleague in the department of English at Adelphi University, Professor Virginia R. Terris. In addition to possessing the combination of talents enumerated above, she is also a poet of distinction, assuring that she would bring to the work a quality of imagination and perceptivity that might prove to be invaluable upon occasion.

It is a great pleasure for me to be able to say that Professor Terris has exceeded my most optimistic expectations in what she has done. I am quite sure that no other volume exists that has even begun to bring together such a mine of information on materials for the study of the part women have played in American civilization as has Professor Terris's book. Her achievement is indeed unique, and I am confident that its value will be appreciated for years to come.

Donald N. Koster
Series Editor

PREFACE

The purpose of this volume is to suggest the possibilities for research into the lives of American women rather than to define the directions the research should take. Since the material that follows will be accessible both to the skilled researcher and to those who are only beginning to familiarize themselves with the subject, I have been faced with difficult decisions regarding selection of material and favored the more general readership but, hopefully, neglected no seeker of information.

No one can argue that the experience of the American woman has not been, in the past, almost completely neglected by American scholarship. The "proper sphere of woman" and the rest of her experiences as well, cornerstones of American history and culture, have been deemed unworthy of record, and, if recorded, unworthy of serious and prolonged consideration. Only today, when the nature of history itself is being redefined, is the significance of woman's experience beginning to receive the attention it deserves.

Because the sources listed in the past have so frequently served to support a narrow view of American experience, the researcher using this bibliography may find fewer of the traditional sources than usual, and obscure and what may seem ephemeral ones in considerable number. Along with the works of "great" women are the modest works of lesser-known or virtually unknown women, along with the histories of white women the lamentably few of black and other minority women.

The newness of the field of women's studies causes it to draw, as suggested, as much on informal as on formal material. Much critical information relating to the history and activities of women is appearing in leaflet and stapled mimeograph form. Securing such material is a problem, since it is frequently available only to local researchers and rapidly goes out of print. Some excellent bibliographies (printed for only a small group that needs specialized information at a certain moment) are, therefore, for all purposes, unavailable.

As this project has moved forward, I have, more than once, trembled before the enormous amount of material confronting me. Most of the material, at one time or another, I have had in hand. In some instances, material that is unannotated indicates that it was unavailable to me; most often, it indicates that the title is self-explanatory. Much of the pamphlet material in print is available upon request. Yet so unpredictable is the economy at present that the reader is advised to write for price information before ordering.

A word about terminology. I wholeheartedly accept Sheila Rowbotham's definition of the word "feminism"--"the assertion of the need to improve the position of women." The phrase "women's movement," as I have used it, refers to the attempts by women since the first half of the nineteenth century to fulfill that need for improvement through social action; "women's liberation" refers to the recent twentieth-century movement.

The lack of regular assistance as I gathered material for this project has created problems for me at times. But whenever I sought assistance, I found it plentiful. In general, as my fellow faculty members at Adelphi University became aware of my seeking out material on American women, they directed many items to me. I wish to thank them for their interest. I gratefully acknowledge the help of librarians at the New York Public Library; at the Galatea Women's Collection of the Boston Public Library; at the Freeport, New York, Memorial Library; at the Nassau Library System center in Garden City, New York; and especially the reference and acquisitions librarians at Adelphi University. Many library items have been made available to me through interlibrary loan. The hundreds of women who have given me information over the telephone I wish now to thank, and, in addition, Dr. Jane Selby of the Northwestern School of Dentistry; Jacqueline G. McGert of the Thomas Holgate Collection, Bennett College, Greensboro, North Carolina; Jane Gould and Emily Kofron at the Barnard Women's Center; Judith Pask of the Kannert Graduate School of Management, Purdue University; and Belita Cowan. At Adelphi University I should like to mention in particular Dr. Jean Graubert, who opened her collection of books on mental health and sexuality to me, and Dr. Marlyn Dalsimer, who helped me in political areas. In the reference section of Adelphi University Library, Carol Schroeder, Lois Novas, Marilyn Sternberg, Marilyn Lesser, and Estelle Herskovitz were helpful, and especially Doris Johnson, head of the reference services, whose knowledge of sources is awesome. In the Acquisitions Department I wish to thank Philip Zingales and Rose Segre. I wish to thank Eleanor Batchelder and the staff at Womanbooks and also Alida Roochvarg, who allowed me to rifle on many occasions the stock of her Paperback Bookseller in Hempstead, New York. I am grateful to Hester Meigs who kept me informed of the bibliographic project she was undertaking for the American Association of University Women.

Of friends I should like to mention Olga Drucker and David Ignatow; of family, Susan and Enoch Terris. Louise Loveall, who made a successful transition from ecology to women's history almost overnight, has been an invaluable assistant in all stages of the work. Ann Gerber and Florence O'Connor have patiently typed, retyped, and deciphered the illegible. And, finally, a store of gratitude goes to Dr. Donald N. Koster, editor of the series, whose patience and support has enabled me to complete this project.

Chapter 1
GENERAL REFERENCES

A. INTRODUCTION TO SOURCES

Research in women's studies derives part of its uniqueness from the inapplicability of traditional source materials that other disciplines draw upon. Sources such as the DICTIONARY OF AMERICAN BIOGRAPHY, that were written by a particular segment of American society for use by its own members, are relatively useless to women's studies projects, though their bias may well serve as a subject for investigation and commentary. Thus, similar material that has long served as a staple in American scholarship has excluded itself from a place in this volume.

At the same time, a renewal of interest in women's place in American life is coinciding with a demand for more efficient means of gathering and distributing information in our mass society. New research tools, among them computers and information centers, are offering to scholarship funds of knowledge that would be otherwise difficult to acquire. Indeed the researcher on the subject of women is faced with bewildering quantities of information--bewildering but also exciting and demanding of investigation.

It is suggested that those using this volume explore, in addition to the sources and resources listed, the SUBJECT GUIDE TO BOOKS IN PRINT, which has been issued continuously since 1957; and the CUMULATIVE PAPERBACK INDEX, 1939-1959: A COMPREHENSIVE BIBLIOGRAPHIC GUIDE TO 14,000 MASS-MARKET PAPERBACK BOOKS OF 33 PUBLISHERS ISSUED UNDER 69 IMPRINTS compiled by Robert Reginald and M.R. Burgess. The first of the two is particularly useful in locating volumes by women currently in print, as are the catalogs issued by publishers, many of whom are now putting out special series of titles relating to women. Reprint houses, such as the Arno Press, Greenwood Press and Source Book Press, are reissuing books that have been long out of print, many of which are listed in the yearly GUIDE TO REPRINTS BULLETIN. It is almost too obvious to mention that women's publishing houses, such as the Feminist Press (see p. 63) and KNOW (see p. 81) engage solely in the printing and reprinting of books and pamphlet material by and about women. Women's bookstores, supplied by distributors such as Ragwomen, thrive in many cities.

Many less specialized bookstores reserve shelves especially for books of interest to women and carry women's periodicals. Shops devoted to rare books are sources of early and first editions for those moved to set up collections or merely to discover what may soon be reprinted.

Government agencies, especially the Women's Bureau (see page 14), and women's organizations, such as the National Organization for Women (see p. 81), are important sources of information in book, pamphlet, and leaflet form. Many periodicals, those appealing to a general readership such as HARPER'S, as well as those aimed at a more specialized group, such as SOCIAL POLICY (see "Women and Health," 6 [September-October 1975]) or the BLACK SCHOLAR (see "The Black Woman," 3 [December 1971]), devote entire numbers to subjects of interest to women. WOMEN'S STUDIES ABSTRACTS lists many of these in its annual index.

Much of the material mentioned above is available at both general and specialized libraries, through interlibrary loan, and, for hard-to-get items particularly, through women's centers (see appendix A). Centers accumulate much material of ephemeral nature, such as clippings and items of local interest, that does not interest less specialized libraries. Some collections, such as the distributed items of the Women's History Research Center (see p. 45) and those in the Sophia Smith Collection and the Arthur and Elizabeth Schlesinger Collection at Radcliffe College, maintain holdings solely on matters relating to women. Many such collections issue catalogs of their holdings, a bibliography in themselves.

Not to be overlooked are microform reproductions of material, the largest collection of which is held by the Women's History Research Center. The NEW YORK TIMES INDEX locates, and summarizes on microfilm, items since 1861. With a little effort, information can be retrieved from the less specialized listings of University Microfilms and other companies engaged in issuing microform reproductions. Audiovisual materials of educational or instructional value through the media of motion pictures, filmstrips, transparencies, and slide sets are listed in FILMS AND OTHER MATERIALS FOR PROJECTION (formerly LIBRARY OF CONGRESS CATALOG: MOTION PICTURES AND FILMSTRIPS), which is issued by the Library of Congress and cumulates annually and quinquennially.

Information sources that list the names of publishers, libraries, government agencies, clearinghouses, consultants, and the like have high potential for women's studies. The ENCYCLOPEDIA OF INFORMATION SYSTEMS AND SERVICES, compiled by Anthony T. Kruzas, has perhaps the widest range of any of these publications. It lists "publishers, computer software and time-sharing companies, micrographic films, libraries, information centers, professional associations, and consultants." The DIRECTORY OF SPECIAL LIBRARIES AND INFORMATION CENTERS, compiled since 1963 and presently in a three-volume fifth edition published by Gale Research Company in 1979, entitles its first volume SPECIAL LIBRARIES AND INFORMATION CENTERS IN THE UNITED

STATES AND CANADA, its second GEOGRAPHICAL-PERSONNEL INDEX, and its third NEW SPECIAL LIBRARIES. Paul Wasserman and Esther Herman are compilers of the 1975 LIBRARY BIBLIOGRAPHY AND INDEXES: A SUBJECT GUIDE TO RESOURCE MATERIAL AVAILABLE FROM LIBRARIES, INFORMATION CENTERS, LIBRARY SCHOOLS AND LIBRARY ASSOCIATIONS IN THE UNITED STATES AND CANADA. The CHICHOREL INDEX TO ABSTRACTING AND INDEXING SERVICES: PERIODICALS IN HUMANITIES AND THE SOCIAL SCIENCES (1974) lists thirty-three thousand journals, serials, services, and yearbooks.

Current and recent information is available from electronic information banks. One of these is the NEW YORK TIMES Information Bank, which abstracts and prints out articles from the NEW YORK TIMES, as well as from sixty periodicals and journals. Facts on File abstracts further current sources in FACTS ON FILE: A WEEKLY WORLD NEWS DIGEST, WITH CUMULATIVE INDEX and EDITORIALS ON FILE also with a cumulative index. Both are bound annually.

Collections are a major source of primary material. SUBJECT COLLECTIONS: A GUIDE TO SPECIAL BOOK COLLECTIONS AND SUBJECT EMPHASES AS REPORTED BY UNIVERSITY, COLLEGE, PUBLIC AND SPECIAL LIBRARIES IN THE UNITED STATES AND CANADA, presently in a fifth edition compiled by Lee Ash and Stephen Calvert, makes material on women more readily available than do other similar volumes. However, other general manuscript and archival listings that are also valuable include Philip M. Hamer's A GUIDE TO ARCHIVES AND MANUSCRIPTS IN THE UNITED STATES, compiled for the U.S. National Historical Publication Commission in 1961; the annual NATIONAL UNION CATALOG OF MANUSCRIPT COLLECTIONS; and the National Archives and Record Service's GUIDE TO THE NATIONAL ARCHIVES OF THE UNITED STATES.

Some bibliographies of bibliographies are Theodore Besterman's A WORLD BIBLIOGRAPHY OF BIBLIOGRAPHIES AND OF BIBLIOGRAPHICAL CATALOGUES, CALENDARS, ABSTRACTS, DIGESTS, INDEXES, AND THE LIKE, now in its fourth revised and enlarged five-volume edition, arranged by subject, and the BIBLIOGRAPHIC INDEX: A CUMULATIVE BIBLIOGRAPHY OF BIBLIOGRAPHIES, which complements Besterman's opus.

Several bibliographies on black Americans are THE NEGRO IN AMERICA: A BIBLIOGRAPHY, compiled by Elizabeth W. Miller and Mary L. Fisher, now in its second revised edition; and THE NEGRO IN THE UNITED STATES: A SELECTED BIBLIOGRAPHY, compiled by Dorothy B. Porter. Between 1965 and 1971 the Negro Bibliographic and Research Center issued the seven-volume NEGRO IN PRINT, which annotates works on blacks and other minorities.

Two specialized bibliographies that require effort but yield some interesting material on obscure women are William Matthews's AMERICAN DIARIES: AN ANNOTATED BIBLIOGRAPHY OF AMERICAN DIARIES WRITTEN PRIOR TO THE YEAR 1861 and Harriette M. Forbes's NEW ENGLAND DIARIES 1602-1800:

A DESCRIPTIVE CATALOGUE OF DIARIES, ORDERLY BOOKS AND SEA JOURNALS, reprinted in 1967.

Information on particular books may be secured from Reader's Advisory Service, whose SELECTED TOPICAL BOOKLISTS is issued in looseleaf form (no. 12, "A Student's Guide to Material on Women," is of special interest). Its quarterly RAS NEWSLETTER prints lists of selected bibliographies and books not included in its regular service. SUBJECT GUIDE TO BOOKS IN PRINT, mentioned above, has an extensive listing of books on women currently in print, as does the BLACK BOOKS BULLETIN.

Reviews of books may be located through BOOK REVIEW INDEX as well as BOOK REVIEW DIGEST; many reviews themselves appear in CHOICE. This monthly journal, issued by the Association of College and Research Libraries, abstracts books in all fields in order to assist college librarians in selecting books for their collections. Many periodicals as diverse as the MONTHLY LABOR REVIEW and MS. regularly review books by and about women.

Guides to earlier periodical literature, an area particularly sensitive to research in relation to "lost" women of the past, include POOLE'S INDEX TO PERIODICAL LITERATURE 1802-1881, and with it, C. Edward Walls's CUMULATIVE AUTHOR INDEX FOR POOLE'S INDEX TO PERIODICAL LITERATURE, 1802-1906; the NINETEENTH CENTURY READERS' GUIDE TO PERIODICAL LITERATURE: 1890-1899, WITH SUPPLEMENTARY INDEXING: 1900-1922, edited by Helen G. Cushing and Adah V. Morris, and the GUIDE TO NEGRO PERIODICAL LITERATURE. The 822-page MAGAZINES FOR LIBRARIES, edited by Berry Gargall, is an annotated guide to periodicals in all fields. An especially useful historical guide to women's magazines is Frank Luther Mott's five-volume A HISTORY OF AMERICAN MAGAZINES, which not only names but also describes women's periodicals.

Ongoing publications include the quarterly SOCIAL SCIENCES AND HUMANITIES INDEX, which covers, in its humanities listing, 260 periodicals in area studies, folklore, history, literature, criticism, performing arts, philosophy, religion, and related subjects. Its social science listing covers 263 periodicals in area studies, economics, law, medicine, political studies, psychology, public administration, sociology, and related subjects. The READERS' GUIDE TO PERIODICAL LITERATURE offers information as does NEW SERIALS TITLES: A UNION LIST OF SERIALS COMMENCING PUBLICATION AFTER DECEMBER 3, 1949, which supersedes the UNION LIST OF SERIALS IN LIBRARIES OF THE UNITED STATES AND CANADA.

Useful also are ULRICH'S INTERNATIONAL PERIODICALS DIRECTORY: A CLASSIFIED GUIDE TO CURRENT PERIODICALS, FOREIGN AND DOMESTIC and IRREGULAR SERIALS AND ANNUALS: AN INTERNATIONAL DIRECTORY, both issued biennially. The latter is of particular help since so much of the material on women is in the ephemeral form. The ESSAY AND GENERAL LITERATURE INDEX, published originally in 1934 and updated by annual and semiannual cumulations, leads the researcher to articles in less scholarly sources.

Those seeking scholarly material that may not be either published or distributed commercially will find useful both University Microfilm International's DISSERTATION ABSTRACTS INTERNATIONAL, for which subject and author indexes were issued 1938-69, with yearly supplements; and its MASTERS ABSTRACTS: ABSTRACTS OF SELECTED MASTERS THESES IN MICROFILM, presently somewhat limited. The Association of Research Libraries issues AMERICAN DOCTORAL DISSERTATIONS.

Several general reference sources are Eugene P. Sheehy's GUIDE TO REFERENCE BOOKS, presently in its ninth edition; Bernard Klein's irregularly issued GUIDE TO AMERICAN DIRECTORIES; and Gale Research Co.'s ENCYCLOPEDIA OF ASSOCIATIONS in three volumes, the second of which includes an executive officers index. The latter is revised annually.

Among the most detailed and authoritative sources for research are government publications. A number of guides to government publications are constantly being issued and updated. The most comprehensive of these, for current purposes, is the MONTHLY CATALOG OF UNITED STATES GOVERNMENT PUBLICATIONS published by the Superintendent of Documents. Aids in using government publications are SUBJECT GUIDE TO GOVERNMENT REFERENCE BOOKS by Sally Wynkoop, to which her GOVERNMENT REFERENCE BOOKS serves as a continuing supplement; and GOVERNMENT PUBLICATIONS AND THEIR USE by Laurence F. Schmeckbier and Roy B. Eastin, now in its second edition, which serves as both guide and survey. For the historian, the COMPREHENSIVE INDEX TO PUBLICATIONS OF THE UNITED STATES GOVERNMENT, 1881-1893, compiled by John G. Ames, and the CATALOG OF THE PUBLIC DOCUMENTS OF CONGRESS AND OF OTHER DEPARTMENTS OF THE GOVERNMENT OF THE UNITED STATES FOR A PERIOD MARCH 4, 1893--DECEMBER 31, 1940, in twenty-five volumes, are invaluable. The Library of Congress issues a MONTHLY CHECKLIST OF STATE PUBLICATIONS which covers not only state agencies but also state universities as well. A specialized bibliography, GOVERNMENT PUBLICATIONS ON THE NEGRO IN AMERICA, 1948-1968, compiled by Ruth M. Davison, was issued in 1969 by Indiana State University and Focus: Black America.

The AMERICAN STATISTICS INDEX: A COMPREHENSIVE GUIDE AND INDEX TO THE STATISTICAL PUBLICATIONS OF THE GOVERNMENT, issued annually since 1973 with monthly supplements, is organized by subject. Although most government divisions issue specialized data, the Bureau of the Census is, of course, an excellent source for statistical information. Since 1878 it has been publishing the STATISTICAL ABSTRACT OF THE UNITED STATES and periodically updates THE STATISTICAL HISTORY OF THE UNITED STATES FROM COLONIAL TIMES TO THE PRESENT. The BUREAU OF CENSUS CATALOG, which includes population reports, appears in quarterly cumulative issues with monthly supplements. A nongovernmental publication, STATISTICS SOURCES: A SUBJECT GUIDE TO DATA IN INDUSTRIAL, BUSINESS, SOCIAL, EDUCA-

TIONAL, FINANCIAL, AND OTHER TOPICS FOR THE UNITED STATES AND INTERNATIONALLY, compiled by Paul Wasserman and Joanne Paskar, is presently in its fifth edition and lists over twelve thousand subjects.

B. WOMEN IN GENERAL

1. Bibliographies

1 Begos, Jane D., comp. "Annotated Bibliography of Published Women's Diaries." Pound Ridge, N.J.: 1977. 67 p. Mimeo., clipped together.

Includes bibliographies, anthologies, general works, fiction, poetry, calendars, almanacs, yearbooks, and journals either in diary form or related to diaries.

2 Cisler, Lucinda, comp. WOMEN: A BIBLIOGRAPHY. 6th ed. New York: 1970. 36 p. Pamph.

Contains fourteen categories briefly annotated. Seventh edition in preparation. Available from Cisler, Box 240, New York, New York 10024.

3 Davis, Audrey B. BIBLIOGRAPHY ON WOMEN: WITH SPECIAL EMPHASIS ON THEIR ROLES IN SCIENCE AND SOCIETY. New York: Science History Publications, 1974. 50 p.

Unannotated and uncategorized.

4 Eichler, Margaret, et al., comps. "An Annotated Selected Bibliography of Bibliographies." 2d rev. ed. Pittsburgh: KNOW, 1976. 33 p. Mimeo., stapled.

Lists ninety readily available annotated listings.

5 Jacobs, Sue-Ellen, comp. WOMEN IN PERSPECTIVE: A GUIDE FOR CROSS-CULTURAL STUDIES. Urbana: University of Illinois Press, 1974. xvi, 299 p. Biblio. Offset, paper.

Part 1, by geographical area; international in scope. The United States section is divided into three categories: Afro-American, Chicana, and general. Part 2, by special topics, includes bibliographies and material on women's roles and status, history, education, sociology (family, marriage, divorce, prostitution, imprisonment) discrimination, sexuality, arts, biographies and autobiographies, publications, collections and centers, feminism, and women in religion.

6 Loader, Jayne. "Women on the Left, 1906-1941: A Bibliography." UNIVERSITY OF MICHIGAN PAPERS IN WOMEN'S STUDIES 2 (September 1975): 9-82.

Annotated. Lists items relating to anarchism, literary Left, Communist party.

7 O'Connor, Patricia. WOMEN: A SELECTED BIBLIOGRAPHY. Women and Human Revolution Series. Springfield, Ohio: Wittenberg University, 1973. vi, 111 p. Offset, pamph.

Revised version of a 1972 unannotated bibliography. Draws on a wide range of material, listing special issues, material of women's studies courses, and library collections on the subject of women. Titles restricted to those in Ohio state universities.

8 WOMEN'S WORK AND WOMEN'S STATUS/1973-1974: A BIBLIOGRAPHY. Edited by Barbara Friedman et al. 3d ed. New York: Barnard College Women's Center, 1975. 370 p. Offset.

Partially annotated. Categorized by subject. Includes bibliography of bibliographies. Noncumulative. Excludes material published outside the United States as well as that of activist groups, of feminist and popular periodicals, and of newspapers. Available from Feminist Press.

2. References

9 Agonito, Rosemary, ed. HISTORY OF IDEAS ON WOMEN: A SOURCE BOOK. New York: G.P. Putnam's Sons, 1977. 414 p.

Contains selections, from the Bible through the United Nations' Declaration of Human Rights, that have shaped women's status and roles in Western culture. Provides headnotes.

10 Beauvoir, Simone de. THE SECOND SEX. Translated and edited by H.M. Parshley. New York: Alfred A. Knopf, 1952. 732 p. Paper.

Presents a broad view of women's awareness, past and present, in patriarchal society.

11 Briffault, Robert. THE MOTHERS: A STUDY OF THE ORIGINS OF SENTIMENTS AND INSTITUTIONS. 3 vols. New York: Macmillan Co., 1927. Reissued by Macmillan in 1931 in a 1-vol. abridged form.

Offers anthropological support for matriarchal theory.

12 Brown, Charles Brockden. ALCUIN: A DIALOGUE. New York:

T. & J. Swords, 1798. 77 p. Reprint. New York: Grossman Publishers, 1971. Paper.

Comprises the first argument supporting rights for women to be published in the United States.

13 Bullough, Vern L., with Bullough, Bonnie. THE SUBORDINATE SEX: A HISTORY OF ATTITUDES TOWARD WOMEN. Urbana: University of Illinois Press, 1973. viii, 375 p. Biblio. Paper.

Explores American experience in chapter 13.

14 Crocker, Hannah. OBSERVATIONS ON THE REAL RIGHTS OF WOMEN, WITH THEIR APPROPRIATE DUTIES, AGREEABLE TO SCRIPTURE, REASON, AND COMMON SENSE. Boston: 1818. viii, 92 p.

15 Davies, Elizabeth G. THE FIRST SEX. New York: G.P. Putnam's Sons, 1971. 382 p.

Attacks myth of female inferiority by tracing its place in "gynocratic" prehistory through pre-Christian and Christian cultures to the present day.

16 Diner, Helen. MOTHERS AND AMAZONS: THE FIRST FEMINIST HISTORY OF CULTURE. Translated by John P. Lundia. Garden City, N.Y.: Doubleday & Co., Anchor Books, 1973. xxiii, 254 p. Paper.

Reviews patriarchies as rather recent cultural development. An anthropological study.

17 Dworkan, Andrea. WOMAN HATING. New York: E.P. Dutton & Co., 1974. 217 p. Biblio. Paper.

Discusses mysogyny as evidenced in fairy tales, pornography, witch figures, and footbinding.

18 Ellman, Mary. THINKING ABOUT WOMEN. New York: Harcourt Brace, 1968. xvi, 240 p.

Maintains that sexist attitudes pervade our literature with specific reference to American Literature.

19 Farnham, Eliza. WOMAN AND HER ERA. 2 vols. 2d ed. New York: A.J. Davis, 1864.

Maintains that although male society views women's physical weakness as evidence of her inferiority, it is evidence of her spiritual superiority.

20 Friedan, Betty. THE FEMININE MYSTIQUE. New York: W.W. Norton & Co., 1964. Paper.

Presents the image versus the reality of the manipulated twentieth-century American women.

Fuller, Margaret. See Ossoli, Margaret Fuller.

21 Gilman, Charlotte Perkins. THE MAN-MADE WORLD: OUR ANDROCENTRIC CULTURE. London: T. Fisher Unwin, 1911. 296 p. Reprint. New York: Source Book Press, 1970.

Discusses male dominance in fields of health, art, literature, sports, society and "fashions," religion, law and government, crime and punishment, politics and warfare, and industry and economics with view to replacing "masculinity" with "humanity."

22 Glazer-Malbin, Nona, and Waehrer, Helen Y., eds. WOMEN IN A MAN-MADE WORLD: A SOCIOECONOMIC HANDBOOK. Chicago: Rand McNally & Co., 1972. xi, 316 p.

Contains articles on psychological, social, and economic differences between men and women, social roles relating to sex differentiation, marriage, economic and labor contributions, myths about women, and sex equality. Authors include Helen Hacker, Juliet Marshall, and Karen Horney as well as Sigmund Freud, Friedrich Engels, and Talcott Parsons.

23 Godwin, Mary A. Wollstonecraft. A VINDICATION OF THE RIGHTS OF WOMAN: WITH STRICTURES ON POLITICAL AND MORAL SUBJECTS. London: J. Johnson, 1792. xix, 452 p. Frequent reprints. Combined with John Stuart Mill's THE SUBJECTION OF WOMEN in Everyman's Library, no. 825. London: Dent; New York: E.P. Dutton & Co., 1965. 317 p. Paper.

Classic. The 1975 reprint of the text, edited by Carol H. Poston and issued as a Norton Critical Edition (New York: W.W. Norton & Co.) includes the authoritative text with background, criticism, and bibliography.

24 Graves, Robert. THE WHITE GODDESS: A HISTORICAL GRAMMAR OF POETIC MYTH. Amended and enl. New York: Farrar, Straus & Giroux, 1948. 511 p. Paper.

Classic. White goddess as source of "true poetry."

25 Greer, Germaine. THE FEMALE EUNUCH. London: MacGibbon & Kee, 1970. 354 p. Biblio. Paper.

Describes the deformation of women within the patriarchal system.

26 Hays, H.R. THE DANGEROUS SEX: THE MYTH OF FEMININE EVIL. New York: G.P. Putnam's Sons, 1964. 316 p. Biblio.

Discusses sources and manifestations of the myth throughout history.

27 Herschberger, Ruth. ADAM'S RIB. New York: Pellegrini & Cudahy, 1948. 238 p. Paper.

Offers a rational and witty attack on myths surrounding stereotyping.

28 Kellen, Konrad. THE COMING AGE OF WOMAN POWER. New York: Peter Wyden, 1972. viii, 367 p. Biblio.

Prognosticates a post-1980 culture after women have brought about social revolution. Appendix contains interviews mostly with women on their views of the future.

29 Klein, Viola. THE FEMININE CHARACTER: HISTORY OF AN IDEOLOGY. New York: International Universities Press, 1946. xviii, 202 p. Biblio. Paper.

Defines "femininity" through various disciplines by experts in the field.

30 Lasky, Ella, ed. HUMANNESS: AN EXPLORATION INTO THE MYTHOLOGIES ABOUT WOMEN AND MEN. New York: MSS Information Corp., 1975. 543 p. Tables, biblio. Paper.

Contains material on sex roles; sexual identity; marriage and family; black, Hispanic, and older women; and mental health.

31 Lenin, Vladimir I. THE EMANCIPATION OF WOMEN. New World Paperbacks. New York: International Publishers Co., 1970. 136 p. Paper.

Includes selections from the writings and letters of Lenin, as well as "Lenin on the Woman Question" by Clara Zetkin.

32 Lundberg, Ferdinand, and Farnham, Marynia. MODERN WOMAN: THE LOST SEX. New York: Grosset & Dunlap, 1947. vii, 497 p. Biblio.

Presents modern women from an obviously negative point of view.

33 Mailer, Norman. THE PRISONER OF SEX. Boston: Little, Brown and Co., 1971. 240 p.

34 Mead, Margaret. MALE AND FEMALE: A STUDY OF THE SEXES IN A CHANGING WORLD. New York: William Morrow & Co., 1949. xii, 477 p.

Note especially part 4, "The Two Sexes in Contemporary America," and appendix 3, "Sources and Experience in Our American Culture."

35 Mencken, Henry L. IN DEFENSE OF WOMEN. New York: Alfred A. Knopf, 1918. Reprint. New York: Octagon Books, 1976. xvi, 210 p.

Points out that the debunker of myths surrounding women sometimes gets caught up in them. Views suffrage as an aberration.

36 Mill, John Stuart, and Mill, Harriet T. ESSAYS ON SEX EQUALITY. Edited by Alice S. Rossi. Chicago: University of Chicago Press, 1970. ix, 242 p. Paper.

Contains an informed analysis of the Mills and their relation to Unitarianism and Unitarian Radicalism. Reprints "Early Essays on Marriage and Divorce," Harriet Mill's "Enfranchisement of Women" and John Stuart Mill's "The Subjection of Women." See also 23.

37 Millett, Kate. SEXUAL POLITICS. New York: Doubleday & Co., 1970. xii, 393 p. Biblio. Paper.

Discusses patriarchal bias in culture and literature especially as it operates in works of D.H. Lawrence, Norman Mailer, Henry Miller and Jean Genet. Traces historical background of the women's movement from 1830 to 1930, and its counterrevolution from 1930 to 1960.

38 O'Neill, Lois D. THE WOMEN'S BOOK OF WORLD RECORDS AND ACHIEVEMENTS. Garden City, N.Y.: Anchor/Doubleday and Co., 1979. xiii, 789 p. Illus. Paper.

Includes many American women.

39 Ossoli, Margaret Fuller. WOMAN IN THE NINETEENTH CENTURY AND KINDRED PAPERS RELATING TO THE SPHERE, CONDITION AND DUTIES OF WOMAN. Edited by Arthur B. Fuller. Introduction by Horace Greeley. New York: Sheldon, Lamport, 1855. Reprint. New York: Source Book Press, 1970. xiv. 420 p.

Greeley's introduction mentions inaccessibility in his time of this prolix but important essay, which presently is widely anthologized and excerpted.

40 "The Political Economy of Women." REVIEW OF RADICAL POLITICAL ECONOMICS 4 (July 1972): special issue.

Uses a Socialist approach to a variety of women's experiences. Includes syllabi and bibliographies.

41 Reed, Evelyn, ed. SEXISM AND SCIENCE. New York: Pathfinder Press, 1978. 190 p. Biblio. Paper.

First printed in INTERNATIONAL SOCIALIST REVIEW, eight articles attack pseudoscientific ideas in life sciences which support myths about women.

42 Roberts, Joan A. BEYOND INTELLECTUAL SEXISM: NEW WOMAN, NEW REALITY. New York: David McKay Co., 1976. xiv, 386 p. Biblios.

Contains twenty-one essays by female scholars. Includes material on social interaction, literature, social institutions, cultural change, role, and many other areas.

43 Roszak, Betty, and Roszak, Theodore, eds. MASCULINE/FEMININE: READINGS IN SEXUAL MYTHOLOGY AND THE LIBERATION OF WOMEN. New York: Harper & Row, 1969. xii, 316 p. Biblio. Paper.

Includes selections reflecting male stereotypical and liberated thinking about women as well as transitional and new attitudes of women toward themselves. Includes current women's movement documents.

44 Schreiner, Olive. WOMAN AND LABOR. London: T.F. Unwin, 1911. 282 p.

Presents social and moral considerations.

45 Scott-Maxwell, Florida. WOMEN AND SOMETIMES MEN. New York: Alfred A. Knopf, 1957. 207 p. Reprint. New York: Harper & Row, 1971.

Discusses self-realization by women as a means of opening up new sex-role concepts and relationships in our society. Jungian in orientation.

46 Stannard, Una. MRS. MAN. San Francisco: Germainebooks, 1977. 384 p. Illus., biblio.

Studies women's surnames as a means to explore historical male biases toward women. Available from Germainebooks, 91 St. Germaine Avenue, San Francisco, California 94114.

47 Tarbell, Ida. THE BUSINESS OF BEING A WOMAN. New York: Macmillan Co., 1912. ix, 242 p.

Claims that the "uneasy woman" is so not because of her traditional role but because of injustices within that role. However the author opposes feminism because it "masculinizes" women.

48 Tripp, Maggie, ed. WOMAN IN THE YEAR 2000. New York: Arbor House, 1974. 352 p. Paper.

Includes Letty Pogrebin, Gloria Steinem, Alvin Toffler, Carolyn Bird, Bella Abzug, and Lois Gould among the twenty-eight contributors.

Wollstonecraft, Mary. See Godwin, Mary Wollstonecraft.

49 Woolf, Virginia. A ROOM OF ONE'S OWN. New York: Fountain; London: Hogarth, 1929. 159 p. Paper.

Maintains that space is necessary for creativity.

3. Films, Tape, Microform

Herstory Films produces and distributes documentary films for and about women.

50 Federal Woman's Program. General Services Administration. FILMS AVAILABLE BY, ABOUT AND FOR WOMEN. Compiled by Janice K. Mendenhall. N.d. 3 p. Offset.

Available from the program.

51 "Women." Pacifica Audiotapes on Reels and Cassettes. Los Angeles: Pacifica Tape Library, Pacifica Library, 1974.

Analyzes the role and status of women including working and black women, lesbians, unwed mothers, and women in the arts, law, and media. Individual tapes on Fanny Wright D'Arusmont, the Grimké sisters, Dorothea Dix, Elizabeth Cady Stanton, Susan Anthony, and Frances Willard. For catalog write Department W 7 4, 5316, Venice Boulevard, Los Angeles, California 90019.

C. AMERICAN WOMEN

1. Sources

Many general sources that have implications for research on American women have already been listed in the introductory essay of this chapter. More specific to our purpose is the material issued by the Women's Bureau of the U.S. Department of Labor. Its "List of Publications" may be secured for a small fee. The leaflet lists bulletins, visual aids, leaflets, and miscellaneous publications, which include information on women workers, women's education and career opportunities, child care, standards and legislation affecting women, fact sheets of all kinds, and reports on both the national and international status of women. The publications in this leaflet are currently available, but the bureau, since its inception, has published an enormous amount of information useful to the researcher. Whatever is out of print is available in federal repositories, several of which are located in each state and a list of which may be had upon request.

The Project on the Status and Education of Women, of the Association of American Colleges, is a major distributor of material on women. For further information on this organization, see the introduction to chapter 5.

As earlier suggested, much material can be obtained from organizations dealing with women's affairs, such as the Women's Action Alliance, or from women's committees, caucuses or divisions of organizations, and government agencies.

Journals such as SIGNS and WOMANSPEAK devote themselves to the general interests of American women, the former to areas of intellectual inquiry, the latter to women at the edge of feminism. (For more specialized journals see subsequent chapters as well as appendix H.)

In addition, general presses, such as the Arno Press, issue a number of books and several series having to do solely with American women, and many presses issue specialized listings of such titles.

2. Bibliographies

a. IN PRINT

52 "Afro-American Women." In AFRICAN AND AFRO-AMERICAN MATERIALS, pp. 18-27. Greensboro, N.C.: Afro-American Institute, Thomas F. Holgate Library, Bennett College, n.d. Offset.

Unannotated.

53 American Association of University Women. Nassau County Branch, New York Division, with Nassau County, New York, Libraries. INTERNATIONAL WOMEN'S YEAR 1975, A SELECTIVE BIBLIOGRAPHY OF PERIODICAL ARTICLES, "WOMEN AROUND THE WORLD." Compiled by Hester Meigs. N.p.: 1975. 47 p. Offset, pamph.

U.S. entries on economics, education, employment, equal rights, status, and organizations. Thirty-three-page index and 208-page supplement issued separately.

54 Cole, Johnneta B., comp. "Black Women in America: An Annotated Bibliography." BLACK SCHOLAR 3 (December 1971): 42-53.

In addition to general listing, includes sections on black women and women's liberation, biographical, autobiographical, and other specialized material.

55 Council of Planning Librarians. SPECIAL ISSUES OF SERIALS ABOUT WOMEN, 1965-1975. Compiled by Susan Cardinale. Exchange Bibliography no. 795. Monticello, Ill.: 1976. 41 p. Offset, stapled.

International in scope. Lists scholarly journals, popular magazines, and alternative presses. Available from Mrs. Mary Vance, P.O. Box 229, Monticello, Illinois 61856.

56 Haber, Barbara, comp. WOMEN IN AMERICA: A GUIDE TO BOOKS, 1963-1975. Boston: G.K. Hall and Co., 1978. 230 p.

Annotated.

57 U.S. Library of Congress. "List of References Relating to Notable American Women." Compiled by Florence S. Hellman. Washington, D.C.: Government Printing Office, 1931. 144 p. Mimeo. Supplements, 1932. Reprint. 1937.

58 Whaley, Sara S., with Eichler, Margrit., comps. "A Bibliography of Canadian and United States Resources on Women." WOMEN'S STUDIES ABSTRACTS (part I) 2, no. 4 (1974): 1-5; (part 2) 3, no. 1 (1974): 1-20.

Annotated. Listings of general reference works, bibliographies of bibliographies in book and pamphlet form, additional library resources, and books and bibliographies in preparation. Available from WOMEN'S STUDIES ABSTRACTS.

See also 78.

b. IN MICROFORM

59 BIBLIOGRAPHY OF AMERICAN WOMEN. Part I. Compiled by H. Carleton Marlow. Woodbridge, Conn.: Research Publications, 1975.

Microfilm includes all monographic materials by and about American women to 1904. Fifty thousand titles arranged chronologically, alphabetically, and topically. Part 2 to be announced. Available in 16 and 33mm silver emulsion film from Research Publications, Inc., 12 Lunar Drive, Woodbridge, Connecticut 06525.

3. References

60 "Achievements of Afro-American Women of the Twentieth Century: A

Checklist." Greensboro, N.C.: 1949. 67 p. Mimeo.

Compiled under the sponsorship of the North Carolina Negro Library Association at Greensboro. Discusses women in arts, business, government, military, sports, and miscellaneous activities.

61 Andreas, Carol. SEX AND CASTE IN AMERICA. Englewood Cliffs, N.J.: Prentice-Hall, 1971. xiv, 146 p. Biblio. Paper.

Concludes that institutions must change before sexism disappears.

62 Breckinridge, Sophonisba P. WOMEN IN THE TWENTIETH CENTURY: A STUDY OF THEIR POLITICAL, SOCIAL AND ECONOMIC ACTIVITIES. New York: McGraw-Hill, 1933. ix, 364 p. Reprint. American Women: Images and Realities series. New York: Arno Press, 1972.

Discusses women engaged in nondomestic activities and their use of spare time in gainful employment and government service. Reprints the Seneca Declaration and the 1932 platform of the National League of Women Voters.

63 Coolidge, Mary R. WHY WOMEN ARE SO. New York: Henry Holt, 1912. viii, 371 p. Reprint. American Women: Images and Realities series. New York: Arno Press, 1972.

Distinguishes "feminine" from "womanly." Discusses beauty, clothing, women who "broke out," and the "new man."

64 [Cooper, Annie J.H.]. A VOICE FROM THE SOUTH, BY A BLACK WOMAN OF THE SOUTH. Xenia, Ohio: Aldine, 1892. iii, 304 p. Reprint. Westport, Conn.: Negro Universities Press, 1969.

Contains remarks on womanhood, higher education for black women, and status and image of black women in America by an ex-slave who founded a university.

65 Crow, Duncan. THE VICTORIAN WOMAN. New York: Stein & Day, 1972. 351 p. Illus.

Analyzes social forces between 1837 and 1901 that affected principally British but also American women.

66 Dorr, Rheta L.C. WHAT EIGHT MILLION WOMEN WANT. Boston: Small, Maynard, 1910. xii, 339 p. Illus. Reprint. Millwood, N.Y.: Kraus Reprint Co., n.d.

Muckraking work discusses women's club movement, women and the law, women in industry, Maude Miner's efforts on behalf of delinquent women, female domestic servants, and suffrage.

67 Eakin, John J. THE NEW ENGLAND GIRL: CULTURAL IDEALS IN HAWTHORNE, STOWE, HOWELLS AND JAMES. Athens: University of Georgia Press, 1976. 252 p.

Explores relationships between realists' characterization of women and interest in "moral reality of American life."

68 Ehrenreich, Barbara, and English, Deirdre. FOR HER OWN GOOD: 150 YEARS OF THE EXPERTS' ADVICE TO WOMEN. Garden City, N.Y.: Anchor/Doubleday, 1978. x, 325 p.

Presents the history of advisors who directed women in areas of health, marriage, housework, motherhood, and child raising, and the forces presently diminishing their power.

69 Farmer, Lydia H., ed. THE NATIONAL EXPOSITION SOUVENIR: WHAT AMERICA OWES WOMEN. Buffalo, N.Y.: Charles Wells Moulton, 1893. 505 p.

Chronicles women's contributions to the arts and humanities, sciences, professions, business, philanthropy, and religion.

70 Gornick, Vivian, and Moran, Barbara K., eds. WOMAN IN SEXIST SOCIETY: STUDIES IN POWER AND POWERLESSNESS. New York: Basic Books, 1971. xxv, 515 p. Tables.

Excellent anthology on wide range of subjects, among them marriage, lesbianism, prostitution, middle-age depression, consumerism, sexist rhetoric. Authors include Kate Millett, Naomi Weisstein, Elaine Showalter, Lucy Komisar.

71 Hacker, Helen M. "Women as a Minority Group." SOCIAL FORCES 30 (October 1951): 60-69. Reprint. Bobbs-Merrill Reprint Series in Social Issues. New York: Bobbs-Merrill Co., 1975. 69 p.

Early study of women as socially marginal.

72 Harbeson, Gladys E. CHOICE AND CHALLENGE FOR THE AMERICAN WOMAN. Rev. ed. Cambridge, Mass.: Schenckman Publishing Co., 1971. xvii, 185 p. Tables, charts, biblio.

Broad approach to place of educated woman in American society as well as to her planning for self-fulfillment.

73 Harley, Sharon, and Terborg-Penn, Rosalyn, eds. THE AFRO-AMERICAN WOMAN: STRUGGLES AND IMAGES. National University Publications. Port Washington, N.Y.: Kennikat Press, 1978. xiii, 137 p.

Focuses on work of, and discrimination against, black women in nineteenth-century America, and their images in poetry and involvement in the blues. Biographical sketches of Anna Cooper, feminist; Nannie Burroughs, educator; and Charlotte Bass, vice-presidential candidate.

74 Higginson, Thomas W. COMMONSENSE ABOUT WOMEN. Boston: Lee & Shepard, 1882. 403 p.

Nineteenth-century feminist's views on women's physiology, education, employment, and suffrage.

75 Hogeland, Ronald W., ed. WOMAN AND WOMANHOOD IN AMERICA. Problems in American Civilization series. Lexington, Mass.: D.C. Heath & Co., 1973. ix, 183 p. Biblio. Paper.

Primary documents from colonial times to the present, with critical essays.

76 Hooker, Isabella B. WOMANHOOD AND ITS SANCTITIES AND FIDELITIES. Boston: Lee & Shepard, 1874. 178 p.

Final section discusses abortion and planned parenthood, with implications for population control.

77 Hunt, Morton M. HER INFINITE VARIETY: THE AMERICAN WOMAN AS LOVER, MATE AND RIVAL. New York: Harper & Row, 1962. 333 p. Biblio.

Complexity of contemporary woman's life reflects that of her historical past.

78 Lerner, Gerda. BLACK WOMEN IN WHITE AMERICA. New York: Pantheon Books, 1972. xxxvi, 630 p. Biblio. Paper.

Major collection of documents 1811 to present. Black woman as slave, educator, sex object, domestic, factory and government worker, politician, and organizer. Includes specialized bibliographies.

79 ______. THE FEMALE EXPERIENCE: AN AMERICAN DOCUMENTARY. American Heritage Series. Indianapolis: Bobbs-Merrill Co., 1977. xxxvi, 509 p. Biblio. Paper.

Primary documents, many previously unpublished, reflect public and private lives of women since 1600s. Sections focus on life cycles (childhood through old age, life-styles), women in a male-defined society (education, domestic and industrial work, labor organizing, politics) and feminist consciousness (woman's sphere, achievement of autonomy).

Lifton, Robert J., ed. THE WOMAN IN AMERICA. See 96.

80 Loewenberg, Bert J., and Bogin, Ruth, eds. BLACK WOMEN IN NINETEENTH-CENTURY AMERICAN LIFE: THEIR WORDS, THEIR THOUGHTS, THEIR FEELINGS. University Park: Pennsylvania State University Press, 1976. xi, 355 p. Biblio.

Selections from primary documents set down private and public events of well- and less well-known women.

81 Lynes, Russell. THE DOMESTICATED AMERICANS. New York: Harper & Row, 1957. xii, 308 p. Illus.

Interaction of manners, architecture, social history, and women from colonial times to present.

82 McBee, Mary L., and Blake, Kathryn A., eds. THE AMERICAN WOMAN: WHO WILL SHE BE? Beverly Hills, Calif.: Glencoe Press; London: Collier-Macmillan, 1974. vii, 164 p. Biblio.

Eleven articles on tasks presently facing American woman. Authors include Ann F. Scott, Judith Bardwick, Juanita Kreps, Jessie Bernard, and Patsy Mink.

83 Marlow, H. Carleton, and Davis, M. Harrison. THE AMERICAN SEARCH FOR WOMAN. Santa Barbara, Calif.: American Bibliographical Center-Clio, 1976. xiv, 539 p. Biblio. Paper.

Analyzes roots of historical attitudes toward women as well as current attitudes and issues.

84 Merriam, Eve. AFTER NORA SLAMMED THE DOOR. Cleveland: World Publishing Co., 1964. 236 p.

Where American women were in the sixties and where they might be going.

85 More, Hannah. THE WORKS OF HANNAH MORE, COMPLETE IN SEVEN VOLUMES. 7 vols. New York: Harper & Brothers, 1845.

English writer of influence on American mores discusses social behavior, sex roles, education, and other matters relating to women.

86 Nearing, Scott, and Nearing, Nellie. WOMAN AND SOCIAL PROGRESS: A DISCUSSION OF THE BIOLOGIC, DOMESTIC, INDUSTRIAL, AND SOCIAL POSSIBILITIES OF AMERICAN WOMEN. New York: Macmillan Co., 1912. xii, 285 p.

Uniqueness of American women and how it demands they contribute to world progress.

87 THE NEGRO HANDBOOK. Compiled by the editors of EBONY. Chicago: Johnson Publishing Co., 1966. 535 p.

Includes vital statistics and sections on education, economy, government, armed forces, professions, sports, creative arts, and press. Biographical dictionary includes some women. Directory of blacks in government and organizations.

88 Pruette, Lorine. WOMEN AND LEISURE: A STUDY OF WASTE. New York: E.P. Dutton & Co., 1924. xxiv, 225 p. Biblio. Reprint. American Women: Images and Realities series. New York: Arno Press, 1972.

Pioneering study of women's frustration stemming from conventional attitudes and withheld rewards. Use of daydream material in diagnostic questionnaire.

89 Reische, Diana L., ed. WOMEN AND SOCIETY. The Reference Shelf, vol. 43, no. 6. New York: H.W. Wilson Co., 1972. 234 p. Biblio.

Anthology focuses on issues, such as women's education and women's studies, women in the church and labor force, abortion, psychological differences between the sexes, and marriage and the family, rather than on personalities. Most selections are anonymous.

90 Roosevelt, Eleanor. IT'S UP TO THE WOMEN. New York: Stokes, 1933. x, 263 p.

Points out the responsibility of women during the Great Depression to initiate new social order in home, politics, public life, business, and professions.

91 Savage, Minot J. MAN, WOMAN AND CHILD. Boston: George H. Ellis, 1884. 211 p.

Views women as intuitive and moral, the kitchen as a barbaric relic, and contemporary dress as ridiculous. Demands suffrage, equal divorce rights, and education.

92 THE VIRGINIA SLIMS AMERICAN WOMEN'S OPINION POLL. Volumes 1 and 2. Conducted by Louis Harris and Associates. New York: n.p., 1970, 1972. Tables. Volume 3. A Study Conducted by the Roper Organization. New York: n.p., 1974. 123 p. Tables.

Volume 1 surveys women's attitudes toward marriage roles, volume 2 toward political and economic roles, and volume 3 toward family roles and sexual morality.

93 Welter, Barbara. "The Cult of True Womanhood." AMERICAN QUARTERLY 18 (Summer 1966): 151-74.

Cardinal virtues include piety, purity, submissiveness, and domesticity.

94 Willard, Frances E. HOW TO WIN: A BOOK FOR GIRLS. 4th ed. New York: Funk & Wagnalls, 1886. 125 p.

Social change demands cultivation of specialty, such as engaging in practical philanthropy (WCTU), journalism, or health activity -- with no novel reading.

95 "Woman/An Issue." Edited by Lee Edwards et al. MASSACHUSETTS REVIEW 15 (Winter 1971-Spring 1972): special issue. Reprinted as WOMAN: AN ISSUE. Boston: Little, Brown and Co., 1972. 299 p. Biblio. Paper.

Articles by Bella Abzug, Anais Nin, and Angela Davis; study of Elizabeth Stuart Phelps; poems by Lucille Clifton, Maxine Kumin, and others. Also short stories, interviews, photographs, and drawings.

96 "The Woman in America." DAEDALUS: A JOURNAL OF THE AMERICAN ACADEMY OF ARTS AND SCIENCES 63 (Spring 1964): special issue. Reprinted as THE WOMAN IN AMERICA. Edited by Robert J. Lifton. Boston: Houghton Mifflin Co., 1964. ix, 293 p. Tables. Paper. Reprint. Westport, Conn.: Greenwood Press, 1977.

Articles that explore genetic as against social and historical roles of American women touch on psychohistory, literature, mother-daughter relationships, status, employment, image, marriage, and choice of professional career. Essays on Jane Addams and Eleanor Roosevelt. By Erik Erickson, Diana Trilling, David Reisman, Alice Rossi, Edna Rostow, Carl Degler, Lotte Bailyn, Esther Peterson, and others.

97 "Women in Public Life." ANNALS OF THE AMERICAN ACADEMY OF POLITICAL AND SOCIAL SCIENCES 56 (November 1914): special issue.

Part 1, "The Feminist Movement," includes articles on economics and changing status and education of women and their conventionality; part 2, "Public Activities of Women," on legislation affecting women, and women in municipal activities, clubs, and juvenile courts; part 3, "Women and the Suffrage," on suffrage and temperance movements.

98 Woolson, Abba G. WOMEN IN AMERICAN SOCIETY. Boston: Roberts Brothers, 1873. vi, 271 p.

Feminist journalist comments on women at summer resorts,

invalidism and physical education, dress reform, and short-comings of compulsive housekeepers.

4. Film, Microform. See chapter 3, section D.

Chapter 2
ROLE, IMAGE, STATUS

A. ROLE

1. Bibliographies, Sources

The Maferr Foundation, 124 East 28 Street, New York, New York 10016, issues material on sex role research. SEX ROLES: A JOURNAL OF RESEARCH, a quarterly issued since 1975, is cross-disciplinary in its approach.

99 Business and Professional Women's Foundation. A SELECTED ANNOTATED BIBLIOGRAPHY: SEX ROLE CONCEPTS. Compiled by Jeanne Spiegel. Washington, D.C.: 1969. 31 p.

Includes periodicals and unpublished dissertations. Available from the foundation.

100 Campen, Jim, comp. "Aspects of American Socialism: Economy, Work. Democracy, Ecology, Sex and Age Roles, Education." In his SOCIALIST ALTERNATIVES FOR AMERICA: A BIBLIOGRAPHY, Chap. 3. Research Materials in Radical Political Economics, Vol. 1. Ann Arbor: Michigan Union for Radical Political Economics, 1974.

Annotated.

101 Council of Planning Librarians. THE CHANGING ROLE OF WOMEN IN AMERICA: A SELECTED ANNOTATED BIBLIOGRAPHY. Compiled by Gale Schlacter and Donna Belli. Exchange Bibliography no. 931. Washington, D.C.: 1975. 36 p. Offset.

Section 1, sources of information; section 2, sources of citations. Available from Mrs. Mary Vance, P.O. Box 229, Monticello, Illinois 61856.

102 Freeman, Leah, comp. THE CHANGING ROLE OF WOMEN: A SELECTED BIBLIOGRAPHY. Bibliographical Series, no. 9. Sacramento,

Calif.: Sacramento State College Library, 1972. 50 p. Offset, paper.

Wide ranging although limited to material in library.

103 U.S. Department of Health, Education and Welfare. National Institute of Mental Health. Center for Human Services. SEX ROLES: A RESEARCH BIBLIOGRAPHY. Compiled by Helen S. Astin. Rockville, Md.: 1975. ix, 362 p. Paper.

Lists titles published between 1960 and 1972 relating to sex differences and sex roles, specialized sex roles, and cultural overview of women's status. Cross-cultural.

2. References

a. ROLE IN GENERAL

104 Chafetz, Janet S[altzman]. MASCULINE, FEMININE OR HUMAN?: AN OVERVIEW OF THE SOCIOLOGY OF SEX ROLES. Itasca, Ill.: F.E. Peacock, 1974. 242 p.

105 Gersoni-Stavn, Diane, ed. SEXISM AND YOUTH. New York: R.R. Bowker Co., 1974. xxviii, 468 p. Biblio.

Part 1 deals with role socialization, part 2 with sexism in schools, part 3 with sexism in texts and children's books, part 4 with sexist toys and games.

106 HARPER STUDIES IN LANGUAGE AND LITERATURE. New York: Harper & Row, 1975. Illus., tables, biblio.

Series of study guides in pamphlet form that include: Helen M. Hacker. THE SOCIAL ROLE OF MEN AND WOMEN: A SOCIOLOGICAL APPROACH. 51 p. Beatrice Taines. WOMEN OF VALOR, MEN OF HONOR. 30 p. Rhoda K. Unger. SEX-ROLE STEREOTYPES REVISITED: PSYCHOLOGICAL APPROACHES TO WOMEN'S STUDIES. Peter N. Weltner. MYTH AND MASCULINITY. 29 p.

107 Heilbrun, Carolyn G. TOWARD A RECOGNITION OF ANDROGYNY. New York: Alfred A. Knopf, 1973. xxi, 189 p. Paper.

Author traces "movement away from sexual polarization" through literary works from the Greeks to the present, viewing liberation from sex roles as essential for survival.

108 Myrdal, Alva, and Klein, Viola. WOMEN'S TWO ROLES: HOME AND WORK. 2d ed., rev. International Library of Sociology and Social Reconstruction. London: Routledge and Kegan Paul, 1968.

xvii, 213 p. Illus.

Integration of roles necessary for survival.

109 Oakley, Ann. SEX, GENDER AND SOCIETY. Towards a New Society Series. New York: Harper & Row, 1972. 220 p. Illus., tables.

Differences between sex and gender. Prejudice rather than biology determines social roles.

110 Reeves, Nancy. WOMANKIND BEYOND THE STEREO-TYPES, WITH PARALLEL READINGS SELECTED AND ANNOTATED BY THE AUTHOR. Chicago: Aldine-Atherton, 1971. xii, 434 p. Illus.

First half of the volume examines assumptions regarding rôle and thinking about women by Caroline Bird, Eleanor Flexner, Margaret Mead and others. Second half anthologizes articles.

111 Yorburg, Betty. SEXUAL IDENTITY: SEX ROLES AND SOCIAL CHANGE. New York: John Wiley, 1974. x, 227 p.

Draws on various disciplines.

b. ROLE AND AMERICAN WOMEN

For research into the role of women in the nineteenth century there exist literally hundreds of books instructing women in their "proper sphere" (i.e., role and duties). For example, see 112.

112 Alcott, William A. LETTERS TO A SISTER: OR, WOMEN'S MISSION. Buffalo, N.Y.: George H. Derby, 1850. xv, 307 p.

Women should serve men better and thus atone for Eve's misdeed.

113 Bernard, Jessie S. WOMEN, WIVES, MOTHERS: VALUES AND OPTIONS. Chicago: Aldine Publishing Co., 1975. 286 p. Tables, figs., biblio.

Reviews research on restructuring of sex roles as well as impact on young women and mothers, influences of age, class, and race on sex roles and future of restructuring.

114 Blake, Lillie D. WOMEN'S PLACE TODAY: FOUR LECTURES, IN REPLY TO THE LENTEN LECTURES ON "WOMAN" BY THE REV. MORGAN DIX. Lovell's Library, vol. 3, no. 105. New York: John W. Lowell, 1883. iv, 173 p.

Suffragist refutes arguments advanced by religionists quoting Scripture in matters relating to religion, home, divorce, and woman's "true mission." Representative of the ongoing debate on woman's role.

115 Chafe, William H., ed. THE AMERICAN WOMAN: HER CHANGING SOCIAL, ECONOMIC, AND POLITICAL ROLES, 1920-1970. New York: Oxford University Press, 1972. xiii, 351 p. Biblio. Paper.

Deals with public attitude toward women, effect of war and depression on women's status, women in politics, the professions and industry, and the Equal Rights Amendment. Extensive listing of collections relating to women.

116 Cott, Nancy F. THE BONDS OF WOMANHOOD: "WOMEN'S SPHERE" IN NEW ENGLAND, 1780-1835. New Haven, Conn.: Yale University Press, 1977. xii, 225 p. Biblio. Paper.

Based on many hitherto unpublished sources, text examines women's experience relating to work, domesticity, education, religion, and sisterhood.

117 Davis, Angela. "Reflections of the Black Women's Role in a Community of Slaves." BLACK SCHOLAR 3 (December 1971): 3-15.

Arguing against premise of Moynihan report (see 623), author points out paradoxical equality between black women and men during slavery.

118 Filene, Peter G. HIM/HER SELF: SEX ROLES IN MODERN AMERICA. New York: Harcourt Brace Jovanovich, 1974. xiv, 351 p. Biblio.

Discusse middle-class men and women, from mid-nineteenth century. Bibliography lists fictional sources as well as personal histories.

119 Hahn, Emily. ONCE UPON A PEDESTAL. New York: Thomas Y. Crowell Co., 1974. 279 p. Biblio.

History of women's freeing themselves from stereotypical roles.

120 Huber, Joan, ed. CHANGING WOMEN IN A CHANGING SOCIETY. Chicago: University of Chicago Press, 1973. 295 p. Biblio. Paper.

Jessie Bernard, Jo Freeman, Hanna Papanek, Cynthia Epstein, Valerie Oppenheimer, Mirra Komarovsky, Helena Z. Lopata, and others survey roots of rationalizations that "keep woman in her place," and suggest adjustments society will have to make to accommodate to changing conditions. Swinging, sex-role conditioning and research, women in graduate education, faculty wives, work and marital patterns, images of women, origins of the current woman's movement, women in public and military service, and black women professionals are among subjects discussed.

121 Janeway, Elizabeth, ed. WOMEN: THEIR CHANGING ROLES. The Great Contemporary Issues series. New York: Arno Press, 1973. x, 556 p. Illus., biblio.

Selected articles from the NEW YORK TIMES include material on social and radical feminism, women's history, women in the arts, day care, abortion, education, family and legal rights under Title VII, and the Equal Rights Ammendment.

122 Mason, K.O., et al. "Change in United States Women's Sex Role Attitudes, 1964-1974." AMERICAN SOCIOLOGICAL REVIEW, 41 (August 1976): 573-646.

123 New York Commission on Human Rights. WOMEN'S ROLE IN CONTEMPORARY SOCIETY, SEPTEMBER 21-25, 1970. New York: Avon, Discus, 1972. 800 p. Paper.

Recommendations concerning equal opportunity in business and industry, the professions and government, fringe benefits, domestic work, taxation, social services, housing and credit practices, education, law (including jury duty), and politics. Contains testimony by Betty Friedan, Mirra Komarovsky, Margaret Mead, Bess Myerson, Mary Ann Krupsak, Bernice Sandler, Wilma Heide, Shirley Chisholm, and others.

124 Rosenberg, Carroll S. "Beauty, the Beast and the Militant Woman: A Case Study in Sex Roles and Social Stress in Jacksonian America." AMERICAN QUARTERLY 23 (October 1971): 562-84.

Fourteen years before the Seneca Falls Convention, the New York Female Moral Reform Society pressed for reforms based on antimale sentiments and attacked woman's subservient role in America. It also espoused cause of working women and demonstrated women's abilities in fields traditionally reserved for men.

125 Rothman, Sheila. WOMAN'S PROPER PLACE: A HISTORY OF CHANGING IDEALS AND PRACTICES, 1870 TO THE PRESENT. New York: Basic Books, 1978. 322 p. Illus.

Discusses interplay between pressures to preserve status quo and pressures for social change as they affect women's lives.

126 "Women: Nine Reports on Role, Image and Message." JOURNAL OF

COMMUNICATION 24 (Spring 1974): special issue.

Material on perception of women's roles on television, in serials, and in children's programs; and on images of women on, and fighting sexism in, television.

3. Audiotape. See 51.

B. IMAGE

1. General

a. SOURCES

Women on Words and Images publishes material on efforts to change the image of women by changing rhetoric relating to them. The National Organization for Women maintains a Task Force on the Image of Women and distributes literature bearing on its activities.

b. BIBLIOGRAPHY

127 Kaiser, Ernest. "Black Images in the Mass Media: A Bibliography." FREEDOMWAYS: A QUARTERLY REVIEW OF THE FREEDOM MOVEMENT 14 (1974): 274-87.

Partially annotated.

c. REFERENCES

128 Axelrod, Janet. "Under My Thumb: A Study of the Image of American Women in Rock 'n' Roll." Unpublished paper, Women's Center, Barnard College, n.d. 35 p. Biblio. Photocopy.

129 Christy, Howard Chandler. THE AMERICAN GIRL AS SEEN AND PORTRAYED BY HOWARD CHANDLER CHRISTY. New York: Moffat, Yard, 1906. 157 p. Illus.

Turn-of-the-century epitome of womanhood.

130 Coffin, Tristram P. THE FEMALE HERO IN FOLKLORE AND LEGEND. New York: Seabury Press, 1975. x, 223 p. Illus.

European and American women.

131 Cohen, Anne B. POOR PEARL, POOR GIRL! THE MURDERED GIRL STEREOTYPE IN BALLAD AND NEWSPAPER. Austin: University of Texas Press, for the American Folklore Society, 1973. xii, 132 p. Illus.

Media's view of turn-of-the-century crime.

132 Cornillon, Susan K., ed. IMAGES OF WOMEN IN FICTION: FEMINIST PERSPECTIVE. Rev. ed. Bowling Green, Ky.: Bowling Green University Populor Press, 1973. xiii, 396 p. Biblio. Paper.

Feminist-oriented literary-critical essays on woman as heroine and hero, on woman as invisible, and on feminist aesthetics.

133 Deegan, Dorothy Y. THE SOCIAL STEREOTYPE OF THE SINGLE WOMAN IN AMERICAN NOVELS: A SOCIOLOGICAL STUDY WITH IMPLICATIONS FOR THE EDUCATION OF WOMEN. New York: King's Crown Press, 1951. xvi, 252 p. Biblio. Reprint. New York: Octagon Books, 1968.

Images of single women in wide range of American novels. Appendix includes listing of books containing single-woman characters by author, date, and character, and classifications categories.

134 Embree, Alice. "Media Images I: Madison Avenue Brainwashing--The Facts." In SISTERHOOD IS POWERFUL: AN ANTHOLOGY OF WRITINGS FROM THE WOMEN'S LIBERATION MOVEMENT, edited by Robin Morgan, pp. 175-91. New York: Random House, 1970. Paper.

Analyzes women's special vulnerability to media advertising.

135 Ferguson, Mary Anne. IMAGES OF WOMEN IN LITERATURE. 2d ed. Boston: Houghton Mifflin Co., 1977. viii, 486 p. Biblio. Paper.

Discusses stereotypical images of submissive wife, mother, bitch, seductress-goddess, sex object, woman alone, and liberated woman.

136 Flora, Cornelia B. "The Passive Female: Her Comparative Image by Class and Culture in Women's Magazine Fiction." In SISTERHOOD IS POWERFUL: AN ANTHOLOGY OF WRITINGS FROM THE WOMEN'S LIBERATION MOVEMENT, edited by Robin Morgan, pp. 435-44. New York: Random House, 1970. Paper.

Concludes that women in working-class fiction are portrayed as being less passive.

137 Fryer, Judith. THE FACES OF EVE: WOMEN IN THE NINETEENTH CENTURY AMERICAN NOVEL. New York: Oxford University Press, 1976. x, 294 p. Illus., biblio.

Discusses women characters as portrayed by Oliver Wendell Holmes, Nathaniel Hawthorne, Herman Melville, Harold

Frederic, Henry James, and Kate Chopin, as well as the social context which shaped them.

138 Goodman, Charlotte. "Images of American Rural Women in the Novel." UNIVERSITY OF MICHIGAN PAPERS IN WOMEN'S STUDIES 1 (June 1975): 57-70.

Serves as corrective to romantic view of farm women.

139 Haskell, Molly. FROM REVERENCE TO RAPE: THE TREATMENT OF WOMEN IN THE MOVIES. New York: Holt, Rinehart & Winston, 1975. 400 p. Illus. Paper.

From the twenties on.

140 Kedesdy, Dierdre A.L. "Images of Women in the American Best Seller: 1870-1900." Unpublished Ph.D. thesis, Tufts University, 1976.

Traditional, to compensate for rapid social change.

141 Millium, Trevor. IMAGES OF WOMEN: ADVERTISING IN WOMEN'S MAGAZINES. New York: Rowman & Littlefield, 1975. 205 p. Illus.

142 Murray, Michele, ed. A HOUSE OF GOOD PROPORTIONS: IMAGES OF WOMEN IN LITERATURE. New York: Simon & Schuster, 1973. 379 p. Biblio. Paper.

Stories categorized by little girl, young girl, virgin, women in love, independent women, wife, mother, family life, women lost, old maid, old woman, and unattainable other.

143 National Advertising Review Board. ADVERTISING AND WOMEN: A REPORT ON ADVERTISING PORTRAYING OR DIRECTED TO WOMEN. New York: 1975. 21 p. Offset, pamph.

"Old ways of thinking . . . outlive changed conditions."

144 Noble, Peter. THE NEGRO IN FILMS. London: Skelton Robinson, 1948. 288 p. Biblio. Reprint. The Literature of the Cinema series. New York: Arno Press, 1970.

Some material on American black women.

145 Pearson, Carol, and Pope, Katherine, eds. WHO AM I THIS TIME? FEMALE PORTRAITS IN BRITISH AND AMERICAN LITERATURE. New York: McGraw-Hill Book Co., 1976. 288 p. Biblio. Paper.

Images of women as heroine, mistress, helpmate, hero, artist, and warrior, in prose and poetry, how they have affected women's lives, and how they reflect social reality.

146 Rogers, Agnes. "The Undivided Appeal of the Gibson Girl." AMERICAN HERITAGE 9 (December 1957): 80-98. Illus.

Ideal upper-class "lady" of pre-World War I America was "feminine without being sexy."

147 Rule, Jane. LESBIAN IMAGES. New York: Doubleday & Co., 1975. xi, 257 p. Biblio. Paper.

American women include Gertrude Stein, Willa Cather, Margaret Anderson, Dorothy Baker, and May Sarton.

148 Scott, Foresman and Company. GUIDELINES FOR IMPROVING THE IMAGE OF WOMEN IN TEXTBOOKS. New York: 1972. 9 p.

Publisher's attempt to eliminate sex role stereotyping. Many publishing houses presently issue such information to their staffs.

149 Trecker, Janice L. "Women in U.S. History High School Textbooks." INTERNATIONAL REVIEW OF EDUCATION 19 (1973): 33-39.

Studies eleven current texts that adhere to traditional images.

150 U.S. President's Commission on the Status of Women. "Two Consultations Sponsored by the Commission: Portrayal of Women by the Mass Media." In AMERICAN WOMEN: REPORT OF THE PRESIDENT'S COMMISSION ON THE STATUS OF WOMEN AND OTHER PUBLICATIONS OF THE COMMISSION, edited by Margaret Mead and Frances B. Kaplan, appendix 3. New York: Scribner's, 1965.

151 Wald, Carol, and Papachristou, Judith, comps. PICTURING WOMEN: 1865-1945. New York: Pantheon Books, 1975. ix, 185 p. Illus.

Popular images in posters, postcards, calendars, paper dolls, steroptican cards, and other visual forms reflecting mythic views of American woman.

152 Warren, Barbara. THE FEMININE IMAGE IN LITERATURE. Harper Humanities Series. Rochelle Park, N.J.: Hayden Book Co., 1973. 280 p.

Dangerous "phantom lady," virgin, masked stereotype, androgyne.

153 Weaver, Marleen E. "Mexican-American Women: Diversity in Depth." ILLINOIS SCHOOL JOURNAL 55 (Fall 1975): 43-49.

Changing image of Chicana as reflected in literature.

154 Wiesenfeld, Cheryl, et al., comps. WOMEN SEE WOMEN: A PHOTOGRAPHIC ANTHOLOGY BY OVER 80 TALENTED PHOTOGRAPHERS. New York: Thomas Y. Crowell Co., 1976. 145 p. Illus. Paper.

155 Women on Words and Images. CHANNELING CHILDREN: SEX STEREOTYPING IN PRIME TIME TV. Prepared by Betty Miles. Princeton, N.J.: 1975. 84 p. Illus., tables. Paper.

Reviews research on children and TV and analyzes programming. Lists resources. Available from Women on Words and Images.

156 Women's Action Alliance. HOW TO MAKE THE MEDIA WORK FOR WOMEN. Prepared by Catherine Samuels. New York: 1974. 29 p. Pamph.

Material on publicity and promotion.

For the image of women in fiction written by men see chapter 9, section D. 2; see also entry 1731.

For the image of women in drama written by men see chapter 9, section D. 4. c. ii.

d. SLIDES

157 Weitzman, Lenore, and Rizzo, Diane. "Images of Males and Females in Elementary School Textbooks: A Slide Show." Washington, D.C.: Resource Center on Sex Roles, n.d.

Analyzes sexism in carousels, tapes, scripts, and pamphlets. Available from the center.

2. Traveler's Views of American Women

a. BIBLIOGRAPHY

158 Monaghan, Frank. FRENCH TRAVELLERS IN THE UNITED STATES 1765-1932: A BIBLIOGRAPHY WITH A SUPPLEMENT BY SAMUEL J. MARINO. New York: Antiquarian, 1961. xii, 130 p.

Scattered entries on women and marriage.

b. REFERENCES

159 Bellegarrique, A. LES FEMMES D'AMÉRIQUE. Paris: Blanchard, 1855. 95 p. Pamph.

American women are self-centered, scornful of men, and love only money.

160 Bird, Isabella L. THE ENGLISHWOMAN IN AMERICA. London: John Murray, 1856. xxv, 464 p. Paper.

Trip from Boston to the Mississippi via Cincinnati and return.

161 Blanc, Marie Therèse de S. [Th. Bentzon]. THE CONDITION OF WOMAN IN THE UNITED STATES: A TRAVELLER'S NOTES. Translated by Abby L. Alger. Boston: Roberts Brothers, 1895. 285 p.

Frenchwoman's views of American society, higher education, women's prisons and industrial schools, and Hampton Institute.

162 Bremer, Frederika. THE HOMES OF THE NEW WORLD: IMPRESSIONS OF AMERICA. 2 vols. New York: Harper, 1853.

Swedish woman's lively account of women's roles in America. Mentions Mrs. Kirkland, Fanny Kemble, Lydia Maria Child, Indian wives, Lowell factory girls, Shaker women, and others.

163 [D'Arusmont, Frances Wright]. VIEWS OF SOCIETY AND MANNERS IN AMERICA IN A SERIES OF LETTERS FROM THAT COUNTRY TO A FRIEND IN ENGLAND, DURING THE YEARS 1818-1819 AND 1820. By an Englishwoman. London: Longmans, Hurst, Rees, Orme, and Browne, 1821. xxiii, 292 p. Reprint. Cambridge, Mass.: Harvard University Press, Belknap Press, 1963.

Popular travel memoir by radical reformer. Enthusiastic about American women.

164 Dixon, William. NEW AMERICA. Philadelphia: J.B. Lippincott Co., 1867. viii, 495 p. Illus.

English traveler comments on Mormon marriage and sexual mores, women of various classes, squatter women, Shakers, especially Mother Ann Lee, female seers and spiritualists, equal rights for women, and Oneida community.

165 Finch, Marianne. AN ENGLISHWOMAN'S EXPERIENCE IN AMERICA. London: R. Bentley, 1853. viii, 386 p.

A black traveler views American women.

166 Longworth, Maria T. [Yelverton, Thérèse, Viscountess Avonmore]. TERESINA IN AMERICA. 2 vols. London: R. Bentley, 1875. Reprint. Foreign Travelers in America 1810-1933 series. New York: Arno Press, 1974.

European travels in regions east of Mississippi River. Note especially chapter 24, volume 1, "Man's Gallantry and Woman's Freedom," and chapter 36, volume 2, "American Marriages."

167 Martineau, Harriet. SOCIETY IN AMERICA. 2 vols. New York: Saunders & Otley, 1837.

Chapter 2 in volume 2, part 2, views position of women in America as betraying democratic ideals. Author discusses marriage, divorce, inheritance, life in boarding houses, domestic employment, and health.

168 Ross, Ishbel. "The Ladies Travel." In her THE EXPATRIATES, chap. 9. New York: Thomas Y. Crowell Co., 1970.

Among the women discussed are Julia Ward Howe, Margaret Fuller Ossoli, Catherine Sedgwick, Kate Field, the Fox sisters, Victoria Woodhull, Tennessee Claflin, Mrs. Frank Leslie, and Dr. Elizabeth Blackwell.

169 Tocqueville, Alexis Charles Henri Maurice Clérel de. DEMOCRACY IN AMERICA. Translated by Henry Reeve. Edited by Henry S. Commager. New York: Oxford University Press, 1947. xxii, 513 p. Biblio. Reprint. New York: Harper & Row, 1966. 802 p. Paper.

Remarks about women and subjects related to women scattered throughout text. Published originally in 1835-40.

170 Trollope, Anthony. "The Rights of Women." In his NORTH AMERICA, chap. 17. New York: Harper & Brothers, 1863. vii, 623 p. Reprint. New York: Alfred A. Knopf, 1951. Illus., biblio.

Nineteenth-century visitor discusses women's rights in regard to employment and political rights which "admit no discussion."

171 Trollope, Frances M. DOMESTIC MANNERS OF THE AMERICANS. 2 vols. London: Whitaker, Treacher, 1832. xxxiii, 454 p. Reprint. New York: Alfred A. Knopf, 1949. Biblio.

Comments by English visitor who lived and worked in America for two years. Material on women scattered but incisive. Various passages on Frances Wright d'Arusmont.

172 Tryon, Warren S., comp. A MIRROR FOR AMERICANS: LIFE AND MANNERS IN THE UNITED STATES, 1790-1870, AS RECORDED BY AMERICAN TRAVELERS. 3 vols. Chicago: University of Chicago Press, 1952. Illus.

Note chapter 5, "A Resolute Woman Observes the Atlantic Cities." Also includes excerpts from Anne Royall's diary and from Frances Lieber's THE STRANGER IN AMERICA.

173 Varigny, Charles V.C. de. LA FEMME AUX ÉTATS-UNIS. Paris: Armand Colin, 1893. 322 p.

French traveler views American women as energetic and materialistic.

C. STATUS

1. General

a. RESOURCES, SOURCES

The Interstate Association of Commissions on the Status of Women pulls together the state organizations working for the improvement of women's status. Its bimonthly newsletter, BREAKTHROUGH, prints general information on legislation for women as well as on organization activities.

b. BIBLIOGRAPHIES

174 Bowling Green State University Library. STATUS OF WOMEN BIBLIOGRAPHY: A SELECTIVE BIBLIOGRAPHY OF GOVERNMENT PUBLICATIONS. Bowling Green, Ohio, Government Documents Department. Bowling Green: 1973. 14 p. Offset, stapled.

Lists documents from 1967 to 1973.

175 U.S. Department of Labor. WOMEN--THEIR SOCIAL AND ECONOMIC STATUS. SELECTED REFERENCES. Compiled by Julia A. Dupont. Washington, D.C.: Government Printing Office, 1970. 46 p.

Lists special libraries as well as individual items.

See note on Women's Bureau on page 14, about the Project for the Status and Education of Women on page 99, about KNOW on page 81.

See also 8, 1157.

c. REFERENCES

Various reports, fact sheets, and recommendations issued by the National Commission on the Observance of International Women's Year 1975 may be had upon request.

176 Addams, Jane. "Position of Women." In JANE ADDAMS: A CENTENNIAL READER, edited by Emily C. Johnson, pp. 100-135. New York: Macmillan Co., 1960.

177 Citizens Advisory Council on the Status of Women. ANNUAL REPORT TO THE PRESIDENT. Washington, D.C.: Government Printing Office, 1970-- . Annual.

Surveys and makes recommendations about fields of major concern to women, including the Equal Rights Amendment, education, employment inside and outside of the home, financial status, child care, female criminal offenders, and other areas. Appendix tabulates and summarizes documents and data.

178 Clarenbach, Kathryn F., and Thompson, Marian L. HANDBOOK FOR COMMISSIONS ON THE STATUS OF WOMEN. Madison: University of Wisconsin-Extension in cooperation with the Women's Bureau, Employment Standards Administration, Department of Labor, 1974. 40 p. Paper.

Includes information on how to establish communications, how to influence legislative processes, how to conduct public hearings and surveys, how to write reports and proposals, and how to run conferences.

179 Ferriss, Abbott L. INDICATORS OF TRENDS IN THE STATUS OF AMERICAN WOMEN. New York: Russell Sage Foundation, 1971. xx, 451 p. Biblio. Offset.

Trends in time series statistics, based on government data, tabulate changes in female population, education and marital status, fertility, women migrants, women at work and unemployed, income status, social participation, recreation, health, and mortality.

180 Grimké, Sarah. LETTERS ON THE EQUALITY OF THE SEXES AND THE CONDITION OF WOMAN. Boston: Isaac Knapp, 1838. Reprint. Burt Franklin Research and Source Work Series, no. 575. New York: Burt Franklin, 1970. 128 p.

Social relations between men and women, status here and abroad, and legal disabilities.

181 Larson, Cedric A. "The Women in WHO'S WHO." In his WHO, SIXTY YEARS OF AMERICAN EMINENCE: THE STORY OF WHO'S WHO IN AMERICA, chap. 16. New York: McDowell, Obolensky, 1958. Illus., tables.

Statistical summary of status of women in America based on WHO'S WHO series.

182 Lerner, Gerda. "New Approaches to the Study of Women in American History." JOURNAL OF SOCIAL HISTORY 3 (Fall 1969): 53-62.

How women's status has been affected by the manner in which she has been recorded.

183 National Commission on the Observance of International Women's Year 1975." . . . TO FORM A MORE PERFECT UNION . . . ": JUSTICE FOR AMERICAN WOMEN. Washington, D.C.: U.S. Department of State, 1976. xi, 382 p. Illus., biblio. Paper.

Reproduces report of the National Commission. Part 1, brief historical introductions; part 2, present status of women: in home, Equal Rights Amendment, mass media, grant allocation, government and union position, law and law enforcement, labor force, discrimination, Indian women, family planning, child care, and government policy toward women; part 3 deals with future of women; part 4, the International Women's Year commission; part 5, recommendations; part 6, appendix, mostly statistical and legal interpretation. Available from the Superintendent of Documents.

184 U.S. President's Commission on the Status of Women. AMERICAN WOMEN: REPORT OF THE PRESIDENT'S COMMISSION ON THE STATUS OF WOMEN AND OTHER PUBLICATIONS OF THE COMMISSION. Edited by Margaret Mead, and Frances B. Kaplan. New York: Scribner's, 1965. xi, 274 p. Tables, charts.

Section 1 is the final report on the status of women in education and counseling; home and community; employment; labor standards; security of widows, single and unemployed women; maternity benefits; women under the law; and women as political participants and office holders. Section 2 contains summaries of committee reports.

d. AUDIOTAPE. See 51.

2. Legal Status

a. SOURCES, RESOURCES

One organization from which information relating specifically to women's legal status may be secured, in addition to the Women's Bureau, is the Women's Equity Action League, which reports on its monitoring of relevant legislation through its monthly newsletter WEAL WASHINGTON REPORT and which also issues kits on a wide variety of subjects. The Women's Lobby issues the bimonthly newsletter ALERT, as well as the WOMEN'S LOBBY QUARTERLY, which analyzes all legislation affecting women, and assorted informational literature. Human Rights for Women publishes the HUMAN RIGHTS FOR WOMEN NEWSLETTER, the JOB DISCRIMINATION HANDBOOK, and, in conjunction with Today Publications, the Law and Women series (see 658, 1029). Women's Law Center (Center for Women's Equality) issues fact sheets on marriage and change of name and also published A WOMAN'S GUIDE TO MARRIAGE AND DIVORCE IN NEW YORK (see 662). Two other helpful groups are the Women's Rights Project of the American Civil Liberties Union and the National Organization for Women Task Force on Legislation.

Several government publications issue the texts of congressional bills and actions surrounding them. These are the CONGRESSIONAL RECORD, which records the daily proceedings of Congress while it is in session; the FEDERAL REGISTER, which reports daily the decisions of regulating agencies and prints sections of laws relevant to the agencies' rulings; and the monthly DIGEST OF PUBLIC GENERAL BILLS, which cumulates through sessions and sets down actions as they take place.

Two private publications are the CQ WEEKLY REPORT, which reviews congressional action and lists key bills and voting records of the members of Congress, and the CONGRESSIONAL AND ADMINISTRATIVE NEWS, which prints histories of leading bills along with actions taken in committee.

Many women's organizations distribute material on the Equal Rights Amendment. Some that do are the League of Women Voters, Women United, National Organization for Women, National Woman's Party, Citizens' Advisory Council on the Status of Women, American Association of University Women, the Young Women's Christian Association, and the Business and Professional Women's Foundation. Some more broadly based organizations making available such information are Common Cause, the American Civil Liberties Union, and the Commission on Civil Rights.

Periodical literature reporting on legislation of importance to women includes the biweekly WOMEN'S LAW REPORT, which comes with a CURRENT DEVELOPMENTS REPORT in a library research binder with supplementary materials that contain the full texts of legislation, and the legislative service WOMEN'S WASHINGTON REPRESENTATIVE, which is published every three weeks while Congress is in session. Monthly publications include the WEAL WASHINGTON

REPORT, a newsletter, and the magazines SPOKESWOMEN, SPEAKOUT, the WOMAN ACTIVIST and the WOMEN LAWYERS JOURNAL. Two quarterlies are the WOMEN'S RIGHTS LAW REPORT and PEER PERSPECTIVE, issued by the Project on Equal Education Rights of the National Organization for Women Legal Defense and Education Fund.

185 Wheeler, Helen R., comp. ALICE IN WONDERLAND, OR THROUGH THE LOOKING GLASS: RESOURCES FOR IMPLEMENTING PRINCIPLES OF AFFIRMATIVE ACTION EMPLOYMENT FOR WOMEN. Washington, D.C.: Educational Resources Information Center, 1975. 14 p.

Annotated. Sixty-four references include printed, audio-visual, and slide material. Available from ERIC Document Reproduction Center, P.O. Box 190, Arlington, Virginia 22210.

b. BIBLIOGRAPHIES

186 Babcock, Barbara, et al., comps. WOMEN AND THE LAW: A COLLECTION OF READING LISTS. Pittsburgh, Pa.: KNOW, 1971. 31 p. Offset, pamph.

187 Greenberg, Hazel, comp. THE EQUAL RIGHTS AMENDMENT: A BIBLIOGRAPHIC STUDY. For Equal Rights Amendment Project. Westport, Conn.: Greenwood Press, 1976. xxviii, 368 p.

Comprehensive. Spans sixty-two years. Includes governmental publications, books, periodicals, journals, indexes to microform collections, and addresses of women's publications and organizations.

Bibliographies on the status of women are available from many of the organizations mentioned in section "a" above. See also 3 and 314.

For further bibliography on the Equal Rights Amendment see 314.

c. REFERENCES

188 Alexander, Shana. STATE-BY-STATE GUIDE TO WOMEN'S LEGAL RIGHTS. Los Angeles: Wollstonecraft, 1975. 224 p.

Laws grouped around categories of age, marriage, children, abortion, divorce, annulment and separation, widowhood, employment, criminal accusation, rape, and citizenship. Formerly titled WOMEN UNDER THE LAW.

189 Babcock, Barbara, et al., eds. SEX DISCRIMINATION AND THE

LAW: CAUSES AND REMEDIES. Boston: Little, Brown and Co., 1975. xlix, 1,975 p.

Casebook. Five sections have to do with constitutional law and feminist history, discrimination on employment and family law, women and criminal law, and women's right to control various aspects of themselves and their lives.

190 Baxter, Ian G. MARITAL PROPERTY. American Family Law Library. Rochester: New York Lawyers' Co-operative, 1973. xxix, 640 p. Offset.

Summary of American marital property law with some historical and geographical background.

191 Bayles, George J. WOMAN AND THE LAW. New York: Century, 1901. xv, 274 p.

Handbook guide to domestic, property, and political rights for nonprofessional women. Appendix includes state-by-state listing of statutes relating to married women.

192 Bernard, Jessie S. WOMAN AND THE PUBLIC INTEREST: AN ESSAY ON POLICY AND PROTEST. Chicago: Aldine-Atherton, 1971. viii, 293 p. Biblios. Paper.

Survey of revolutionary changes going on in our society and resulting paradoxes of policy as they relate to women. Includes discussion on employment, women's rights, and discrimination.

193 Breckinridge, Sophonisba P. MARRIAGE AND CIVIC RIGHTS OF WOMEN: SEPARATE DOMICIL [sic] AND INDEPENDENT CITIZENSHIP. Social Service Monograph, no. 13. Chicago: University of Chicago Press, 1931. xi, 158 p.

The Cable Act and how it affected both native and foreign-born women.

194 Bres, Rose F. MAIDS, WIVES, AND WIDOWS: THE LAW OF THE LAND AND OF VARIOUS STATES AS IT AFFECTS WOMEN. New York: E.P. Dutton & Co., 1918. 267 p.

First-aid legal handbook on women's legal status covers general matters as well as state laws on marriage and divorce, pensions for mothers, and minimum wages. Includes legislative digest.

195 Brown, Barbara A., et al., eds. WOMEN'S RIGHTS AND THE LAW: THE IMPACT OF THE ERA ON STATE LAWS. Praeger Special Studies.

New York: Published for the Women's Law Project by Praeger, 1977. 448 p. Paper.

Theoretical as well as pragmatic effects of the Equal Rights Amendment on criminal and antidiscrimination law, domestic relations, employment, civil rights, and public obligations.

196 California Commission on the Status of Women. Equal Rights Amendment Project. IMPACT ERA: LIMITATIONS AND POSSIBILITIES. Edited by Hazel Greenberg. Millbrae, Calif.: Les Femmes, 1976. xii, 287 p. Paper.

Eighteen articles discuss political, economic, social, and psychological impact of the amendment.

197 Davidson, Kenneth, et al. TEXTS, CASES AND MATERIALS ON SEX BASED DISCRIMINATION. American Casebook Series. St. Paul, Minn.: West, 1974. xxxv, 1,031 p.

Includes constitutional aspects, those having to do with sexual interaction within family, with employment, with educational opportunity, and with innovative aspects of criminal law in delineating sex roles.

198 DeCrow, Karen. SEXIST JUSTICE. New York: Random House, 1974. xii, 329 p. Paper.

Documents "legal misogyny" in employment, estate law, marriage, abortion, naming, and education. Notes cite cases.

199 Jongeward, Dorothy, and Scott, Dru. AFFIRMATIVE ACTION FOR WOMEN: A PRACTICAL GUIDE FOR WOMEN AND MANAGEMENT. Reading, Mass.: Addison-Wesley Publishing Co., 1975. ix, 334 p. Illus.

Includes interpretation of laws, how they relate to women in government, religion, and management, with sections also on black women, women in psychotherapy, and sexist language.

200 Kanowitz, Leo. SEX ROLES IN LAW AND SOCIETY: CASES AND MATERIALS. Albuquerque: University of New Mexico Press, 1973. xiv, 706 p. Paper.

Designed as text for courses in women and the law. Material on sex roles, the law and marriage, employment, the Constitution, public accommodation, education, pornography, the media, sex preference, appearance, the military, and poverty. Cases illustrate each. Appendix includes amended text of Title VII of Civil Rights Act. Supplement issued in 1974.

201 _____. WOMEN AND THE LAW: THE UNFINISHED REVOLUTION. Albuquerque: University of New Mexico Press, 1969. ix, 312 p. Paper.

Law as it relates to single and married women. Examines Title VII and the Equal Rights Amendment as well as constitutional aspects of discrimination. Includes texts of Title VII, Executive Order 11246, and two court opinions.

202 Kelley, Florence. SOME ETHICAL GAINS THROUGH LEGISLATION. Citizens' Library of Economics, Politics and Sociology. New York: Macmillan Co., 1905. x, 341 p. Reprint. New York: Arno Press, 1969.

Material on child labor, right to leisure for women, consumers' rights. Appendix includes court cases.

203 Morris, Richard B. "Women's Rights in Early American Law." In his STUDIES IN THE HISTORY OF AMERICAN LAW, WITH SPECIAL REFERENCE TO THE SEVENTEENTH AND EIGHTEENTH CENTURIES, chap. 3. 2d ed. Studies in History, Economics and Public Law, no. 316. London: P.S. King; New York: Columbia University, 1930. 285 p. Biblio. Reprint. New York: Octagon Books, 1964.

Includes primary and secondary material.

204 Murphy, Irene L. PUBLIC POLICY ON THE STATUS OF WOMEN: AGENDA AND STRATEGY FOR THE 70S. Lexington Books. Lexington, Mass.: D.C. Heath & Co., 1973. xi, 129 p. Biblio.

Studies inadequate response to feminism as political movement by White House and Congress during the Nixon administration. Discusses women's lobby and future activism.

205 New York Coalition for Equal Rights. "ERA Campaign Kit." Prepared by League of Women Voters of New York State. New York: 1975. 94 p. Mimeo.

Theoretical and practical concerns.

206 Rembaugh, Bertha, comp. THE POLITICAL STATUS OF WOMEN IN THE UNITED STATES: A DIGEST OF LAWS CONCERNING WOMEN IN THE VARIOUS ESTATES AND TERRITORIES. New York: G.P. Putnam's Sons, 1911. xiii, 164 p.

Historical glimpse into confusion surrounding women's status. From report sponsored by Women's Political Union.

207 Ross, Susan C. THE RIGHTS OF WOMEN: THE BASIC ACLU GUIDE TO WOMEN'S RIGHTS. New York: Discus, 1973. 384 p. Charts. Paper.

Covers legal means to cope with sex discrimination in question and answer form. Includes charts of state antidiscrimination laws, information on name changing, listings of sources for legal help, and women's organizations and publications.

208 Smith, Julia E. ABBY SMITH AND HER COWS, WITH A REPORT OF THE LAW CASE DECIDED CONTRARY TO THE LAW. Hartford, Conn.: n.p., 1877. 94 p. Reprint. American Women: Images and Realities series. New York: Arno Press, 1972.

Resisting taxation without representation, two unmarried sisters fought, and won, their case, becoming suffragists in the process.

209 Sprague, Henry H. WOMEN UNDER THE LAW IN MASSACHUSETTS: THEIR RIGHTS, PRIVILEGES AND DISABILITIES. 2d ed. Boston: Little, Brown and Co., 1903. xi, 100 p.

Lists cases. First published in 1884.

210 Stimpson, Catharine A., ed. in conjunction with the Congressional Information Service. "Discrimination against Women: Congressional Hearings on Equal Rights in Education and Employment." Bowker/CIS Document Series. New York: R.R. Bowker Co., 1973. xvii, 558 p. Tables. Photocopy.

Part 1, testimony by Anne Scott, Wilma Heide, Ann Harris, Shirley Chisholm, Lucy Komisar, and others on sex discrimination. Part 2, documents on women and work and women in the professions and government, with model remedies for discrimination suggested by various women's organizations.

211 Switzer, Ellen, and Susco, Wendy. THE LAW FOR A WOMAN. REAL CASES AND WHAT HAPPENED. New York: Charles Scribner's Sons, 1975. x, 246 p. Paper.

Surveys cases having to do with civil, educational, employment, family, property, and medical rights. Appendix lists employment commissions, grounds for divorce, and information on law schools in the United States.

212 U.S. Commission on Civil Rights. SEX BIAS IN THE UNITED STATES CODE: A REPORT . . . APRIL, 1977. Washington, D.C.: Government Printing Office, 1977. vii, 230 p. Biblio. Offset, paper.

Discusses women's status under the Constitution, analyzes bias in army and social security system, and relation of language to discriminatory practices. Offers recommendations.

213 U.S. Department of Health, Education and Welfare. TITLE IX GRIEVANCE PROCEDURES: AN INTRODUCTORY MANUAL. Prepared by Martha Matthews and Shirley McCune. Washington, D.C.: 1977. 102 p. Illus., biblio.

214 Wasserman, Richard. "Racism, Sexism and Preferential Treatment." UCLA LAW REVIEW 24 (February 1977): 581-622.

Necessity of affirmative action programs to combat racism and sexism.

See also 594.

d. IN MICROFORM

215 Women's History Research Center. WOMEN AND THE LAW: A COLLECTION ON MICROFILM. Berkeley, Calif.: 1975.

In six sections: 1, Law/General (ERA, credit, divorce); 2, Politics; 3, Employment; 4, Education; 5, Rape/Prison/Prostitution; 6, Black and Third World Women. Available from the center. Reel guides and annotated catalogs included.

For the economic status of women see chapter 7, section B.

Chapter 3
HISTORY

A. RESOURCES

Major collections of women's history are held at the Arthur and Elizabeth Schlesinger Library on the History of Women in America, previously known as the Women's Archives at Radcliffe College, Cambridge, Massachusetts. A printed catalog of the collection entitled MANUSCRIPT INVENTORIES AND THE CATALOGS OF THE MANUSCRIPTS, BOOKS AND PICTURES may be obtained by writing the library, Cambridge, Massachusetts.

Another major collection of women's history is held by the Women's History Research Center Library at Berkeley, California. Because of lack of funding, the collection had to be divided among institutions that have facilities for its upkeep, although a few of these documents are still in "cold storage." All dispersed items are available in microfilm from the center from which instructions for ordering may be secured. The International Women's History (Periodical) Archives, consisting of newsletters, newspapers, and journals, are housed at the Special Collections Library, Northwestern University, Evanston, Illinois. The topical files collection, consisting of WOMEN'S HEALTH/MENTAL HEALTH (see 1470), and WOMAN AND THE LAW (see 215) files, are housed at the Archives of Contemporary History, University of Wyoming, Laramie, Wyoming. These have not yet been entirely microfilmed. The collection of major pamphlets is housed at Princeton University, Princeton, New Jersey.

Many collections are becoming available through microfilm. See 311.

For further listings of women's collections see page 3; and 218 and 280.

B. BIBLIOGRAPHIES

216 Common Women Collective. WOMEN IN U.S. HISTORY: AN ANNOTATED BIBLIOGRAPHY. Cambridge, Mass.: 1976. iii, 114 p. Paper.

Includes material on women's movement (suffrage, abolition, reform movements), employment, native American women and Chicanas, sexuality and lesbianism, and autobiography.

217 Harrison, Cynthia E., comp. WOMEN IN AMERICAN HISTORY: A BIBLIOGRAPHY. Clio Bibliographical Series. Santa Barbara, Calif.: American Bibliographical Center, Clio Press, 1978. About 1,000 p.

Three chronological sections--1783 to 1865, Civil War to World War II, and 1945 to the present--further subdivided into subject divisions.

218 Hinding, Andrea, and Chambers, Clarke A., comps. WOMEN'S HISTORY SOURCES: A GUIDE TO ARCHIVES AND MANUSCRIPT COLLECTIONS IN THE UNITED STATES. 2 vols. New York: R.R. Bowker, 1979. 2,600 p.

Lists twenty thousand sources located in two thousand repositories. Introduction discusses origins and status of women's history, as well as historical methodology.

219 Lerner, Gerda, comp. BIBLIOGRAPHY IN THE HISTORY OF AMERICAN WOMEN. 3d rev. ed. Bronxville, N.Y.: Sarah Lawrence, 1975. 19 p. Offset, stapled.

Unannotated. Listings in bibliography; historiography; theories regarding women; general history; family; motherhood; work; education; sexuality; women, law, and crime; women and art; black and other minority, and immigrant women; biography and autobiography.

220 ten Houten, Elizabeth S., comp. "Collections of Special Use for Women History Resources in the United States." AAUW JOURNAL 67 (April 1974): 35-36.

Includes general listing as well as more specialized listings in medicine, religion, organizations, religion, and oral history sources.

221 Thomas, Roy R., comp. "Women in American History, 1896-1920: Their Manuscripts in the Library of Congress." Bowie, Md.: Bowie Street College, 1972. 9 leaves.

Prepared for Workshop in Archival and Manuscript Sources for the Study of Women's History, Organization of American Historians.

222 Wilson, Joan H., and Donnan, Lynn B., comps. "Women's History: A Listing of West Coast Archival and Manuscript Sources--Part 1." CALIFORNIA HISTORICAL QUARTERLY 55 (September 1976): 74-83.

223 Winsor, Justin. THE LITERATURE OF WITCHCRAFT IN NEW ENGLAND. Reprinted from PROCEEDINGS OF THE AMERICAN ANTIQUARIAN SOCIETY, October 1895. Worcester, Mass.: Hamilton, 1896. 25 p. Pamph.

Numerous seventeenth-century, as well as nineteenth-century sources.

See also 293, 298, 299.

C. REFERENCES

224 Adams, Charles F. ANTINOMIANISM IN THE COLONY OF MASSACHUSETTS BAY, 1636-1638; INCLUDING THE SHORT STORY AND OTHER DOCUMENTS. Boston: Prince Society, 1894. 415 p. Reprint. Burt Franklin Research and Source Work Series, no. 131; American Classics in History and Social Sciences, no. 2. New York: Burt Franklin, 1967.

Includes, among other issues, Anne Hutchinson as a woman in a man's world, evidenced in the direct questioning in "The Examination of Mrs. Anne Hutchinson" (p. 235-84) and "Trial of Mrs. Hutchinson before the Church in Boston" (pp. 285-336).

225 Adams, John, and Warren, Mercy Otis. In CORRESPONDENCE BETWEEN JOHN ADAMS AND MERCY WARREN RELATING TO HER "HISTORY OF THE AMERICAN REVOLUTION," JULY-AUGUST 1807, pp. 315-511. Collections of the Massachusetts Historical Society, 5th series, vol. 4. Boston: 1878. Reprint. American Women: Images and Realities series. New York: Arno Press, 1972.

Close friends cross swords over scholarly matters.

226 Alexander, William. THE HISTORY OF WOMEN, FROM THE EARLIEST ANTIQUITY TO THE PRESENT TIMES, GIVING THE ACCOUNT OF ALMOST EVERY INTERESTING PARTICULAR CONCERNING THE SEX, AMONG ALL NATIONS ANCIENT AND MODERN. 2 vols. 3d ed. Philadelphia: J.H. Dobelbower, 1796.

Early women's history from feminist point of view. American women are native American.

227 Altbach, Edith H., ed. WOMEN IN AMERICA. Lexington, Mass.: D.C. Heath & Co., 1974. x, 205 p.

Focus on working and middle-class women employed inside and outside of the home from colonial period. Includes chronology 1617-1973.

228 Aptheker, Herbert, ed. A DOCUMENTARY HISTORY OF THE NEGRO PEOPLE IN THE UNITED STATES. New York: Citadel Press, 1969. xviii, 942 p.

Numerous documents relate to black women in a wide variety of roles, 1661-1910.

229 _____. A DOCUMENTARY HISTORY OF THE NEGRO PEOPLE IN THE UNITED STATES: 1910-1932. Secaucus, N.J.: Citadel Press, 1973. xii, 754 p.

Among 145 documents, a few relate to women.

230 Armstrong, Margaret. FIVE GENERATIONS: LIFE AND LETTERS OF AN AMERICAN FAMILY, 1750-1900. New York: Harper, 1930. ix, 425 p. Illus.

Women's lives revealed through detailed account of upper-class New York family life.

231 Banner, Lois. WOMEN IN MODERN AMERICA: A BRIEF HISTORY. The Harbrace History of the United States. New York: Harcourt Brace Jovanovich, 1974. xii, 276 p. Illus. Paper.

From 1890 to the present.

232 Battis, Emery J. SAINTS AND SECTARIES: ANNE HUTCHINSON AND THE ANTINOMIAN CONTROVERSY IN THE MASSACHUSETTS BAY COLONY. Chapel Hill: University of North Carolina, 1962. xv, 379 p. Illus., tables, biblio.

Intellectual history through biography.

233 Baxter, Annette, with Jacobs, Constance. TO BE A WOMAN IN AMERICA 1850-1930. New York: Times Books, 1978. 240 p. Illus.

Unusual photographs of women's lives, many of them anonymous.

234 Beard, Mary R. WOMAN AS A FORCE IN HISTORY: A STUDY OF THE TRADITIONS AND REALITIES. New York: Macmillan Co., 1946. viii, 369 p. Biblio. Paper.

Claims that women's role as a subject throughout history has conditioned attitudes and behavior toward them.

235 _____, ed. AMERICA THROUGH WOMEN'S EYES. New York: Macmillan Co., 1933. 558 p. Biblio.

Discusses women as participants in American history. This volume served as an early spur to feminist history.

236 Bell, Margaret. WOMEN OF THE WILDERNESS. New York: E.P. Dutton & Co., 1938. 384 p.

Hardships of women's lives in Massachusetts Bay Colony. Material on Anne Bradstreet. No documentation.

237 Bell, Margaret V.H. [Dwight]. A JOURNEY TO OHIO IN 1810, AS RECORDED IN THE JOURNAL OF MARGARET VAN HORN DWIGHT. Yale History Manuscripts, no. 1. New Haven, Conn.: Yale University Press, 1941. vi, 64 p. Reprint. 1941.

Wagon trip made by the granddaughter of Jonathan Edwards.

238 Benson, Mary S. WOMEN IN EIGHTEENTH-CENTURY AMERICA: A STUDY OF OPINION AND SOCIAL USAGE. Columbia Studies in History, Economics, and Public Law, no. 405. New York: Columbia University, 1935. 343 p. Biblio. Reprint. Port Washington, N.Y.: Kennikat Press, 1966.

Upper- and middle-class women in literature, law, politics, and religion. Includes commentaries by foreign visitors.

239 Bergman, Peter M., et al. THE CHRONOLOGICAL HISTORY OF THE NEGRO IN AMERICA. New York: Harper & Row, 1969. 698 p. Biblio.

Black women in context of American black history.

240 Blumenthal, Walter H. WOMEN CAMP FOLLOWERS OF THE AMERICAN REVOLUTION. Philadelphia: G.S. McManus, 1952. 104 p. Reprint. Women in America: From Colonial Times to the 20th Century series. New York: Arno Press, 1974.

241 Booth, Sally S. THE WITCHES OF EARLY AMERICA. Rev. ed. New York: Hastings House, 1975. 238 p. Biblio.

Studies in detail the institution of witchcraft.

242 ______. THE WOMEN OF '76. New York: Hastings House, Publishers, 1973. 329 p. Illus, biblio.

Includes European, as well as American women, involved in the Revolutionary War.

243 Botkin, Benjamin A. LAY MY BURDEN DOWN: A FOLK HISTORY OF SLAVERY. Chicago: University of Chicago Press, 1945. xxi, 298 p. Illus. Paper.

Complete narratives, as well as excerpts, many by women, from the Slave Narrative Collection of the Federal Writers' Project.

244 Boyer, Paul, and Nissenbaum, Stephen, eds. SALEM-VILLAGE WITCHCRAFT: A DOCUMENTARY RECORD OF LOCAL CONFLICT IN COLONIAL NEW ENGLAND. American History Research Series. Belmont, Calif.: Wadsworth Publishing Co., 1972. xxv, 416 p. Illus., biblio.

Primary documents set witch trials in sociological context.

245 Branch, E. Douglas. "Garlands and Chains." In his THE SENTIMENTAL YEARS: 1836-1860, chap. 7. New York: D. Appleton, 1934. Illus. Paper.

Focuses on women in philanthropy, professions, and politics; on women's clothing and education; and on women as family members. Presents material also on women in arts, in medicine, and in Lowell mills.

246 Brockett, Linus P., and Vaughan, Mary C. WOMAN'S WORK IN THE CIVIL WAR: A RECORD OF HEROISM, PATRIOTISM AND PATIENCE. Philadelphia: Ziegler, McCurdy; Boston: R.H. Curran, 1867. 799 p. Illus.

Biographical sketches include those of Dorothea Dix, Clara Barton, Mary Ann Bickerdyke, and Mary Livermore. Material on philanthropic and relief work, Hospital Transport Corps, and Women's Central Relief Association.

247 Brown, Dee. THE GENTLE TAMERS: WOMEN OF THE OLD WILD WEST. New York: G.P. Putnam's Sons, 1958. 317 p. Illus., biblio. Paper.

Frontier women from wives to prostitutes with some material on Calamity Jane and Lola Montez.

248 Buhle, Mari Jo, et al. "Women in American Society: An Historical Contribution." RADICAL AMERICA 5 (July-August 1971): 3-66.

Interprets woman's role and status from colonial times to present with view to correcting shortcomings of conventional historical approach.

249 Carroll, Berenice A., ed. LIBERATING WOMEN'S HISTORY: THEORETICAL AND CRITICAL ESSAYS. Urbana: University of Illinois Press, 1976. xiv, 434 p. Paper.

Twenty-three scholarly essays with international as well as American focus.

250 Conrad, Susan P. PERISH THE THOUGHT: INTELLECTUAL WOMEN IN ROMANTIC AMERICA, 1830-1860. New York: Oxford University Press, 1976. vi, 292 p. Illus., biblio. Paper.

Material on Lydia Child, Caroline Dall, Elizabeth Ellett, Margaret Fuller, Sarah Grimké, Elizabeth Peabody, Elizabeth Cady Stanton, Sara Whitman, and many others.

251 Demos, John. A LITTLE COMMONWEALTH: FAMILY LIFE IN THE PURITAN COLONY. New York: Oxford University Press, 1970. xvi, 201 p. Illus. Paper.

Includes material on status of women, their clothing, and their property rights.

252 Dick, Everett. "The Frontier Women." In his THE DIXIE FRONTIER: A HISTORY OF THE SOUTHERN FRONTIER FROM THE FIRST TRANS-MONTANE BEGINNINGS TO THE CIVIL WAR, chap. 26. New York: Alfred A. Knopf, 1948. xix, 374, xxv p. Illus. Reprint. New York: G.P. Putnam's Sons, Capricorn Books, 1964.

253 Douglas, Ann. THE FEMINIZATION OF AMERICAN CULTURE. New York: Alfred A. Knopf, 1977. x, 403 p.

The alliance between ladies and ministers and its pervasive literary and cultural influence.

254 Earle, Alice M. COLONIAL DAMES AND GOODWIVES. Boston: Houghton Mifflin Co., 1895. 315 p. Reprint. American Classics Series. New York: Frederick Ungar, 1962.

Chapters on women in business, and on witches, travelers (Sarah Kemble Knight), women in religion (Jeremiah Wilkinson), women's amusements, Daughters of Liberty, and home life in the northern and southern colonies. Undocumented.

255 Ellett, Elizabeth F. THE PIONEER WOMEN OF THE WEST. Philadelphia: Porter & Coates, 1852. ix, 434 p. Reprint. Freeport, N.Y.: Books for Libraries, 1973.

First history of women in the Western movement.

256 _____. THE WOMEN OF THE AMERICAN REVOLUTION. 3 vols. American History and Americana Series, no. 47. New York: Baker & Haskell, 1848. Reprint. New York: Haskell House, 1969.

Domestic history. Early attempt to define women's place in American history.

257 Evans, Elizabeth. WEATHERING THE STORM: WOMEN OF THE AMERICAN REVOLUTION. New York: Charles Scribner's Sons, 1975. 372 p. Illus., biblio.

Introductions and headnotes to diaries and journals of eleven personalities of the period.

258 Farnham, Eliza W.B. LIFE IN PRAIRIE LAND. New York: Harper & Brothers, 1846. xii, 408 p. Reprint. American Women: Images and Realities series. New York: Arno Press, 1972.

Intimate view of prairie life by woman who later became women's warden at Sing Sing and teacher of the blind in Boston.

259 Fass, Paula S. THE DAMNED AND THE BEAUTIFUL: AMERICAN YOUTH IN THE 1920S. New York: Oxford University Press, 1977. xii, 497 p.

Middle-class American college women and men in broad social context.

260 Fischer, Christiane, ed. LET THEM SPEAK FOR THEMSELVES: WOMEN IN THE AMERICAN WEST 1849-1900. Hamden, Conn.: Archon Books, 1977. 346 p. Biblio. Paper.

Seven sections contain selections from personal writings of women arranged around life in mining towns and camps, on farms and ranches, with the army, in cities, and pursuing careers, as well as women growing up and travelers' views of such lives.

261 Fowler, Samuel P. SALEM WITCHCRAFT: COMPRISING MORE WONDERS OF THE INVISIBLE WORLD, COLLECTED BY ROBERT CALEF: AND WONDERS OF THE INVISIBLE WORLD BY COTTON MATHER. London: n.p., 1700. Reprint. Boston: William Veazie, 1865. xxi, 446 p.

Published with a view to establishing truth about witchcraft. Note especially part 1, "An Account of the Sufferings of Margaret Rule. . . ." Appendix lists those convicted of witchcraft, some of whom were executed.

262 Fowler, William H. WOMAN ON THE AMERICAN FRONTIER: A VALUABLE AND AUTHENTIC HISTORY OF THE HEROISM, ADVENTURES, PRIVATIONS, CAPTIVITIES, TRIALS, AND NOBLE LIVES AND DEATHS OF THE "PIONEER MOTHERS OF THE REPUBLIC." Hartford Conn.: S.S. Scranton, 1879. 527 p. Illus. Reprint. New York: Source Book Press, 1970.

Unusual account of frontier woman and her various roles.

263 Friedman, Jean E., and Shade, William G., eds. AMERICAN SISTERS: WOMEN IN AMERICAN LIFE AND THOUGHT. 2d ed. Boston:

Allyn & Bacon, 1976. ix, 446 p. Biblio. Paper.

Reprints of twenty-four essays grouped in four sections--"Women in Colonial America," "Victorian Images," "The Progressive Impulse," and "The Illusion of Equality."

264 Froiseth, Jennie A., ed. THE WOMEN OF MORMONISM: THE STORY OF POLYGAMY, AS TOLD BY THE VICTIMS THEMSELVES. Introduction by Frances Willard. Detroit: C.G.C. Paine, 1882. xiii, 416 p. Illus.

Subscription book that printed purported Mormon histories set down by the vice-president of the Women's Anti-Polygamy Society.

265 George, Carol V.R., ed. "REMEMBER THE LADIES": NEW PERSPECTIVES ON WOMEN IN AMERICAN HISTORY--ESSAYS IN HONOR OF NEILSON MANFRED BLAKE. Syracuse, N.Y.: Syracuse University Press, 1975. xvi, 201 p.

Section 1 contains material on Anne Hutchinson, eighteenth-century feminist theorists, and relation of Protestant ethnic to feminist thought; section 2, women and the nativist movement, male midwifery, and Harriet Tubman; section 3, divorce, the flapper, American cult feminism in Japan, and the founding of the Women's Bureau.

266 Grant, Anne. MEMOIRS OF AN AMERICAN LADY: WITH SKETCHES OF MANNERS AND SCENES IN AMERICA AS THEY EXISTED PREVIOUS TO THE REVOLUTION. London: Longmans, Hurst, Rees & Ormo, 1807. xxxvi, 300 p. Illus. Reprint. New York: Dodd, Mead, 1901.

Upper-class woman's view that delighted Irving, Scott, Thackeray, and many others.

267 Greene, Lorenzo J. THE NEGRO IN COLONIAL NEW ENGLAND, 1620-1776. New York: Columbia University Press, 1942. Biblio. Reprint. New York: Atheneum Press, 1968. 404 p. Paper.

Occupations, legal rights, crimes, and punishments of colonial black women, as well as their sexual and marital roles. Appendix includes population statistics on black women in Massachusetts towns.

268 Groves, Ernest R. THE AMERICAN WOMAN: THE FEMININE SIDE OF A MASCULINE CIVILIZATION. New York: Greenberg, 1937. vii, 465 p. Reprint. American Women: Images and Realities series. New York: Arno Press, 1972.

Detailed social history of American women in the first half

of the twentieth century discusses regional characteristics of women's lives as well as political, economic, and social advances.

269 Hague, Parthenia A. A BLOCKADED FAMILY: LIFE IN SOUTHERN ALABAMA DURING THE CIVIL WAR. Boston: Houghton Mifflin Co. 1888. v, 176 p. Reprint. The Black Heritage Library Collection. Freeport, N.Y: Books for Libraries, 1971.

Unique, intimate view of war by black woman.

270 Hartman, Mary S., and Banner, Lois, eds. CLIO'S CONSCIOUSNESS RAISED: NEW PERSPECTIVES ON THE HISTORY OF WOMEN. New York: Harper Torchbook, Harper & Row, 1974. xii, 253 p.

Articles on American Victorian women regarding their health--birth control, medical treatment, venereal disease; professions in library and the church; prostitution, and effects of timesaving machines on their lives.

271 Holliday, Carl. WOMEN'S LIFE IN COLONIAL DAYS. Boston: Cornhill, 1922. xvi, 319 p. Biblio. Reprint. Williamstown, Mass.: Corner House Publishers, 1968.

Chapters on religion, education, the home, dress, social life, marriage, and women's initiative. Based largely on contemporary documents.

272 Hulton, Ann. LETTERS OF A LOYALIST LADY, BEING THE LETTERS OF ANN HULTON, SISTER OF HENRY HULTON, COMMISSIONER OF CUSTOMS AT BOSTON, 1767-1776. Cambridge, Mass.: Harvard University Press, 1927. Reprint. Eyewitness Accounts of the American Revolution series. New York: Arno Press, 1970. xi, 106 p.

273 Hunter, Alexander. THE WOMEN OF THE DEBATABLE LAND. Washington, D.C.: Dobden, 1912. viii, 261 p. Illus. Reprint. Middle Atlantic States Historical Publications series, no. 1. Port Washington, N.Y.: Kennikat Press, 1972.

Confederate soldier's somewhat sentimental account of Virginian women during Civil War.

274 James, Janet W. "History and Women at Harvard: The Schlesinger Library." HARVARD LITERARY BULLETIN 16 (1968): 385-99.

275 Jones, Katharine M., ed. HEROINES OF DIXIE: CONFEDERATE WOMEN TELL THEIR STORY OF THE WAR. Indianapolis: Bobbs-Merrill Co., 1955. xiv, 430 p. Illus., biblio.

Women's view of the Civil War through their public and private writings.

276 Knight, Sarah Kemble. THE JOURNAL OF MADAME KNIGHT. THE PRIVATE JOURNAL KEPT BY MADAME KNIGHT, ON A JOURNEY FROM BOSTON TO NEW YORK, IN THE YEAR 1704. FROM AN ORIGINAL MANUSCRIPT. Boston: Small, Maynard, 1920. xiv, 72 p.

Journey by horseback through the backwoods of New England into the sophistication of New York.

277 Leonard, Eugenie A. THE DEAR-BOUGHT HERITAGE. Philadelphia: University of Pennsylvania Press, 1965. 658 p. Illus., biblio.

Women's roles inside and outside of the home in colonial America.

278 Lerner, Gerda. THE WOMAN IN AMERICAN HISTORY. Specialized Studies in American History Series. Menlo Park, N.J.: Addison-Wesley Publishing Co., 1971. 207 p. Illus., biblio. Paper.

Overview from colonial period to present.

279 Logan, Mary S. [Mrs. John A.], et al. THE PART TAKEN BY WOMEN IN AMERICAN HISTORY. Wilmington, Del.: Perry-Nalle Publishing Co., 1912. xii, 927 p. Illus., biblio. Reprint. American Women: Images and Realities series. New York: Arno Press, 1972.

Background and biographical material. Special attention to "aboriginal," Catholic, and Jewish women.

280 Massey, Mary E. BONNET BRIGADES. The Impact of the Civil War Series. New York: Alfred A. Knopf, 1966. xxi, 371 p. Illus.

Well-researched history of white and black women during Civil War. Lists manuscript collections with locations.

281 Millstein, Beth, and Bodin, Jeanne. WE, THE AMERICAN WOMEN: A DOCUMENTARY HISTORY. Chicago: SRA, 1977. xii, 331 p. Illus., biblio. Offset.

Twelve chapters from Civil War to the present divided into background information on women's roles and excerpts from women's writing. Popular in tone.

282 Mulder, William, and Mortensen, A. Russell, eds. AMONG THE MORMONS: HISTORIC ACCOUNTS BY CONTEMPORARY OBSERVERS. New York: Alfred A. Knopf, 1958. xiv, 482, xiv p.

Anthology includes several first-hand accounts by Mormon wives.

283 Putnam, Emily J. "The Lady of the Slave States." In her THE LADY: STUDIES OF CERTAIN SIGNIFICANT PHASES OF HER HISTORY, pp. 282-323. New York: G.P. Putnam's Sons, 1910. Reprint. Chicago: University of Chicago Press, 1970. Paper.

The devitalizing life of the antebellum woman.

284 Read, Georgia W. "Women and Children on the California-Oregon Trail in the Gold Rush." MISSOURI HISTORICAL REVIEW 39 (October 1944): 1-23.

285 Richards, Caroline C. VILLAGE LIFE IN AMERICA, 1852-1872, INCLUDING THE PERIOD OF THE CIVIL WAR, AS TOLD IN THE DIARY OF A SCHOOL-GIRL. Rev. and enl. New York: Henry Holt, 1913. x, 225 p. Reprint. Williamstown, Mass.: Corner House Publishers, 1972.

Small upstate New York town.

286 Rowbotham, Sheila. HIDDEN FROM HISTORY: REDISCOVERING WOMEN IN HISTORY FROM THE 17TH CENTURY TO THE PRESENT. New York: Vintage Books, Random House, 1974. xxxvi, 183 p. Paper.

Marxist-feminist approach comes out of English experience but with implications for research into the history of American women.

287 Rowlandson, Mary. THE SOVEREIGNTY AND GOODNESS OF GOD, TOGETHER WITH THE FAITHFULNESS OF THE PROMISES DISPLAYED, BEING A NARRATIVE OF THE CAPTIVITY AND RESTORATION OF MRS. MARY ROWLANDSON. 2d ed. Cambridge, Mass.: n.p., 1682. 80 p. Reprint. Boston: Houghton Mifflin Co., 1930.

Long-time best seller records white woman's life with Indian tribe.

288 Royall, Anne. SKETCHES OF LIFE, HISTORY, AND MANNERS IN THE UNITED STATES. New Haven, Conn.: 1826. Reprint. New York: Johnson Reprint Co., 1971. 392 p.

By America's first female journalist.

289 Ryan, Mary P. WOMANHOOD IN AMERICA FROM COLONIAL TIMES TO THE PRESENT. New York: New Viewpoints, 1975. 496 p. Paper.

Social and cultural factors that have molded the American woman. Thematic.

290 Scott, Ann F. THE AMERICAN WOMAN: WHO WAS SHE. Spectrum Book. Englewood Cliffs, N.J.: Prentice-Hall, 1971. vii, 182 p. Paper.

Wealth of short selections and excerpts that have not been available (cf. Millay's letter to New York University). Editorial introductions to sections on work, education, reform, marriage, family, sex, and so on in perspective.

291 _____. THE SOUTHERN LADY: FROM PEDESTAL TO POLITICS: 1830-1930. Chicago: University of Chicago Press, 1970. xv, 247 p. Biblio. Paper.

Study of the Southern woman before and after the Civil War demonstrates how image and reality influenced one another.

292 _____. WOMEN IN AMERICA: SELECTED READING. The Life in America Series. Boston: Houghton Mifflin Co., 1970. x, 214 p. Illus., biblio.

Anthology drawn from writings of white and Indian women from colonial times to present. Special section on the women's movement. Includes student "paperback library" and questions for study and discussion.

293 Simkins, Frances B., and Patton, James W. THE WOMEN OF THE CONFEDERACY. Richmond, Va.: Garrett & Massie, 1936. ix, 306 p. Illus., biblio.

Wide range of contributions. Bibliography includes many primary sources.

294 Smith, Helen E. COLONIAL DAYS AND WAYS, AS GATHERED FROM THE FAMILY PAPERS. N.p.: 1900. 376 p. Reprint. American Classics Series. New York: Ungar, 1966.

Discusses Huguenot, Puritan, and other minority women and the way they lived.

295 Smith, Page. DAUGHTERS OF THE PROMISED LAND: WOMEN IN AMERICAN HISTORY. Women in American History Series. Boston: Little, Brown and Co., 1970. x, 392 p. Paper.

White women, illustrious and obscure. Author believes American "new woman" has persisted since 1620. Commentary on hippies, "manipulation girls," and unorthodox living arrangements.

296 Sochen, June. HER STORY: A WOMAN'S VIEW OF AMERICAN HISTORY. New York: Alfred, 1974. 448 p. Illus. Paper.

Appendix includes Seneca Declaration, excerpts from the WOMAN'S BIBLE, THE NOW BILL OF RIGHTS and the National Women's Caucus platform.

297 _____. MOVERS AND SHAKERS: AMERICAN WOMEN THINKERS AND ACTIVISTS, 1900-1970. New York: Quadrangle, 1973. xi, 320 p. Biblio. Paper.

Twentieth-century history from feminist point of view.

298 Sprague, William. WOMEN AND THE WEST: A SHORT SOCIAL HISTORY. Boston: Christopher, 1940. 294 p. Illus., biblio. Reprint. American Women: Images and Realities series. New York: Arno Press, 1972.

Texture and range of life and struggles for political and economic rights. Appendix includes first-hand accounts. Bibliography lists contemporary manuscripts, government publications, and newspapers.

299 Spruill, Julia C. WOMEN'S LIFE AND WORK IN THE SOUTHERN COLONIES. Chapel Hill: University of North Carolina Press, 1938. viii, 426 p. Illus., biblio. Reprint. New York: W.W. Norton and Co., 1972. Paper.

Everyday life inside and outside of home. Bibliography includes many primary sources.

300 Starkey, Marion L. THE DEVIL IN MASSACHUSETTS: A MODERN INQUIRY INTO THE SALEM WITCH TRIALS. New York: Alfred A. Knopf, 1949. 310 p. Biblio. Paper.

Psychological insights.

301 Stenhouse, Fanny [Mrs. T.B.H.]. A LADY'S LIFE AMONG THE MORMONS. A RECORD OF PERSONAL EXPERIENCE AS ONE OF THE WIVES OF A MORMON ELDER, DURING A PERIOD OF MORE THAN TWENTY YEARS. New York: Russell Brothers, 1872. 221 p.

The first of many reissues of the same volume under many titles, both here and abroad, that detailed the horrors of polygamy. First published in 1872 under title of POLYGAMY IN UTAH.

302 Swint, Henry L., ed. DEAR ONES AT HOME: LETTERS FROM CONTRABAND CAMPS. Nashville, Tenn.: Vanderbilt University Press, 1966. 274 p.

Letters of Quaker sisters Lucy and Sarah Chase, who were first relief workers and later teachers among freed blacks on the South Carolina Islands during the Civil War.

303 Tullidge, Edward W. WOMEN OF MORMONDOM. New York: n.p., 1877. x, 552 p.

Defensive recounting of high position Mormon women held under polygamy. Excerpts journals of both sexes.

304 Van Rensselaer, May [Mrs. John King]. THE GOEDE VROUW OF MANA-HA-TA AT HOME AND IN SOCIETY 1609-1760. New York: Charles Scribner's Sons, 1898. xxii, 418 p. Reprint. American Women: Images and Realities series. New York: Arno Press, 1972.

Drawn from family records and traditions. Feminist approach to history.

305 Welter, Barbara. DIMITY CONVICTIONS: THE AMERICAN WOMAN IN THE NINETEENTH CENTURY. Athens: Ohio University Press, 1976. 230 p.

The conditioning of young women to the sexist social norms. Intellectual and social history.

306 Weston, Jeane. MAKING DO: HOW WOMEN SURVIVED THE '30S. Chicago: Follett Publishing Co., 1976. xi, 331 p.

Interviews with women about their experience in the home, at work, growing up, in church and organizations, and elsewhere during the Great Depression.

307 Wharton, Anne H. COLONIAL DAYS AND DAMES. Philadelphia: J.B. Lippincott Co., 1894. Illus. 248 p.

People and manners of the colonies. Note "A Group of Early Poetesses." Undocumented.

308 Wiley, Bell I. CONFEDERATE WOMEN. Contributions in American History, no. 38. Westport, Conn.: Greenwood Press, 1974. xiv, 204 p. Paper.

Letters and diaries of Mary Chestnut, Virginia Clay, and Varina Davis reflect roles women played in the Civil War.

309 Williams, Selma R. DEMETER'S DAUGHTERS: THE WOMEN WHO

FOUNDED AMERICA, 1587-1787. New York: Atheneum Publishers, 1975. xii, 359 p. Illus., biblio.

Women's roles in settlement of and growth of independence of America. Includes all social classes and native American women.

310 "Women and the American West." MONTANA: MAGAZINE OF WESTERN HISTORY 24 (Summer 1974): special issue.

See also 620, 637, 882.

D. FILM, MICROFORM

311 HISTORY OF WOMEN: A COMPREHENSIVE COLLECTION ON MICROFILM. Woodbridge, Conn.: Research Publications, 1975-- . In process.

Includes sources in all fields relating to women, both American and international, printed prior to 1920. Draws on nine major public and private archives. For information write Research Publications, 12 Lunar Drive, Woodbridge, Connecticut 06525.

312 Women's Film Project. "The Emerging Woman: A Film About the History of Women in the United States." 40 min. 16mm soundfilm, in black and white.

History from early 1800s includes women's place in Industrial Revolution, abolition, Victorian society, and suffrage movement. Also images of women in early twentieth century, as workers in World War II, and development of women's liberation. Available from Film Images, 17 West 60th Street, New York, New York 10023.

313 Women's History Research Center. HERSTORY. Berkeley, Calif.: 1974.

Reproduces material issued by women's liberation, civic, religious, professional, and peace groups. In two sections of three reels each. HERSTORY includes titles between 1956 and September 1971. SUPPLEMENTARY SET I includes titles from October 1971 through June 1973. SUPPLEMENTARY SET 2 includes titles from July 1973 through June 1974. Includes reel guides and directories. Available from the center.

E. ORAL HISTORY

The regional Oral History Office of the Bancroft Library at the University of California at Berkeley is presently taping and transcribing a series of interviews with selected women who have made some significant contributions to Western development. Some careers covered are those of photographer, community health worker, teacher, artist, writer, religious, and suffrage worker. Bound, illustrated, and indexed copies of these interviews are available in repositories, the names of which may be secured from the Regional Oral History Office.

Chapter 4
WOMEN'S MOVEMENT

A. RESOURCES, SOURCES

Three major publishers of information on the women's movement are the Feminist Press, the National Organization for Women, and KNOW. The Feminist Press originally published only women's biographies from a feminist point of view and children's books challenging the usual sexual stereotypes, but the press has since branched into reprinting books by and about women and pamphlets on various topics. It also issues a newsletter, NEWS/NOTES, and, with the Clearinghouse on Women's Studies, WOMEN'S STUDIES NEWSLETTER. In addition, it has cooperated with KNOW in publishing FEMALE STUDIES (see 474). For information on publications of the National Organization of Women and KNOW see page p. 81. See also the resource section of chapter 3 and similar sections in chapters on more specialized areas.

Periodicals of the past that document the women's movement are listed in 314. For the contents of thirteen of these periodicals in microform see 354. Some of the periodicals related to the current movement are listed in section 1 of this chapter and others in appendix H.

Manuscript collections having to do with women's rights in a variety of areas are listed in Ash and Calvert, page 3. Those having to do with the women's rights movement in the United States between 1848 and 1970 are listed in 314.

NOTE: Where a clear distinction exists in the references themselves between the women's movement in general and the recent women's liberation movement, I have observed this distinction by placing them appropriately in either the women's movement or the women's liberation section. Where such distinction does not exist, references have been placed in the first category.

B. BIBLIOGRAPHIES

314 Krichmar, Albert, et al. comps. THE WOMEN'S RIGHTS MOVEMENT IN THE UNITED STATES 1848-1970: A BIBLIOGRAPHY AND SOURCE-BOOK. Metuchen, N.J.: Scarecrow Press, 1972. ix, 445 p.

Lists material on general matters (legal and political status, Equal Rights Amendment, and suffrage), economic status (business and the professions, and wages), education, religion, and biography. Also general background reference sources, manuscript sources and collections, women's liberation serials of both the nineteenth and twentieth centuries, with an index. Includes some entries on 1840 World Anti-Slavery Convention. Partially annotated.

315 Schuman, Pat, and Detlefsen, Gay, comps. "Sisterhood is Serious." LIBRARY JOURNAL 96 (September 1971): 2587-94.

Selected short annotated listing on the women's movement as well as on American women in a broader context.

For bibliographies focusing on current movement see section I.1 of this chapter.

See also 342.

C. ANTHOLOGIES, DOCUMENTS

316 Kraditor, Aileen S., ed. UP FROM THE PEDESTAL: SELECTED DOCUMENTS IN THE HISTORY OF AMERICAN FEMINISM. Chicago: Quadrangle, 1968. 372 p. Biblio. Paper.

Focuses on early arguments about woman's sphere, issues of the women's movement, and the struggle to gain the vote. Introduction deals with woman's image in history and historiography.

317 Martin, Wendy. THE AMERICAN SISTERHOOD: WRITINGS OF THE FEMINIST MOVEMENT FROM COLONIAL TIMES TO THE PRESENT. New York: Harper & Row, 1972. ix, 367 p. Illus., biblio. Paper.

Historical selections on political, legal, economic, social, sexual, and psychological problems.

318 Papachristou, Judith. WOMEN TOGETHER: A HISTORY IN DOCUMENTS OF THE WOMEN'S MOVEMENT IN THE UNITED STATES. New York: Alfred A. Knopf, 1976. xiv, 273, vii. Illus., tables, biblio.

Primary documents from the 1830s to the present.

319 Parker, Gail, ed. THE OVENBIRDS: AMERICAN WOMEN ON WOMANHOOD, 1820-1920. Garden City, N.Y.: Doubleday & Co., 1972. 397 p. Paper.

Introduction discusses strengths and weaknesses of early feminism in light of antebellum sentimental literature. Selections by Lydia Sigourney, Lydia Maria Child, Angelina Weld, Catharine Beecher, Harriet Beecher Stowe, Sarah Orne Jewett, Elizabeth Cady Stanton, Jane Addams, and Charlotte Perkins Gilman.

320 Rossi, Alice S., ed. THE FEMINIST PAPERS: FROM ADAMS TO BEAUVOIR. New York: Columbia University, 1973. xix, 716 p. Biblio. Paper.

Extensive.

D. GENERAL REFERENCES

321 Deckard, Barbara S. THE WOMEN'S MOVEMENT: POLITICAL, SOCIOECONOMIC AND PSYCHOLOGICAL ISSUES. 2d ed. New York: Harper & Row, 1979. 484 p. Biblio. Paper.

Material on stereotyping, current patterns of discrimination, employment and the professions, and women before the law. Includes also historical prospectives of the women's movement in various societies, with emphasis on American movement.

322 Dell, Floyd. WOMEN AS WORLD BUILDERS: STUDIES IN MODERN FEMINISM. Chicago: Forbes, 1913. 104 p. Reprint. Pioneers of the Woman's Movement: An International Perspective Series. Westport, Conn.: Hyperion Press, 1976.

Interpretive essays on Charlotte Perkins Gilman, Jane Addams, Isadora Duncan, Emma Goldman, and others by a male feminist.

323 Douglass, Frederick. FREDERICK DOUGLASS ON WOMEN'S RIGHTS. Edited by Philip S. Foner. Contributions of Afro-American and African Studies, no. 25. Westport, Conn.: Greenwood Press, 1976. x, 192 p.

Includes newspaper pieces, speeches, tributes to individual women, and commentary by Rosa Hazel and Mary Terrell.

324 Eisenstein, Zillah R., ed. CAPITALIST PATRIARCHY AND THE CASE FOR SOCIALIST FEMINISM. New York: Monthly Review Press, 1979. vii, 394 p. Tables.

Presents broad context and then goes on to analyze various aspects of the history of the nineteenth-century American women.

325 Klagsbrun, Francine, ed. THE FIRST MS. READER. New York: Warner Press, 1973. 282 p.

Reprints most of the articles in the first issue of MS. with additional selections. Appends a history of MS. magazine.

326 O'Neill, William L. EVERYONE WAS BRAVE: THE RISE AND FALL OF FEMINISM IN AMERICA. Chicago: Quadrangle Books, 1969. xi, 369 p.

Presents feminism as self-defeating. Preface discusses feminist rhetoric and social feminism.

327 Steinem, Gloria, et al., eds. WONDER WOMAN. New York: Holt, Rinehart & Winston Warner, 1972. Unpaged. Biblio.

Feminism in 1940 comics.

328 Todd, John. WOMAN'S RIGHTS. Tracts for the People, no. 4. Boston: Lee & Shepard, 1867. 27 p. Dodge, Mary A. [Gail Hamilton, pseud.]. WOMAN'S WRONGS: A COUNTER-IRRITANT. Boston: Ticknor & Fields, 1868. 212 p. Reprint. American Women: Images and Realities series. New York: Arno Press, 1972.

Two pamphlets: a widely read pamphlet by a clergyman posing classical antifeminist arguments and the response to it by a Washington feminist.

329 Violette, Augusta G. ECONOMIC FEMINISM IN AMERICAN LITERATURE PRIOR TO 1848. University of Maine Studies, 2d series, no. 2. Orono: University of Maine, 1925. 114 p.

As evidenced in Thomas Paine, Angelina Grimké, Margaret Fuller, and others.

330 Walsh, Correa M. FEMINISM. New York: Sturgis & Watton, 1917. 393 p.

The theory of feminism, like that of socialism, is based on a false belief in future peace, prosperity, and plenty.

331 Wortis, Helen, and Rabinowitz, Clara, eds. THE WOMAN'S MOVEMENT: SOCIAL AND PSYCHOLOGICAL PERSPECTIVES. New York: Published for the American Orthopsychiatric Association by AMS Press, 1972. xv, 151 p. Biblio.

Shows the relation of woman to roles of wife, mother, sex partner, and single person to the women's movement.

E. HISTORY

1. References

332 Adams, Mildred. THE RIGHT TO BE PEOPLE. Philadelphia: J.B. Lippincott Co., 1967. 248 p. Biblio.

Surveys the women's movement, 1840-1966, gauging social and political gains by terms set forth in the Seneca Falls Declaration.

333 Berg, Barbara J. THE REMEMBERED GATE: ORIGINS OF AMERICAN FEMINISM; THE WOMEN AND THE CITY, 1810-1860. New York: Oxford University Press, 1978. xvi, 334 p. Biblio.

Purports that urbanization rather than abolitionism was the source of American feminism.

334 Cooper, James L., and Cooper, Sheila M.I. THE ROOTS OF AMERICAN FEMINIST THOUGHT. Boston: Allyn & Bacon, 1973. vi, 298 p.

Historical-biographical backgrounds precede essays by Margaret Fuller Ossoli, Angelina Grimké, Charlotte Perkins Gilman, and others.

335 Davis, Pauline, comp. A HISTORY OF THE NATIONAL WOMEN'S RIGHTS MOVEMENT FOR TWENTY YEARS. WITH THE PROCEEDINGS OF THE DECADE MEETING HELD AT APOLLO HALL, OCTOBER 20, 1870; and Stanton, Elizabeth Cady, ADDRESS AT THE DECADE MEETING, ON MARRIAGE AND DIVORCE. New York: Journeyman Printers' Cooperative Association, 1891. 119 p., and additional pages 40 F-J, 28 p.

Includes as appendix various speeches and reports as well as a memorial by Victoria C. Woodhull.

336 Evans, Richard J. THE FEMINISTS: WOMEN'S EMANCIPATION MOVEMENTS IN EUROPE, AMERICA AND AUSTRALIA, 1840-1920. New York: Harper & Row, 1977. 256 p.

Comparative study.

337 Flexner, Eleanor. CENTURY OF STRUGGLE: THE WOMAN'S RIGHTS MOVEMENT IN THE UNITED STATES. Cambridge, Mass.: Harvard University Press, Belknap Press, 1959. xiv, 384 p. Illus.

Classic.

338 Green, Arnold W., and Milbrick, Eleanor. "What Has Happened to the Feminist Movement?" In STUDIES IN LITERATURE: LEADERSHIP

AND DEMOCRATIC ACTION, edited by Alvin Gouldner, pp. 227-302. New York: Harper's, 1950. Reprint. New York: Russell & Russell Publishers, 1965.

Discusses the weakness of the feminist movement in the 1950s.

339 Gurko, Miriam. THE LADIES OF SENECA FALLS: THE BIRTH OF THE WOMEN'S MOVEMENT. New York: Macmillan Co., 1974. ix, 328 p. Illus., biblio. Paper.

Written to inform the "new generation" that nothing is new.

340 Janeway, Elizabeth. BETWEEN MYTH AND MORNING: WOMEN AWAKENING. New York: William Morrow & Co., 1974. 279 p. Biblio.

Background history of the women's movement and where it's going at present.

341 Jensen, Oliver. REVOLT OF AMERICAN WOMEN. New York: Harcourt, Brace, 1971. 224 p. Illus. Paper.

Pictorial history, 1860s to 1950s.

342 Lemons, J. Stanley. THE WOMAN CITIZEN: SOCIAL FEMINISM IN THE 20S. Urbana: University of Illinois Press, 1973. xiii, 266 p. Biblio. Paper.

Social feminism links Progressive movement and the New Deal. Excellent listing of private papers, organization archives, periodical material, and unpublished articles and theses.

343 Mann, Arthur. "The New and the Newer Women." In his YANKEE REFORMERS IN THE URBAN AGE, chap. 9. Cambridge, Mass.: Harvard University Press, Belknap Press, 1954. x, 314 p. Biblio.

Detailed study compares the women's movement in Boston between 1880 and 1900 to feminist reforms elsewhere.

344 Melder, Keith. BEGINNINGS OF SISTERHOOD: THE AMERICAN WOMAN'S RIGHTS MOVEMENT, 1800-1858. Studies in the Life of Women. New York: Schocken Books, 1977. 199 p. Biblio.

Material on woman's sphere, role in reform movements, church and female societies and organizations, and personalities of early women's movement.

345 MORMON WOMEN'S PROTEST: AN APPEAL FOR FREEDOM, JUSTICE AND EQUAL RIGHTS. FULL ACCOUNT OF GREAT MASS MEETING, HELD IN THE THEATRE, SALT LAKE CITY, UTAH. SATURDAY, MARCH 6, 1886. 91 p. Pamph.

Includes correspondence arising out of the 1886 meeting as well as a memorial to Congress in Washington.

346 National Woman Suffrage Association. REPORT OF THE INTERNATIONAL COUNCIL OF WOMEN ASSEMBLED BY THE NATIONAL WOMAN'S SUFFRAGE ASSOCIATION, WASHINGTON, D.C., UNITED STATES OF AMERICA, MARCH 25 TO APRIL 1, 1888. Washington, D.C.: Rufus H. Darby, 1888. vii, 471 p.

Reports of women in professional education, philanthropy, industry, religion, and politics as well as discussions on legislation and women as moral pillars by leading American feminists in international context.

347 O'Neill, William L. THE WOMAN MOVEMENT: FEMINISM IN THE UNITED STATES AND ENGLAND. New York: Barnes & Noble; London: Allen & Unwin, 1969. 208 p. Biblio.

Part 1 traces parallel movement in two countries. Part 2 reproduces documents by nineteenth- and twentieth-century feminists.

348 REPORT OF THE WOMEN'S RIGHTS CONVENTION HELD AT SENECA FALLS, N.Y. JULY 19TH AND 20TH, 1848. Rochester, N.Y.: John Dick, 1848. 12 p. Pamph.

Original report. Women's rights meetings and conventions were held throughout the nineteenth century and reports of them printed in pamphlet form. Many are available in larger libraries.

349 Riegel, Robert E. AMERICAN FEMINISTS. Lawrence: University of Kansas Press, 1963. 223 p. Illus., biblio.

Chapter 10 analyzes forces creating feminism.

350 Sinclair, Andrew. THE BETTER HALF: THE EMANCIPATION OF THE AMERICAN WOMAN. New York: Harper & Row, 1965. xxix, 401 p. Reprinted as THE EMANCIPATION OF THE AMERICAN WOMAN. New York: Harper & Row, Colophon Books, 1965.

Of special interest is material on health, dress, genteel and working women, and the new Victorians.

351 Sochen, June. THE NEW WOMEN: FEMINISM IN GREENWICH VILLAGE 1910-1920. New York: Quadrangle, 1972. xi, 175 p. Paper.

Earlier twentieth-century women as prototypes of those involved in the recent movement.

352 Stanton, Elizabeth Cady. THE WOMAN'S BIBLE. 2 vols. New York:

European Publishing, 1895-98. Reprint, 2 vols. in 1. Introduction by Barbara Welter. American Woman: Images and Realities series. New York: Arno Press, 1972. xlii, 217 p.

Revision of many books of the Bible challenged long-held views and precipitated schism within the American women's movement. Introduction to the reprint supplies background and history.

353 Tremaine, Rose. THE FIGHT FOR FREEDOM FOR WOMEN. Politics in Action, no. 9. Ballantine's History of the Violent Century. New York: Ballantine Books, 1973. 157 p. Illus., biblio.

Brief history ties British and American movements together. Interestingly illustrated.

For listings on current movement see section 1 of this chapter.

2. In Microform

354 PERIODICALS ON WOMEN AND WOMEN'S RIGHTS. Westport, Conn.: Greenwood Press, 1975. Microfiche.

Near complete contents of thirteen periodicals between 1853 through end of World War I reflecting diversity of the women's movement. Titles include FORERUNNER, LIBERAL REVIEW, LILY, LOWELL OFFERING, LUCIFER THE LIGHTBEARER, MOTHER EARTH BULLETIN, THE NATIONAL CITIZEN AND BALLOT BOX, THE REVOLUTION, STILETTO, UNA, WESTERN WOMAN VOTER, WOMAN VOTER, and WOMAN'S PROTEST. For information write Greenwood Press.

F. SUFFRAGE

1. Sources

For collections of manuscripts having to do with woman's suffrage see Ash and Calvert, page 3.

For biographical sources see 2234, 2252, 2281, 2392, 2441, 2442, and 2447.

For periodicals coming out of the nineteenth-century suffrage movement see volumes 3 and 4 in Mott, page 4.

2. Bibliographies

355 Franklin, Margaret L. THE CASE FOR WOMAN SUFFRAGE: A BIB-

LIOGRAPHY. New York: National College Equal Suffrage League, 1913. 315 p.

Unannotated.

356 Krichmar, Albert, et al., comps. "Suffrage." In THE WOMEN'S RIGHTS MOVEMENT IN THE UNITED STATES 1848-1970: A BIBLIOGRAPHY AND SOURCEBOOK, compiled by Albert Kirchmar, pp. 78-120. Metuchen, N.J.: Scarecrow Press, 1972.

Partially annotated.

3. References

357 Beecher, Catharine E. "Address on Female Suffrage." In PIONEERS OF WOMEN'S EDUCATION IN THE UNITED STATES: EMMA WILLARD, CATHERINE [sic] BEECHER, MARY LYON, edited by Willystine Goodsell, pp. 190-124. New York: McGraw Hill Book Co., 1931. Reprint. New York: AMS Press, 1970.

Author's belief in "woman's sphere" underlines conservatism of one branch of the nineteenth-century women's movement.

358 Buhle, Mari Jo, and Buhle, Paul, eds. THE CONCISE HISTORY OF WOMAN SUFFRAGE: SELECTIONS FROM THE CLASSIC WORK OF STANTON, ANTHONY, GAGE AND HARPER. Urbana: University of Illinois Press, 1978. xxii, 468 p. Paper.

359 Bushnell, Horace. WOMEN'S SUFFRAGE: THE REFORM AGAINST NATURE. New York: Charles Scribner, 1869. 184 p.

Maintains that woman's happiness lies in fulfilling traditional role and not in achieving political voice.

360 Catt, Carrie Chapman, and Shuler, Nellie R. WOMAN SUFFRAGE AND POLITICS: THE INNER STORY OF THE SUFFRAGE MOVEMENT. New York: Charles Scribner's Sons, 1923. xii, 504 p.

Interrelation of American politics and suffrage campaign that caused delay in passage of the Nineteenth Amendment. Appendix includes chronology of passage of amendment.

361 Gluck, Sherna, ed. FROM PARLOR TO PRISON: FIVE SUFFRAGISTS TALK ABOUT THEIR LIVES: AN ORAL HISTORY. New York: Vintage Books, 1976. 288 p. Illus. Paper.

Based on materials in section 4, below.

362 Grimes, Alan P. THE PURITAN ETHIC AND WOMAN SUFFRAGE. New York: Oxford University Press, 1967. xiii, 159 p.

In viewing Puritan-Mormon revival of the West as a means

of maintaining economic, social, and racial status quo, the author sees suffrage as conservative rather than radical phenomenon.

363 Howe, Julia Ward. JULIA WARD HOWE AND THE WOMEN SUFFRAGE MOVEMENT: A SELECTION FROM HER SPEECHES AND ESSAYS. Edited by Florence H. Hull. Boston: Dana, Estes, 1913. 241 p. Reprint. Women's Rights and Liberation: Essential Documents series. New York: Arno Press, 1969.

364 Kraditor, Aileen S. THE IDEAS OF THE WOMAN SUFFRAGE MOVEMENT, 1890-1920. New York: Columbia University, 1965. xii, 313 p. Biblio. Paper.

Suffrage as intellectual history.

365 Maule, Frances. WOMAN SUFFRAGE: HISTORY, ARGUMENTS AND RESULTS. Ed. by Frances M. Bjorkman, and Annie G. Porritt. The Blue Book. Rev. ed. New York: National Woman Suffrage Publishing, 1917. 244 p.

Reference handbook. Early antecedent of women's studies programs.

366 Miller, Leo. WOMEN AND THE DIVINE REPUBLIC. Buffalo, N.Y.: Haas & Navert, 1874. vi, 213 p.

Woman's "moral sublimity" fits her for work in temperance, peace activities, and prison reform rather than for involvement with suffrage movement.

367 Morgan, David. SUFFRAGISTS AND DEMOCRATS: THE POLITICS OF WOMAN SUFFRAGE IN AMERICA. East Lansing: Michigan State University Press, 1972. 225 p.

Study of period 1916-20 and its multilevel politics.

368 National American Woman Suffrage Association. VICTORY, HOW WOMEN WON IT: A CENTENNIAL SYMPOSIUM, 1840-1940. New York: H.W. Wilson Co., 1940. 174 p. Illus., biblio.

History of women's rights movement based on records of the association. Appendix includes chronology of events, congressional action, and "directions for lobbyists."

369 National Woman Suffrage Association. WOMAN'S SUFFRAGE AND THE POLICE: THREE SENATE DOCUMENTS. Reprint. The Police in America series. New York: Arno Press, 1971. Separately paged.

1. U.S. [63d] Senate Committee on the District of Colum-

bia. "Interference with the Suffrage Procession." 20 p.

2. U.S. Senate [63d] Senate Committee on the District of Columbia. "Suffrage Parade." Report of the Committee on the District of Columbia, U.S. Senate Report no. 53. May 29, 1913. xvi p. "Suffrage Parade." 16 p.

3. U.S. [63d] Senate Committee. "Hearings . . . March 6-17, April 16-17, 1913." 749 p. Illus.

370 Park, Maud W. FRONT DOOR LOBBY. Edited by Edna L. Stantia. Boston: Beacon Press, 1960. 278 p. Illus.

Introduction overviews suffrage campaigns. Text details maneuverings in Congress of the National American Women's Suffrage Association from 1915 through passage of the amendment.

371 Paulson, Ross E. WOMEN'S SUFFRAGE AND PROHIBITION: A COMPARATIVE STUDY OF EQUALITY AND SOCIAL CONTROL. Glenview, Ill.: Scott, Foresman, 1973. 212 p.

Prohibition and suffrage as complex responses to social change. In international context.

372 Robinson, Harriet Jane H. MASSACHUSETTS IN THE WOMEN SUFFRAGE MOVEMENT: A GENERAL POLITICAL, LEGAL AND LEGISLATIVE HISTORY FROM 1774 TO 1881. Boston: Roberts Brothers, 1881. xi, 265 p.

Conventions of and early influences on focal organization. Appendix includes Crocker's OBSERVATIONS ON THE REAL RIGHTS OF WOMEN and material on World Anti-Slavery Convention, LOWELL OFFERING, and suffrage laws.

373 Scott, Anne F., and Scott, Andrew M. ONE HALF THE PEOPLE. THE FIGHT FOR WOMAN'S SUFFRAGE. America's Alternatives Series. Philadelphia: J.B. Lippincott Co., 1975. xiii, 173 p. Biblio.

374 Seawall, Molly E. "The Ladies' Battle." ATLANTIC MONTHLY 106 (1910): 289-303.

Antisuffragist attacks woman suffrage on grounds of woman's physical weakness, exposure to unsuitable company at polls, lack of legislative experience, and possible forfeiture of property rights.

375 Stanton, Elizabeth Cady, et al. HISTORY OF WOMAN SUFFRAGE. New York: Fowler & Wells, 1881-1922. Reprint. New York: Arno Press, 1969; New York: Source Book Press, 1970.

Classic. Volume 1, 1848-61; volume 2, 1861-76; volume 3, 1876-85; volume 4, 1883-1900; volume 5, 1900-20. Appendixes contain documents. Available in THE CONCISE HISTORY OF WOMAN SUFFRAGE: SELECTIONS FROM THE CLASSIC WORK OF STANTON, ANTHONY, GAGE AND HARPER. Edited by Mari Jo Buhle and Paul Buhle. Urbana: University of Illinois Press, 1978. xxii, 468 p.

376 Stevens, Doris. JAILED FOR FREEDOM: THE STORY OF THE MILITANT AMERICAN SUFFRAGIST MOVEMENT. New York: Boni & Liveright, 1920. Reprint. New York: Schocken Books, 1976. xii, 388 p. Illus. Paper.

Political militance by suffragists, 1913-19. Appendix contains text of National Suffrage Amendment.

4. Oral History

The Regional Oral History Office of the Bancroft Library at the University of California at Berkeley is completing interviews with suffragists, among them Alice Paul and Jeannette Rankin, as unit 1 of its Women in Politics Oral History Project. Ten have been completed. These will be available in printed form in repositories designated by the project.

G. CAUSES RELATED TO THE WOMEN'S MOVEMENT

1. Reform in General

377 Chambers, Clarke A. SEEDTIME OF REFORM: AMERICAN SOCIAL SERVICE AND SOCIAL ACTION 1918-1933. Minneapolis: University of Minnesota Press, 1963. xviii, 326 p. Biblio.

Women in general context of early twentieth-century reform movements such as women's rights, child labor, and settlement house action.

378 Conway, Jill. "Women Reformers and American Culture, 1870-1930." JOURNAL OF SOCIAL HISTORY 5 (Winter 1971-72): 164-77.

Failure of reformers rooted in their essentially romantic view of women.

379 O'Connor, Lillian. PIONEER WOMEN ORATORS: RHETORIC IN THE ANTE-BELLUM REFORM MOVEMENT. New York: Vantage, 1952. xvii, 264 p. Biblio.

Rhetorical criteria and considerations about individual speakers in historical context.

380 Stearns, Bertha-Monica. "Reform Periodicals and Female Reformers, 1830-1860." AMERICAN HISTORICAL REVIEW 37 (July 1923): 678-99.

Reports on issues of temperance, chastity, and dress reform espoused by women's periodicals. Covers period from 1830 to the advent of the Civil War.

381 Tyler, Alice F. FREEDOM'S FERMENT: PHASES OF AMERICAN SOCIAL HISTORY. Minneapolis: University of Minnesota Press, 1944. x, 608 p. Illus., biblio. Paper.

Religious, utopian, and humanitarian crusades and reforms in pre-Civil War America in which women were active. Covers the relation of the women's movement to temperance and abolition.

See also chapter 7, section E. 12.

2. Abolition

382 Beecher, Catharine E. ESSAY ON SLAVERY AND ABOLITIONISM, WITH REFERENCES TO THE DUTY OF AMERICAN FEMALES. Philadelphia: Henry Perkins, 1833. 152 p. Reprint. Black Heritage Library Collection Series. Freeport, N.Y.: Books for Libraries, 1970.

Letters to Angelina Grimké argue against adversary position of Abolition Society viewing women as mediators.

383 Child, Lydia Maria. LETTERS OF LYDIA MARIA CHILD WITH A BIOGRAPHICAL INTRODUCTION BY JOHN G. WHITTIER AND AN APPENDIX BY WENDELL PHILLIPS. Boston: Houghton Mifflin Co., 1883. xxv, 280 p. Reprint. Anti-Slavery Crusade in America series. New York: Arno Press, 1969.

Abolition sympathies of popular writer. Contains bibliography of Child's works, 1824-78.

384 Grimké, Angelina. AN APPEAL TO THE WOMEN OF THE NOMINALLY FREE STATES. 2d ed. Issued by the Anti-Slavery Convention of American Women. Boston: Isaac Knapp, 1838. 70 p. Microfiche. Bettsville, Md.: Women and the Church in America Series, no. 79. American Sociological Library Association, Board of Microtexts, 1978. 1 sheet.

Views women as instigators and maintainers, as well as victims of, slave system.

385 Grimké, Sarah. LETTERS ON THE EQUALITY OF THE SEXES AND

THE CONDITION OF WOMEN ADDRESSED TO MARY S. PARKER, PRESIDENT OF THE BOSTON FEMALE ANTI-SLAVERY SOCIETY. Boston: n.p., 1838. 128 p. Reprint. Burt Franklin Research and Source Works Series, no. 575. New York: Burt Franklin, 1970.

Historical series of letters, numbers 7, 8, and 9 relating specifically to conditions in the United States.

386 Hersh, Blanche G. THE SLAVERY OF SEX: FEMINIST-ABOLITIONISTS IN AMERICA. Urbana: University of Illinois Press, 1978. 280 p. Biblio.

Discusses parallels and interactions between abolitionism and women's movement in broad context through studying characteristics of fifty-one women actively involved.

387 Lutz, Alma. CRUSADE FOR FREEDOM: WOMEN OF THE ANTI-SLAVERY MOVEMENT. Boston: Beacon Press, 1968. 338 p. Illus., biblio.

Material on Elizabeth Chandler, Prudence Crandall, Abby Foster, Lucy Stone, and many others, as well as on male feminists James Mott and Theodore Weld.

388 Mott, Lucretia. SLAVERY AND THE "WOMAN QUESTION": LUCRETIA MOTT'S DIARY OF HER VISIT TO GREAT BRITAIN TO ATTEND THE WORLD'S ANTI-SLAVERY CONVENTION OF 1840. Edited by Frederick B. Tolles. Supplement 23 to the JOURNAL OF THE FRIENDS' HISTORICAL SOCIETY. London and Haverford, Pa.: Friends' Historical Society; Friends' Historical Association, 1952. 81 p.

Seminal meeting between Lucretia Mott and Elizabeth Cady Stanton. Introduction supplies background.

389 Wyman, Lillie B.C. "Women in Philanthropy--Work of Anti-Slavery Women." In WOMAN'S WORK IN AMERICA, edited by Annie N. Meyer, chap. 16. New York: Henry Holt, 1891. Reprint. American Women: Images and Realities series. New York: Arno Press, 1972.

Summary listing of women in the abolition movement.

3. Miscellaneous Causes—Peace, Prison Reform, Temperance, Purity Crusade, and Consumerism

a. BIBLIOGRAPHIES

390 Cook, Blanche W., comp. BIBLIOGRAPHY ON PEACE RESEARCH IN HISTORY. Santa Barbara, Calif.: University Bibliographical Center, 1969. v, 72 p. Paper.

Annotated. Includes manuscript collections, peace organizations, biography, and autobiography.

Collections relating to women's involvement in the peace movement are listed in Ash and Calvert, see page 3.

391 "Temperance and Women's Rights, 1865-1900." In HARVARD GUIDE TO AMERICAN HISTORY, edited by Oscar Handlin, et al., pp. 440-42. Cambridge, Mass.: Harvard University Press, Belknap Press, 1963.

b. REFERENCES

392 Degen, Marie L. THE HISTORY OF THE WOMEN'S PEACE PARTY. The Johns Hopkins University Studies in Historical and Political Science, series 57, no. 3. Baltimore: Johns Hopkins University Press, 1939. Reprint. New York: Burt Franklin, 1974. 266 p. Biblio. Paper.

Documentary history of the organization that became the Women's International League for Peace and Freedom, from its inception under Jane Addams and Cattie Chapman Catt in 1915 through the signing of World War I peace treaties.

393 Dix, Dorothea L. MEMORIAL TO THE LEGISLATURE OF MASSACHUSETTS [IN BEHALF OF THE PAUPER INSANE AND IDIOTS IN JAILS AND POORHOUSES THROUGH THE COMMONWEALTH]. Boston: Munroe & Frances, 1843. 32 p. Pamph.

Report of investigations that produced immediate reforms in prisons and other institutions.

394 ______. REMARKS ON PRISONS AND PRISON DISCIPLINES IN THE UNITED STATES. Philadelphia: Joseph Kite, 1845. 108 p. Reprint. Montclair, N.Y.: Patterson Smith, 1967.

Short, informative introduction points out that Dorothea Dix's goal was not social revenge, as many charged.

394 Gusfield, Joseph R. SYMBOLIC CRUSADE: STATUS POLITICS AND THE AMERICAN TEMPERANCE MOVEMENT. Urbana: University of Illinois Press, 1963. viii, 198 p. Tables. Paper.

Interpretive study contains much material on Women's Christian Temperance Union and its leaders.

396 Kyvig, David E. "Women against Prohibition." AMERICAN QUARTERLY 28 (Fall 1976): 465-82.

Traces history of Women's Organization for National Prohibition Reform and the efforts of its founder, Pauline Morton Sabin.

397 Moritzen, Julius. THE PEACE MOVEMENT IN AMERICA. New York: G.P. Putnam's Sons, 1912. xix, 419 p. Illus.

398 Nathan, Maud. THE STORY OF AN EPOCH-MAKING MOVEMENT. New York: Doubleday, Page, 1926. xx, 245 p.

History of the National Consumers' League.

399 Pivar, David J. PURITY CRUSADE, SEXUAL MORALITY AND SOCIAL CONTROL, 1868-1900. Contributions to American History, no. 23. Westport, Conn: Greenwood Press, 1973. 308 p.

Attempts at nineteenth-century sexual reform (prostitution and the white slave trade) and their relation to the woman's movement.

400 Stewart, Eliza D. [Mother Stewart]. MEMORIES OF THE CRUSADE, A THRILLING ACCOUNT OF THE GREAT UPRISING OF THE WOMEN OF OHIO IN 1873, AGAINST THE LIQUOR CRIME. 2d ed. Columbus, Ohio: William G. Hubbard, 1889. 535 p. Reprint. American Women: Images and Realities series. New York: Arno Press, 1972.

Stewart subsequently founded, with Frances Willard, the Women's Christian Temperance Union.

401 Willard, Frances E. WOMAN AND TEMPERANCE: OR, THE WORK AND WORKERS OF THE WOMEN'S CHRISTIAN TEMPERANCE UNION. Hartford, Conn.: Park Publishing, 1883. 648 p. Reprint. American Women: Images and Realities series. New York: Arno Press, 1972.

By the founder of the union.

For additional information on the peace movement, see 1398, 1399, 2223; on temperance, see 2487; on prison reform, see 1401; on child labor, see 1043, 1404; on dress reform, see 947, 2235.

H. CLUBS AND ORGANIZATIONS

1. Sources

Most established societies and associations issue listings of members; some have published official histories. Central offices maintain files or organizational records and minutes. For collections of organizational records and related manuscripts see the NATIONAL UNION CATALOG OF MANUSCRIPT COLLECTIONS, page 3. Most organizations publish monthly or quarterly magazines and/or newsletters. Some organizations, such as the Young Women's Christian Association, issue lists of their publications.

402 Barrer, Myra E., ed. WOMEN'S ORGANIZATIONS & LEADERS 1975-1976 DIRECTORY. Washington, D.C.: Today Publications & News Service, 1976. Sectional pagination. Supplement, Fall 1976.

Lists activist women and their organizations. Alphabetical, geographical, and subject area index. Printed material issued by each organization is also listed and indexed. Being updated.

403 ENCYCLOPEDIA OF ASSOCIATIONS. Edited by Nancy Yakes and Denise Akey. 3 vols. 13th ed. Detroit: Gale Research Co., 1979.

Volume 1 lists national U.S. organizations by category and key word; volume 2 by geographical location with executive's index; volume 3 lists new associations and projects.

2. Bibliographies

For periodicals issued by nineteenth-century women's clubs see volume 4, chapter 21 in Mott, page 4.

For articles about nineteenth-century women's clubs see NINETEENTH CENTURY READER'S GUIDE, page 4.

3. References

404 Anderson, Pegg. THE DAUGHTERS: AN UNCONVENTIONAL LOOK AT AMERICA'S FAN CLUB--THE DAR. New York: St. Martin's Press, 1974. 360 p. Biblio.

405 Brumbaugh, Sara B. DEMOCRATIC EXPERIENCE AND EDUCATION IN THE NATIONAL LEAGUE OF WOMEN VOTERS. Contributions to Education, no. 916. New York: Teachers College, Columbia University, Bureau of Publications, 1946. x, 115 p. Biblio.

History, philosophy, and goals of the organization.

406 "The Club Movement among Colored Women of America." In A NEW NEGRO FOR A NEW CENTURY, chap. 17. Chicago: American Publishing House, 1900. 428 p. Illus. Reprint. Miami, Fla.: Mnemosyne, 1969.

See also chapter 18 which lists individual clubs within the National Association of Colored Women.

407 Croly, Jane C. [Jennie C.]. HISTORY OF THE WOMAN'S CLUB MOVEMENT IN AMERICA. New York: Henry Gallin, 1898. xi, 1184 p. Illus.

Official history. Largely membership listings and state minutes.

408 Davis, Elizabeht L. LIFTING AS THEY CLIMB. Washington, D.C.: National Association of Colored Women, n.d. 424 p. Illus.

Gives the history of the National Association of Colored Women since its founding in 1896. Special chapter on black women in music.

409 Parker, Marjorie. ALPHA KAPPA ALPHA: 1908-1958. N.p.: 1958. iii, 140 p.

Outlines the development of the oldest Greek letter society for black women.

410 Sims, Mary S. THE NATURAL HISTORY OF A SOCIAL INSTITUTION--THE YOUNG WOMEN'S CHRISTIAN ASSOCIATION. New York: Woman's Press, 1936. x, 251 p.

Documented. The same author recorded the subsequent history of the organization in THE YWCA--AN UNFOLDING PURPOSE (New York: Woman's Press, 1950. xv, 157 p.) and THE PURPOSE WIDENS (New York: National Board, YWCA, 1969. iv, 100 p.).

411 Strayer, Martha. THE DAR: AN INFORMAL HISTORY. Washington, D.C.: Public Affairs Press, 1958. vi, 262 p. Reprint. Westport, Conn.: Greenwood Press, 1975. Paper.

Investigative journalist's eye turned on history and policies of the DAR since its founding in 1890.

412 Talbot, Marion, and Rosenberry, Lois K. THE HISTORY OF THE AMERICAN ASSOCIATION OF UNIVERSITY WOMEN, 1881-1931. Boston: Houghton Mifflin Co., 1931. viii, 479 p.

Talbot was a founder of the organization.

413 Wells, Mildred W. UNITY IN DIVERSITY: THE HISTORY OF THE GENERAL FEDERATION OF WOMEN'S CLUBS. Washington, D.C.: 1953. xiv, 525 p. Illus.

Incorporates material from 407 and includes additional records, archives, and membership lists, as well as constitution and bylaws.

I. WOMEN'S LIBERATION

1. Resources, Sources, Bibliographies

A major publisher of information on the current women's movement is KNOW. This press issues reprints of feminist articles, original articles, and book lists of women's books put out by other publishing houses. Its catalog lists material on feminism, mental and physical health, sexuality, education, employment, religion, sex-role stereotyping, child care, art, language, literature and poetry, politics and law, history, images, and humor as well as books for children and women's studies. It maintains the KNOW News Service, which issues a monthly bulletin to feminist publications, and cooperates with the Feminist Press in publishing FEMALE STUDIES (see 474).

The National Organization for Women (NOW), while not primarily a publishing house, nevertheless issues a considerable amount of informational material in the form of both pamphlets and bibliographies. Kits on the following topics are available: sex discrimination, women in religion, child care and nonsexist books for children, marriage and divorce, woman's financial status, minority women, and masculine mystique. In addition, NOW task forces on current issues send out information sheets about their activities. The national organization puts out the quarterly NOW ACTS and a monthly newsletter, DO IT NOW, which includes information on legislative matters. The directory of the newsletter is available in microfilm from the Women's Historical Research Center. Many state and local NOW organizations issue their own publications. The Arthur and Elizabeth Schlesinger Library at Radcliffe is the official repository of the papers of this organization.

The Congressional Clearinghouse on Women's Rights issues a newsletter that lists and annotates current legislation, news items, articles, and reports. It is available from the clearinghouse, 722 House Annex Building, No. 1, Washington, D.C. 20515.

Booklists are available not only from presses but also from feminist bookstores and feminist book distributors, such as the Feminist Bookmart. For addresses of feminist presses see appendix I. For addresses of bookstores and distributors see appendix E.

A few of the serials coming out of the present movement are AMAZON, AURORA, BIG MAMA RAG, BOOTLEGGER (check for bibliographies; also a press), BLACK WOMEN'S LOG, CONCILIO MUJERES, THE FEMINIST, 51%, LESBIAN VOICE, MAJORITY REPORT, MONTHLY EXTRACT, MS., OFF OUR BACKS, THE SPOKESWOMAN, UP FROM UNDER, and WOMANSPEAK. See also appendix H.

The contents of many feminist journals are available in the HERSTORY microfilm series issued by the Women's Historical Research Center.

Women's Movement

For a listing of collections relating to the recent movement see Ash and Calvert, page 3.

Most of the following resources include or are made up entirely of bibliographies.

414 Boston Women's Collective. WOMEN'S YELLOW PAGES: THE ORIGINAL SOURCE BOOK FOR WOMEN. Boston: 1974. 159 p.

Available from the collective, 490 Beacon Street, Boston, Massachusetts 02115.

415 Gager, Nancy, ed. WOMEN'S RIGHTS ALMANAC, 1974: A UNIQUE REFERENCE GUIDE ABOUT AND FOR ALL AMERICAN WOMEN. Bethesda, Md.: Elizabeth Cady Stanton Publishing, 1974. 620 p. Illus., tables, biblio.

Statistical and factual information on women's status state by state; statistical and summary information on demography, women in government, employment, marriage and divorce, child care, education, health, financial matters, poverty and welfare, lesbianism, abortion, and women's organizations. Backgrounds and history. Bibliographies of periodicals and bibliography. Feminist terms. Sources of legal assistance. Being updated.

416 Grimstad, Kirsten, and Rennie, Susan, eds. THE NEW WOMAN'S SURVIVAL CATALOG. A woman-made Book. New York: Coward, McCann & Geoghegan, 1973. 223 p. Illus., biblios. Paper.

Self-help resource book on communications, arts, health, children, education and learning, self-defense, work and money, discrimination, and the women's movement. Lists presses, directories, bibliographies, and publications in all areas including mixed and nonprint media. Lack of indexes makes reference difficult.

417 ______. THE NEW WOMAN'S SURVIVAL SOURCEBOOK. Another woman-made Book. New York: Alfred A. Knopf, 1975. 245 p. Illus., biblio. Paper.

Successor to 416. SOURCEBOOK updates and rearranges material of the earlier volume to clarify the diversity in the current women's movement. Well indexed. Superseded by CHRYSALIS, a feminist periodical.

418 Harrison, Cynthia E., comps. WOMEN'S MOVEMENT MEDIA: A SOURCE GUIDE. New York: R.R. Bowker Co., 1975. xi, 269 p. Biblio. Paper.

Annotated. Lists distributors, news services, products, centers, collections, organizations, agencies, and resources in all areas. By state.

419 Krichmar, Albert, et al., comps. THE WOMEN'S MOVEMENT IN THE SEVENTIES: AN INTERNATIONAL-ENGLISH LANGUAGE BIBLIOGRAPHY. Metuchen, N.J.: Scarecrow Press, 1977. xvi, 891 p. Biblio.

Partially annotated. Over eighty-six hundred cross-cultural items with emphasis on changing conditions. Includes review articles. Limited resources listing.

420 Rowbotham, Sheila. WOMEN'S LIBERATION AND REVOLUTION: A BIBLIOGRAPHY. Bristol, Engl.: Falling Wall, 1972. 24 p. Reprint. Old Westbury, N.Y.: Feminist Press, 1973. Excerpted in hardcover edition of entry 454.

421 Switchboard, Inc. WHOLE WOMEN CATALOGUE: A GUIDE TO RESOURCES FOR WOMEN IN NORTH CAROLINA. Chapel Hill, N.C.: 1974. 118 p. Illus., biblios. Offset, paper.

Informal reports on health and athletics, politics, lesbians, women's studies, women and the law, and other issues of interest to women. Appendix prints name change form.

422 Wheeler, Helen R. WOMANHOOD MEDIA: CURRENT RESOURCES ABOUT WOMEN. Metuchen, N.J.: Scarecrow Press, 1972. v, 335 p. Offset.

Includes Liberation Awareness Inventory, analysis of library reference tools in context of women's movement, list of books for starting nonsexist collection, directory of sources issuing directories, and other material of interest to women. Appendix includes out-of-print titles of interest, sexist rhetoric, and audiovisual resources.

423 The Womanpower Project. THE NEW YORK WOMAN'S DIRECTORY. New York: Workman Publishing, 1973. 262 p. Paper.

Where to find help for any problems ranging from day care centers and abortions to plumbers and credit cards. Similar sourcebooks are being issued by women's groups in various other cities.

See also 428, 452, 459.

2. Anthologies

424 Adams, Elsie, and Briscoe, Mary L. UP AGAINST THE WALL: ON WOMEN'S LIBERATION. Beverly Hills, Calif.: Glencoe Press, 1971. xx, 521 p. Biblio. Paper.

Selections cover traditional views, women's "nature," modes of adjustment, and women's liberation.

425 Adelstein, Michael E., and Pival, Jean G., eds. WOMEN'S LIBERATION. Perspective Series. New York: St. Martin's Press, 1972. 150 p. Tables. Paper.

Presents pros and cons of women's dilemmas centering on stereotyping, motherhood, politics, and occupational consideration. Suggests solutions. Topics for discussion and review conclude each selection.

426 Cooke, Joanne, et al., eds. THE NEW WOMEN: AN ANTHOLOGY OF WOMEN'S LIBERATION. A MOTIVE Anthology on Women's Liberation. Indianapolis: Bobbs-Merrill Co., 1970. 217 p.

Controversial anthology of "prose, poetry and polemics" refused publication by United Methodist Church which had originally sponsored it. Printed as special issue of MOTIVE, March-April 1969.

427 Epstein, Cynthia F., and Goode, William J., eds. THE OTHER HALF: ROADS TO WOMEN'S EQUALITY. Spectrum Book. Englewood Cliffs, N.J.: Prentice-Hall, 1971. viii, 207 p.

Focuses on issues of interest to current movement. Reprints documents associated with current movement.

428 Morgan, Robin, ed. SISTERHOOD IS POWERFUL: AN ANTHOLOGY OF WRITINGS FROM THE WOMEN'S LIBERATION MOVEMENT. New York: Random House, 1970. xl, 602 p. Paper.

Sections on discrimination in professions, office, church, and before the law; images and nonimages in media and elsewhere, consciousness changing, emerging ideologies, poetry, documents, SCUM Manifesto, principles of New York Radical Feminists, and songs. Bibliography includes films listing.

429 Myron, Nancy, and Bunch, Charlotte, eds. LESBIANISM AND THE WOMAN'S MOVEMENT. Baltimore: Diana Press, 1975. 104 p. Illus., biblio.

Ten articles selected from the FURIES. Lesbianism as essentially political.

430 Thompson, Mary Lou, ed. VOICES OF THE NEW FEMINISM. Boston: Beacon Press, 1970. viii, 146 p. Biblio.

Includes bibliography by Lucinda Cisler (see 2).

3. References

431 Allen, Pam. FREE SPACE: A PERSPECTIVE ON THE SMALL GROUP IN WOMEN'S LIBERATION. New York: Times Change, 1971. 63 p. Illus. Pamph.

Means of achieving a sense of effectiveness.

432 Atkinson, Ti-Grace. AMAZON ODYSSEY. New York: Links Books, 1974. xxiv, 258 p. Illus. Paper.

Writings from 1967 to 1972 deal with "ideological" and "tactical" concerns.

433 Beal, M.F. SAFE HOUSE: A CASEBOOK STUDY OF REVOLUTIONARY FEMINISM IN THE 1970'S. Eugene, Oreg.: Northwest Matrix, 1977. 154 p. Illus., biblio. Offset, paper.

Focuses on factors radicalizing women. Material on the Symbionese Liberation Army.

434 Borun, Minda, et al., comps. WOMEN'S LIBERATION: AN ANTHROPOLOGICAL VIEW. Pittsburgh: KNOW, 1971. 69 p. Pamph.

Covers period 1861-1969. Available from KNOW.

435 Burton, Gabrielle. I'M RUNNING AWAY FROM HOME BUT I'M NOT ALLOWED TO CROSS THE STREET. Pittsburgh: KNOW, 1972. 207 p. Paper.

Family's response to self-growth. Available from KNOW.

436 Carden, Maren L. THE NEW FEMINIST MOVEMENT. New York: Russell Sage Foundation, 1974. xviii, 234 p.

Organizational study.

437 De Crow, Karen. THE YOUNG WOMEN'S GUIDE TO LIBERATION: ALTERNATIVES TO A "HALF-LIFE" WHILE THE CHOICE IS STILL YOURS. New York: Pegasus, 1971. 200 p. Biblio.

438 Decter, Midge. THE NEW CHASTITY AND OTHER ARGUMENTS AGAINST WOMEN'S LIBERATION. New York: Coward, McCann & Geoghegan, 1972. 256 p.

Contemporary woman suffers from too much rather than from too little freedom.

439 Ellis, Julie. REVOLT OF THE SECOND SEX. New York: Lancer Books, 1970. 189 p.

Handbook format. After a brief historical introduction, the focus is on the sixties and after.

440 Firestone, Shulamith. THE DIALECTIC OF SEX: THE CASE FOR THE FEMINIST REVOLUTION. New York: William Morrow & Co., 1970. 242 p. Paper.

Outlines the philosophical foundations of radical feminism.

441 Freeman, Jo. THE POLITICS OF WOMEN'S LIBERATION: A CASE STUDY OF AN EMERGING SOCIAL MOVEMENT AND ITS RELATION TO THE POLICY PROCESS. New York: David McKay Co., 1975. xvi, 268 p. Biblio.

In-depth study of symbiotic relationship between the current movement and the American political system.

442 Gonzalez, Sylvia. "The White Feminist Movement: The Chicana Perspective." SOCIAL SCIENCE JOURNAL 14 (April 1977): 67-76.

Discusses backgrounds of Chicana oppression, stereotyping, and need for support from Anglo feminists, partly through women's studies courses.

443 Hole, Judith, and Levine, Ellen. REBIRTH OF FEMINISM. New York: Quadrangle, 1971. xiii, 488 p. Illus., tables, charts, biblio.

Part 1: Origins and development of women's movement; part 2, ideas and issues; part 3, areas of action in media, abortion, child care, education, professions, and church. Reprints Seneca Falls Declaration, as well as some documents associated with the current movement. Includes an annotated chronology of the women's movement in America, 1961-71.

444 Koedt, Ann, et al., eds. RADICAL FEMINISM. New York: Quadrangle, 1973. viii, 424 p. Illus. Paper.

Five sections deal with history of women's movement in America, political nature of radical feminism, its theories and organization, and its effects on the arts. Reprints documents associated with the movement.

445 Lerner, Gerda. "Women's Rights and American Feminism." AMERICAN

SCHOLAR 40 (Spring 1971): 235-48.

Defines the differences in the meaning of women's liberation to different classes.

446 McBride, Angela B. LIVING WITH CONTRADICTIONS: A MARRIED FEMINIST. New York: Harper & Row, 1976. 244 p. Paper.

Discusses the conflicts and resolutions regarding body, parents, marriage, motherhood, employment, and other issues.

447 Mitchell, Juliet. WOMAN'S ESTATE. New York: Pantheon Books, 1972. 182 p.

Analyzes the relation of radical feminism to black power, the third world, student movements, draft resistance, marriage, sex, family, and education.

448 Moulton, Ruth. "Psychoanalytic Reflections on Women's Liberation." CONTEMPORARY PSYCHOANALYSIS 8 (Spring 1972): 197-228.

Attempts to understand the psychological forces of the current movement.

449 NOTES FROM THE FIRST YEAR. Edited by Kathy Amatinek et al. New York: New York Radical Women, 1968. Unpaged.

Includes "The Women's Rights Movement in the United States" by Shulamith Firestone.

450 NOTES FROM THE SECOND YEAR, MAJOR WRITINGS OF THE RADICAL FEMINISTS. Edited by Shulamith Firestone. New York: Radical Feminism, 1969. 126 p. Illus.

Includes Joreen, "The Bitch Manifesto"; Pat Mainardi, "The Politics of Housework"; Ti-Grace Atkinson, "Radical Feminism"; Anne Koedt, "The Myth of the Vaginal Orgasm"; Ellen Willis, "Consumerism and Women"; and articles on consciousness raising and manifestos.

451 NOTES FROM THE THIRD YEAR. Edited by Anne Koedt. New York: Notes from the Third Year, 1971. 142 p. Illus.

Includes articles on history from a feminist point of view; woman experience which includes aging, lesbianism, prostitution, men, and violence; experience of black women; children's books; theoretical material on marriage, rape, media, and other; "The Independent Female," a play by Joan Holden; "Women Writers and Female Experience" by Elaine Showalter.

452 Paulsen, Kathryn, and Kuhn, Ryan A., comps. WOMAN'S ALMANAC: TWELVE HOW-TO HANDBOOKS IN ONE. New York: J.B. Lippincott Co., 1976. 624 p. Biblio.

Practical information on money and finance, politics, sexuality and anatomy, motherhood, employment, psychology, and legal problems. Directory lists over fifteen hundred services and organizations.

453 Reid, Inez S. "TOGETHER" BLACK WOMEN. Prepared for the Black Women's Community Development. New York: Emerson Hall, 1972. xiii, 383 p.

Investigates attitudes of militant black women and their alienation from white women's movement and American social life.

454 Rowbotham, Sheila. WOMEN: RESISTANCE AND REVOLUTION: A HISTORY OF WOMEN AND REVOLUTION IN THE MODERN WORLD. New York: Pantheon Books, 1972. 288 p. Biblio. Paper.

"Liberation of women necessitates liberation of all human beings."

455 Sheehan, Valeria H., ed. UNMASKING: TEN WOMEN IN METAMORPHOSIS. Chicago: Swallow Press, 1973. 286 p.

Taped sessions of consciousness-raising group.

456 Solanas, Valeria. S.C.U.M. (SOCIETY FOR CUTTING UP MEN) MANIFESTO. New York: Olympia Press, 1968. 105 p.

Includes informative preface by the publisher, Paul Krassner.

457 Vetterberg-Braggin, Mary, et al., eds. FEMINISM AND PHILOSOPHY. Totowa, N.J.: Littlefield, Adams, 1977. xii, 452 p. Biblio.

Thirty-three contemporary thinkers discuss moral issues, role, rhetoric, employment, marriage, rape, and abortion.

458 Ware, Celestine. WOMAN POWER: THE MOVEMENT FOR WOMEN'S LIBERATION. New York: Towers Public Affairs Books, 1970. 176 p. Biblio. Paper.

Radical feminist discusses parallels between nineteenth- and twentieth-century feminism as well as the relation of black woman to women's liberation.

459 Woman's Action Alliance. A PRACTICAL GUIDE TO THE WOMAN'S MOVEMENT. Edited by Deena Peterson. New York: 1974. 224 p. Biblio.

Includes an overview of the current women's movement, national directory of women's organizations, and a listing of books, bookstores, and consciousness-raising guidelines.

460 "Women's Liberation as One of the Seven Polarizing Issues." ANNALS, AMERICAN ACADEMY OF POLITICAL ARTS AND SCIENCES 97 (September 1971): 118-39.

461 "The Women's Movement." JOURNAL OF THE NATIONAL ASSOCIATION OF WOMEN DEANS AND COUNSELORS 36 (Winter 1973): special issue.

Discusses the movement's relationship to counseling and counselors.

See also 1366, 1562, 1696.

J. WOMEN'S STUDIES

1. Sources, Resources

The Clearinghouse on Women's Studies, an educational project of the Feminist Press, publishes and distributes resources, guides, pamphlets, curricular materials, bibliographies, and the quarterly WOMEN'S STUDIES NEWSLETTER. It regularly publishes and updates lists of institutions offering women's studies programs. The National Organization for Women's Committee to Promote Women's Studies distributes information on workshops and also the WOMEN'S STUDIES NEWS SHEET which includes general information and bibliography.

Among the periodicals in the field of women's studies are FEMINIST STUDIES, SIGNS, WOMEN'S STUDIES: AN INTERDISCIPLINARY JOURNAL, and the UNIVERSITY OF MICHIGAN'S PAPERS IN WOMEN'S STUDIES.

462 Berkowitz, Tamar, et al. WHO'S WHO AND WHERE IN WOMEN'S STUDIES. Old Westbury, N.Y.: Clearinghouse on Women's Studies, Feminist Press, 1974. 256 p. Paper.

Lists by name, institution, and subject. Supersedes GUIDE TO CURRENT FEMALE STUDIES.

463 Froschl, Merle, and Williamson, Jane. FEMINIST RESOURCES FOR SCHOOLS AND COLLEGES: A GUIDE TO CURRICULAR MATERIALS. Rev. ed. Old Westbury, N.Y.: Clearinghouse on Women's Studies, Feminist Press, 1977. 67 p. Biblio. Paper.

Lists items relating to sex bias on state and federal levels, guides for rhetoric, analyses of media, women's studies programs, books by and about women, multimedia materials, organizations, periodicals, and publishers. Preschool through higher education.

2. Abstracts, Bibliographies

The Women's History Research Center issues bibliographies on women's studies courses and indexes them by topic.

464 Gerstenberger, Donna, and Allen, Carolyn, comps. "Women Studies/American Studies, 1970-1975." AMERICAN QUARTERLY 29 (1977): 261-79. Bibliography issue.

Bibliographical essay precedes listing. Emphasis on special issues, literary criticism, and women's history.

465 McKim, Joanna, comp. "Basic Feminism: Introduction to Women's Studies." Santa Ana, Calif.: Santa Ana College, 1974. 60 p. Mimeo.

Extensive. Material on immigrant, black, Chicana, Asian-American, and native American women.

466 Rosenfelt, Deborah S., comp. STRONG WOMEN: AN ANNOTATED BIBLIOGRAPHY OF LITERATURE FOR THE HIGH SCHOOL CLASSROOM. Old Westbury, N.Y.: Feminist Press, 1976. 58 p. Paper.

Lists autobiographies, biographies, dramas, novels, short stories, and poetry. Includes topical indexes.

467 WOMEN'S STUDIES ABSTRACTS. Rush, N.Y.: 1972-- . Quarterly.

Annotates periodicals, including bibliographies.

468 Zangrando, Joanna S. "Women's Studies in the United States: Approaching Reality." AMERICAN STUDIES INTERNATIONAL 14 (Autumn 1975): 15-26.

Lists wide variety of sources in traditional as well as non-print media, and artifacts.

See also section 1 above, as well as 220, 470, 476.

3. Course Resources, References

Women's studies syllabi are available from KNOW and from the Women's History Research Center, indexed by subject.

469 Blumhagan, Kathleen O'C., and Johnson, Walter D., eds. WOMEN'S STUDIES: AN INTERDISCIPLINARY COLLECTION. Contributions in Women's Studies, no. 2. Westport, Conn.: Greenwood Press, 1978. xi, 142 p.

Relates specific issues to broader issues of women's movement.

470 California University. University Extension. "New Directions: Estudios Femeniles de la Chicana." Edited by Anna Nieto-Gomez. Berkeley, Calif.: n.d. v, 65 p. Biblio. Offset, paper.

Source outlines in history, sociology, higher education of the Chicana, image in literature, and extensive bibliography that includes nonprint materials.

471 Chmaj, Betty E., comp. AMERICAN WOMEN AND AMERICAN STUDIES. Somerville, Mass.: Women's Free Press, 1971. xvi, 258 p. Biblio. Offset, paper.

Prepared for the Commission on the Status of Women, American Studies Association. Part 1: commission report; part 2: twenty-seven syllabi, bibliographies, and commentary; part 3: summary and reaction. Available from KNOW.

472 Chmaj, Betty E., et al., comps. IMAGE, MYTH AND BEYOND: AMERICAN WOMEN AND AMERICAN STUDIES II. Pittsburgh: KNOW, 1974. 375 p. Illus., charts. Paper.

Part 1: report on status of academic women; part 2: syllabi, bibliographies, and program listings; part 3: images and myths about women. Available from KNOW.

473 College Art Association of America. WOMEN'S STUDIES IN ART AND ART HISTORY. Compiled by Athena T. Spear. New York: 1974. 67 p. Offset, paper.

Includes studio and art history courses, catalog of group shows by women, and organizations listing.

474 FEMALE STUDIES. 1-10. Available from KNOW. Offset, paper.

Number 1: A COLLECTION OF COLLEGE SYLLABI AND READING LISTS. Edited by Shelia Tobias. September 1970. 73 p.

Includes seventeen course descriptions and bibliographies mostly in social sciences.

Number 2: FEMALE STUDIES II: Collected by the Commission on the Status of Women of the Modern Language Association. Edited by Florence Howe, and Carol Ahlum. December 1970. 165 p.

Includes sixty-five syllabi for college courses.

Number 3: FEMALE STUDIES III: Prepared for the Commission on the Status of Women of the Modern Language Association. Edited by Florence Howe, and Carol Ahlum. December 1971. 181 p.

Includes "New Guide to Current Female Studies," fifty-four syllabi for college courses, and seventeen women's studies programs.

Number 4: TEACHING ABOUT WOMEN. Prepared for Modern Language Association Commission on the Status of Women. Edited by Elaine Showalter, and Carol Ohmann. December 1971. 71 p.

Twelve essays on teaching of women's studies.

Number 5: PROCEEDINGS OF THE CONFERENCE ON WOMEN AND EDUCATION: A FEMINIST PERSPECTIVE. Edited by Rae Lee Siporin. July 1972. 160 p.

Conference cosponsored by University of Pittsburgh and the Modern Language Association. Seventeen essays on various aspects and problems of teaching women's studies.

Number 6: CLOSER TO THE GROUND: WOMEN'S CLASSES, CRITICISMS, PROGRAMS, 1972. Edited by Nancy Hoffman, et al. 1972. 235 p.

Focuses on teaching of women's studies, especially literature, in the classroom. Includes detailed study of women's program at Portland State University.

Number 7: GOING STRONG--NEW PROGRAMS, NEW COURSES. Edited by Deborah S. Rosenfelt. 1973. 256 p.

Includes sixty women's courses and twelve women's studies programs. Bibliographies on women, art and feminism, and on women in biology, anthropology, and psychology.

Number 8: DO-IT-YOURSELF WOMEN'S STUDIES. Edited by Sarah Slavin Schramm. 1975. 256 p. Biblio.

Articles on women's studies at all educational levels and how they were effected. This volume put out by the Committee to Promote Women's Studies of the National Organization of Women. Includes listing of addresses of women's studies groups.

Number 9: TEACHING ABOUT WOMEN IN THE FOREIGN LANGUAGES. Edited by Sidonie Cassirer. Prepared for the Commission on the Status of Women of the Modern Language Association. 1976. 256 p. Biblios.

Ninety listings and course outlines for women's courses in French, Spanish, and German given in U.S. colleges.

Number 10: STUDENT WORK/LEARNING TO SPEAK. Edited by Deborah S. Rosenfelt. 1976. 256 p.

Includes produced play, group autobiographies, poems, short stories, and articles drawn from undergraduate women's studies courses.

475 Leavitt, Ruby R. PEACEABLE PRIMATES AND GENTLE PEOPLE: ANTHROPOLOGICAL APPROACHES TO WOMEN'S STUDIES. Harper's Studies in Language and Literature. New York: Harper & Row, 1975. 38 p. Biblio. Paper.

Study guide. Note especially "The Role and Status of Women," pages 24-36.

476 Leonard, Eugenie A., et al. THE AMERICAN WOMAN IN COLONIAL AND REVOLUTIONARY TIMES, 1565-1800: A SYLLABUS WITH BIBLIOGRAPHY. Philadelphia: University of Pennsylvania Press, 1962. 169 p. Reprint. Westport, Conn.: Greenwood Press, 1975.

Reflects a wide range of women's experience. Extensive bibliography.

477 Lynn, Naomi, et al., comps. RESEARCH GUIDE IN WOMEN'S STUDIES. Morristown, N.J.: General Learning, 1974. ix, 194 p. Biblio. Paper.

Deals with problems on how to write a women's studies paper and how to use statistical information. Lists general and specialized research tools, information and research centers, and women's studies offerings.

478 McGuigan, Dorothy G., ed. A SAMPLER OF WOMEN'S STUDIES. Ann Arbor: Center for Continuing Education, University of Michigan, 1973. 116 p. Illus. Paper.

Material on dance, general and political status, biographies of feminists, and education.

479 Turner, Maryann. BIBLIOTECA FEMINA: A HISTORY OF BOOK COLLECTIONS CONCERNING WOMEN. New York: Tower Press, 1978. 117 p. Illus. Paper.

In addition to history includes also methods of setting up collections. Appends listing of women's studies courses and topical files.

K. NONSEXIST READING, EDUCATIONAL, AND VISUAL MATERIAL FOR CHILDREN

Nonsexist children's books and material about them are available from, among other sources, KNOW, the Feminist Press, the Women's Action Alliance, and Lollipop Power. MS. publishes nonsexist short stories for children in each issue.

480 Adell, Judith, and Klein, Hilary D., comps. A GUIDE TO NON-SEXIST CHILDREN'S BOOKS. Chicago: Academy, 1976. 149 p.

Bibliography of fiction and nonfiction for preschool through the twelfth grade.

481 BOYS AND GIRLS TOGETHER. Beechhurst, N.Y.: Feminist Book Mart. 1974. 27 p. Pamph.

Annotated bibliography. Update projected. Available from Book Mart.

482 Davis, Enid. THE LIBERTY CAP: A CATALOGUE OF NON-SEXIST MATERIALS FOR CHILDREN. Chicago: Academy, 1977. viii, 236 p. Biblio.

Lists wide range of printed matter as well as publishers, distributors, and organizations for preschoolers through young adults. Bibliographies are collected from the bimonthly THE LIBERTY CAP and updated.

483 DICK AND JANE AS VICTIM: SEX STEREOTYPING IN CHILDREN'S READERS. Princeton, N.J.: Women in Words and Images, 1972. 57 p. Biblio. Pamph.

Analyzes children's readers statistically, discusses implications of the study, and offers recommendations for change. Available from Women in Words and Images.

484 Johnson, Laurie O. NONSEXIST CURRICULAR MATERIALS FOR ELEMENTARY SCHOOL. Old Westbury, N.Y.: Feminist Press, 1974. 96 p. Looseleaf.

Comprehensive. Being revised.

485 LITTLE MISS MUFFET FIGHTS BACK. Rev. ed. New York: Feminists on Children's Media, 1974. 62 p.

Annotated bibliography lists children's books as well as articles on sex discrimination in children's books. Available from Feminists on Children's Media.

486 Sprung, Barbara. NONSEXIST EDUCATION FOR YOUNG CHILDREN: A PRACTICAL GUIDE. Englewood Cliffs, N.J.: Prentice-Hall, 1977. 128 p. Biblio., illus. Paper.

Includes annotated bibliography of picture books and unannotated bibliography of readings.

487 Wengraf, Susan, and Artel, Linda, comps. POSITIVE IMAGES: NON-SEXIST FILMS FOR YOUNG PEOPLE. San Francisco: Bootlegger Press, 1976. 167 p. Illus. Paper.

Lists films, video, filmstrips and slide shows, photographs, distributors' addresses, and selected resources. Includes subject index.

L. RHETORIC

1. Bibliography

488 Thorne, Barrie, and Henley, Nancy, comps. "Sex Differences in Language, Speech, and Nonverbal Communication: An Annotated Bibliography." In their LANGUAGE AND SEX: DIFFERENCE AND DOMINANCE, pp. 205-311. Rawley, Mass.: Newbury House, 1975. xii, 311 p.

See also 491.

2. References

489 APA Task Force on Issues of Sexual Bias in Graduate Education. "Guidelines for the Nonsexist Use of Language." AMERICAN PSYCHOLOGIST 30 (June 1975): 682-84.

490 Gershung, H. Lee. "Sexist Semantics in the Dictionary." ETC: A REVIEW OF GENERAL SEMANTICS 31 (1974): 159-69. Tables, biblio.

491 Key, Mary R. MALE/FEMALE: WITH A COMPREHENSIVE BIBLIOGRAPHY. Metuchen, N.J.: Scarecrow Press, 1974. vii, 200 p. Illus., biblio.

Linguist discusses differences in communication between the sexes in a broad context.

492 Lakoff, Robin. LANGUAGE AND WOMAN'S PLACE. New York: Harper & Row, Colophon Books, 1975. 83 p. Biblio. Paper.

Portrays sexist nature of language as a symptom rather than a problem.

493 Marshall, Joan K. ON EQUAL TERMS: A THESAURUS FOR NONSEXIST INDEXING AND CATALOGING. New York: Neal-Schuman, 1977. viii, 152 p. Paper.

Offers alternatives to the sexist bias of the system in the Library of Congress subject headings offered by Committee on Sexism in Subject Headings of American Library Association.

494 Miller, Casey, and Swift, Kate. WORDS AND WOMEN: NEW LANGUAGE IN NEW TIMES. Garden City, N.Y.: Doubleday & Co., Anchor Books, 1977. viii, 177 p.

Historical perspective.

495 Thorne, Barrie, and Henley, Nancy, eds. LANGUAGE AND SEX: DIFFERENCE AND DOMINANCE. Sociolinguist Series. Rawley, Mass.: Newbury House, 1975. xii, 311 p.

Contains twelve articles on general issues, including the making of nonsexist dictionary.

496 Wilson, Robert A. PLAYBOY'S BOOK OF FORBIDDEN WORDS: A LIBERATED DICTIONARY OF IMPROPER ENGLISH, CONTAINING OVER 700 UNINHIBITED DEFINITIONS OF EROTIC AND SCATALOGICAL TERMS. Chicago: Playboy Press Book, 1972. xi, 302 p.

Shows how women appear in nonacademic rhetoric.

497 Young Woman's Christian Association. AN INTELLIGENT WOMAN'S GUIDE TO DIRTY WORDS: THE FEMINIST ENGLISH DICTIONARY. Chicago: 1973. 50 p.

Available from YWCA, Loop Center, 37 South Wabash, Chicago, Illinois.

M. MALE LIBERATION

498 David, Deborah S., and Brannon, Robert, eds. THE FORTY-NINE PERCENT MAJORITY: THE MALE SEX ROLE. Reading, Mass.: Addison-Wesley Publishing Co., 1976. xiv, 338 p. Paper.

Image and role in American society.

499 Farrell, Warren. THE LIBERATED MAN. BEYOND MASCULINITY: FREEING MEN AND THEIR RELATIONSHIPS WITH WOMEN. New York: Random House, 1974. xxxii, 380 p. Biblio. Paper.

500 Komarovsky, Mirra. DILEMMA OF MASCULINITY: A STUDY OF COLLEGE YOUTH. New York: W.W. Norton & Co., 1976. x, 274 p. Tables, biblio.

Study of Ivy League men includes relationships with women.

501 Nichols, Jack. MEN'S LIBERATION: A NEW DEFINITION OF MASCULINITY. New York: Penguin Books, 1975. 333 p. Paper.

502 Snodgrass, Jon, ed. A BOOK OF READINGS FOR MEN AGAINST SEXISM. New York: Times Change Press, 1977. 240 p. Biblio. Paper.

In part 1 men write about the part they play in the oppression of women, in part 2 about the related oppressions of gay, class, and general social oppression.

Chapter 5
EDUCATION

This chapter has to do with the education of women and discrimination against their education. For women as educators and discrimination against their employment in educational institutions see chapter 7, section E. 2.

A. GENERAL BACKGROUND

1. Resources

The Project on the Status and Education of Women of the Association of American Colleges acts as a clearinghouse for information on all matters affecting women's education. In addition to issuing the monthly newsletter ON CAMPUS WITH WOMEN, the project also puts out either original or reprints of bibliographies, reports, interpretations and summaries of federal and state laws and court decisions affecting women's education, recruitment listings, and material on minority women and affirmative action. Items are free upon request.

Other organizations that issue material having to do with the education of women and discrimination against women in education are the Clearinghouse on Women's studies (see p. 89), the National Organization for Women Education Task Force (see p. 81), the Women's Equity Action League, and the Women's Bureau (see p. 14). The Resource Center on Sex Roles in Education issues a newsletter containing information on recent research, law actions, and so on. Material is also available from educational organizations, such as the National Education Association and the American Federation of Teachers AFL-CIO. For a listing of educational organizations see 403. The biweekly ADULT CONTINUING EDUCATION carries items of interest; the quarterly PEER PERSPECTIVE, published by the National Organization for Women Legal Defense and Education Fund, monitors federal enforcement progress in educational discrimination. The Educational Resources Information Center (ERIC) is a nationwide information network which acquires and abstracts significant reports related to a wide range of educational topics. It issues the monthly RESOURCES IN EDUCATION that indexes by subject, author, and institution the material it abstracts.

For a listing of collections having to do with education see Ash and Calvert, page 3.

See also 519, 524.

2. Sources

503 College Entrance Examination Board. THE NEW YORK TIMES GUIDE TO CONTINUING EDUCATION IN AMERICA. Edited by Frances C. Thomson. New York: Quadrangle, 1972. 911 p. Biblio.

Education courses that are "academic and vocational, traditional and new, in the classroom and through the mail, for credit and for fun."

504 EDUCATION INDEX. New York: H.W. Wilson Co., 1929-- . Monthly. Annual and triennial cumulations.

Lists periodicals, books, pamphlets, monographs, and reports.

505 ENCYCLOPEDIA OF EDUCATIONAL RESEARCH: A PROJECT OF THE AMERICAN EDUCATION RESEARCH ASSOCIATION. 4th ed. xxviii, 1,522, xliv p. London: Collier-Macmillan, 1969.

By subject. Updates bibliography and activity in each field. Note particularly "Sex Differences" and "Education of Women."

506 NORTH AMERICAN EDUCATOR'S WORLD: THE STANDARD GUIDE TO AMERICAN-CANADIAN EDUCATIONAL ASSOCIATIONS, PUBLICATIONS, CONVENTIONS, RESEARCH CENTERS & FOUNDATIONS. CURRENT DATES THROUGH 1974. 3d ed., rev. Philadelphia: North American, 1972. 627 p.

507 Ohles, John F., comp. BIOGRAPHICAL DICTIONARY OF AMERICAN EDUCATORS. 3 vols. Westport, Conn.: Greenwood Press, 1978.

Includes educators in specialized, as well as general fields of education.

508 STANDARD EDUCATIONAL ALMANAC. Orange, N.J.: Academic Media, 1968-- . Annual.

Guide to education facts and statistics.

509 U.S. Office of Education. DIGEST OF EDUCATIONAL STATISTICS. Washington, D.C.: Government Printing Office, 1962-- . Annual.

Provides general, as well as specific information relating to all educational levels. Includes federal programs and related activities.

510 WHO'S WHO AMONG STUDENTS IN AMERICAN UNIVERSITIES. Washington, D.C.: Randall, 1935-- .

See also the listing of who's who among faculty and staff at colleges and universities (chapter 7, section E.2.c).

511 Young, Margaret L., et al., eds. EDUCATION AND INFORMATION SCIENCE LIBRARIES. Vol. 2 of SUBJECT DIRECTORY OF SPECIAL LIBRARIES AND INFORMATION CENTERS. 5th ed. Detroit: Gale Research Co., 1979. xvii, 149 p.

3. Bibliographies

The Education Commission of the United States issues a wide range of bibliographies for seminars and clinics available from its office at 1800 Lincoln Street, Denver, Colorado 50203.

The Educational Resources information Center (ERIC) indexes and abstracts the contents of all journals listed in the CURRENT INDEX TO JOURNALS OF HIGHER EDUCATION. It also prepares bibliographies of and abstracts research documents announced in RESOURCES IN EDUCATION and disseminated through the ERIC Document Reproduction Service. It is invaluable in locating items published informally.

512 Astin, Helen S., et al., comps. WOMEN: A BIBLIOGRAPHY ON THEIR EDUCATION AND CAREERS. New York: Behavioral Publications, 1974. 243 p.

Sponsored by University Research Corporation and the Institute of Life Insurance. Lists and abstracts 352 items, most of which were written after 1966. Categories include determinants of career choice, women in the world of work and their adjustment to it, work policies studies, sex roles and socialization, education and continuing education for women.

513 Dweck, Susan, comp. WOMEN: A BIBLIOGRAPHY ON THEIR EDUCATION AND CAREERS. Washington, D.C.: Human Service Press, 1971. 243 p.

Annotated.

514 U.S. Office of Education. BIBLIOGRAPHY RESEARCH STUDIES IN EDUCATION (1926-1940). Compiled by Francesco Cordasco. 4 vols. Detroit: Gale Research Co., 1974.

Mostly annotated. Originally issued as UNITED STATES OFFICE OF EDUCATION BULLETIN Series, 1928-41.

See also 524.

4. References

515 Coleman, James S. THE ADOLESCENT SOCIETY: THE SOCIAL LIFE OF THE TEENAGER AND ITS IMPACT ON EDUCATION. New York: Free Press; London: Collier-Macmillan, 1961. xvi, 368 p. Tables, figs. Paper.

Teenage status system and educational achievement.

516 Emma Willard Task Force on Education. SEXISM IN EDUCATION. 3d ed. Minneapolis: 1972. 87 p. Biblio. Paper.

Views sexism in the classroom as the root of sexism in society. Material on educational proposals, rhetoric, lesbianism, American history, sports, and so on.

517 Frazier, Nancy, and Sadker, Myra. SEXISM IN SCHOOL AND SOCIETY. Critical Issues in Education Series. New York: Harper & Row, 1973. xv, 215 p. Illus., biblio. Paper.

Autobiographical, from elementary school through college. Suggestions for eliminating discriminatory attitudes and practices.

518 Goodsell, Willystine. THE EDUCATION OF WOMEN: ITS SOCIAL BACKGROUND AND ITS PROBLEMS. New York: Macmillan Co., 1923. 378 p.

History of women's education and its relation to marriage; sex differentiation; vocational, social, and moral training; and health problems.

519 Guttentag, Marie, et al., eds. UNDOING SEX STEREOTYPES: RESEARCH AND RESOURCES FOR EDUCATION. New York: McGraw-Hill Book Co., 1976. ix, 342 p. Biblio. Paper.

Project supported by Ford Foundation reports on current activities being used to combat sexism through junior high school levels, and means of effecting further attitudinal change.

520 Harrison, Barbara G. UNLEARNING THE LIE: SEXISM IN SCHOOL. New York: Liveright, 1973. xiii, 174 p. Biblio. Paper.

Account of the attempt to eliminate sexist-racist biases in

educational practices of the Woodward School in Brooklyn, New York.

521 Komarovsky, Mirra. WOMEN IN THE MODERN WORLD: THEIR EDUCATION AND THEIR DILEMMAS. Boston: Little, Brown and Co., 1953. xv, 319 p.

Sociologist's somewhat equivocal position toward the women's choice of education-career and home life.

522 "Sex Discrimination." INEQUALITY IN EDUCATION 18 (October 1974): special issue.

Articles on sexism in public education with specific cases and judicial guides relating to sexism in education.

523 Sexton, Patricia C. THE FEMINIZED MALE: CLASSROOMS, WHITE COLLARS AND THE DECLINE OF MANLINESS. New York: Random House, 1969. 240 p. Paper.

Destructive sexist forces in educational organizations diminish humanity of both men and women.

524 Stacey, Judith, et al., eds. AND JILL CAME TUMBLING AFTER: SEXISM IN AMERICAN EDUCATION. Laurel Original. New York: Dell Publishing Co., 1974. 461 p. Biblio. Paper.

Articles on sexism at all educational levels. Appendix includes annotated bibliography, list of special issues, materials, resources, organizations, audiovisual aids, and government legislative sources of educational materials.

525 U.S. Congress. House. Committee on Education and Labor. THE WOMEN'S EDUCATIONAL EQUITY ACT OF 1973. HEARINGS BEFORE THE SUBCOMMITTEE ON EDUCATION OF THE COMMITTEE ON LABOR AND PUBLIC WELFARE, UNITED STATES SENATE, 93RD CONGRESS, FIRST SESSION . . . OCTOBER 17 AND NOVEMBER 9, 1973. Washington, D.C.: Government Printing Office, 1973. 426 p.

Text of the act, statements of witnesses, and supplementary material that includes reports, articles, and research summaries.

526 U.S. Department of Health, Education and Welfare. "Nondiscrimination on the Basis of Sex: Education, Programs and Activities Receiving or Benefiting from Federal Assistance." FEDERAL REGISTER 40 (4 June 1975): 24128-45.

Reprinted by the department as "Final Title IX Regulation Implementing Education Amendments of 1972 Prohibiting

Discrimination in Education. Effective Date: July 21, 1975." Contains summary of provisions with interpretation of measure, questions, and answers.

527 WE'LL DO IT OURSELVES: COMBATTING SEXISM IN EDUCATION. Edited by David Rosen, et al. Lincoln: Nebraska Curriculum Center, University of Nebraska, 1974. xvi, 321 p. Biblios. Paper.

Articles on minority women, lesbians, child care, the women's movement, health, and law. Available from the Nebraska Curriculum Development Center, Andrews Hall, University of Nebraska, Lincoln, Nebraska 68588.

B. HISTORY

Histories of women's colleges of both the nineteenth and twentieth centuries are available in many libraries.

529 Beecher, Catharine E. THE TRUE REMEDY FOR THE WRONGS OF WOMAN: WITH A HISTORY OF AN ENTERPRISE HAVING THAT FOR ITS OBJECT. Boston: Phillips, Sampson, 1851. viii, 263 p.

Author urges young women to realize potential to become effective citizens through acquiring education.

530 Blandin, Irma M.E. THE HISTORY OF HIGHER EDUCATION FOR WOMEN IN THE SOUTH PRIOR TO 1860. New York: Neale Publishing, 1909. Reprint. New York: Zenger Publishing Co., 1976. 328 p.

531 Boas, Louise S. WOMEN'S EDUCATION BEGINS: THE RISE OF WOMEN'S COLLEGES. Norton, Mass.: Wheaton College, 1935. 295 p. Biblio. Reprint. American Education: People, Ideas and Institutions series. New York: Arno Press, 1971.

Social and religious milieu in which women's education coalesced in the nineteenth century. Discusses founding and curricula of Smith, Vassar, Mount Holyoke, Wellesley, and other institutions. Bibliography includes listing of catalogs of colleges and seminaries.

532 Brackett, Anne A., ed. THE EDUCATION OF AMERICAN GIRLS CONSIDERED IN A SERIES OF ESSAYS. New York: G.P. Putnam's Sons, 1874. 401 p.

Thirteen essays include histories of women's colleges and essays on women in England and America. By Ednah

Cheney, Caroline Dall, Mary Jacobi, Mary Nutting, and others.

533 Burstall, Sara A. THE EDUCATION OF GIRLS IN THE UNITED STATES. New York: Macmillan Co.; London: Swan Sonnenschein, 1894. xii, 204 p. Reprint. American Education: People, Ideas and Institutions series. New York: Arno Press, 1970.

534 Clarke, Edward H. SEX AND EDUCATION: OR, A FAIR CHANCE FOR GIRLS. Boston: J.R. Osgood, 1873. 181 p. Reprint. Medicine and Society in America series. New York: Arno Press, 1972.

Classic biological argument supports case for discrimination against women's education. See 540, 551, 1056.

535 Cross, Barbara M., ed. THE EDUCATED WOMAN IN AMERICA: SELECTED WRITINGS OF CATHARINE BEECHER, MARGARET FULLER AND M. CAREY THOMAS. Classics in Education series, no. 25. New York: Teachers College Press, 1965. viii, 175 p. Illus. Paper.

"Unfeminine" women who became models for the "new woman." Informative introduction.

536 Earle, Alice M. "Women Teachers and Girl Scholars." In her CHILD LIFE IN COLONIAL DAYS, chap. 4. New York: Macmillan, 1899. xxi, 418 p. Illus.

Female education at the end of the seventeenth and beginning of the eighteenth centuries.

537 Frankfort, Roberta. COLLEGIATE WOMEN: DOMESTICITY AND CAREER IN TURN-OF-THE-CENTURY AMERICA. New York: New York University Press, 1977. xix, 121 p.

Focuses on Bryn Mawr and Wellesley. Material on Elizabeth Peabody, Alice Palmer, Martha Thomas, Ellen Richards. Appendix supplies statistics.

538 Goodsell, Willystine, ed. PIONEERS OF WOMEN'S EDUCATION IN THE UNITED STATES: EMMA WILLARD, CATHERINE [sic] BEECHER, MARY LYON. New York: McGraw-Hill Book Co., 1931. viii, 311 p. Illus. Reprint. New York: AMS Press, 1970.

Introductory essay on women's education in America prior to 1820. Includes Willard's "A Plan for Approving Female Education" and excerpts from her textbooks; various of Beecher's writings on education, suffrage, domesticity, and health; and Lyon's first published appeal on behalf of Mount Holyoke, description of the early seminary and comparison of its curriculum with that of Ipswich Female Academy. Biographical essay precedes each excerpt.

539 Hanscom, Elizabeth D., and Greene, Helen F. SOPHIA SMITH AND THE BEGINNINGS OF SMITH COLLEGE. Smith College Fiftieth Anniversary Publications, vol. 2. Northampton, Mass.: Smith College, 1925. x, 120 p.

Based mostly on private papers.

540 Howe, Julia Ward, ed. SEX AND EDUCATION: A REPLY TO DR. E.H. CLARKE'S "SEX IN EDUCATION." Boston: Roberts Brothers, 1874. 203 p. Reprint. American Women: Images and Realities series. New York: Arno Press, 1972.

Contains replies to 534 by Thomas Wentworth Higginson, Caroline Dall, Elizabeth Stuart Phelps, and others.

541 Jex-Blake, Sophia. A VISIT TO SOME AMERICAN SCHOOLS AND COLLEGES. London: Macmillan & Co., 1867. xii, 250 p. Reprint. Westport, Conn.: Hyperion Press, 1976.

Reactions of visiting British doctor.

542 Kendall, Elaina. PECULIAR INSTITUTIONS: AN INFORMAL HISTORY OF THE SEVEN SISTERS COLLEGES. New York: G.P. Putnam's Sons, 1975. 272 p. Illus.

543 Kuhn, Annel. THE MOTHER'S ROLE IN CHILDHOOD EDUCATION: NEW ENGLAND CONCEPTS 1830-1860. Yale Studies in Religious Education, no. 19. New Haven, Conn.: Yale University Press, 1947. x, 224 p. Illus., biblio.

Mother as agent of social control.

544 Newcomer, Mable. A CENTURY OF HIGHER EDUCATION FOR AMERICAN WOMEN. New York: Harper, 1959. xii, 266 p. Tables, biblio.

Broad view of problems and triumphs.

545 Orton, James, ed. THE LIBERAL EDUCATION OF WOMEN: THE DEMAND AND THE METHOD. CURRENT THOUGHT IN AMERICA AND ENGLAND. New York: A.S. Barnes, 1873. x, 328 p.

Pros and cons of the necessity of education for women as well as education offered by specific colleges. Appendix includes remarks by Thomas Wentworth Higginson, Wendell Phillips, and others.

546 Phelps, Almira H.L. HOURS WITH MY PUPILS. New York: A.S. Barnes, 1868. xxix, 363 p.

Phelps, the sister of Emma Willard, founder of Pataposco Female Institute, and an active antisuffragist, instructs her pupils in principles of virtue and piety through a series of lectures.

547 Rush, Benjamin. THOUGHTS ON FEMALE EDUCATION, ACCOMMODATED TO THE PRESENT STATE OF SOCIETY, AND GOVERNMENT IN THE UNITED STATES OF AMERICA. Philadelphia: Prichard & Hall, 1787. 32 p. Pamph.

Conditions peculiar to America make education for women a necessity.

548 Sewall, May W. "The Education of Women in the Western United States." In WOMAN'S WORK IN AMERICA, edited by Annie N. Meyer, chap. 3. New York: Henry Holt, 1891. Reprint. New York: American Women: Images and Realities series. New York: Arno Press, 1972.

To end of nineteenth century. Passages on Oberlin. See also appendix B of same volume.

549 Stock, Phyllis. BETTER THAN RUBIES: A HISTORY OF WOMEN'S EDUCATION. New York: G.P. Putnam's Sons, 1978. 252 p. Biblio.

Good general background. Covers women's education from antiquity.

550 Thompson, Eleanor W. EDUCATION FOR LADIES, 1830-1860: IDEAS ON EDUCATION IN MAGAZINES FOR WOMEN. New York: King's Crown, 1947. ix, 170 p. Biblio.

Discusses curricula, private and public education, child training, normal school education, medical training, and training of handicapped and males.

551 Trecker, Janice L. "Sex, Science and Education." AMERICAN QUARTERLY 26 (October 1974): 352-66.

Discusses theories underlying sexism in education as set forth in 534 and similar nineteenth-century works.

552 Woody, Thomas. A HISTORY OF WOMEN'S EDUCATION IN THE UNITED STATES. 2 vols. Science and Education Series. New York: Science Press, 1929. Biblio., vol. 2.

Volume 1 contains material on attitudes toward women's

education; early regional, teacher, and secondary education of women; academies and seminaries and their texts; and courses of study in seminaries and high schools. Volume 2 contains material on women's changing economic status, vocational, physical, and professional education, colleges for women, coeducation, suffrage, and women's clubs. Includes listing of college texts.

See also 2152.

C. HIGHER EDUCATION, CURRENT

1. Resources

Most of the organizations and institutions mentioned in section A.1 at the beginning of this chapter issue material also on higher education for women. In addition, the American Association of University Women publishes a monthly journal and focuses specifically on higher education as do the caucuses and committees of professional organizations relating to academic disciplines. Informational items that they print are frequently reprinted by, and are available from, the Project on the Status and Education of Women. Committee W of the American Association of University Professors functions on both national and state levels and material is available from the national office and from many of its state organizations and chapters. The CHRONICLE OF HIGHER EDUCATION and the newsletters EQUAL OPPORTUNITY IN EDUCATION, ON CAMPUS WITH WOMEN, and ADULT AND CONTINUING EDUCATION may be of assistance.

See also 573.

2. Bibliographies

553 Association of Collegiate Alumnae. CONTRIBUTIONS TOWARDS A BIBLIOGRAPHY OF THE HIGHER EDUCATION OF WOMEN. Boston: Trustees of the Boston Public Library, 1897. vii, 42 p. Paper.

Lists history, health, coeducation, law, medicine, postgraduate study, occupations, colleges, universities, and professional societies open to women. Items limited to those in the library.

554 Harmon, Linda A., comp. STATUS OF WOMEN IN HIGHER EDUCATION 1963-1972: A SELECTIVE BIBLIOGRAPHY. Series in Bibliography, no. 2. Ames: Iowa State University Library, 1972. xix, 124 p. Illus. Offset, paper.

Mostly annotated. Material on status, historical perspectives, and future ramifications. Introduction provides overview. Generic rather than subject categories. Includes ephemera and Educational Resources Information Center materials. Appendix prints text of Title VII and a list of institutions charged with discrimination. Available from the library, attention Photoduplication Center, Ames, Iowa 50010.

555 Oltman, Ruth M. STATUS OF GRADUATE AND PROFESSIONAL EDUCATION OF WOMEN 1974. A VIEW OF THE LITERATURE AND BIBLIOGRAPHY. Paper prepared for the American Association of University Women Conference on Graduate and Professional Education of women, 10 May, 1974. Urbana, Ill.: Educational Resources Information Center, 1974. 14 p.

556 Westervelt, Esther M., et al. WOMEN'S HIGHER EDUCATION AND CONTINUING EDUCATION: AN ANNOTATED BIBLIOGRAPHY WITH SELECTED REFERENCES IN RELATED ASPECTS OF WOMEN'S LIVES. New York: College Entrance Board, 1971. 67 p. Paper.

Annotated. Listings on status, research, behavior and aspirations, employment, and bibliography.

See also 1171.

3. References

557 American Association of State Colleges and Universities. WOMEN'S STAKE IN LOW TUITION. Compiled by Minnie Bengelsdorf. Washington, D.C.: 1974. Unpaged. Pamph.

Available from the association.

558 Astin, Helen S. THE WOMAN DOCTORATE IN AMERICA: ORIGINS, CAREER AND FAMILY. New York: Russell Sage Foundation, 1969. xii, 196 p. Tables, biblio.

Sampling of women doctorate recipients of 1957-58 reveals ways in which subjects used training, their degree of commitment to careers, and professional contributions.

559 Bond, Horace M. BLACK AMERICAN SCHOLARS. Detroit: Balamp, 1972. v, 209 p. Tables, maps. Paper.

Family history and relationships vital to acquisition of doctorates. Genetic table of African princess leads through eight generations to three doctorates.

560 Bushnell, John H. "Student Culture at Vassar." In THE AMERICAN

COLLEGE: A PSYCHOLOGICAL AND SOCIAL INTERPRETATION OF THE HIGHER LEARNING, edited by Nevitt Sanford, chap. 14. New York: John Wiley, 1962.

Anthropological analysis of the life of the class of 1958 throughout its four years on campus.

561 Carnegie Commission on Higher Education. ESCAPE FROM THE DOLL'S HOUSE: WOMEN IN GRADUATE AND PROFESSIONAL SCHOOL EDUCATION. A REPORT PREPARED FOR THE COMMISSION. Prepared by Saul D. Feldman. New York: McGraw-Hill Book Co., 1974. xvi, 208 p.

Study of prejudice against women in higher education, and their self-images and career expectations.

562 Centra, John A., with Kaykendall, Nancy M. WOMEN, MEN AND THE DOCTORATE. Princeton, N.J.: Educational Testing Service, 1974. viii, 214 p. Tables, fig. Offset, paper.

Sponsored by the Graduate Record Examinations Board. Study of current status and professional development.

563 Henderson, Jean G., and Henderson, Algo D. MS. GOES TO COLLEGE. Carbondale: Southern Illinois University; London: Feffer & Simons, 1975. x, 180 p. Tables, biblio. Paper.

Realistic, well-researched presentation of realities of college life. Based on interviews.

564 Hiestand, Dale L. CHANGING CAREERS AFTER 35: NEW HORIZONS THROUGH PROFESSIONAL AND GRADUATE STUDY. New York: Columbia University, 1971. xiv, 170 p.

Part of Conservation of University's Human Resources Project.

565 Howe, Florence, ed. WOMEN AND THE POWER TO CHANGE. New York: McGraw-Hill Book Co., 1975. xvii, 182 p.

Sponsored by the Carnegie Commission on Higher Education. Adrienne Rich writes on women-centered universities, Arlie Hochschild on the shaping of the universities to the male image, Aleta Wallach on women in law school, and Florence Howe on how to gain power for women without extending oppression to other groups.

566 HOW HARVARD RULES WOMEN, BEING A TOTAL CRITIQUE OF HARVARD UNIVERSITY, INCLUDING: NEW LIBERATED DOCUMENTS, GOVERNMENT RESEARCH, THE EDUCATIONAL PROCESS EPISODE, AND A FREE POWER CHART. Cambridge, Mass.: Africa Research Group, 1970. 88 p. Illus.

567 Hutchinson, Emilie J. WOMEN AND THE PH.D: FACTS FROM THE EXPERIENCES OF 1,025 WOMEN WHO HAVE TAKEN THE DEGREE OF DOCTOR OF PHILOSOPHY SINCE 1877. Institute of Women's Professional Relations, Bulletin no. 2. Greensboro: North Carolina College for Women, 1929. x, 212 p. Tables.

568 Lever, Janet, and Schwartz, Pepper. WOMEN AT YALE. Indianapolis: Bobbs-Merrill Co., 1971. 274 p. Illus.

Two women graduates conclude that chauvinism at Yale reflects that in American culture. Academic rituals analyzed for sexist orientation.

569 Miller, Ann, ed. A COLLEGE IN DISPERSION: WOMEN OF BRYN MAWR 1876-1975. Boulder, Colo.: Westview 1976. xi, 315 p. Tables.

Profiles of undergraduates, graduates, and alumnae based on statistical surveys.

570 Noble, Jeanne L. THE NEGRO WOMAN'S COLLEGE EDUCATION. Studies in Education Series. New York: Bureau of Publications, Teachers College, Columbia University, 1956. x, 163 p. Tables, biblio.

First survey of college education of black woman. Includes history to 1950, survey of graduates, interviews with professionals, and evaluation of needs.

571 Richardson, Betty. SEXISM IN HIGHER EDUCATION. New York: Seabury Press, 1975. 221 p.

Childhood conditioning and social prejudice working together produce failure in bright women.

572 U.S. Congress. House. Committee on Education and Labor. SEX DISCRIMINATION REGULATIONS BEFORE SUBCOMMITTEE ON POST-SECONDARY EDUCATION, REVIEW OF REGULATIONS TO IMPLEMENT TITLE IX . . . JUNE 17-26. 94th Cong. 1st sess. Washington, D.C.: Government Printing Office, 1975. xi, 664 p.

General but with some stress on collegiate athletics. Available from the Superintendent of Documents.

573 U.S. Department of Health, Education and Welfare. AVAILABILITY DATA: MINORITIES AND WOMEN. Rev. ed. Washington, D.C.: 1973. Variously paged. Tables. Offset, paper.

Aggregate of assorted information in the field of higher education. Lists resources.

574 U.S. Office of Education. EARNED DEGREES CONFERRED. Washington, D.C.: Government Printing Office, 1947/48-- .

A publication of the National Center for Educational Statistics. Since 1966/67 issued in two parts: A, SUMMARY DATA, and B, INSTITUTIONAL DATA. Volume for 1974/75 includes EARNED DEGREES CONFERRED: ANALYSES OF TRENDS, 1965-66 through 1943-75. For information on degrees conferred at earlier dates, see ANNUAL REPORTS OF THE COMMISSIONER OF EDUCATION 1867-1917 and BIENNIAL SURVEY OF EDUCATION IN THE UNITED STATES, 1916/18-- 1956/58 (Washington, D.C.: Government Printing Office, 1921-63). Available from the Superintendent of Documents.

575 WOMEN ON CAMPUS: THE UNFINISHED LIBERATION. Edited by the editors of CHANGE magazine. New Rochelle, N.Y.: CHANGE, 1975. 256 p. Paper.

Reprints twenty-one articles from CHANGE having to do with numerous problems still to be solved.

576 Women's Equity Action League (WEAL) Education and Legal Defense Fund. WOMEN AND FELLOWSHIPS. Compiled by Judith Nies. Washington, D.C.: 1976. 35 p. Offset, stapled.

Past history of discrimination in the distribution of fellowships, pressures for change, and case histories demonstrating possibilities for change. Being updated. Available from the WEAL Education and Legal Defense Fund, 805 15th Street, N.W., Suite 822, Washington, D.C. 20005.

For information of women's studies programs see chapter 4, section J.

Chapter 6
SOCIOLOGY

A. SOURCES, BIBLIOGRAPHIES

1. Sources

A guide to libraries with holdings of special interest to the social sciences is SOCIAL SCIENCES AND HUMANITIES LIBRARIES, INCLUDING . . . ART . . . HISTORY . . . MUSIC, RELIGION/THEOLOGY, THEATER, volume 4 of SUBJECT DIRECTORY OF SPECIAL LIBRARIES AND INFORMATION CENTERS, published in 1974 by Gale Research.

Periodicals that carry articles of interest to women, some of which have put out special issues bearing on women's issues, are the AMERICAN JOURNAL OF SOCIOLOGY, the JOURNAL OF MARRIAGE AND THE FAMILY, SOCIAL FORCES, and JOURNAL OF SOCIAL ISSUES.

Relevant reviews are available in CONTEMPORARY SOCIOLOGY: A JOURNAL OF REVIEWS and SOCIOLOGY, REVIEW OF BOOKS.

For abstracts see SOCIOLOGICAL ABSTRACTS which is published five times a year with an annual cumulative index.

2. Bibliographies

578 American Library Association. SOURCES OF INFORMATION IN THE SOCIAL SCIENCES: A GUIDE TO THE LITERATURE. Compiled by Carl M. White, et al. Chicago: 1973. xviii, 702 p.

Annotated.

579 Family Service Association of America. READING REFERENCES. Offset, stapled.

Separate lists on marriage, parenthood, and family relationships; early marriage; one-parent families; and divorce and remarriage. Lists are available from the association.

580 Institute of Pluralism and Group Identity. NOWHERE TO BE FOUND: A LITERATURE REVIEW AND ANNOTATED BIBLIOGRAPHY ON WHITE WORKING CLASS WOMEN. Compiled by Victoria Samuels. New York: 1975. 28 p. Offset, stapled.

Available from the institute.

See also 2, 5, 586, and chapter 2, section A.1.

B. GENERAL REFERENCES

581 AMERICAN JOURNAL OF SOCIOLOGY 78 (January 1973): special issue. Reprinted as 120.

582 Chafe, William H. WOMEN AND EQUALITY: CHANGING PATTERNS IN AMERICAN CULTURE. New York: Oxford University Press, 1977. xiii, 207 p. Biblio.

Underlying social and economic changes affecting women.

583 "Feminist Perspective: The Sociological Challenge." Edited by Lillian B. Rubin. SOCIAL PROBLEMS 23 (April 1976): special issue. Tables, biblio.

Twelve articles in sections entitled "The Woman's Movement in Theoretical, Historical and Comparative Perspective," "Women in the Occupational Structure," "Psychosexual Development and Conflict," "Sexual Stereotyping of Children and the Aged," and "Problems of Children in Divorce and Prison Situations."

584 Millman, Marcia, and Kanter, Rosabeth M., eds. ANOTHER VOICE: FEMINIST PERSPECTIVES ON SOCIAL LIFE AND SOCIAL SCIENCE. Garden City, N.Y.: Doubleday & Co., Anchor Books, 1975. xvii, 382 p. Biblio. Paper.

Feminists question assumptions of traditional sociological concepts of gender roles, public versus private individuals, "single society," sex as social variable, and status quo as well as methodologies.

585 Mott, Frank Luther, et al. WOMEN, WORK, AND FAMILY: DIMENSIONS OF CHANGE IN AMERICA. Lexington, Mass.: D.C. Heath & Co., 1978. xii, 153 p. Tables, figs., biblios.

Studies the experiences of five-thousand women between 1968 and 1973.

586 Rosenberg, Marie B., and Bergstrom, Len V. WOMEN AND SOCIETY: A CRITICAL REVIEW OF THE LITERATURE WITH A SELECTED ANNOTATED BIBLIOGRAPHY. Beverly Hills, Calif.: Sage Publications, 1975. 360 p.

Material on sociology, political science, and history of women. WOMEN AND SOCIETY: CITATIONS 3601 TO 6000; AN ANNOTATED BIBLIOGRAPHY, issued by the same publisher in 1978, updates the original volume.

587 Safilos-Rothschild, Constantina, ed. TOWARD A SOCIOLOGY OF WOMEN. Lexington, Mass.: Xerox College Publishing, 1972. xii, 406 p. Biblio. Paper.

Articles centered on sex roles as they shape men and women, women's images and attitudes toward money; options open to women; and women's liberation.

588 Seifer, Nancy. NOBODY SPEAKS FOR ME: SELF-PORTRAITS OF AMERICAN WORKING CLASS WOMEN. New York: Simon & Schuster, 1976. 477 p. Illus.

Includes oral histories having to do with community and women's concerns, unionism, and practical politics.

See also chapter 2, section A.2.

C. MODES OF LIVING

1. Life-Styles

Files of so called "women's magazines" such as HARPER'S BAZAAR (1867--) or GOOD HOUSEKEEPING (1885--) are a fruitful source of information on the life-styles of women. See Mott, page 4, for further titles.

589 Atkeson, Mary M. THE WOMAN ON THE FARM. The Century Rural Life Books. New York: Century, 1924. ix, 331 p. Biblio.

Compares the twentieth-century farm woman to her pioneer predecessor; discusses how she lives.

590 Crow, Martha F. THE AMERICAN COUNTRY GIRL. New York: Frederick A. Stokes, 1915. viii, 367 p. Reprint. Women in America:

From Colonial Times to the 20th Century series. New York: Arno Press, 1974.

The girl who didn't leave home.

591 Ginzberg, Eli, et al. LIFE STYLES OF EDUCATED WOMEN. Carnegie Corporation Conservation of Human Resources Project, no. 2. New York: Columbia University Press, 1966. 224 p. Tables, biblio. Paper ed. published as EDUCATED AMERICAN WOMEN: LIFE-STYLES AND SELF-PORTRAITS, 1971.

Concludes that educated women cope more adequately than uneducated women.

592 Kahn, Kitty. HILLBILLY WOMEN. Garden City, N.Y.: Doubleday & Co., 1973. viii, 230 p. Illus. Paper.

Taped conversations with Southern Appalachian women detail daily experience. Excellent introduction. Appendix lists grassroots organizations and publications of area.

593 Keats, John. THE CRACK IN THE PICTURE WINDOW. New York: Ballantine, 1957. xviii, 196 p. Illus., biblio.

Chapter 3 deals with abrasion of women in suburban developments.

594 Lavori, Nora. LIVING TOGETHER, MARRIED OR SINGLE: YOUR LEGAL RIGHTS. New York: Harper & Row, 1976. 255 p. Tables. Paper.

595 Le Masters, E.E. BLUE-COLLAR ARISTOCRATS: LIFE STYLES AT A WORKING CLASS TAVERN. Madison: University of Wisconsin Press, 1975. 228 p. Paper.

Considerable material on women regarding particularly marriage, family, and sexuality.

596 Lynd, Robert, and Lynd, Helen. MIDDLETOWN: A STUDY IN AMERICAN CULTURE. New York: Harcourt, Brace, 1929. x, 550 p. Tables. Paper.

Women in context of small American city. See entry 597 for follow-up study.

597 _____. MIDDLETOWN IN TRANSITION: A STUDY IN CULTURAL CONFLICTS. New York: Harcourt, Brace, 1937. xviii, 604 p. Tables. Paper.

A sequel to entry 596. Study of middle American ten years later reveals patterns of change in women's lives.

598 Roberts, Ron E. THE NEW COMMUNES: COMING TOGETHER IN AMERICA. Englewood Cliffs, N.J.: Prentice-Hall, 1971. 144 p. Paper.

Comparison of today's communes with those of the nineteenth century.

599 Seeley, John, et al. CRESTWOOD HEIGHTS: A STUDY OF THE CULTURE OF SUBURBAN LIFE. New York: Basic Books, 1956. xv, 505 p. Paper.

The complex roles women play in suburban life within larger context. Title varies.

600 Stephens, Kate. "The New England Woman." ATLANTIC MONTHLY 88 (1901): 60-66.

Characteristics of, and social forces that go to make up, the "New England woman," particularly the New England "spinster."

601 Van Deusen, Edmund L. CONTRACT COHABITATION: AN ALTERNATIVE TO MARRIAGE. New York: Grove Press, 1974. 190 p. Paper.

602 Yellis, Kenneth A. "Prosperity's Child." AMERICAN QUARTERLY 21 (Spring 1969): 44-64.

Asserts that the flapper, as the idealized type of the 1920s was the antithesis of Gibson girl. Surveys her rhetoric, sexuality, dress, behavior, and social origins.

See also section I of this chapter.

2. Women as Family Members

a. GENERAL

i. Bibliographies

603 Davis, Lenwood G., with Sims, Janet, comps. THE BLACK FAMILY IN THE UNITED STATES: A SELECTED BIBLIOGRAPHY OF ANNOTATED BOOKS, ARTICLES, AND DISSERTATIONS ON BLACK FAMILIES IN AMERICA. Westport, Conn.: Greenwood Press, 1978. xii, 132 p.

Comprehensive.

604 Keiffer, Miriam G., and Warren, Patricia A., comps. "Resource

Bibliography." In THE WOMAN'S MOVEMENT: SOCIAL AND PSYCHOLOGICAL PERSPECTIVES, edited by Helen Nortis and Clara Rabinowitz, pp. 111-47. New York: AMS Press for American Orthopsychiatric Association, 1972.

American studies approach to American family.

605 Klotman, Phyllis R., and Baatz, Wilmer H., comps. THE BLACK FAMILY AND THE BLACK WOMAN: A BIBLIOGRAPHY. Rev. ed. New York: Arno Press, 1972. x, 231 p.

Unannotated. Includes a listing of slave narratives.

606 Minnesota Council on Family Relations. FAMILY LIFE: LITERATURE AND FILMS, AN ANNOTATED BIBLIOGRAPHY. Minneapolis: 1951-- . Offset, paper.

Frequent revisions. Supplement issued 1976. Available from the council, 1219 University Avenue, S.E., Minneapolis, Minnesota 54414.

See also 628.

ii. References

The JOURNAL OF MARRIAGE AND THE FAMILY (formerly MARRIAGE AND FAMILY LIVING) and the JOURNAL OF ORTHOPSYCHIATRY are among the many journals printing articles on aspects of family life.

607 Angell, Robert C. THE FAMILY ENCOUNTERS THE DEPRESSION. New York: Charles Scribner's Sons, 1936. 309 p.

Impact of the Great Depression on wide range of family groups. Female roles of interest.

608 Bell, Norman W., and Vogel F., eds. A MODERN INTRODUCTION TO THE FAMILY. Rev. ed. Glencoe, Ill.: Free Press, 1968. xi, 758 p.

Articles on psychological and social relationships of family.

609 Bernard, Jessie S., ed. SELF-PORTRAIT OF A FAMILY: LETTERS BY JESSIE, DOROTHY LEE, CLAUDE, AND DAVID BERNARD. Boston: Beacon Press, 1978. 288 p. Illus.

Feminist-sociologist examines through family correspondence her role as professional and family member.

610 Breckinridge, Sophonisba P. THE FAMILY AND THE STATE: SELECT DOCUMENTS. Social Service Series. Chicago: University of

Chicago Press, 1934. Reprint. Family in America series. New York: Arno Press, 1972. xiv, 565 p.

Judicial decisions and commission reports relating to marriage, divorce, rights of spouses, and property rights, children's guardianship, apprenticeship, adoption, and illegitimacy.

611 Calhoun, Arthur W. A SOCIAL HISTORY OF THE AMERICAN FAMILY FROM COLONIAL TIMES TO THE PRESENT. 3 vols. Cleveland: Arthur H. Clark, 1917-19. Biblios. Reprint. Family in America series. New York: Arno Press, 1973.

Of particular relevance to women are volume 1, chapters 1, 5, and 16; volume 2, chapter 4; and volume 3, chapter 6.

612 Cavan, Ruth S. THE AMERICAN FAMILY. 3d ed. New York: Thomas Y. Crowell Co., 1963. xii, 548 p. Tables, biblio.

Contains both general and detailed material on women in marital roles, their education and employment. Appendix includes vital statistics.

613 Engels, Friedrich. THE ORIGINS OF FAMILY, PRIVATE PROPERTY AND THE STATE. Translated by Ernest Unterman. Standard Socialist Series. Chicago: Charles Kerr, 1902. Reprint. New York: International Publishers Co., 1972. 217 p. Paper.

614 Eshleman, J. Ross, ed. PERSPECTIVES AND THE FAMILY: TEXT AND READINGS. Boston: Allyn & Bacon, 1969. viii, 770 p. Tables, charts. Paper.

Material on women's role in family organization and family patterns as they relate to minority groups, such as the Amish and to middle-aged women.

615 Ferriss, Abbott L. INDICATORS OF CHANGE IN THE AMERICAN FAMILY. New York: Russell Sage Foundation, 1970. xii, 145 p. Figs., tables, biblio. Paper.

Statistical time series based on government data, arranged topically under marriage, fertility, marital status, households, dependency, divorce, work, and income and poverty.

616 Frazier, E. Franklin. THE NEGRO FAMILY IN THE UNITED STATES. New York: Macmillan Co., 1949. xxi, 767 p. Illus., maps, biblio. Paper.

Pioneering study supported by wealth of documentary material. Early view of black woman as wife and mother.

617 Glazer-Malbin, Nona, ed. OLD FAMILY/NEW FAMILY: INTERPERSONAL RELATIONSHIPS. New York: D. Van Nostrand Co., 1975. vi, 282 p. Tables.

Includes ten articles on pair, two-couple, and network family arrangements.

618 Halmstrom, Lynda L. THE TWO-CAREER FAMILY. Cambridge, Mass.: Schenckman Publishing Co., 1972. vii, 203 p. Tables. Paper.

Points out that today's two-career family is still viewed as a deviation from the middle-class norm.

619 Howe, Louise K., ed. THE FUTURE OF THE FAMILY: MOTHERS, FATHERS AND CHILDREN; SEX ROLES AND WORK. New York: Simon & Schuster, 1972. 387 p. Paper.

Anthology covers position of women in all aspects of family life.

620 Morgan, Edmund S. VIRGINIANS AT HOME: FAMILY LIFE IN THE 18TH CENTURY. Williamsburg in America Series. Williamsburg, Va.: Colonial Williamsburg, 1952. 99 p. Illus. Reprint. Charlotteville: University Press of Virginia, 1963.

Women's lives in general social context.

621 Otto, Herbert A., ed. THE FAMILY IN SEARCH OF A FUTURE: ALTERNATE MODELS FOR MODERNS. Sociology Series. New York: Appleton-Century-Crofts, 1970. xiv, 204 p.

Discusses a wide variety of alternate family structures, including progressive monogamy, group marriage, polyandry and polygyny, with some focus on arrangements for older people.

622 Rainwater, Lee. BEHIND GHETTO WALLS: BLACK FAMILIES IN A FEDERAL SLUM. Chicago: Aldine Publishing Co., 1970. x, 446 p. Tables, biblio. Paper.

"Private life as it is lived" in the Pruitt-Igo housing project in St. Louis. Much direct interview.

623 Rainwater, Lee, and Yancey, William L. THE MOYNIHAN REPORT AND THE POLITICS OF CONTROVERSY. A Trans-Action Social Science and Public Poly Report. Including the Full Text of THE NEGRO FAMILY: THE CASE FOR NATIONAL ACTION by Daniel Patrick Moynihan. Cambridge, Mass.: MIT Press, 1967. xviii, 493 p. Tables, figs. Paper.

Analyzes reactions to controversial report that hypothesized the instability of the lower-class black family.

624 Rapaport, Rhona, and Rapaport, Robert. DUAL-CAREER FAMILIES RE-EXAMINED: NEW INTEGRATIONS OF WORK AND FAMILY. New York: Harper, 1976. 382 p. Biblio. Paper.

Examines working families in general as well as those in particular lines of work.

625 Reed, Evelyn. WOMAN'S EVOLUTION: FROM MATRIARCHAL CLAN TO PATRIARCHAL FAMILY. New York: Pathfinder Press, 1975. xviii, 491 p. Biblio.

Hypothesizes replacement of original, collective matriarchal society by patriarchal society.

626 Reiss, Ira L. THE FAMILY SYSTEM IN AMERICA. New York: Holt, Rinehart & Winston, 1971. xvi, 493 p. Tables, biblio. Paper. Published as READINGS ON THE AMERICAN FAMILY SYSTEM.

Anthropological-historical approach. Note part 5, chapter 23, "Feminism and Equalitarianism: Women's Liberation."

627 Ross, Heather L., and Sawhill, Isabelle V. TIME OF TRANSITION: THE GROWTH OF FAMILIES HEADED BY WOMEN. Washington, D.C.: Urban Institute, 1975. xii, 223 p. Tables, figs., biblio.

Includes information on marriage, race and family, welfare families, and children. Appendix supplies statistics.

628 Rubin, Lillian B. WORLDS OF PAIN: LIFE IN THE WORKING-CLASS FAMILY. New York: Basic Books, 1976. ixv, 268 p. Biblio.

629 Rudwick, Bracey M. BLACK MATRIARCHY: MYTH OR REALITY? Belmont, Calif.: Wadsworth Publishing Co., 1971. 217 p. Tables, figs. Paper.

Eleven scholars examine most important issues relating to Moynihan report (see 623).

630 "Sexism in Family Studies." JOURNAL OF MARRIAGE AND THE FAMILY 33 (August 1971): special issue.

Articles on female culture and tolerance of domestication, stereotyping, male "sisters," images of women in literature, sex roles, negative views of marriage, women in psychotherapy, and women's history.

631 Skolnick, Arlene, and Skolnick, Jerome H., comps. THE FAMILY IN TRANSITION: RETHINKING MARRIAGE, SEXUALITY, CHILD REARING AND FAMILY ORGANIZATION. Boston: Little, Brown and Co., 1971. xii, 542 p.

See also 251.

b. WOMEN IN THE HOME

i. Bibliography

632 Business and Professional Women's Foundation. WORKING WOMEN: HOMEMAKERS AND VOLUNTEERS: AN ANNOTATED SELECTED BIBLIOGRAPHY. Compiled by Jenrose Felmley. Washington, D.C.: 1975. 25 p.

Few entries prior to 1970.

ii. References

633 Abbott, Lyman. THE HOME BUILDER. Boston: Houghton Mifflin Co., 1908. 129 p.

Antifeminist views woman's home as her "unique monument."

634 Bacon, Elizabeth N. "The Growth of Household Appliances." Ph.D. dissertation, Radcliffe College, 1944.

635 Beecher, Catharine E., and Stowe, Harriet Beecher. THE AMERICAN WOMAN'S HOME, OR, PRINCIPLES OF DOMESTIC SCIENCE, BEING A GUIDE TO THE FORMATION AND MAINTAINANCE OF ECONOMICAL, HEALTHFUL, BEAUTIFUL, AND CHRISTIAN HOMES. New York: Ford; Boston: H.A. Brown; Philadelphia: Charles S. Greene; Chicago: J.A. Stoddard; San Francisco: Francis Dewing, 1869. xii, 500 p. Illus., glossary. Reprint. American Education: People, Ideas and Institutions series, series 2. New York: Arno Press, 1972.

Moral and practical guidance for woman's "supreme duty." Most popular revision of A TREATISE ON DOMESTIC ECONOMY, FOR THE USE OF YOUNG LADIES AT HOME AND AT SCHOOL, published originally in 1841. Reprinted by Source Book Press, 1970.

636 Child, Lydia Maria. THE AMERICAN FRUGAL HOUSEWIFE, DEDICATED TO THOSE WHO ARE NOT ASHAMED OF ECONOMY. 12th ed. Boston: American Stationers', 1836. 141 p. Reprint. New York: Harper & Row, 1972.

Best seller of mid-nineteenth century.

637 Earle, Alice M. HOME LIFE IN COLONIAL DAYS. New York: Macmillan, 1899. Reprint. Stockbridge, Mass.: Berkshire Traveller Press, 1974. xvi, 470 p.

Detailed though undocumented account.

638 Gilman, Charlotte Perkins. THE HOME, ITS WORK AND INFLUENCE. New York: McClure, Phillips, 1903. xi, 347 p. Reprint. New York: Source Book Press, 1970..

Home has lagged behind other social institutions. Women should go to work and children to child care centers.

639 Hechtlinger, Adelaide. THE SEASONAL HEARTH: THE WOMAN AT HOME IN EARLY AMERICA. Woodstock, N.Y.: Overbook, 1977. 255 p. Illus.

Detailed view of women's work, with economic implications, includes material on recipes, preserving, gardening, laundering, doctoring, and much else.

640 Hooks, Janet M. "The Contribution of Household Production to the National Income." Ph.D. thesis, University of Illinois, 1960. Available from University Microfilms, Ann Arbor, Mich.

641 LIBERATING THE HOME. Women in America: From Colonial Times to the 20th Century series. New York: Arno Press, 1974.

Includes two nineteenth-century publications: WOMAN AND HER NEEDS by Elizabeth Oakes Smith (New York: Fowler & Wells, 1851. 120 p.); and A DOMESTIC PROBLEM: WORK AND CULTURE IN THE HOUSEHOLD by Abby M. Diaz (Boston: J.R. Osgood, 1875. 120 p.) Both discuss the intellectual poverty of housework and the need to surmount it.

642 Lopata, Helena Z. OCCUPATION: HOUSEWIFE. New York: Oxford University Press, 1971. xvi, 387 p.

Upper-middle-class women. Based on indepth interviews.

643 Myerson, Abraham. THE NERVOUS HOUSEWIFE. Boston: Little, Brown and Co., 1927. 273 p. Reprint. American Women: Images and Realities series. New York: Arno Press, 1972.

Early psychiatric approach to housework foresees later change in women's role.

644 Oakley, Ann. THE SOCIOLOGY OF HOUSEWORK. New York: Pantheon Books, 1974. x, 242 p. Tables.

Probes attitudes and working conditions of the housewife.

645 Parloa, Maria. HOME ECONOMICS: A GUIDE TO HOUSEHOLD MANAGEMENT INCLUDING THE PROPER TREATMENT OF MATERIALS ENTERING INTO THE CONSTRUCTION AND THE FURNISHING OF THE HOUSE. New York: Century, 1898. xii, 378 p. Illus.

Woman's duties in the nineteenth century, from care of gas and oil lamps to the straightening of whalebone.

646 Randolph, Mrs. Mary. THE VIRGINIA HOUSE-WIFE; OR, METHODICAL COOK. Baltimore: John Maskitt, 1836. 180 p.

Usable today. Cookbooks of the nineteenth century and earlier are available in libraries and may include material on the running of the household.

647 Stowe, Harriet Beecher. HOUSEHOLD PAPERS AND STORIES. In THE WRITINGS OF HARRIET BEECHER STOWE, vol. 8. Riverside edition. Boston: Houghton Mifflin Co., 1896. ix, 493 p. Illus.

Literary woman's solution to problems of household management.

648 Warrior, Betsy, and Leghorn, Lisa. HOUSEWORKER'S HANDBOOK. 3d exp. ed. Cambridge, Mass.: Women's Center, 1975. 109 p. Illus. Pamph.

Includes material on social and economic aspects of housework as well as listing of inventions by women.

649 Widmer, Kingsley. "Reflections of a Male Housewife: On Being a Feminist Fellow-Traveller." VILLAGE VOICE, 10 June 1971, p. 8.

Available from KNOW.

See also 450.

c. MARRIAGE

i. Sources

650 U.S. Bureau of the Census. MARRIAGE AND DIVORCE 1867-1906. SPECIAL REPORTS. 2 vols. Washington, D.C.: Government Printing Office, 1909.

Volume 1 is a statistical summary of marriage and divorce laws of each state, U.S. territory, and selected foreign countries. Volume 2 contains tables of divorce according to specific cause and libellant of each state and territory by year and periods of years.

See also 664.

ii. Bibliographies

651 Aldous, Joan, and Hill, Reuben. INTERNATIONAL BIBLIOGRAPHY OF RESEARCH IN MARRIAGE AND THE FAMILY, 1900-1964. Vol. 1. Minneapolis: University of Minnesota Press, 1967. 508 p.

Includes listing of periodicals. Volume 2, covering the years 1965-72, was issued in 1974. Volume 3, entitled INVENTORY OF MARRIAGE AND FAMILY LITERATURE, covering the years 1973-74, was issued in 1975, and since 1975, has been issued annually.

See also 3.

iii. References

652 Barron, Milton L., ed. THE BLENDING AMERICAN: PATTERNS OF INTERMARRIAGE. Chicago: Quadrangle Books, 1972. xiv, 357 p. Biblio.

Anthologizes articles on current problems, research, and consequences, as well as religious implications of intermarriage.

653 Bernard, Jessie S. THE FUTURE OF MARRIAGE. New York: World Publishing Co., 1972. xvi, 367 p. Tables, biblio. Paper.

Asserts that the institution of marriage will persist though forms will become flexible.

654 _____. REMARRIAGE: A STUDY OF MARRIAGE. New York: Dryden, 1956. xii, 372 p. Tables.

Interviews and statistical evidence focus on characteristics and problems of older divorced and widowed population.

655 Breedlove, William, and Breedlove, Jerrye. SWAP CLUBS: A STUDY IN CONTEMPORARY SEXUAL MORES. Los Angeles: Sherbourne Press, 1964. 256 p.

656 Carlier, Auguste. MARRIAGE IN UNITED STATES. Translated by B. Joy Jeffries. Boston: de Vries, Ibarra; New York: Leypold & Holt, 1867. xv, 179 p.

Nineteenth-century French writer compares American with English and French marriages. Remarks on divorce, celibacy, marriage in various religious sects and among women doctors.

657 Chapman, Jane R., and Gates, Margaret, eds. WOMEN INTO WIVES: THE LEGAL AND ECONOMIC IMPACT OF MARRIAGE. Sage Yearbooks in Women's Policy Studies, vol. 2. Beverly Hills, Calif.: Sage Publications, 1977. Biblios. Paper.

Analyzes the relationships between marriage and the economic dependency of women, and explores means and implication of social changes relating to them.

658 Chotiner, Renée D. MARRIAGE AND THE SUPREME COURT. The Law and Women Series, no. 2 (Law-2). Washington, D.C.: Today Publications & News Service, 1974. 41 p. Pamph.

Analyzes the influence of court decisions on sex stereotyping and discrimination, on the right of woman to control her own body, and on employment and property rights after marriage. Available from Today Publications & News Service, which cosponsored the series with Human Rights for Women.

659 Constantine, Larry L., and Constantine, Joan M. GROUP MARRIAGE: A STUDY OF CONTEMPORARY MULTILATERAL MARRIAGE. New York: Macmillan Co., 1973. xii, 299 p. Biblio. Paper.

Looks at monogamy as an American myth. Appendix includes statistics on family size, economic structure, and attitudes toward religion.

660 DeLora, Jack R., and DeLora, Joann S., eds. INTIMATE LIFE STYLES: MARRIAGE AND ITS ALTERNATIVES. 2d ed. Pacific Palisades, Calif.: Goodyear Publishing Co., 1975. xv, 421 p. Biblio. Paper.

Discusses dating and mate selection; sex as a social, personal, and interpersonal concern; the contemporary family, and current alternatives.

661 Duvall, Evelyn. IN-LAWS PRO AND CON: AN ORIGINAL STUDY OF INTERPERSONAL RELATIONS. New York: Association Press, 1954. 400 p. Charts, biblio.

662 Erickson, Nancy. A WOMAN'S GUIDE TO MARRIAGE AND DIVORCE IN NEW YORK. New York: Woman's Law Center, 1974. 42 p. Biblio. Pamph.

Answers questions most often asked in crises on procedures, terms of alimony, child care, property rights, name change, and so on. Available from the center.

663 Figes, Eva. PATRIARCHAL ATTITUDES. Women in Revolt: A Series on the Emancipation of Women. New York: Stein & Day, 1970. 191 p. Biblio. Paper.

Discusses attitudes that prevent society from viewing marriage as anachronistic institution.

664 Fleming, Jennifer B., and Washburne, Carolyn K. FOR BETTER, FOR WORSE: A FEMINIST HANDBOOK ON MARRIAGE AND OTHER OPTIONS. New York: Charles Scribner's Sons, 1977. ix, 406 p. Biblio., illus. Offset, paper.

Discusses personal, legal, financial, and maternal aspects of marriage, as well as lesbianism and bisexuality as alternatives to marriage. Resources listing. Appendix on common-law marriage.

665 Gove, Walter R. "Sex Roles, Marital Status and Suicide." JOURNAL OF HEALTH AND SOCIAL BEHAVIOR 13 (June 1972): 204-13. Tables, biblio.

Gives suicide statistics which support the view that marriage is more advantageous for men than for women, and widowhood and divorce for women than for men.

666 Herman, Sondra R. "Loving Courtship or the Marriage Market? The Ideal and the Critics 1871-1911." AMERICAN QUARTERLY 25 (May 1973): 235-54.

Examines attitudes toward marriage from Puritan times to the liberal thinkers Charlotte Gilman Perkins, Lester Ward, Theodore Dreiser, and others.

667 Hirsch, Arthur H. SEXUAL MISBEHAVIOR OF THE UPPER CULTURED: A MID-CENTURY STUDY OF THE BEHAVIOR TRENDS OUTSIDE MARRIAGE IN THE UNITED STATES SINCE 1930. (LIMITED TO WHITE PERSONS). Human Relations Research Publications in Human Behavior Trends, vol. 1. New York: Vantage Press, 1955. 512 p.

Based on cooperation of forty-thousand subjects. Note particularly chapter 8, "The Woman as Aggressor."

668 Howard, George E. A HISTORY OF MATRIMONIAL INSTITUTIONS CHIEFLY IN ENGLAND AND THE UNITED STATES. 3 vols. Chicago: University of Chicago Press; London: T. Fisher Unwin, 1904. Reprint. Atlantic Highlands, N.J.: Humanities Press, 1964. Biblio.

Volume 2, part 3, deals with marriage in the United States from colonial times by region. Volume 3, part 1 (continued), deals with divorce and problems of marriage and family.

669 Hunt, Morton M. THE AFFAIR: A PORTRAIT OF EXTRAMARITAL LOVE IN CONTEMPORARY AMERICA. New York: World Publishing Co., 1969. xvi, 317 p. Biblio. Paper.

Based on interviews, diaries, and questionnaires.

670 Komarovsky, Mirra. BLUE-COLLAR MARRIAGE. New York: Random House, 1964. xv, 395 p. Tables, biblio. Paper.

Intensive study of fifty-eight blue-collar families.

671 Muncy, Raymond L. SEX AND MARRIAGE IN UTOPIAN COMMUNITIES. Bloomington: Indiana University Press, 1973. 275 p. Paper.

Unique forms and practices. Note especially "Women's Rights in Utopian Communities."

672 Oberholzer, Emil J. DELINQUENT SAINTS: DISCIPLINARY ACTION IN THE EARLY CONGREGATIONAL CHURCHES OF MASSACHUSETTS. Columbia Studies in History, Economics, and Public Law, no. 590. New York: Columbia University, 1956. x, 379 p. Tables, biblio. Reprint. New York: AMS Press, 1968.

See especially chapter 6, "Domestic and Marital Relations," and chapter 7, "Extramarital Relations."

673 Oneida Community. BIBLE COMMUNISM: A COMPILATION FROM THE ANNUAL REPORTS AND OTHER PUBLICATIONS OF THE ONEIDA ASSOCIATION AND BRANCHES; PRESENTING, IN CONNECTION WITH THEIR HISTORY, A SUMMARY VIEW OF THEIR RELIGIOUS AND SOCIAL THEORIES. Brooklyn: Office of the Circular, 1853. Reprint. American Utopian Adventure Series. Philadelphia: Porcupine, 1972.

Detailed documentation of biblical applications of relations between men and women as viewed by members of the community.

674 Robertson, Constance. ONEIDA COMMUNITY: AN AUTOBIOGRAPHY, 1851-1876. Syracuse, N.Y.: Syracuse University Press, 1970. xvi, 364 p. Illus., biblio.

Studies group marriage in a utopian community as well as management of quantity and quality of offspring through a unique system of birth control.

675 Scanzoni, John H. "Husband-Wife Relationships." In his THE BLACK FAMILY IN MODERN SOCIETY: PATTERNS OF STABILITY AND SECURITY, chap. 6. Chicago: University of Chicago Press, 1977.

Variations in black-white conjugal patterns come about from discrimination rather than from bio-racial differences.

676 _____. SEXUAL BARGAINING: POWER POLITICS IN THE AMERICAN MARRIAGE. Englewood Cliffs, N.J.: Prentice-Hall, 1972. ix, 180 p. Biblio. Paper.

Conflict intrinsic to marriage has positive as well as negative results.

677 Seidenberg, Robert. MARRIAGE IN LIFE AND LITERATURE. New York: Philosophical Library, 1970. ix, 340 p. Paper ed. published as MARRIAGE BETWEEN EQUALS: STUDIES FROM LIFE AND LITERATURE. Garden City, N.Y.: Doubleday & Co., Anchor Press, 1973.

Covers positive and negative effects of marriage, supported by reference to works of literature.

678 Sickels, Robert J. RACE, MARRIAGE, AND THE LAW. Albuquerque: University of New Mexico Press, 1972. viii, 167 p. Biblio.

Gives the history of the legal status of interracial marriage in America.

679 Stuart, Irving R., and Abt, Lawrence E. INTERRACIAL MARRIAGE: EXPECTATIONS AND REALITIES. New York: Grossman Publishers, 1973. xiv, 355 p.

Section 1 deals with emotional, social, and economic aspects; section 2, with Indian and Hawaiian intermarriage.

680 "To Love, Honor, and . . . Share: A Marriage Contract for the Seventies." MS 1 (June 1973): 62-64, 102-3.

Gives the text of an egalitarian marriage contract.

681 Weeks, John R. TEENAGE MARRIAGES: A DEMOGRAPHIC ANALYSIS. Westport, Conn.: Greenwood Press, 1976. xxi, 171 p. Illus.

Prepared under auspices of International Population and Urban Research, University of California at Berkeley.

See also 594, 601, 732.

d. WOMEN AS WIVES

682 Alcott, William A. THE YOUNG WIFE; OR, DUTIES OF WOMAN IN THE MARRIAGE RELATION. Boston: G.W. Light, 1837. 376 p. Reprint. Family in America series. New York: Arno Press, 1972.

"The first duty being submission. . . ."

683 Gelles, Richard J. THE VIOLENT HOME: A STUDY OF PHYSICAL AGGRESSION BETWEEN HUSBANDS AND WIVES. Sage Library of Special Research, vol. 13. Beverly Hills, Calif.: Sage Publications, 1972. 219 p. Tables, figs. Paper.

Semantic differences in defining violence may shape women's reaction to it. Uses a sociological rather than pathological approach.

684 Morris, Pauline. PRISONERS AND THEIR FAMILIES. A RESEARCH PROJECT UNDER THE AUSPICES OF POLITICAL AND ECONOMIC PLANNING. New York: Hartt, 1965. 327 p. Tables.

See especially chapter 4, "The Wives"; chapter 5, "The Wives Separated before Imprisonment"; and chapter 6, "Discrepancies between Husbands and Wives."

685 Rainwater, Lee, et al. WORKING MAN'S WIFE: HER PERSONALITY, WORLD, AND LIFE STYLE. New York: Oceana Publications, 1959. xiv, 238 p. Biblio.

Studies in detail the psychological world of the blue-collar wife.

686 Schwartz, Gwen G., and Wyden, Barbara. THE JEWISH WIFE. New York: Peter H. Wyden, Publisher, 1969. vi, 308 p.

Counters stereotypical image with information gathered from interviews.

687 Seidenberg, Robert. CORPORATE WIVES--CORPORATE CASUALTIES? New York: AMACOM, 1973. ix, 177 p. Biblio. Paper.

Mistreatment of corporate wives.

e. WOMEN AS MOTHERS

i. General

688 Bernard, Jessie S. THE FUTURE OF MOTHERHOOD. New York: Dial Press, 1974. xiii, 426 p.

Salvages the role from the destructive institutions of the past.

689 Child, Lydia Maria. THE MOTHER'S BOOK. 2d ed. Boston: Carter & Hendee, 1831. x, 169 p.

Instructs mothers on care and feeding of infants, on cultivation of their "bodily senses," and on their attitudes toward supernatural appearances. Includes reading lists for children and other aids for child care.

690 Gibson, Gay G., with Risher, Mary Jo. BY HER OWN ADMISSION: A LESBIAN MOTHER'S FIGHT TO KEEP HER SON. Garden City, N.Y.: Doubleday & Co., 1977. ix, 276 p.

691 Hagood, Margaret J. MOTHERS OF THE SOUTH: PORTRAITURE OF THE WHITE TENANT FARM WOMAN. Chapel Hill, N.C.: University of North Carolina Press, 1939. 252 p. Reprint. Westport, Conn.: Greenwood Press, 1969; Family in America series. New York: Arno Press, 1972.

Farm mothers of southern Piedmont seem to nullify negative effects of their culture on their children.

692 Hammer, Signe. DAUGHTERS AND MOTHERS: MOTHERS AND DAUGHTERS. New York: Quadrangle, 1975. 196 p.

Revealing interviews on relationships between women.

693 Hope, Karol, and Young, Nancy, ed. MOMMA: THE SOURCEBOOK FOR SINGLE MOTHERS. New York: New American Library, 1976. xi, 388 p. Paper.

Expands on earlier published MOMMA project to include more interviews and personal experiences. Appends history of MOMMA, an organization for single mothers.

694 Kammerer, Percy G. THE UNMARRIED MOTHER: A STUDY OF FIVE HUNDRED CASES. Boston: Little, Brown and Co., 1918. xv, 342 p. Biblio., tables. Reprint. Patterson Reprint Series in Criminology, Law Enforcement, and Social Problems, no. 58. Montclair, N.J.: Patterson Smith, 1969.

695 Klein, Carole. THE SINGLE-PARENT EXPERIENCE. New York: Walker & Co., 1973. 241 p. Paper.

Details problems facing single-by-choice (mostly women) parents. Appendix lists helpful state resources on adoption, pregnancy, and related counseling.

696 Klerman, Lorraine V.M., and Jekel, James F. SCHOOL-AGE MOTHERS: PROBLEMS, PROGRAMS, AND POLICY. Hamden, Conn.:

Shoe String Press, 1973. xiv, 152 p. Tables. Paper.

Includes material on maternal health services, dropouts, and poverty.

697 Kriesburg, Louis. MOTHERS IN POVERTY: A STUDY OF FATHERLESS FAMILIES. Chicago: Aldine Publishing Co., 1970. x, 356 p. Tables.

Discusses factors that maintain conditions of poverty and cause its generational transmission.

698 Peck, Ellen, and Senderowitz, Judith. PRONATALISM: THE MYTH OF MOM & APPLE PIE. New York: Thomas Y. Crowell Co., 1974. xii, 333 p. Biblio. Paper.

Anthology challenges pronatalist myths and biases of both society and the women's movement.

699 Rains, Prudence M. BECOMING AN UNWED MOTHER: A SOCIOLOGICAL ACCOUNT. Observations Series. Chicago: Aldine Publishing Co., 1971. vii, 207 p. Biblio.

Focus on consequence rather than cause.

700 Rice, Susan T. MOTHER'S DAY: ITS HISTORY, ORIGIN, CELEBRATION, SPIRIT, AND SIGNIFICANCE AS RELATED TO PROSE AND VERSE. Our American Holidays Series. New York: Moffat, Yard, 1915. 363 p.

701 Rich, Adrienne. OF WOMAN BORN: MOTHERHOOD AS EXPERIENCE AND INSTITUTION. New York: W.W. Norton & Co., 1976. 318 p.

In-depth exploration of motherhood as "potential relationship" and "institution." By American poet-feminist.

702 Sigourney, Lydia H. LETTERS TO MOTHERS. Hartford, Conn.: Hudson & Skinner, 1838. vii, 240 p.

Motherhood as "be all and end all."

703 Strecker, Edward A. THEIR MOTHERS' SONS: THE PSYCHIATRIST EXAMINES AN AMERICAN PROBLEM. Philadelphia: J.B. Lippincott Co., 1946. 237 p.

Rejections of draftees caused by momism, which can be eliminated by more realistic attitudes toward motherhood.

704 Weiss, Nancy P. "Mother: The Invention of Necessity: Dr. Benjamin

Spock's BABY AND CHILD CARE." AMERICAN QUARTERLY 29 (Winter 1977): 519-46.

How Spock's best seller influenced the lives of women.

705 Wilson, Otto. FIFTY YEARS' WORK WITH GIRLS: 1883-1933. THE STORY OF THE FLORENCE CRITTENDEN HOMES. Alexandria, Va.: National Florence Crittenden Mission, 1933. 513 p.

Homes for unwed mothers.

706 Wylie, Philip. "Common Women." In his GENERATION OF VIPERS, chap. 9. New York: Farrar & Rinehart, 1942. xxiii, 318 p.

Momism with a vengeance.

See also 11, 16, 543, 629, 1546.

ii. Working Mothers

(a). SOURCES, BIBLIOGRAPHIES

707 Business and Professional Women's Foundation. WORKING MOTHERS: A SELECTED ANNOTATED BIBLIOGRAPHY. Compiled by Jeanne Spiegel. Washington, D.C.: 1968. 24 p. Pamph.

Includes audiovisual sources. Available from the foundation.

See also Women's Bureau, page 14 above.

(b). REFERENCES

708 Anthony, Katherine. MOTHERS WHO MUST EARN. Russell Sage Foundation, West Side Studies, vol. 2, part 2. New York: Survey Associates, 1914. vii, 222 p. Tables, illus.

Early study of 370 West Side New York mothers covers wages, hours, regularity of work, and effect on health and family life.

709 Callahan, Sidney C., ed. THE WORKING MOTHER. New York: Macmillan Co., 1971. 264 p. Biblio.

Assembles fifteen articles on self-realization in the working mother.

710 Curley, Jayme, et al. THE BALANCING ACT: A CAREER AND A BABY. Chicago: Chicago Review, Swallow Press, 1976. 217 p.

Five young women discuss their lives.

711 Etaugh, C.E. "Effects of Maternal Employment on Children: A Review of Recent Research." MERRILL-PALMER QUARTERLY 20 (April 1974): 20-93.

712 Hoffman, Lois W., et al. WORKING MOTHERS: AN EVALUATION REVIEW OF THE CONSEQUENCES FOR WIFE, HUSBAND AND CHILD. The Jossey-Bass Behavioral Science Series. San Francisco: Jossey-Bass, 1974. xiv, 272 p. Tables, biblio.

Research findings on psychological factors, commitment to work, child care arrangements, effects on child and family, and familial relationships.

See also Women's Bureau, page 14.

iii. Child Care

(a). RESOURCES, SOURCES, BIBLIOGRAPHIES

Information on child care is available from the Women's Bureau, the Child Welfare League of America, and the Office of Child Development, Department of Health, Education and Welfare. For a listing of sources and organizations see 417. Women's organizations interested especially in child care are the Women's Action Alliance and the National Organization for Women Task Force on Child Care. KNOW issues a useful bibliography on child care.

713 Day Care and Child Development Council of America. RESOURCES FOR CHILD CARE: A CATALOG OF PUBLICATIONS. Washington, D.C.: 1973. Unpaged.

Has listings of organizations, services, and audiovisual aids. Material on minorities, relation of day care and social policy, systems of day care, and more. Available from the council.

714 Howard, Norma K., comp. DAY CARE: AN ANNOTATED BIBLIOGRAPHY. Urbana, Ill.: ERIC Clearinghouse on Early Childhood Education, 1971. 19 p.

Lists reports, papers, and articles of practical use in establishing day care centers.

715 Wells, Albert, comp. AN ANNOTATED BIBLIOGRAPHY. VOLUME I. FINAL REPORT: PART X. Minneapolis: Institute for Interdisciplinary Studies, 1971. 367 p.

Includes congressional acts and hearings examined by Day Care Policy Studies Group. Updates 1970, 1971 bibliographies.

(b). REFERENCES

716 Bernard, Jacqueline. THE CHILDREN YOU GAVE US: A HISTORY OF 150 YEARS OF SERVICES TO CHILDREN. New York: Jewish Child Care Association of New York, 1973. viii, 186 p. Illus., biblio.

History of major child welfare agency.

717 Breitbart, Vicki, ed. THE DAY CARE BOOK: THE WHY, WHAT, AND HOW OF COMMUNITY DAY CARE. New York: Alfred A. Knopf, 1974. ix, 209 p. Illus., biblio.

Overview. Resource section lists equipment and financial needs in detail and includes listing of books, periodicals, films, and other sources.

718 Evans, E. Belle. DAY CARE FOR INFANTS: THE CASE FOR INFANT DAY CARE AND A PRACTICAL GUIDE. Boston: Beacon Press, 1972. xii, 216 p. Illus., biblio.

719 Howes, Ethel P., and Beach, Dorothea. "The Co-operative Nursery School: What it Can Do For Parents." Institute for the Co-ordination of Women's Interest, publication no. 3. Northampton, Mass.: Smith College, 1928. 74 p.

Early child care arrangements for women interested in continuing intellectual and professional projects.

720 Levine, James A. WHO WILL RAISE THE CHILDREN? NEW OPTIONS FOR FATHERS AND MOTHERS. Philadelphia: J.B. Lippincott Co., 1976. 192 p.

Role reversal in caring for children.

721 Roby, Pamela, ed. CHILD CARE--WHO CARES? FOREIGN AND DOMESTIC INFANT AND EARLY CHILDHOOD DEVELOPMENT POLICIES. New York: Basic Books, 1973. xxii, 456 p. Biblio.

Anthology.

722 Ruderman, Florence A. CHILD CARE AND WORKING MOTHERS: A STUDY OF ARRANGEMENTS MADE FOR THE DAYTIME CARE OF CHILDREN. New York: Child Welfare League of America, 1968. xv, 387 p. Tables.

Investigative study that led to improved day care services.

723 Steinfels, Margaret O'Brien. WHO'S MINDING THE CHILDREN? THE HISTORY AND POLITICS OF CHILD CARE IN AMERICA. New

York: Simon & Schuster, 1974. 281 p. Biblio.

724 U.S. Children's Bureau. CHILD CARE ARRANGEMENTS OF WORKING MOTHERS IN THE UNITED STATES. Prepared by Seth Low, and Pearl G. Spindler. Washington, D.C.: Government Printing Office, 1968. 123 p. Paper.

Available from the superintendent of documents.

725 U.S. Congress. Senate. COMPREHENSIVE CHILD DEVELOPMENT ACT OF 1971. JOINT HEARINGS BEFORE THE SUBCOMMITTEE ON EMPLOYMENT, MANPOWER, AND POVERTY AND THE SUBCOMMITTEE ON CHILDREN AND YOUTH OF THE COMMITTEE ON LABOR AND PUBLIC WELFARE. 92d Cong. 1st sess. Washington, D.C.: Government Printing Office, 1971. 930 p. Tables.

Federal child care bills with testimony and statements by individuals and organizations.

726 U.S. Women's Bureau. DAYCARE CENTERS: INDUSTRY'S INVOLVEMENT. Bulletin no. 296. Washington, D.C.: Government Printing Office, 1971. v, 33 p. Chart.

Programs, costs, tax allowances, exemptions, and history of centers sponsored since World War II.

3. Divorce

a. RESOURCES, BIBLIOGRAPHIES

Packets containing information on divorce are available from Women's Equity Action League and the National Organization for Women Task Force on Divorce.

The Family Service Association of America distributes a bibliography on divorce and remarriage.

727 Israel, Stanley, comp. BIBLIOGRAPHY ON DIVORCE. New York: Bloch Publishing Co., 1974. xiv, 300 p.

Annotates and gives chapter heads for each book listed. Unannotated listing of books published prior to those annotated, as well as relevant worldwide publications.

728 McKenny, Mary. DIVORCE: A SELECTED ANNOTATED BIBLIOGRAPHY. Metuchen, N.J.: Scarecrow Press, 1975. 163 p.

Significant materials in English. Appendix includes resources and divorce laws state by state.

See also 740.

b. REFERENCES

729 Barnett, James H. DIVORCE AND THE AMERICAN DIVORCE NOVEL, 1858-1937: A STUDY IN LITERARY REFLECTIONS ON SOCIAL INFLUENCES. New York: Russell & Russell, 1939. 168 p. Biblio.

730 Blake, Nelson M. THE ROAD TO RENO: A HISTORY OF DIVORCE IN THE UNITED STATES. New York: Macmillan Co., 1962. vii, 259 p.

First overview since Howard's in 1904 (see 668). Emphasis on changing climate of opinion.

731 Bohannon, Paul, ed. DIVORCE AND AFTER. Garden City, N.Y.: Doubleday & Co., 1970. vi, 301 p. Figs., biblio. Paper.

Changing attitudes toward marriage, divorce, sexuality, and divorce reform. Cross-cultural.

732 Carter, Hugh, and Glick, Paul C. MARRIAGE AND DIVORCE: A SOCIAL AND ECONOMIC STUDY. Vital Health Statistics Monograph. Cambridge, Mass.: Harvard University Press, 1970. xxix, 451 p. Illus.

Trends and variations revealed by government statistics form basis of demographic study.

733 Eisler, Riane T. DISSOLUTION: NO-FAULT DIVORCE, MARRIAGE, AND THE FUTURE OF WOMEN. New York: McGraw-Hill Book Co., 1977. xiv, 279 p. Paper.

Sections on child custody, social and legal aspects of divorce, and alternatives. Includes divorce checklist and sample marriage contract.

734 Hunt, Morton M. THE WORLD OF THE FORMERLY MARRIED. New York: Macmillan Co., 1966. xiii, 326 p.

Based on interviews, questionnaires.

735 Koster, Donald N. THE THEME OF DIVORCE IN AMERICAN DRAMA, 1871-1939. Philadelphia: 1942. x, 117 p. Biblio. Paper.

Includes a survey of laws and public attitudes toward divorce. Lists plays.

736 Martin, John R. DIVORCE AND REMARRIAGE: A PERSPECTIVE FOR

COUNSELING. Scottsdale, Pa.: Herald Press, 1974. 136 p. Biblio.

737 O'Neill, William L. DIVORCE IN THE PROGRESSIVE ERA. New York: Yale University Press, 1967. Reprint. New York: Franklin Watts, 1973. xii, 295 p. Biblio. Paper.

Divorce in the ideological context of the period and its relation to family change.

738 Sherwin, Robert V. COMPATIBLE DIVORCE. New York: Crown Publishers, 1969. xi, 308 p. Paper.

Divorce with minimal psychic and legal abrasion.

739 Wheeler, Michael. NO-FAULT DIVORCE. Boston: Beacon Press, 1974. 194 p. Biblio.

Divorce reform and how it works.

740 Women in Transition. WOMEN'S SURVIVAL: A FEMINIST HANDBOOK ON SEPARATION AND DIVORCE. Rev. and enl. ed. New York: Charles Scribner's Sons, 538 p. Illus., biblio. Paper.

Resource book dealing with legal, financial, emotional, consumer, housing, and other problems. Appendix lists centers, clinics, rape crises groups, and so on.

See also 662.

4. Women Alone, Widowhood

741 Adams, Margaret. SINGLE BLESSEDNESS: OBSERVATIONS ON THE SINGLE STATUS IN A MARRIED SOCIETY. New York: Basic Books, 1976. viii, 264 p.

Attacks myths surrounding single people.

742 Beck, Frances. DIARY OF A WIDOW. Boston: Beacon Press, 1965. 142 p.

743 Bequaert, Lucia H. SINGLE WOMEN: ALONE AND TOGETHER. Boston: Beacon Press, 1976. xvi, 256 p. Biblio.

Reports on interviews with twenty-seven women who come from various economic and social groups and who head households. Lists resources and useful addresses.

744 Caine, Lynn. WIDOW: THE PERSONAL CRISIS OF A WIDOW IN

AMERICA. New York: William Morrow & Co., 1974. 222 p.

745 Keyssar, Alexander. "Widowhood in Eighteenth-Century Massachusetts: A Problem in the History of the Family." PERSPECTIVES IN AMERICAN HISTORY 8 (1974): 80-119. Tables.

746 La Barre, Harriet. A LIFE OF YOUR OWN: A WOMAN'S GUIDE TO LIVING ALONE. New York: David McKay Co., 1972. xi, 209 p.

747 Lopata, Helena Z. WIDOWHOOD IN AN AMERICAN CITY. Cambridge, Mass.: Schenckman Publishing Co., 1973. xii, 369 p. Tables, biblio. Paper.

Focuses on social and personal factors in lives of widows over fifty living in Chicago. Available from General Learning Press, 250 James Street, Morristown, New Jersey.

748 O'Brien, Patricia. THE WOMAN ALONE. New York: Quadrangle, 1973. xii, 285 p. Biblio.

Epilogue reports on interviews with eight women.

749 Paine, Harriet E. [Eliza Chester]. THE UNMARRIED WOMAN. Portia Series. New York: Dodd, Mead & Co., 1892. 253 p.

American woman alone has problems peculiar to her status.

750 Silverman, Phyllis R., et al. HELPING EACH OTHER IN WIDOWHOOD. New York: Health Sciences Publishing Corp., 1974. xviii, 212 p. Biblio.

Report of proceedings at Laboratory of Community Psychiatry, Harvard Medical School.

751 SINGLE BLESSEDNESS; OR, SINGLE LADIES AND GENTLEMEN, AGAINST THE SLANDERS OF THE PULPIT, THE PRESS, AND THE LECTUREDOM. New York: C.S. Francis; Boston: Crosby, Nichols, 1852. xxiv, 297 p.

752 Strugnell, Cecile. ADJUSTMENT TO WIDOWHOOD AND SOME RELATED PROBLEMS: A SELECTED AND ANNOTATED BIBLIOGRAPHY. New York: Health Sciences Publishing Corp., 1974. 201 p. Biblio. Paper.

Discusses nature of bereavement, problems related to it, and helping relationships such as the Widow to Widow program begun at Harvard.

753 Taves, Isabella. WOMEN ALONE. New York: Funk & Wagnalls, 1968. 316 p.

Discusses personal relationships, pros and cons of single living, and role of women's liberation in changing attitudes toward single living.

5. Women in Middle and Old Age

a. RESOURCES, SOURCES, BIBLIOGRAPHIES

The Information Center on the Mature Woman serves as a clearinghouse for information on women over the age of forty. The center maintains a library of lay and professional books for use by researchers. It also issues bibliographies on health and appearance, marriage, sexuality, the women's movement, employment, education, retirement, and leisure.

The National Council on Aging issues a "Selected Bibliography," which contains information on some topics frequently neglected, and A GENERAL BIBLIOGRAPHY ON AGING; both are annotated. It also publishes a quarterly journal, CURRENT LITERATURE ON AGING, that lists books and articles. The council also issues films. Information on all of these publications is available from the council. PRIME TIME, a journal for older women, is published eleven times a year. The University of Florida Institute of Gerontology issues a series of monographs that touch on matters of interest to the aging population, both male and female. The National Organization for Women maintains a task force on older women.

Although much material has been written in the field of gerontology, many of the sources do not make a distinction between men and women. Thus, relatively few have been included here.

754 National Organization for Women. Task Force on Older Women. AGE IS BECOMING: AN ANNOTATED BIBLIOGRAPHY ON WOMEN AND AGING. Prepared by Interface Bibliographers. Oakland, Calif.: 1976. 35 p. Offset, stapled.

Selected items relating to status, role, finances, sexual and physical matters, and life-styles. Includes note on bibliographical method. Available from interface Bibliographies, 3018 Hillegass Avenue, Berkeley, California 94705.

755 SOURCEBOOK ON AGING. Chicago: Marquis Academic Media, Marquis Who's Who, 1977. 662 p. Tables, figs., charts, biblios.

Deals with aging in general; health; economic status;

housing; employment; education; transportation; leisure and retirement; special concerns, such as minorities, consumer product safety and credit; and the names and addresses of governmental and nongovernmental agencies and offices.

See also 743, 760, 761, 762.

b. REFERENCES

756 Harris, Janet. THE PRIME OF MS AMERICA: THE AMERICAN WOMAN AT 40. New York: G.P. Putnam's Sons, 1975. 250 p. Biblio.

Economic, social, and sexual aspects of middle-aged women.

757 Jacoby, Susan. "'What Do I Do for the Next 20 Years?': Feminism in the $12,000-a-Year Family." NEW YORK TIMES MAGAZINE, 17 June 1973, pp. 10-11, 39-43, 49.

Remarks by members of consciousness-raising group made up of Brooklyn blue-collar wives.

758 Jones, Rochelle. THE OTHER GENERATION: THE NEW POWER OF OLDER PEOPLE. Englewood Cliffs, N.J.: Prentice-Hall, 1977. xi, 264 p. Paper.

Impact of older women and men on American society.

759 Meltzer, Leslie M. "The Aging Female." Master's thesis, Adelphi University, 1974. viii, 151 p. Biblio.

Available from University Microfilms, Ann Arbor, Michigan.

760 Smith, Bert K. AGING IN AMERICA. Boston: Beacon Press, 1973. xii, 239 p. Paper.

General overview includes information on 1971 White House Conference on Aging. Lists resources and directory of state agencies on aging.

761 Tripp, Mary J. SENIOR CITIZENS: A GUIDE TO ENTITLED BENEFITS. San Carlos, Calif.: White Oak Publishing House, 1977. xiv, 181 p. Biblio. Offset, paper.

Sections on services, opportunities, social security, supplementary income, medicare, and information and referral services. Available from White Oak Publishing House, P.O. Box 566, San Carlos, California 94070.

762 Troll, Lillian, et al., eds. LOOKING AHEAD: A WOMAN'S GUIDE TO THE PROBLEMS AND JOYS OF GROWING OLDER. Englewood Cliffs, N.J.: Prentice-Hall, 1977. viii, 216 p. Paper.

Twenty-five articles include material on physical aging, adjustment to widowhood, new experiences, problems facing minority women, sources of assistance, and personal resources of older women.

763 U.S. Federal Council on the Aging. NATIONAL POLICY CONCERNS FOR OLDER WOMEN: COMMITMENT TO A BETTER LIFE. Washington, D.C.: 1975[?]. iv, 51 p. Illus.

Includes testimony and recommendations bearing on economic, social, health, and legal matters of concern that were presented in hearings held before the council, as well as on minority women, homemakers and widows.

6. Women in Poverty

a. SOURCES

The Welfare Reform Information Service Community, which serves as a clearinghouse on welfare reform and related matters, issues a newsletter, FOR OUR WELFARE, to its members.

Information is available also from the National Welfare Rights Organization, the Women's Bureau, and the Women's Equity Action League.

See also 777.

b. BIBLIOGRAPHIES

764 Glenn, Norval, et al., comps. SOCIAL STRATIFICATION: A RESEARCH BIBLIOGRAPHY. Berkeley, Calif.: Glendessary, 1970. xi, 466 p.

International in scope but emphasis is on the United States.

765 Spiker, Barry K., comp. COMPREHENSIVE BIBLIOGRAPHY ON POVERTY AND WELFARE IN THE UNITED STATES. Marquette: Northern Michigan University, Forensic Union, 1973. 209 p.

766 Tompkins, Dorothy C. POVERTY IN THE UNITED STATES DURING THE SIXTIES: A BIBLIOGRAPHY. Berkeley: University of California, Institute of Governmental Studies, 1970. ix, 542 p. Offset.

Partially annotated.

c. REFERENCES

767 Berman, Susan K. "Two American Welfare Mothers." MS. 1 (June 1973): 74-81.

Interviews.

768 Campbell, Helen S., et al. DARKNESS AND DAYLIGHT: OR LIGHTS AND SHADOWS OF NEW YORK LIFE. A WOMAN'S NARRATIVE OF MISSION AND RESCUE WORK IN TOUGH PLACES, WITH PERSONAL EXPERIENCE AMONG THE POOR IN REGIONS OF POVERTY AND VICE; AN ALL-NIGHT MISSIONARY'S EXPERIENCE IN GOSPEL WORK IN THE SLUMS; A JOURNALIST'S ACCOUNT OF LITTLE-KNOWN PHASES OF METROPOLITAN LIFE; AND A DETECTIVE'S EXPERIENCE AND OBSERVATIONS AMONG THE DANGEROUS AND CRIMINAL CLASSES, THE WHOLE PORTRAYING LIFE IN DARKEST NEW YORK BY DAY AND BY NIGHT. Hartford, Conn.: A.D. Worthington, 1899. xii, 740 p.

Subscription work claiming to portray women's lives in slums and jail and as shop girls.

769 _____. PRISONERS OF POVERTY: WOMEN WAGE EARNERS, THEIR TRADES AND THEIR LIVES. The Social History of Poverty, The Urban Experience Series. Boston: Roberts Brothers, 1887. Reprint. New York: AMS Press, 1972. v, 257 p.

Sketches of individual working women including domestics. Author considers improving their lot through general and industrial education, and introduction of socialistic principles of management.

770 Carey, Matthew. ESSAY ON THE PUBLIC CHARITIES IN PHILADELPHIA, INTENDED TO VINDICATE THE BENEVOLENT SOCIETIES OF THIS CITY FROM THE CHARGE OF ENCOURAGING ILLNESS, AND TO PLACE IN STRONG RELIEF BEFORE AN ENLIGHTENED PUBLIC, THE SUFFERINGS AND OPPRESSION UNDER WHICH THE GREATER PART OF THE FEMALES LABOUR, WHO DEPEND ON THEIR INDUSTRY FOR A SUPPORT FOR THEMSELVES AND THEIR CHILDREN. 4th ed. Philadelphia: J. Clarke, 1830. xiv, 24 p. Table. Pamph.

Preface recounts conditions of grinding poverty. Text surveys public charities reformation, relief of physical wants, and promotion of education.

771 Coles, Robert, and Coles, Jane H. WOMEN OF CRISIS. New York: Delacorte & Seymour, Lawrence, 1978. xii, 304 p. Biblio.

First-person accounts by five migrant workers.

772 Milwaukee County Welfare Rights Organization. WELFARE MOTHERS SPEAK OUT: WE AIN'T GONNA SHUFFLE ANYMORE. New York: W.W. Norton & Co., 1972. 190 p. Biblio., illus., tables.

Inside view of welfare experience. Appendixes contain statistics of activities of U.S. welfare assistance programs.

773 Piven, Francis F., and Cloward, Richard A. REGULATING THE POOR: THE FUNCTION OF PUBLIC WELFARE. New York: Pantheon Books, 1971. xvii, 389 p. Tables.

Background. Statistics.

774 Sheehan, Susan. A WELFARE MOTHER. Boston: Houghton Mifflin Co., 1975. xvi, 144 p. Paper.

Carmen Santana's story first appeared in a less detailed version in the NEW YORKER.

775 Smith, Mary R. ALMSHOUSE WOMEN: A STUDY OF TWO HUNDRED TWENTY-EIGHT WOMEN IN THE CITY AND COUNTRY ALMSHOUSE OF SAN FRANCISCO. Leland Stanford Junior University Publications: History and Economics 3. Stanford, Calif.: Stanford University, 1896. 44 p. Biblio., tables. Pamph.

Statistical study. Administrative inefficiency creates more dependents than "charitable workers" can provide for.

776 Stein, Bruno. ON RELIEF: THE ECONOMICS OF POVERTY AND PUBLIC WELFARE. New York: Basic Books, 1971. xii, 211 p.

History of poor laws, public support measures, implications for policy, and possible positive approaches.

777 U.S. Commission on Civil Rights. WOMEN AND POVERTY. Washington, D.C.: 1974. v, 81 p. Tables. Paper.

Includes demographic profiles and information on public assistance, the impact of federal assistance, child care legislation, and means maintenance. Statistics comprise appendix.

778 Wirt, Sykes. "Among the Poor Girls." PUTNAM'S MAGAZINE 1 (1868): 423-43. Reprinted in DEMOCRATIC VISTAS, 1860-1880, edited by Alan Trachtenburg, pp. 150-59. The American Culture Series, 4. New York: George Braziller, 1970.

Sympathetic close-up.

See also 691.

D. DEMOGRAPHY, BIRTH CONTROL, ABORTION

1. Demography

a. SOURCES, BIBLIOGRAPHY

The Katherine Dexter McCormick Library of Planned Parenthood-World Population issues a guide to sources in population and family planning, as well as a selected bibliography on population and family planning, fertility studies, abortion, sexuality, birth control, and marriage. Available from the organization.

b. REFERENCES

779 Bogue, Donald J. POPULATION OF THE UNITED STATES. Glencoe, Ill.: Free Press, 1959. vi, 873 p. Tables, figs.

Reports in population development in the United States. See especially chapter 8, "Sex Composition of the Population."

780 DeJong, Gordon F. APPALACHIAN FERTILITY DECLINE: A DEMOGRAPHIC AND SOCIOLOGICAL ANALYSIS. Lexington: University of Kentucky Press, 1968. xii, 138 p. Tables, figs. Paper.

Concludes that cultural factors and changes in them affect fertility rates.

781 Farley, Reynolds. GROWTH OF THE BLACK POPULATION: A STUDY OF DEMOGRAPHIC TRENDS. Markham Sociology Series. Chicago: Markham Publishing Co., 1970. v, 286 p. Tables, figs.

Discusses sociological, ecological, and health conditions affecting demographic patterns from colonial times to the present.

782 Freedman, Ronald, et al. FAMILY PLANNING, STERILITY AND POPULATION GROWTH. New York: McGraw-Hill Book Co., 1959. 515 p. Illus.

First study to relate fertility to demographic factors. Undertaken by Survey Research Center, University of Michigan and Scripps Foundation for Research in Population Problems. For a follow-up study, see 795.

783 Grabill, Wilson H., et al. THE FERTILITY OF AMERICAN WOMEN. Census Monograph Series. New York: John Wiley & Sons, 1958; London: Chapman & Hall, 1958. xvi, 448 p. Tables, figs.

Discusses fertility trends since colonial times. Includes

material on contraceptive practices and social and psychological factors that bear on fertility.

784 Greene, Evarts B., and Harrington, Virginia D. AMERICAN POPULATION BEFORE THE FEDERAL CENSUS OF 1790. New York: Columbia University, 1932. Reprint. Gloucester, Mass.: Peter Smith, 1966. xxii, 228 p. Biblio.

Assembles earlier census compilations and adds material from scattered sources. Provide estimates as well as official figures for both local and summary tallies.

785 Kiser, Clyde V., et al. TRENDS AND VARIATIONS IN FERTILITY IN THE UNITED STATES. American Public Health Association--Vital and Health Statistics Monograph. Cambridge, Mass.: Harvard University Press, 1968. xxvii, 338 p. Tables, figs., biblio.

Based on 1960 census. Pioneering study on medical and biological aspects of fertility, fecundity, and family planning. Also deals with fertility by ethnic grouping. Personal, marital, educational, occupation, and economic factors are related to fertility and illegitimacy.

786 Mazie, Sara M. POPULATION, DISTRIBUTION AND POLICY. In POPULATION GROWTH AND THE AMERICAN FUTURE RESEARCH REPORTS, vol. 5. Washington, D.C.: Government Printing Office, 1972. xvi, 719 p.

Covers population distribution trends, migration, social and economic aspects of urban size, and national and local growth and policy.

787 Parke, Robert, Jr., and Westoff, Charles F. ASPECTS OF POPULATION GROWTH AND THE AMERICAN FUTURE RESEARCH REPORTS, vol. 6. Washington, D.C.: Government Printing Office, 1972. xvii, 607 p.

Note chapter 7 by Frederick S. Jaffe, "Family Planning Services in the United States." In addition to detailed data on public and private avenues of service, material on government and broad social policies toward fertility control is included. Also, part 2 by Parke and Westoff, "Fertility Control," offers information on fertility research, teenage sexuality, and abortion. Available from the Superintendent of Documents.

788 Ryder, Norman B., and Westoff, Charles F. REPRODUCTION IN THE UNITED STATES 1965. Princeton, N.J.: Princeton University Press, 1971. 464 p.

Measures aspects of reproductive behavior. Part of National Fertility Study.

789 Silverman, Anna. THE CASE AGAINST HAVING CHILDREN. New York: David McKay Co., 1971. ix, 212 p.

Maintains that neither all women nor the world population need more children.

790 Thompson, Warren S., and Whelpton, Pascal K. POPULATION TRENDS IN THE UNITED STATES. Demographic Monographs, vol. 9. New York: Gordon & Breach, 1969. 415 p.

Provides the most complete picture of U.S. population between 1790 and 1930. Derived from President's Research Committee on Social Trends.

791 Tucker, George. PROGRESS OF THE UNITED STATES IN POPULATION & WEALTH IN FIFTY YEARS AS EXHIBITED BY THE DECENNIAL CENSUS FROM 1790 TO 1840 . . . WITH AN APPENDIX CONTAINING AN ABSTRACT OF THE CENSUS OF 1850. New York: Press of Hunt's Merchant's Magazine, 1843. xii, 211 p. Appendix, vii, 68 p. Reprint. Economics Classics Series. New York: Augustus M. Kelly, 1964.

Contains general statistics on women. Provides more specialized statistics on the decreasing birth rate in the nineteenth century, on the slave population, and the growing immigrant population.

792 Westoff, Charles F., and Parke, Robert, Jr., eds. DEMOGRAPHIC AND SOCIAL ASPECTS OF POPULATION GROWTH. Commission on Population Growth and the American Future Research Reports, vol. 1. Washington, D.C.: Government Printing Office, 1972. 674 p. Tables, figs., biblio.

Presents material on minority groups, teenage childbearing, illegitimacy, abortion, and sterility. See especially part 3, "Family and Women"; and part 4, "Unwanted Fertility."

793 Westoff, Charles F., and Potvin, Raymond H. COLLEGE WOMEN AND FERTILITY VALUES. Office of Population Research Series. Princeton, N.J.: Princeton University Press, 1967. xx, 237 p. Tables.

Discusses the influence of education on fertility.

794 Westoff, Leslie A., and Westoff, Charles F. FROM NOW TO ZERO: FERTILITY, CONTRACEPTION AND ABORTION IN AMERICA. Boston: Little, Brown and Co., 1971. 358 p.

Based on 1965 National Fertility Study.

795 Whelpton, Pascal K., et al. FERTILITY AND FAMILY PLANNING IN THE UNITED STATES. Fertility and Family Planning, no. 2. Princeton, N.J.: Princeton University Press, 1966. 443 p. Tables, figs., biblio.

Presents follow-up results on 782. First study to include material on blacks, Asiatics, and native Americans.

2. Birth Control, Family Planning

a. SOURCES

Many private organizations issue material on family planning and birth control. A few of these are Planned Parenthood-World Population, Zero Population Growth, National Organization for Non Parents, International Childbirth Association, Family Planning and Information Service, and Association of Voluntary Sterilization. A major government source is the U.S. Maternal and Child Health Service and the National Center for Family Planning Services of the Department of Health, Education and Welfare.

b. BIBLIOGRAPHIES

796 National Committee on Maternal Health. BIBLIOGRAPHY OF FERTILITY CONTROL, 1950-1965. Edited and compiled by Christopher Tietze. Publication no. 23. New York: 1965. iv, 198 p.

797 Planned Parenthood-World Population. CURRENT LITERATURE IN FAMILY PLANNING. New York: 1973-- . Monthly.

Available from the Katherine Dexter McCormick Library, 810 Seventh Avenue, New York, New York 10019.

798 U.S. Maternal and Child Health Service. SELECTED REFERENCES FOR SOCIAL WORKERS ON FAMILY PLANNING: AN ANNOTATED LIST. Compiled by Mary E. Watts. Rev. ed. Washington, D.C.: 1971. 38 p. Pamph.

Available from the Superintendent of Documents.

c. REFERENCES

799 Alcott, William A. THE PHYSIOLOGY OF MARRIAGE. Boston: Dinsmoor, 1866. vi, 259 p. Reprint. Medicine and Society in America series. New York: Arno Press, 1972.

Early discussion of contraception.

800 BIRTH CONTROL AND FAMILY PLANNING IN NINETEENTH-CENTURY AMERICA. Sex, Marriage and Society series. New York: Arno Press, 1974. Separately paged.

Four nineteenth-century publications are bound together in the following order: James Ashton. THE BOOK OF NATURE (New York: Brother Jonathan Office, 1865. iv, 64 p.); E.B. Foote. THE RADICAL REMEDY IN SOCIAL SCIENCE; OR, BORNING BETTER BABIES THROUGH REGULATING REPRODUCTION BY CONTROLLING CONTRACEPTION (New York: Murray Hill Publishing, 1886. 122 p. Biblio.); An American Physician. REPRODUCTIVE CONTROL, OR A GUIDE TO MATRIMONIAL HAPPINESS (Cincinnati, Ohio: n.p., 1855. 64 p.); and Dr. J. Soule. SCIENCE OF REPRODUCTION AND REPRODUCTIVE CONTROL (Stereotype ed. New York: n.p., 1856. 70 p.).

801 Bogue, Donald J., ed. SOCIOLOGICAL CONTRIBUTIONS TO FAMILY PLANNING RESEARCH. Chicago: University of Chicago Community and Family Study Center, 1967. 409 p. Tables. Offset.

Includes exploration of attitudes of black and white women toward childbearing and birth control.

802 Cisler, Lucinda. "Unfinished Business: Birth Control and Women's Liberation." In SISTERHOOD IS POWERFUL: AN ANTHOLOGY OF WRITINGS FROM THE WOMEN'S LIBERATION MOVEMENT, edited by Robin Morgan, pp. 245-89. New York: Random House, 1970.

Overview of history, practice, and attitudes toward birth control.

803 Dennitt, Mary W. BIRTH CONTROL LAWS: SHALL WE KEEP THEM, CHANGE THEM, OR ABOLISH THEM. New York: Frederick H. Hitchcock, 1926. ix, 309 p. Illus.

Birth control legislation in the 1920s. Appendix lists state laws, jail sentences for advocates, and assorted relevant documents.

804 Dienes, C. Thomas. LAW, POLITICS AND BIRTH CONTROL. Urbana: University of Illinois Press, 1972. vii, 374 p. Biblio.

805 Fryer, Peter. THE BIRTH CONTROLLERS. London: Secker & Warburg, 1965. 384 p. Illus., biblio.

History of birth control since Egyptian times includes material on American movement.

806 Gordon, Linda. WOMAN'S BODY, WOMAN'S RIGHT: A SOCIAL HISTORY OF BIRTH CONTROL IN AMERICA. New York: Grossman Publishers, 1976. xviii, 479 p.

Study of birth control as social history, its "ideas, its constituency, the motivations and needs of its advocates and opponents."

807 Jennings, Samuel K. THE MARRIED LADY'S COMPANION; OR, THE POOR MAN'S FRIEND. 2d rev. ed. New York: L. Dow, 1808. Reprint. Medicine and Society in America series. New York: Arno Press, 1972. iv, 304 p.

808 Owen, Robert Dale. MORAL PHYSIOLOGY: TREATISE ON POPULATION QUESTIONS, OR MEANS DEVISED TO CHECK PREGNANCY. By a Physician. New York: 1836. vi, 76 p.

Early influential book on contraception.

809 Peck, Ellen. THE BABY TRAP. New York: Pinnacle Books, 1971. vii, 270 p. Paper.

"Children by choice, not coercion."

810 Rainwater, Lee, and Weinstein, Karol. AND THE POOR GET CHILDREN: SEX, CONTRACEPTION, AND FAMILY PLANNING IN THE WORKING CLASS. Social Research Studies in Contemporary Life Series. Chicago: Quadrangle Books, 1960. xiv, 202 p. Biblio. Paper.

Study of attitudes in working-class Chicago.

811 Reed, James. FROM PRIVATE VICE TO PUBLIC VIRTUE: THE BIRTH CONTROL MOVEMENT AND AMERICAN SOCIETY SINCE 1830. New York: Basic Books, 1978. xvi, 456 p. Illus., biblio.

Includes sections on Margaret Sanger, Robert Dickinson, and James Gamble.

812 Reed, Ritchie H., and McIntosh, Susan. "Costs of Children." In ECONOMIC ASPECTS OF POPULATION CHANGE, edited by Elliott R. Morss and Ritchie H. Reed, pp. 333-51. The Commission in Population Growth and the America Future Research Reports, vol. 11. Washington, D.C.: Government Printing Office, 1972. 379 p.

Compares indirect costs in earnings foregone by mother with those related to uncontrolled fertility and family size. Available from the Superintendent of Documents.

813 Sanger, Margaret H. WOMAN AND THE NEW RACE. New York:

Brentano's, 1920. xii, 234 p.

Urges birth control as moral necessity in world society.

814 Stuart, Martha, and Liu, W.T. eds. THE EMERGING WOMAN: THE IMPACT OF FAMILY PLANNING. AN INFORMAL SHARING OF INTERESTS, IDEAS, AND CONCERNS, HELD AT THE UNIVERSITY OF NOTRE DAME. Boston: Little, Brown and Co., 1970. xxiii, 329 p.

Presents discussions of contraception, woman's self-image, sexuality, marriage, and education.

815 Weisbord, Robert G. "Blacks on the Distaff Side." In his GENOCIDE: BIRTH CONTROL AND THE BLACK AMERICAN, chap. 8. Westport, Conn.: Greenwood Press, Two Continents, 1975. ix, 219 p. Biblio.

Black feminists' view of birth control and abortion.

See also 783, 2428.

d. IN MICROFORM

See 1470.

e. ORAL HISTORY

The Schlesinger Library Oral History Project on Women in Birth Control and Maternal Health Movements, being conducted by the Arthur and Elizabeth Schlesinger Library on the History of Women in America at Radcliffe, is in the process of interviewing women who have been active in the birth control movement, family planning, marriage counseling, and sex education. It has an exchange arrangement with the Oral History Office of Bancroft Library, University of California at Berkeley. The memoirs are for public use.

3. Abortion

a. BIBLIOGRAPHIES

816 Association for the Study of Abortion. BIBLIOGRAPHY. New York: 1965-- . Irregular.

Lists publications, reprints of articles, chapters, lectures, and judicial opinions having to do with abortion cases. The association also publishes the ASA NEWSLETTER and informational pamphlets at irregular intervals.

817 Dollen, Charles, comp. ABORTION IN CONTEXT: A SELECT BIB-

LIOGRAPHY. Metuchen, N.J.: Scarecrow Press, 1970. 150 p.

Indexed by subject and resource.

See also 3.

b. REFERENCES

818 ABORTION IN NINETEENTH CENTURY AMERICA. Sex, Marriage and Society series. New York: Arno Press, 1974. Separately paged.

Four nineteenth-century pamphlets are bound together in the following order: Hugh L. Hodge. FOETICIDE, OR CRIMINAL ABORTION (Philadelphia: University of Pennsylvania, 1869. 44 p.); E. Frank Howe. SERMON ON ANTE-NATAL INFANTICIDE (Terre Haute, Ind.: Allen & Andrews, 1869. 32 p.); H.S. Pomeroy. IS MAN TOO PROLIFIC? (New York: Funk & Wagnalls, 1891. 64 p.); and Ely V. de Warker. THE DETECTION OF CRIMINAL ABORTION AND A STUDY OF FOETICIDAL DRUGS (Boston: James Campbell, 1872. 88 p.).

819 Callahan, Daniel. ABORTION: LAW, CHOICE AND MORALITY. New York: Macmillan Co.; London: Collier-Macmillan, 1970. xv, 524 p. Tables.

Provides background on moral and social issues.

820 Denes, Magda. IN NECESSITY AND SORROW: LIFE AND DEATH IN AN ABORTION HOSPITAL. New York: Basic Books, 1976. xvii, 247 p. Paper.

Personal experience triggered study based on interviews.

821 Lader, Lawrence. ABORTION II: MAKING THE REVOLUTION. Boston: Beacon Press, 1973. xiii, 242 p. Biblio.

History of movement.

822 Lee, Nancy. THE SEARCH FOR AN ABORTIONIST. Chicago: University of Chicago Press, 1969. xv, 207 p. Tables, biblio.

Sociological study of process of searching for an abortionist in America in the 1960s.

823 Mohr, James C. ABORTION IN AMERICA: THE ORIGINS AND EVOLUTION OF NATIONAL POLICY, 1800-1900. New York: Oxford, 1978. ixx, 331 p.

Reports the effects of changing social attitudes on once-approved medical practice. Appendix includes case studies.

824 Rosen, Harold, ed. ABORTION IN AMERICA: MEDICAL, PSYCHIATRIC, LEGAL, ANTHROPOLOGICAL AND RELIGIOUS CONSIDERATIONS. Boston: Beacon Press, 1967. xix, 368 p. Tables, biblio.

Published in 1954 as THERAPEUTIC ABORTION.

825 Sklar, June, and Berkov, Beth. "Abortion, Illegitimacy, and the Annual Birth Rate." SCIENCE 185 (13 September 1974): 909-25.

Reports that abortion prevented more illegitimate births than the total of legitimate births during 1971.

See also 815, 910.

c. IN MICROFORM

See 1470.

E. MINORITY WOMEN

1. Black Women

a. SOURCES, BIBLIOGRAPHIES

The National Council of Negro Women, a coalition of a variety of black women's organizations, issues information on a wide range of topics.

826 Council of Planning Librarians. "Black Women in the Cities, 1872-1875: A Bibliography of Published Works on the Life and Achievement of Black Women in Cities of the United States." 2d ed. Compiled by Lenwood G. Davis. Exchange Bibliography nos. 751-52. Washington, D.C.: 1975. 75 p. Mimeo.

Variety of references deals with urban affairs, lists collections, organizations, and elected black women officials from local through national levels. Available from Mrs. Mary Vance, P.O. Box 229, Monticello, Illinois 61856.

827 Davis, Lenwood G., comp. THE BLACK WOMAN IN AMERICAN SOCIETY: A SELECTED ANNOTATED BIBLIOGRAPHY. Boston: G.K. Hall & Co., 1975. xi, 159 p. Offset.

Lists a wide range of printed material. Includes listings of collections, organizations, publishers and editors, and elected officials as well as statistics on women in rural and urban areas.

828 Dumond, Dwight L. A BIBLIOGRAPHY OF ANTISLAVERY IN AMERICA. Ann Arbor: University of Michigan Press, 1961. 119 p.

Useful though it has neither a table of contents nor an index.

829 Miller, Elizabeth, W., and Fisher, Mary L., comps. THE NEGRO IN AMERICA: A BIBLIOGRAPHY. 2d ed. rev. and enl. by Mary L. Fisher. Cambridge: Harvard University Press, 1970. xx, 351 p.

Unannotated. Contains material in women although it is not listed in a separate category.

830 Sweet, Charles E., comp. SOCIOLOGY OF THE AMERICAN NEGRO. Focus: Black American Bibliographical Series, Indiana University Libraries and Focus: Black America. Bloomington: 1969. 53 p. Paper.

See also 52, 54, 1146, 1197.

For a listing of organizations for black and Third World women see 402, 403.

b. REFERENCES

831 Albert, Octavia V.R. THE HOUSE OF BONDAGE, OR CHARLOTTE BROOKS AND OTHER SLAVES, ORIGINAL AND LIFELIKE, AS THEY APPEARED IN THEIR PLANTATION AND CITY SLAVE LIFE; TOGETHER WITH TEN PICTURES OF THE PECULIAR INSTITUTION, WITH SIGHTS AND INSIGHTS INTO THEIR NEW RELATIONS AS FREED MAN, FREE-MAN, AND CITIZENS. New York: Hunt & Eaton, 1890; Cincinnati: Cranston & Stone, 1890. xiv, 161 p. Reprint. Black Heritage Library Collection. Freeport, N.Y.: Books for Libraries Press, 1972.

Focuses on horrors of lives of slave women.

832 American Council on Education. American Youth Commission. CHILDREN OF BONDAGE: THE PERSONALITY DEVELOPMENT OF NEGRO YOUTH IN THE URBAN SOUTH. Prepared by John Dollar, and Allison Davis. Washington, D.C.: 1940. xxviii, 299 p.

Study focuses on personalities and their socialization. Note especially case histories of two lower-class young women, chapters 2, 3; of two middle-class young women, chapters 6, 7.

833 AUNT SALLY; OR, THE CROSS, THE WAY TO FREEDOM: A NARRATIVE OF THE SLAVE-LIFE AND PURCHASE OF THE MOTHER OF

REV. ISAAC WILLIAMS, OF DETROIT, MICHIGAN. Cincinnati: American Reform Tract and Book Society, 1858. Reprint. Miami, Fla.: Mnemosyne, 1969. vii, 216 p. Illus.

Written for Sabbath schools in order to involve the young in "spirit of Liberty."

834 Carson, Josephine. SILENT VOICES: THE SOUTHERN NEGRO WOMAN. New York: Delacorte Press, 1969. 273 p. Paper.

Well-researched study of the black Southern women of all classes.

835 Crummell, Alexander. THE BLACK WOMAN OF THE SOUTH: HER NEGLECTS AND HER NEEDS. Washington, D.C.: B.S. Adams, 1883. 16 p. Pamph.

836 Halsell, Grace. SOUL SISTER. New York: World Publishing Co., 1969. 211 p. Paper.

Southern white woman becomes black in order to discover human values in Harlem and in the South.

837 Johnson, Charles S. SHADOW OF THE PLANTATION. Chicago: University of Chicago Press, 1934. xxii, 215 p. Illus., tables, charts. Paper.

Studies black women in context of family, economic, and religious life in rural Macon County, Alabama.

838 Ladner, Joyce A. TOMORROW'S TOMORROW: THE BLACK MANNER. Garden City, N.Y.: Doubleday & Co., 1971. xxvi, 304 p. Biblio. Paper.

Study of black girls becoming women challenges the white academic view of normality.

839 Robinson, Pat, ed. LESSONS FROM THE DAMNED. New York: Times Change, 1973. 156 p.

Autobiographical chronicles of lower-middle-class black women living in Rochester, New York, housing projects.

840 Schulz, David. "Coming Up as a Girl in the Ghetto." In his COMING UP BLACK: PATTERNS OF GHETTO SOCIALIZATION, chap. 2. Englewood Cliffs, N.J.: Prentice-Hall, 1969. xiv, 209 p. Tables, biblio.

Study of poor immigrants and how they cope.

841 Smith, Lillian. KILLERS OF THE DREAM. Rev. and enl. ed. New York: W.W. Norton & Co., 1961. 253 p. Paper.

Maintains that contradictory views of sex and segregation make humane society impossible. Autobiographical.

842 Staples, Robert. THE BLACK WOMAN IN AMERICA: SEX, MARRIAGE AND THE FAMILY. Professional-Technical Series. Chicago: Nelson Hall, 1973. 269 p. Biblio. Paper.

Drawing upon historical past of Afro-American, author refutes assumptions of Moynihan Report (see 623). Links black and feminist movements as challenge to male power elite.

843 Wallace, Michelle. BLACK MACHO AND THE MYTH OF SUPERWOMAN. New York: Dial Press, 1979. viii, 182 p.

Views black women as vulnerable rather than powerful figures, as projected in the Moynihan Report (see 623). Details author's involvement in social movements of the 60s.

See also 78, 622, 623, 1301.

c. IN FILM, MICROFORM

844 GUIDE TO FILMS (16mm) ABOUT NEGROES. Alexandria, Va.: Serina Press, 1970. 67 p. Pamph.

Limited listing, with sources, of films about American black women, including Harriet Tubman, Lena Horne, and Marian Anderson. Available from Serina Press, 70 Kennedy Street, Alexandria, Virginia 22305.

2. Minority Women Other Than Black

a. BIBLIOGRAPHIES, MISCELLANEOUS SOURCES

845 Carey, Emily A., et al., comps. WOMEN, ETHNICITY AND COUNSELING (A RESOURCE LIST). Boston: Womanspace, 1977. 24 p. Offset, stapled.

Unannotated. Listing drawn up for 1977 Boston Conference on Women, Ethnicity and Counseling. Cross-cultural items as well as items on black, native American, and Hispanic women. Available from Womanspace Feminist Therapy Collective, Inc., 636 Beacon Street, Boston, Massachusetts 02215.

846 Cantor, Aviva, comp. BIBLIOGRAPHY ON THE JEWISH WOMAN: A COMPREHENSIVE AND ANNOTATED LISTING OF WORKS PUBLISHED 1900-1978. Fresh Meadows, N.Y.: Doris B. Gold, 1979. 53 p., with additional pages. Offset, stapled. Paper.

Includes general titles in history, nonsexist children's books, and poetry, with more specialized one relating to women in American history. Lists Jewish publications and organizations, and feminist presses. Available from Biblio Press, P.O. Box 22, Fresh Meadows, New York 11365.

847 Durran, Pat H., and Cabella-Argendona, comps. THE CHICANA: A BIBLIOGRAPHIC STUDY. Los Angeles: University of California, Chicano Studies Center, 1973. 51 p.

848 Klein, Bernard, and Icolari, Daniel, eds. REFERENCE ENCYCLOPEDIA OF THE AMERICAN INDIAN. 2d ed. Rye, N.Y.: Todd, 1973. 536 p. Biblio.

Who's who section contains biographical and professional information on native American women. Numerous women listed in bibliography. Update of 1967 volume.

849 Medicine, Beatrice. "The Role of Women in Native American Societies: A Bibliography." INDIAN HISTORIAN 8 (Summer 1975): 50-54.

Unannotated.

850 Murdock, George P. ETHNOGRAPHIC BIBLIOGRAPHY OF NORTH AMERICA. 3d ed. New Haven, Conn.: Human Relations Area Files, 1960. xxiii, 393 p. Offset.

Lists material on puberty rites, child care, woman rituals, native American women, and Eskimo women. Also includes biography and autobiography.

851 Talbot, Jane M., and Cruz, Gilbert R., comps. A COMPREHENSIVE CHICANO BIBLIOGRAPHY, 1960-1970. Austin, Tex.: Jenkins Publishing Co., 1973. xvi, 375 p.

Note "Women, Marriage, and the Family" and "Machismo" in the index.

See also 3, 853, 1146, 1197.

b. REFERENCES

852 "Chicana." DE COLORES: JOURNAL OF EMERGING RAZA PHILOSOHIES 3 (1975): special issue.

Contains articles, documents, poetry, diction.

853 Cotera, Martha P. THE CHICANA FEMINIST. Austin, Tex.: Information Systems Development, 1977. 68 p. Biblio. Pamph.

Presents material on heritage, role, identity, issues, and other. Bibliography partially annotated.

854 ______. DIOSA Y HEMBRA: THE HISTORY AND HERITAGE OF CHICANA IN THE U.S. Austin, Tex.: Information Systems Development, 1976. 202 p. Offset.

Draws a socioeconomic profile of the Chicana and views her as a member of the family and of society at large.

855 Garbarino, Merwyn S. "Seminole Girl." TRANS-ACTION 7 (February 1970): 40-46.

Describes problems facing young Floridian woman who was born into tribal life and later graduated from college.

856 Hamamsy, Laila S. "The Role of Women in a Changing Navaho Society." AMERICAN ANTHROPOLOGIST 59 (1957): 101-11. Biblio.

Discusses pressures challenging economic position and functioning of family affect women more than men. Discusses traditional and new patterns related to marriage ceremonies, household duties, and so on.

857 Katz, Jane B., ed. I AM THE FIRE OF TIME: THE VOICES OF NATIVE AMERICAN WOMEN. New York: E.P. Dutton & Co., 1977. xix, 201 p. Illus. Paper.

Fourteen selections divided equally between tribal and twentieth-century experience, much of it oral history.

858 Landes, Ruth. THE OJIBWA WOMAN. Columbia University Contributions to Anthropology, vol. 31. New York: Columbia University Press, 1938. viii, 247 p. Reprint. New York: W.W. Norton & Co., 1971.

Flexible structure of women's as against men's lives that causes wide variation in female behavior patterns. Taped interviews.

859 Lewis, Oscar. LA VIDA: A PUERTO RICAN FAMILY IN THE CULTURE OF POVERTY--SAN JUAN AND NEW YORK. New York:

Vintage Books, 1965. lix, 669 p. Paper.

Classic.

860 Linton, Ralph, ed. ACCULTURATION IN SEVEN AMERICAN INDIAN TRIBES. New York: Appleton-Century, 1940. xiii, 526 p.

Includes discussion of sexual mores, marriage, and division of labor as they relate to women.

861 Lurie, Nancy O. "Indian Women: A Legacy of Freedom." In LOOK TO THE MOUNTAIN, edited by Robert L. Iacopi, pp. 29-36. San Jose, Calif.: Gousha Publications, 1972. 121 p. Illus.

Attacks myths surrounding status of native American women and mentions today's outstanding Indian women.

862 Marriott, Alice L. THE TEN GRANDMOTHERS. The Civilizations of the American Indian Series, no. 2. Norman: University of Oklahoma Press, 1945. Reprint. New York: Source Book Press, 1977. xiv, 306 p. Illus., biblio.

Kiowa women.

863 Mason, Otis T. WOMAN'S SHARE IN PRIMITIVE CULTURE. The Anthropological Series. New York: D. Appleton, 1894. xiii, 295 p. Illus.

Considerable material on native American women.

864 Mathur, Mary E.F. "Who Cares That a Woman's Work is Never Done?" INDIAN HISTORIAN 4 (Summer 1971): 11-16. Biblio.

Life and economic role of native American woman.

865 O'Meara, Walter. DAUGHTERS OF THE COUNTRY: THE WOMEN OF THE FUR TRADERS. New York: Harcourt, Brace, & World, 1968. xii, 368 p. Illus., biblio.

Study of the relations between the white men and native American women.

866 Reichard, Gladys A. SPIDER WOMAN: A STORY OF NAVAJO WEAVERS AND CHANTERS. New York: Macmillan Co., 1934. x, 282 p. Illus.

Autobiographical account of woman who lives with Navajos and learns their crafts.

867 Richards, C. "The Role of the Iroquois Women." Ph.D. thesis, Cornell University, 1969.

868 Terrell, John J., and Terrell, Donna M. INDIAN WOMEN OF THE WESTERN MORNING: THEIR LIFE IN EARLY AMERICA. New York: Dial Press, 1974. 214 p. Biblio. Paper.

Covers all aspects of the native American woman's life when white people first arrived.

869 Witt, Shirley H. "Native Women Today: Sexism and the Indian Woman." CIVIL RIGHTS DIGEST 6 (Spring 1974): 29-35.

See also 920, 1301.

c. IN MICROFORM

See 215, 1470.

F. IMMIGRANT WOMEN

1. Sources

The University of Minnesota Immigration History Research Center holds collections on Czech, Finnish, Italian, Polish, and Slovene women. Included are letters, scrapbooks, and newspaper clippings, some on microfilm. Among the papers is the primary material of 872.

2. References

870 Abbott, Edith. IMMIGRATION: SELECT DOCUMENTS AND CASE RECORDS. Chicago: University of Chicago Press, 1924. Reprint. American Immigration Collection series, no. 1. New York: Arno Press, 1969. xxii, 809 p.

Documents relating to passage, admission, exclusion, and expulsion of aliens, and domestic migration problems, many of them involving women from a wide range of European countries.

871 Baum, Charlotte, et al., comps. THE JEWISH WOMAN IN AMERICA. New York: Dial Press, 1975. xiii, 290 p. Illus., biblio. Paper.

Relates the experience of the Jewish woman from the 1840s to the present.

872 Ets, Marie H. ROSA: THE LIFE OF AN ITALIAN IMMIGRANT. Minneapolis: University of Minnesota Press, 1970. xi, 254 p.

Gives an unusual first-person account of an Italian cleaning woman from Milan. Written down by a Chicago social worker in 1884.

873 Gans, Herbert J. THE URBAN VILLAGERS: GROUP AND CLASS IN THE LIFE OF ITALIAN-AMERICANS. New York: Free Press of Glencoe, 1962. xvi, 367 p. Biblio.

Discusses life in Boston's West End.

874 McLean, Annie M. "Life in the Pennsylvania Coal Fields, With Particular Reference to Women." AMERICAN JOURNAL OF SOCIOLOGY 14 (November 1908): 329-51. Tables.

Social life of Slavic immigrants. Tabulation of material on amusements, clubs and centers, and church efforts to ameliorate women's lives under aegis of Young Women's Christian Association.

875 Neidle, Cecyle S. AMERICA'S IMMIGRANT WOMEN: THEIR CONTRIBUTION TO THE DEVELOPMENT OF A NATION FROM 1609 TO THE PRESENT. Boston: G.K. Hall & Co., 1975. 312 p. Biblio, illus. Paper.

Show how women's contributions parallel those of men from the colonial period on.

876 U.S. Treasury Department. TABLES SHOWING ARRIVALS OF ALIEN PASSENGERS AND IMMIGRANT IN THE UNITED STATES FROM 1820 TO 1888. Prepared by the Bureau of Statistics. Washington, D.C.: Government Printing Office, 1889. 173 p. Tables, diagram.

Includes breakdowns by sex according to nationality and numbers, by quarter and financial years.

877 U.S. Woman's Bureau. THE IMMIGRANT WOMAN AND HER JOB. Prepared by Caroline Manning. Bulletin no. 74. Washington, D.C.: Government Printing Office, 1930. ix, 179 p. Tables. Reprint. The American Immigration Collection. New York: Arno Press, 1970.

Early study of central European women in Philadelphia and Lehigh Valley. Focuses on work in factories and at home and attendance in evening schools. Extensive use of statistics.

G. CRIMES BY AND AGAINST WOMEN

1. General

The National Council on Crime and Delinquency maintains an information center that acquires, organizes, and disseminates information from more than one-hundred and fifty journals and two-thousand documents, excepting only unpublished or statistical matter in the criminal justice field.

a. RESOURCES, BIBLIOGRAPHIES

878 Chamliss, William J., and Seidman, Robert B. SOCIOLOGY OF THE LAW: A RESEARCH BIBLIOGRAPHY. Berkeley, Calif.: Glendessary, 1970. viii, 113 p.

879 Protano, Emanual T., and Piccirillo, Martin L. LAW ENFORCEMENT: A SELECTIVE BIBLIOGRAPHY. Littleton, Colo.: Libraries Unlimited, 1974. 203 p.

880 Rosenzweig, Marianne, and Brodsky, Annette, comps. THE PSYCHOLOGY OF THE FEMALE OFFENDER: A RESEARCH BIBLIOGRAPHY. University: University of Alabama, Center for Correctional Psychology, 1976. iii, 45 p. Biblio.

Lists selected materials from the period 1950-75. Covers research and treatment of juveniles and adults. Available from the University of Alabama, Box 2968, University, Alabama 35486.

For resources listing see also 890.

b. REFERENCES

881 Adler, Freda, with Adler, Herbert M. SISTERS IN CRIME: THE RISE OF THE FEMALE CRIMINAL. New York: McGraw-Hill Book Co., 1976. 287 p. Paper.

Views female criminality as arising out of new female assertiveness.

882 Blumenthal, Walter H. BRIDES FROM BRIDEWELL: FEMALE FELONS SENT TO COLONIAL AMERICA. Rutland, Vt.: Charles E. Tuttle Co., 1962. Reprint. Westport, Conn.: Greenwood Press, 1973. 139 p. Illus.

Colonial antecedents of many present-day Americans. Well documented.

883 Breckenridge, Sophonisba P. "The Woman Offender." In her SOCIAL WORK AND THE COURTS, chap. 7. Social Service Series. Chicago: University of Chicago Press, 1934.

Material on venereal disease, prostitution, the court as public health agency, and the American Health Association.

884 Davidson, Terry. CONJUGAL CRIME: UNDERSTANDING AND CHANGING THE WIFEBEATING PATTERN. New York: Hawthorn Books, 1978. 274 p.

Research, interviews, and personal experience form the basis for this insightful study.

885 Chapman, Jane R., and Gates, Margaret, eds. THE VICTIMIZATION OF WOMEN. Sage Yearbooks in Women's Policy Studies, vol. 3. Beverly Hills, Calif.: Sage Publications, 1978. 282 p. Paper.

Discusses victimization of women as inevitable in sexist social order in its general aspects as well as in the more particular ones of rape, battering, sexual abuse of children, prostitution, sexual harassment, and effects on women's health.

886 [Ellington, George]. THE WOMEN OF NEW YORK, OR THE UNDERWORLD OF THE GREAT CITY. ILLUSTRATING THE LIFE OF THE WOMEN OF FASHION, WOMEN OF PLEASURE, ACTRESSES AND BALLET GIRLS, PICKPOCKETS AND SHOPLIFTERS, ARTISTS' FEMALE MODELS, WOMEN OF THE TOWN, ETC. New York: New York Book, 1869. 650 p. Illus. Reprint. New York: Arno Press, 1972.

Epitome of Victorian attitudes toward women. Includes as suspect women doctors and "strongminded women."

887 "The Female Offender." Edited by Annette M. Brodsky. CRIMINAL JUSTICE AND BEHAVIOR 1 (December 1974): special issue. Biblio.

Articles on research and programs.

888 Langley, Roger, and Levy, Richard C. WIFE BEATING: THE SILENT CRISIS. New York: E.P. Dutton & Co., 1977. x, 242 p. Biblio.

Investigative journalistic approach includes many first-person narratives.

889 Martin, Del. BATTERED WIVES. San Francisco: New Glide, 1976. xix, 288 p. Paper.

Provides an overview of personal, legal, and legislative aspects of battering. Lists refuges for battered wives.

890 National Commission on the Observance of International Women's Year. FEMALE OFFENDERS. Prepared by Female Offender Resource Center. Washington, D.C.: Government Printing Office, 1977. Variously paged. Biblio. Paper.

Includes workshop guide, fact sheet, film listing, resource people, organizations, and programs. By section of country.

891 Pollak, Otto. THE CRIMINALITY OF WOMEN. Philadelphia: University of Pennsylvania Press, 1967. Reprint. Westport, Conn.: Greenwood Press, 1978. xii, 180 p. Tables, biblio.

"Criminality of women reflects their biological nature in a given cultural society."

892 Reston, James, Jr. THE INNOCENCE OF JOAN LITTLE: A SOUTHERN MYSTERY. New York: Times Books, 1977. xii, 340 p.

Chapters from differing points of view of those involved point up complexities of social currents at work.

893 Shultz, Gladys D. HOW MANY MORE VICTIMS? SOCIETY AND THE SEX CRIMINAL. Philadelphia: J.B. Lippincott Co., 1965. ix, 363 p.

Studies men who assault women and children.

894 Simon, Rita J. WOMEN AND CRIME. Lexington, Mass.: D.C. Heath & Co., 1975. xvi, 126 p. Tables, biblio.

Discusses history of attitudes toward women criminals, relevance to them of the current women's movement and the Equal Rights Amendment, and parole.

895 Steinmetz, Suzanne K., and Straus, Murray A., eds. VIOLENCE IN THE FAMILY. New York: Harper & Row, 1974. ix, 337 p. Paper.

Has sections on violence between spouses and kin and violence by parents. Discusses the family as a training ground for violence.

896 Vedder, Clyde B., and Sommerville, Dora B. THE DELINQUENT GIRL. 2d ed. Springfield, Ill.: Charles C Thomas, Publisher, 1975. xiv, 174 p. Biblio.

Surveys different kinds of problems involving young women and explores factors contributing to delinquency.

2. Rape

a. RESOURCES, BIBLIOGRAPHY

897 Chapelle, Duncan, et al., comps. "Forcible Rape: Bibliography." JOURNAL OF CRIMINAL LAW 65 (1974): 248-63.

Unannotated. Sections on general information, victims, offenders, legal, and medical issues.

898 New York Radical Feminists. RAPE: THE FIRST SOURCEBOOK FOR WOMEN. Compiled by Noreen Cornell, and Cassandra Wilson. New York: New American Library, 1974. 283 p. Biblio. Paper.

Information on consciousness raising, speakout, legal and feminist action, such as rape crisis centers, self-defense, and political action.

See also 906.

b. REFERENCES

899 Amir, Menachem. PATTERNS IN FORCIBLE RAPE. Chicago: University of Chicago Press, 1971. ix, 394 p. Biblio.

Studies rapes in Philadelphia.

900 Brownmiller, Susan. AGAINST OUR WILL: MEN, WOMEN AND RAPE. New York: Simon & Schuster, 1975. 472 p. Paper.

Carefully researched study of past and current attitudes toward rape and of legal handling of rape.

901 Burgess, Ann W., and Holmstrom, Linda L. RAPE: VICTIMS OF CRISIS. Bowie, Md.: Robert J. Brady, 1974. xii, 308 p. Tables.

Presents victim's and rapist's views of the act of rape. Materials on reactions, crisis intervention, and counseling of victims.

902 Gager, Nancy, and Schurr, Cathleen. SEXUAL ASSAULT: CONFRONTING RAPE IN AMERICA. New York: Grosset & Dunlap, 1976. xiv, 336 p. Biblio.

Material on victims and rapists, legal procedures, organizations to assist rape victims, and suggestions for ultimate solutions.

903 Goldberg, Jacob A., and Goldberg, Rosamund W. GIRLS OF THE

CITY STREETS: A STUDY OF 1400 CASES OF RAPE. New York: Distributed by American Social Hygiene, 1935. 384 p. Reprint. Women in America: From Colonial Times to the 20th Century series. New York: Arno Press, 1974.

Clinical approach based on the premise that mental health directly relates to social justice.

904 Hilberman, Elaine. THE RAPE VICTIM. New York: Basic Books, 1976. xii, 105 p.

Study by Project of American Psychological Association Committee on Women investigates the legal, social, and medical aspects of rape as well as reactions of and toward the victim, and the role of the therapist.

905 MacDonald, John M. RAPE: OFFENDERS AND VICTIMS. Springfield, Ill.: Charles C Thomas, Publisher 1971. xvi, 342 p. Biblio.

906 Meden, Andra, and Thompson, Kathleen. AGAINST RAPE: A SURVIVAL MANUAL FOR WOMEN. HOW TO AVOID ENTRAPMENT AND HOW TO COPE WITH RAPE PHYSICALLY AND EMOTIONALLY. New York: Farrar, Straus and Giroux, 1974. 152 p. Illus., biblio.

Appendix includes statistics, resource material.

907 Russell, Diana E.H. THE POLITICS OF RAPE: THE VICTIM'S PERSPECTIVE. New York: Stein & Day, 1975. 311 p. Biblio.

Interviews with rapists and their victims as well as political interpretation of rape.

c. IN MICROFORM

See 215.

3. Prostitution

a. BIBLIOGRAPHY

908 Bullough, Vern, et al. A BIBLIOGRAPHY OF PROSTITUTION. New York: Garland Publishing Co., 1977. x, 419 p.

Focuses on prostitution on pages 60-78, but includes scattered references also in subject areas.

b. REFERENCES

909 Chicago. City. Vice-Commission. THE SOCIAL EVIL IN CHICAGO: A STUDY OF EXISTING CONDITIONS. WITH RECOMMENDATIONS

BY THE VICE-COMMISSIONER OF CHICAGO. Chicago: Gunthorp-Warren, 1911. Reprint. New York: Arno Press, 1970. 399 p. Illus., tables.

910 Crapsey, Edward. THE NETHER SIDE OF NEW YORK, OR, THE VICE, CRIME AND POVERTY OF THE GREAT METROPOLIS. New York: Sheldon, 1872. 185 p.

Reprints articles first appearing in the GALAXY. Note chapter 16, "Prostitution," and chapter 17, "The Abortionist."

911 Greenwald, Harold. THE ELEGANT PROSTITUTE: A SOCIAL AND PSYCHOLOGICAL STUDY. New York: Walker & Co., 1970. xii, 305 p. Biblio.

Revised edition of THE CALL GIRL: A SOCIAL AND PSYCHOLOGICAL STUDY. New York: Ballantine Press, 1958.

912 Haft, Marilyn. "Hustling for Rights." CIVIL LIBERTIES REVIEW 1 (Winter-Spring 1974): 8-26.

Discusses historical background, legal and constitutional considerations, and licensing. Excellent "Note on Sources."

913 Hall, Susan. LADIES OF THE NIGHT. A Prairie House Book. New York: Trident, 1973. 249 p. Illus.

Based on interviews.

914 Kneeland, George J., with Davis, Katharine B. COMMERCIALIZED PROSTITUTION IN NEW YORK CITY. Publications of the Bureau of Social Hygiene. New York: Century, 1913. xii, 334 p. Tables.

Reports on conditions of prostitution and on corrective agencies.

915 McDowell, J.R. MAGDALEN FACTS. New York: n.p., 1832. vi, 104 p. Pamph.

Early anecdotal study of "fallen women" in New York. Speculates about causes and cures of "licentiousness."

916 Millett, Kate. THE PROSTITUTION PAPERS: A CANDID DIALOGUE. New York: Basic Books, 1973. 149 p. Paper.

Reports on interviews with two prostitutes and a lawyer who defends them. Raises basic feminist issues.

917 Murtagh, John, and Harris, Sara. CAST THE FIRST STONE. New York: McGraw-Hill Book Co., 1957. viii, 307 p.

World of prostitution through the eyes of New York's chief magistrate. Glossary of prostitute's lingo.

918 Powell, Aaron M. STATE REGULATION OF VICE. REGULATION EFFORTS IN AMERICA. THE GENEVA CONFERENCE, NEW YORK. New York: Wood & Holbrook, 1878. 127 p.

Possibility of licensing prostitutes in America.

919 Rosen, Ruth, and Davidson, Sue, eds. THE MAIMIE PAPERS. Old Westbury, N.Y.: Feminist Press, in cooperation with the Arthur and Elizabeth Schlesinger Library on the History of Women in America, 1977. li, 439 p. Paper.

Letters exchanged between a young Philadelphia prostitute and a Bostonian social worker result in rehabilitation.

920 Samuels, Gertrude. THE PEOPLE VS. BABY. Garden City, N.Y.: Doubleday & Co., 1967. 292 p.

Journalistic account of a Puerto Rican woman involved with prostitution, drugs, and prison.

921 Sanger, William W. THE HISTORY OF PROSTITUTION: ITS EXTENT, CAUSES, AND EFFECTS THROUGHOUT THE WORLD. New York: Harper, 1858. xiv, 709 p. Reprint. American Women: Images and Realities series. New York: Arno Press, 1972.

Presents one-third of the surveys based on an official report devoted to New York City.

922 Sheehy, Gail. HUSTLING: PROSTITUTION IN OUR WIDE-OPEN SOCIETY. New York: Delacorte Press, 1971. 273 p. Paper.

Author cooperating with police witnesses prostitution at first hand. Attitudes of prostitutes toward feminists.

923 Strong, Ellen. "The Hooker." In SISTERHOOD IS POWERFUL: AN ANTHOLOGY OF WRITINGS FROM THE WOMEN'S LIBERATION MOVEMENT, edited by Robin Morgan, pp. 289-97. New York: Random House, 1970.

Radical orientation toward prostitution by an ex-prostitute.

924 "The Whore Issue." APHRA (Spring 1971): special issue.

Contains fiction, poetry, interviews, and essay on the place of prostitution in a male-oriented society.

925 Winick, Charles, and Kinsie, Charles M. THE LIVELY COMMERCE: PROSTITUTION IN UNITED STATES. New York: Quadrangle, 1971. ix, 320 p.

Discusses the individuals involved, the ways in which the business is conducted, the relation between prostitution and law, and prostitution and the military, and efforts at control.

926 Woolston, Harriet B. PROSTITUTION IN THE UNITED STATES. Publications of the Bureau of Social Hygiene. New York: Century, 1921. Reprint. Patterson Smith Reprint Series in Criminology, Law Enforcement and Social Problems, no. 29. Montclair, N.J.: Patterson Smith, 1969. ix, 360 p.

Focuses on prostitution in the United States prior to World War I.

See also 3, 2200, 2242, 2343.

c. IN FILM, MICROFORM

927 "Ain't Nobody's Business." 16mm soundfilm, in color, sound. Evergreen, Colo.: Tomato Productions, 1977.

Documentary on female prostitution features six prostitutes, male members of vice squad, and footage from the World Meeting of Prostitutes. Available from Tomato Productions.

928 Child, Abigail, and Child, Jon, producers and eds. "Game, A Film about Hustling." 38.5 mins. 16 mm, black and white, sound. Film Image, 1973.

Winner of CINÉ Golden Eagle Award tells of life of street hustler and her pimp in cinema verité style.

See also 215.

4. Women in Prison

a. RESOURCES, BIBLIOGRAPHY

929 California University. Institute of Governmental Studies. THE PRISON AND THE PRISONER: A BIBLIOGRAPHY. Public Policies Bibliographies, no. 1. Berkeley, Calif.: 1972. 156 p.

See also 938.

b. REFERENCES

930 Burkhart, Kathryn W. WOMEN IN PRISON. Garden City, N.Y.: Doubleday & Co., 1973. viii, 465 p. Biblio. Paper.

Relates personal histories.

931 Cheney-Lind, Meta. "Judicial Enforcement of the Female Sex Role: The Family Court and the Female Delinquent." ISSUES AND CRIMINOLOGY 8 (Fall 1973): 51-69. Tables, biblio.

Maintains that sexism, with resultant violation of civil rights, is rampant.

932 Deming, Barbara. PRISON NOTES. New York: Grossman Publishers, 1966. 185 p. Illus.

Relates experience in an Albany, Georgia, jail by a woman involved in civil libertarian demonstrations.

933 District of Columbia. Commission on the Status of Women. FROM CONVICT TO CITIZEN: PROGRAMS FOR THE WOMAN OFFENDER. Prepared by Virginia A. McArthur. Washington, D.C.: 1974. ii, 38 p. Biblio.

Presents overview, programs, and recommendations. Available from the commission, Room 204, District Building, 14th and E Streets, N.W., Washington, D.C. 20004; and from National Technical Information Service, Springfield, Virginia 22151.

934 Giallombardi, Rose. SOCIETY OF WOMEN: A STUDY OF A WOMEN'S PRISON. New York: John Wiley, 1966. ix, 244 p. Biblio.

Study coming out of a year-long observation at the Federal Reformatory for Women, Alderson, West Virginia.

935 Harris, Sara. HELLHOLE: THE SHOCKING STORY OF THE INMATES AND LIFE IN THE NEW YORK CITY HOUSE OF DETENTION FOR WOMEN. New York: E.P. Dutton & Co., 1967. 288 p.

936 Heffernan, Esther. MAKING IT IN PRISON: THE SQUARE, THE COOL AND THE LIFE. New York: Wiley-Interscience, 1972. xvi, 231 p. Biblio.

Study of the Women's Reformatory of the District of Columbia at Occoquan, Virginia, 1961 to 1963.

937 Moseley, William H., and Gerould, Mary H. "Sex and Parole: A

Comparison of Male and Female Prisoners." JOURNAL OF CRIMINAL JUSTICE 3 (1975): 47-58. Tables, biblio.

Survey of personal attitudes, time served, and parole outcome.

938 Resources for Community Change. WOMEN BEHIND BARS: AN ORGANIZING TOOL BY RESOURCES FOR COMMUNITY CHANGE. Washington, D.C.: 1975. 56 p. Illus., biblio.

Surveys problems. Lists groups offering assistance to women in prison as well as a wide variety of resources having to do with legal and personal problems of women in prison.

939 U.S. Department of Justice. Law Enforcement Assistance Administration. NATIONAL STUDY OF WOMEN'S CORRECTIONAL PROGRAMS. Compiled by Ruth M. Glick, and Virginia V. Neto. Washington, D.C.: Government Printing Office, 1977. xxx, 358 p. Tables, charts, illus., biblio.

Available from the Superintendent of Documents.

940 Ward, D., and Kassebaum, G. WOMEN'S PRISONS: SEX AND SOCIAL STRUCTURE. Chicago: Aldine Publishing Co., 1965. xi, 269 p.

941 Zalba, Serapio R. WOMEN PRISONERS AND THEIR FAMILIES: A MONOGRAPH ON A STUDY OF THE RELATIONSHIPS OF A CORRECTIONAL INSTITUTION AND SOCIAL AGENCIES WORKING WITH INCARCERATED WOMEN AND THEIR CHILDREN. Sacramento: California Department of Social Welfare and Department of Corrections, 1964. xiv, 124 p. Tables, biblio.

Undertaken to clarify problems and practices with view to ameliorating conditions.

c. IN MICROFORM

See 215.

d. FILM

942 "Like a Rose." 16 mm soundfilm, in black and white. Evergreen, Colo.: Tomato Productions, 1975.

Award-winning documentary film on experience of two women serving twenty-five-year sentences in state penitentiary. Available from Tomato Productions.

H. DRESS, FASHIONS

1. Sources

For names of fashion periodicals see chapter 3, volume 2; chapter 4, volume 3; chapter 11, volume 4 in Mott, page 4.

For the names of collections on dress and costume see Ash and Calvert, page 3.

2. References

943 Bender, Marilyn. THE BEAUTIFUL PEOPLE. New York: Coward-McCann, 1967. 320 p. Illus. Paper.

High fashion, then and now, with its social implications.

944 Corson, Bender. FASHIONS IN HAIR: THE FIRST FIVE THOUSAND YEARS. London: Peter Owen, 1965. 701 p. Illus., biblio.

Although international in scope, this work provides much material on American women in the nineteenth and twentieth centuries.

945 Fairchild, John. THE FASHIONABLE SAVAGES. Garden City, N.Y.: Doubleday & Co., 1965. viii, 200 p. Illus.

Covers the world of high fashion that includes many American designers.

946 Hawes, Elizabeth. FASHION IS SPINACH. New York: Random House, 1938. x, 336 p.

Irreverent remarks by a top designer.

947 Jones, Marie M. WOMAN'S DRESS: ITS MORAL AND PHYSICAL RELATIONS, BEING AN ESSAY DELIVERED BEFORE THE WORLD'S HEALTH CONVENTION, NEW YORK CITY, NOVEMBER, 1864. New York: Miller, Wood, 1865. 29 p. Pamph.

Attacks contemporary dress design for women. Includes a pattern for "reform dress," the forerunner of today's slack suit.

948 Kushner, Trucia. "Finding a Personal Style." MS. 2 (February 1974): 45-51, 82-86.

The look of the seventies and the effect of the women's

movement on style.

949 McClellan, Elisabeth. HISTORIC DRESS IN AMERICA, 1607-1870. 2d ed. New York: Tudor, 1937. 661 p. Illus., glossary, biblio.

Contains illustrations which are not always trustworthy.

950 Riegel, Robert E. "Women's Clothes and Women's Rights." AMERICAN QUARTERLY 15 (Fall 1963): 390-401.

Surveys dress reform between 1851 and 1920.

951 Ross, Mary S. AMERICAN WOMEN IN UNIFORM: COMPLETE DESCRIPTION, DUTIES, QUALIFICATIONS, AND REQUIREMENTS OF 37 WOMEN'S ORGANIZATIONS, INCLUDING 27 OFFICIAL UNIFORMS, INSIGNIA, AND RANK OF ALL GROUPS IN FULL COLOR. Garden City, N.Y.: Garden City Publishing, 1943. 72 p. Illus.

Note particularly the last two chapters.

952 U.S. National Museum. WOMEN'S BATHING AND SWIMMING COSTUMES IN THE UNITED STATES. Compiled by Claudia B. Kidwell. Washington, D.C.: Government Printing Office, 1969. 32 p. Illus.

953 Veblen, Thorstein. "The Economic Theory of Women's Dress." POPULAR SCIENCE MONTHLY 46 (November 1894): 198-205.

Views dress as "conspicuous consumption."

954 Warwick, Edward P., et al. EARLY AMERICAN DRESS. Rev. ed. New York: Benjamin Blom, 1965. 428 p. Illus., plates, biblio.

Views costume as an integral part of a complex national life. Excellent plates.

I. MANNERS

1. Sources

Women's magazines offer funds of information on manners. See Mott, page 4 for listings of women's periodicals since colonial times. See 314 for a more abbreviated listing of periodicals prior to 1968.

2. References

955 Amory, Cleveland. THE PROPER BOSTONIANS. American Society

Series. New York: E.P. Dutton & Co., 1947. 381 p. Biblio.

Note especially chapter 5, "The Boston Women," and chapter 6, "Belles and Grandes Dames."

956 Aretz, Gertrude [Kuntze-Dolten]. THE ELEGANT WOMAN FROM THE ROCOCO PERIOD TO MODERN TIMES. Translated by James Lever. New York: Harcourt, Brace, 1932. 314 p. Biblio., plates.

957 Butler, Charles. THE AMERICAN LADY. Philadelphia: Hogan & Thompson, 1845. ix, 288 p.

Summarizes upper-class female duties including the place of operas, concerts, dancing, reading, and conversation in young women's lives.

958 Cable, Mary, et al. AMERICAN MANNERS AND MORALS: A PICTURE HISTORY OF HOW WE BEHAVED AND MISBEHAVED. New York: American Heritage, 1969. 399 p. Illus.

Contains a wealth of material drawn from popular and fine arts, advertising, book illustrations, and elsewhere. Informed text discusses woman's dominance in society.

959 Carson, Gerald. THE POLITE AMERICANS: A WIDE-ANGLE VIEW OF OUR MORE OR LESS GOOD MANNERS OVER 300 YEARS. New York: William Morrow & Co., 1966. vi, 346 p. Illus., biblio.

Much material but scattered. Note especially chapter 5, "Women: Theirs Not to Reason Why."

960 Day, Charles W. HINTS OF ETIQUETTE AND THE USAGES OF SOCIETY WITH A GLANCE AT BAD HABITS. New York: A.V. Blake, 1844. 157 p.

Formalities of life between the sexes before the Civil War.

961 Furness, Clifton J., ed. THE GENTEEL FEMALE: AN ANTHOLOGY. New York: Alfred A. Knopf, 1931. xiv, 306. Biblio.

Anthologizes selections organized into chapters on frailty, sentiment, melancholy, piety, decorum, sphere and influence, the literary lady, and so on. Excellent introduction.

962 Hale, Sarah J. MANNERS: OR, HAPPY HOMES AND GOOD SOCIETY ALL YEAR ROUND. Boston: J.E. Tilton, 1868. 377 p. Reprint. American Women: Images and Realities series. New York: Arno Press, 1972.

Based on Hale's columns in GODEY'S LADIES' BOOK. Hints on reading, correct speech, and avoidance of divorce as well as on details of etiquette.

963 Kingsland, Florence [Mrs. Burton]. ETIQUETTE FOR ALL OCCASIONS. New York: Doubleday, Page, 1901. vi, 531 p.

Gives rules for respectable society of the early 1900s. Published also under the title THE BOOK OF GOOD MANNERS: ETIQUETTE FOR ALL OCCASIONS.

964 Mansfield, Blanche McM. THE AMERICAN WOMAN ABROAD. New York: Dodd, Mead, 1911. vi, 534 p. Illus.

Contains everything a lady needs to know for a trip abroad.

965 Markun, Leo. MRS. GRUNDY. New York: D. Appleton, 1930. xii, 658 p.

Part 2 deals with the proprieties of American life from Plymouth colony to the 1930s, all wryly told.

966 Post, Emily. EMILY POST'S ETIQUETTE: THE BLUE BOOK OF SOCIAL USAGE. 11th rev. ed. New York: Funk & Wagnalls, 1965. 707 p.

967 Putnam, Emily J. THE LADY: STUDIES OF CERTAIN SIGNIFICANT PHASES OF HER HISTORY. New York: G.P. Putnam's Sons, 1910. xxv, 323 p. Reprint. Chicago: University of Chicago Press, 1969. Paper.

Note especially "The Lady of the Slave States."

968 Sherwood, John. MANNERS AND SOCIAL USAGES. New York: Harper, 1884. 325 p.

Passages on "good" and "bad" society and on "elderly girls" (unmarried women over thirty).

969 Stiles, Henry R. BUNDLING: ITS ORIGIN, PROGRESS AND DECLINE IN AMERICA. J. Munsell, 1869. 139 p.

Amusing survey of the practice of bundling in New England.

See also chapter 2, section B.2.b.

Chapter 7
EMPLOYMENT

A. EMPLOYMENT IN GENERAL

1. Sources, Resources

The major government agency to issue material on women's employment is the U.S. Women's Bureau which offers a variety of material from leaflets to full-size volumes (see also page 14). Other agencies that are of assistance are the Equal Employment Opportunity Commission, the Office of Federal Contract Compliance, the Federal Women's Program, the U.S. Bureau of the Census, the U.S. Bureau of Labor Statistics, the Wage and Hour division of the U.S. Department of Labor, the U.S. Civil Service Commission, the National Labor Relations Board, and the Citizen's Advisory Council on the Status of Women. The Office of Information, Publications, and Reports of the U.S. Department of Labor, maintains a news service and, in addition, issues the bimonthly WOMEN & WORK, which prints regular columns on employment trends and ideas and much other related information. The publication lists career opportunities inside and outside of government as well as federal activities and legislation having to do with women's employment.

Many private organizations of broad scope, such as the AFL-CIO, have established women's caucuses or committees. For the names of specialized organizations having to do with specific businesses or professions, see the headnotes of the following sections. A number of women's organizations such as the National Organization for Women have task forces devoted to specialized aspects of women's work. Most of them distribute information on their activities. The Women's Action Alliance has resources of various kinds to help working women in matters of sex discrimination and child care, distributes kits having to do with specific areas, and issues the monthly WOMEN'S AGENDA. The Woman's Equity Action League is also an important source of material. The Center for Vocational Education, Ohio State University, produces and distributes a variety of pamphlets having to do with women at work.

A periodical that may be of use is the MONTHLY LABOR REVIEW, which prints current information and reviews books on women and also issues special sections of women's employment from time to time. The FEDERAL REGISTER prints texts of congressional legislation. The SPOKESWOMAN carries material of more general interest to working women.

For a listing of collections having to do with labor material see Ash and Calvert, page 3.

See also 974, 979, 988, 991, 998.

2. Bibliographies

970 Business and Professional Women's Foundation. WORK FORCE ENTRY BY MATURE WOMEN: REVIEW AND BIBLIOGRAPHY. Washington, D.C.: 1977. 20 p. Pamph.

Annotated. Includes material on needs of women re-entering labor market and on counselor's role. Available from foundation.

971 California University. Institute of Industrial Relations. WOMEN AT WORK: AN ANNOTATED BIBLIOGRAPHY. Compiled by Mei Liang Bickner. Los Angeles: 1974. Unpaged. Offset.

The eight sections are (1) general, (2) historical development, (3) education and training (counseling, educational attainment, continuing education), (4) working women (statistics, characteristics, unions), (5) occupations (from professional to unskilled trades), (6) special groups (teenagers, minority women, and other), (7) public policy (federal and state laws), and (8) bibliography. Indexed by subject.

972 Feminist Theory Collective. AMERICAN WOMEN: OUR LIVES AND LABOR: AN ANNOTATED BIBLIOGRAPHY ON WOMEN AND WORK IN THE UNITED STATES, 1900-1975. Eugene, Oreg.: 1976. 36 p. Pamph.

Available from the Amazon Reality Collective, P.O. Box 95, Eugene, Oregon 97401.

973 Koba Associates. WOMEN IN NON-TRADITIONAL OCCUPATIONS. Washington, D.C.: U.S. Department of Health, Education and Welfare; Bureau of Occupational and Adult Education, 1977. iii, 189 p. Biblio. Offset, paper.

Annotated. Includes overview and lists material on skilled, vocational, and professional occupations. Extensive listings of sources of further information.

974 Phelps, Ann, et al., comps. NEW CAREER OPTIONS FOR WOMEN: A SELECTED ANNOTATED BIBLIOGRAPHY. Women Studies Series. New York: Human Sciences, 1977.

Focuses on women's access to higher education and patterns of professional employment. Items at women at work, present opportunities in education, personal considerations, counseling, and legal issues.

See also 8, 512, 513, 984.

3. References

975 Baker, Elizabeth F. TECHNOLOGY AND WOMAN'S WORK. New York: Columbia University Press, 1964. xvi, 460 p. Biblio.

Traces women's place in the labor force from colonial times. Covers changing occupational patterns and protective labor legislation beginning in the nineteenth century.

976 Bancroft, Gertrude. THE AMERICAN LABOR FORCE: ITS GROWTH AND CHANGING COMPOSITION. Prepared for the Social Science Research Council in cooperation with the U.S. Department of Commerce and Bureau of the Census. New York: John Wiley; London: Chapman & Hall, 1958. xiv, 256 p. Tables.

Analyzes 1950 Census Bureau statistics. Provides figures on part-time labor force and family employment patterns. Appendix includes statistics of years 1890-1955.

977 Baxandall, Rosalyn, et al., eds. AMERICA'S WORKING WOMEN: A DOCUMENTARY HISTORY, 1600-PRESENT. New York: Vintage Books, 1976. xxii, 448 p. Illus.

Includes sections on native American, immigrant, and black women.

978 Bird, Caroline. ENTERPRISING WOMEN: THEIR CONTRIBUTION TO THE AMERICAN ECONOMY, 1776-1876. New York: W.W. Norton & Co., 1976. 216 p. Paper.

Women in industry, business, and the professions.

979 _____. EVERYTHING A WOMAN NEEDS TO KNOW TO GET PAID WHAT SHE'S WORTH. Edited by Helen Mandelbaum. New York: David McKay Co., 1973. Paper.

Provides material on opportunities for women in men's jobs as well as nonsexist jobs, tactics for securing all kinds of employment, affirmative action programs, and legal and collective action. Source section includes bibliographies, listing of trade and professional associations, and sources for guidance, training, and counseling for employed and self-employed women.

980 Blatch, Harriet S. MOBILIZING WOMANPOWER. New York: Women's Press, 1918. 195 p. Illus.

Reports on women in World War I work.

981 Bowen, William G., and Finegan, T. Aldrich. THE ECONOMICS OF LABOR FORCE PARTICIPATION. Princeton, N.J.: Princeton University Press, 1969. xxvi, 897 p. Illus.

Includes information on rates and trends of participation and their relation to demographic factors, characteristics of men, and young, single, and older women as labor force participants, problems of unemployment, and so on. Much statistical material.

982 Cantor, Milton, and Laurie, Bruce, eds. CLASS, SEX, AND THE WOMEN. Contributions in Labor History, no. 1. Westport, Conn.: Greenwood Press, 1977. ix, 253 p.

Ten contemporary views of nineteenth-century mill and immigrant (Italian and Jewish) women, women in the West, and the Women's Trade Union League.

983 Caplow, Theodore. "Occupations of Women." In his SOCIOLOGY OF WORK, chap. 10. Minneapolis: University of Minnesota Press, 1954. Reprint. Westport, Conn.: Greenwood Press, 1978. viii, 330 p. Tables, biblio. Paper.

Concise statement of situation at mid-century.

984 Farmer, Helen S., and Backer, Thomas E. NEW CAREER OPTIONS FOR WOMEN: A COUNSELOR'S SOURCEBOOK. Women's Studies Series. New York: Human Sciences Press, 1977. 349 p. Tables, charts, biblio.

Funded by National Institute of Education. Discusses women's employment in the seventies, opportunities in training and education, as well as theories, concepts, and techniques and methods of counseling.

985 Filene, Catherine, ed. CAREERS FOR WOMEN. Boston: Houghton Mifflin Co., 1920. xiii, 134 p. Diagrams. Reprint. Women in America: From Colonial Times to the 20th Century series. New York: Arno Press, 1974.

Contains 174 career descriptions under 32 general headings. By-product of expanding opportunities for women in early twentieth century.

986 Foxley, Cecilia H. LOCATING, RECRUITING AND EMPLOYING WOMEN. Garrett Park, Md.: Garrett Park, 1976. 357 p. Charts, tables, biblio. Offset, paper.

Background material as well as information on legal and educational issues. Appendixes include documents having to do with equal employment opportunities, guidelines, and so on.

987 Hard, W.I., and Dorr, Rheta, L.C. "Woman's Invasion." EVERYBODY'S MAGAZINE 19-20 (November 1908-April 1909).

Series of articles dealing with issues relating to employment of working and middle-class women of the period.

988 Higginson, Margaret V., and Quick, Thomas L. THE WOMAN'S GUIDE TO A SUCCESSFUL CAREER. New York: AMACOM, 1975. vii, 230 p. Biblio.

Detailed strategies. Includes listing of resources.

989 Kreps, Juanita. SEX IN THE MARKETPLACE: AMERICAN WOMEN AT WORK. Policy Studies in Employment and Welfare, no. 11. Baltimore: Johns Hopkins University Press, 1971. x, 117 p. Tables, figs., biblio. Paper.

Survey of working women at both professional and nonprofessional levels. Discusses demand and supply, earnings, and laws dealing with discrimination. Statistics.

990 Kundsin, Ruth B., ed. WOMEN AND SUCCESS: THE ANATOMY OF ACHIEVEMENT. New York: William Morrow & Co., 1974. 256 p. Biblio.

Successful women--Millicent McIntosh, Mary Calderone, Esther Peterson, Mary Bunting, and Patricia Albjorg Graham among them--discuss personal and family attitudes and relationships, impact of education, and economic factors as determinants of success.

991 Loring, Rosalind K., and Otto, Hubert A., eds. NEW LIFE OPTIONS: THE WORKING WOMAN'S RESOURCE BOOK. New York: McGraw-Hill Book Co., 1976. vii, 487 p.

Issues, new career opportunities, family and health problems, personal relationships, and managing options including retirement.

992 Medsger, Betty. WOMEN AT WORK: A PHOTOGRAPHIC DOCUMENTARY. New York: Sheed & Ward, 1975. xii, 212 p.

993 National Manpower Council. WOMANPOWER. New York: Columbia University, 1975. xxxiii, 371 p. Tables, figs., biblio.

Draws upon contributions of government departments, organizations, and individuals to gain fuller understanding of "role of women in working population." Includes chapters on women in labor force, trends in employment, impact of World War II on employment of women, education for girls, women in armed forces, and public policy issues relating to women.

994 Ohio. State University. Center for Human Resource Research. LONGITUDINAL SURVEYS OF LABOR MARKET EXPERIENCE OF WOMEN. U.S. Department of Labor, Manpower Administration. Manpower Research Monograph Series, no. 21. Washington, D.C.: Government Post Office, 1970-- . Irregular. Illus., biblio.

Reports on interviews and mail surveys with women between 30 and 44 for the years 1967 through 1974, and women between 14 and 24 for the years 1968 through 1971. Covers labor force participation, unemployment, job histories, formative influences, education and training, health, marital, family and financial characteristics, military service, work attitudes and aspirations, and psychological and environmental variables. A handbook, issued in a revised edition in 1976, serves as a guide to the project, indexes, and questionnaires, and includes bibliographies of the reports, grouping them under the headings of preretirement years, careers thresholds, dual careers and special reports. The indexes, issued in looseleaf form, are keys to the over ten thousand interviews.

995 O'Neill, William L., ed. WOMEN AT WORK. Chicago: Quadrangle Books, 1972. xix, 360 p. Paper.

Editor contributes informative introduction to "The Long Day" by Dorothy Richardson (see 1090) and "Inside the New York Telephone Company" by Elinor Langer.

996 Oppenheimer, Valerie K. THE FEMALE LABOR FORCE IN THE UNITED STATES: DEMOGRAPHIC AND ECONOMIC FACTORS GOVERNING ITS GROWTH AND CHANGING COMPOSITION. Institute of International Studies, Population Monograph Series, no. 5. Berkeley, Calif.: University of California, 1970. xii, 197 p. Illus., biblio.

Paper. Reprint. Westport, Conn.: Greenwood Press, 1976.

997 Penny, Virginia. EMPLOYMENTS OF WOMEN: CYCLOPEDIA OF WOMEN'S WORK. Boston: Weller, Wise, 1863. xxiii, 500 p.

Pioneer work. Lists 533 occupations for women as well as wages paid to men and women for same work, qualifications, effects on health, occupations in the South and in Europe. Includes professional, industrial, and domestic categories as well as those in which no women were then employed.

998 Pogrebin, Lotty. GETTING YOURS: HOW TO MAKE THE SYSTEM WORK FOR THE WORKING WOMAN. New York: David McKay Co., 1975. 312 p. Biblio. Paper.

Sections on specializations, conditions to expect, information to use to combat myths, and resources.

999 Richings, G.F. "Prominent Colored Women." In his EVIDENCES OF PROGRESS AMONG COLORED PEOPLE, chap. 26. Philadelphia: George S. Ferguson, 1902. xvi, 575 p. Illus.

Short overview of black women and their accomplishments in the professions, business, and the arts in the nineteenth century.

1000 Schwartz, Felice, et al. HOW TO GO TO WORK WHEN YOUR HUSBAND IS AGAINST IT, YOUR CHILDREN AREN'T OLD ENOUGH, AND THERE'S NOTHING YOU CAN DO ANYHOW. New York: Simon & Schuster, 1972. 350 p. Paper.

Part-time professional "career Baedeker" covers fifty-two specialized fields.

1001 Seed, Susan, ed. SATURDAY'S CHILD: 36 WOMEN TALK ABOUT THEIR JOBS. New York: Bantam Books, 1975. viii, 184 p. Illus.

Interviews with women in arts, communications, trades, services, business, science, medicine, commerce, and government. Includes listing of related organizations.

1002 Smith, Georgiana M. HELP WANTED--FEMALE: A STUDY OF DEMAND AND SUPPLY IN A LOCAL JOB MARKET FOR WOMEN. Research program, Institute of Management and Labor Relations. New Brunswick, N.J.: Rutgers University, 1964. iv, 94 p. Tables, charts. Pamph. Paper.

Detailed study of Middlesex County, New Jersey. Made with view to understanding what was happening from point of view of both employers and employees. Surveys recruiting practices, kinds of work, wages, and characteristics of women employees and their reasons for working.

1003 Smuts, Robert W. WOMEN AND WORK IN AMERICA. New York: Columbia University Press, 1959. Reprint. New York: Schocken Books, 1971. 180 p. Biblio. Paper.

Investigates kinds of women who work, and the personal qualities and social attitudes underlying employment. Parts of Conservation of Human Resources Project.

1004 Stern, Madeleine B. WE THE WOMEN: CAREER FIRSTS OF NINETEENTH CENTURY AMERICAN WOMEN. New York: Schulte Publishing Co., 1962. x, 403 p. Illus., biblio. Reprint. New York: Burt Franklin, 1974.

Sketches of twelve women who broke down barriers in the arts, in science and technology, in the professions and trades, and in business and industry.

1005 Stetson, Damon. STARTING OVER. New York: Macmillan Co., 1971. 258 p.

Problems arising from change in occupation.

1006 Sweet, James A. WOMEN IN THE LABOR FORCE. Studies in Population. New York: Seminar Press, 1973. viii, 211 p.

Shows how family opposition affects women workers.

1007 U.S. Bureau of Labor Statistics. OCCUPATIONAL OUTLOOK HANDBOOK: EMPLOYMENT INFORMATION ON MAJOR OCCUPATIONS FOR WOMEN IN GUIDANCE. Washington, D.C.: 1949-- . Biennial.

Supplements are available.

1008 U.S. Equal Employment Opportunity Commission. EMPLOYMENT PROFILES OF WOMEN AND MINORITIES IN 23 METROPOLITAN AREAS, 1974. Ed. by Joan Hannan. U.S. Research Report, no. 49. Washington, D.C.: 1976. 4, 314 p. Tables. Paper.

Presents material on women in general, as well as black, Hispanic, and Asian-American women, based on reports of private employers and state and local governments.

1009 ______. REPORT 1975: JOB PATTERNS OF MINORITIES AND WOMEN IN PRIVATE INDUSTRY. 2 vols. Washington, D.C.:

1977-- . Annual. Tables, illus. Paper.

Contains mostly tabulated material. Available from the Superintendent of Documents.

1010 U.S. Women's Bureau. 1975 HANDBOOK FOR WOMEN WORKERS. Bulletin no. 297. Washington, D.C.: Government Printing Office, 1975. xiii, 435 p. Tables, charts, biblio.

Part 1 contains information on occupational and financial status of working mothers, child care, minority and unemployed women, employment by occupation and industry, and education and training; part 2 deals with laws governing employment and civil and political status; part 3 covers state, federal, and international mechanisms established to advance women. Being updated.

1011 _____. WOMEN'S OCCUPATIONS THROUGH SEVEN DECADES. Prepared by Janet Hooks. Bulletin no. 218. Washington, D.C.: Government Printing Office, 1947. vii, 260 p. Tables, charts, biblio.

Study of women workers in 1940 as well as changes in women's occupations 1870-1940 (white collar, labor, service occupations, business, profession, agriculture, trades and crafts).

1012 "Women in the Workplace: A Special Section." MONTHLY LABOR REVIEW 97 (Mary 1974): special section. Biblio.

Articles on where women work, sex stereotyping, women's earnings, women in the professions 1870 to 1970, temporary help, and children of working mothers.

See also 769, 970.

B. ECONOMIC STATUS, DISCRIMINATION

1. Sources

Information on women's economic status is available from those sources listed in section A of this chapter, and also from the U.S. Equal Employment Opportunity Commission, the Interstate Association of Commissions on the Status of Women, which publishes BREAKTHROUGH, and the Citizens' Advisory Council on the Status of Women, which issues material on fringe and maternity benefits. Documents relating to compliance are available from the Office of Federal Compliance, Department of Labor.

The Bureau of National Affairs maintains a regular bimonthly reporting service which issues the FAIR EMPLOYMENT PRACTICES MANUAL, a guide to federal and state laws, and FAIR EMPLOYMENT PRACTICES CASES, the full texts of cases and digest of Equal Employment Opportunity Commission decisions.

The Women's Equity Action League distributes "Equal Pay" and "Credit" kits. Federally Employed Women issues THE ABC'S OF YOUR JOB, a series of fact sheets on laws relating to and rights accorded to federally employed women. These fact sheets translate complex regulations into easily understood terms.

The AFFIRMATIVE ACTION REGISTER is a monthly newsletter that prints information about openings in business and the professions.

2. Bibliographies

1013 Krichmar, Albert, et al., comps. "Economic Status." In his THE WOMEN'S RIGHTS MOVEMENT IN THE UNITED STATES, pp. 121-203. Metuchen, N.J.: Scarecrow Press, 1972.

Partially annotated. Categories include "Business and Professions" (law, medicine, politics, sciences), "Wages," "Equal Wages" in relation to women's movement.

1014 Ohio. State University. Center for Human Resource Research. WOMEN AND THE ECONOMY: A BIBLIOGRAPHY AND A REVIEW OF THE LITERATURE ON SEX DIFFERENTIATION IN THE LABOR MARKET. Compiled by Andrew I. Kohen, et al. Columbus, Ohio: 1975. 93 p.

1015 Minnesota University. Industrial Relations Center. PROBLEMS AND ISSUES IN THE EMPLOYMENT OF MINORITY, DISADVANTAGE, AND FEMALE GROUPS: AN ANNOTATED BIBLIOGRAPHY. Compiled by Patrick R. Pinto, and Jeanne O. Buchmeier. Bulletin no. 59. Minneapolis: 1973. 62 p. Pamph.

Lists reporting and abstracting services, legal references, and general references having to do with staffing, training, compensation, and unions.

1016 Pask, Judith M., comp. "Women and the Economy: A Selected Bibliography." Prepared for Indiana Council for Economic Education. West Lafayette, Ind.: Krannert Graduate School of Management, Purdue University, 1977. 14 p. Mimeo., stapled.

Unannotated. Lists bibliographies, periodicals, and audiovisual sources relatingto role career planning, money management, and women in the working world. Available from the compiler, Library, Krannert Graduate School of Industrial Administration, Purdue University, West Lafayette, Indiana 47907.

3. References

1017 Ahern, Dee Dee, with Bliss, Betty. THE ECONOMICS OF BEING A WOMAN. New York: Macmillan Co., 1976. xii, 212 p.

Discriminatory practices that affect women's lives and what to do about them.

1018 Alexander, Rodney, and Sapery, Elizabeth. SHORTCHANGED: WOMEN AND MINORITIES. Prepared for the Council on Economic Priorities, University Press of Cambridge, Massachusetts, Series on Social Sciences. New York: Dunellen Publishing Co., 1972. xii, 186 p. Tables, biblio.

Documents patterns of discrimination in employment (recruitment, affirmative action, training, maternity) and banking (lending) practices. Eighteen individual bank profiles.

1019 Baer, Judith A. THE CHAINS OF PROTECTION: THE JUDICIAL RESPONSE TO WOMEN'S LABOR LEGISLATION. Contributions to Women's Studies, no. 1. Westport, Conn.: Greenwood Press, 1978. x, 238 p.

Asserts that protective legislation for women has contributed to male predominance in labor. Scholarly analysis of materials.

1020 Bird, Caroline, with Briller, Sara W. BORN FEMALE: THE HIGH COST OF KEEPING WOMEN DOWN. Rev. ed. New York: David McKay Co., 1970. xiv, 302 p.

Overview of waste resulting from job discrimination. Includes discussion of legislation affecting women's employment, history of women workers, various adaptations and escape mechanisms of employed women, and remedies to end present discriminations.

1021 Blaxall, Martha, and Reagen, Barbara, eds. WOMEN AND THE WORKPLACE: THE IMPLICATIONS OF OCCUPATIONAL SEGREGATION. Chicago: University of Chicago Press, 1976. x, 326 p. Tables, charts. Paper.

Comes out of a conference held in 1976 by the American Economic Association and Center for Research in Higher Education and the Professions, Wellesley. Originally published as a supplement to SIGNS (Spring 1976).

1022 Boseworth, Louise M. THE LIVING WAGE OF WOMEN WORKERS: A STUDY OF INCOME AND EXPENDITURES OF 450 WOMEN IN THE CITY OF BOSTON. Philadelphia: American Academy of Political and Social Sciences, 1911. vi, 90 p. Tables. Pamph. Reprint. Social Problems and Social Policy: The American Experience series. New York: Arno Press, 1976.

Information on nominal and actual income as well as expenditures for lodging, food, clothing, health, savings, and debt. Offers insight into urban living conditions.

1023 Branch, Mary S. WOMEN AND WEALTH: A STUDY OF ECONOMIC STATUS OF AMERICAN WOMEN. Chicago: University of Chicago Press, 1934. xvii, 153 p. Biblio.

Pioneering survey of women's wealth in the United States, with interpretations of roles of women as taxpayers, property owners, wage earners, buyers, and managers of family income. Statistics comprise the appendix.

1024 Brownlee, W. Elliott, and Brownlee, Mary M., eds. WOMEN IN THE AMERICAN ECONOMY: A DOCUMENTARY HISTORY, 1675-1925. New Haven, Conn.: Yale University Press, 1976. viii, 360 p. Tables. Paper.

Contains primary documents related to women's economic roles and status on farms, in factories and professions, and as consumers.

1025 Campbell, Helen S. WOMEN WAGE-EARNERS: THEIR PAST, THEIR PRESENT, AND THEIR FUTURE. Boston: Roberts Brothers, 1893. xii, 313 p. Tables, biblio. Reprint. American Women: Image and Realities series. New York: Arno Press, 1972.

History of conditions of employment and wages in factories in America through the nineteenth century as compared with those in Europe. Includes text of Factory Inspection Act of 1886 with amendments.

1026 Chapman, Jane R., ed. ECONOMIC INDEPENDENCE FOR WOMEN: THE FOUNDATION FOR EQUAL RIGHTS. Sage Yearbooks in Women's Policy Studies, vol. 1. Beverly Hills, Calif.: Sage Publications, 1976. 320 p. Tables, figs., biblios. Paper.

Focuses on current issues that include economic role, poverty, blue collar jobs, trade unions, working wives and credit discrimination.

1027 Chesler, Phyllis, and Goodman, Emily J. WOMEN, MONEY & POWER. New York: William Morrow & Co., 1976. 288 p. Paper.

"Psychoeconomic" discussion.

1028 Clark, Sue A., and Wyatt, Edith. MAKING BOTH ENDS MEET: THE INCOME AND OUTLAY OF NEW YORK WORKING GIRLS. New York: Macmillan Co., 1911. xiii, 270 p. Illus.

Reports investigations made for the National Consumers' League of abysmal conditions of women workers, many of them immigrants, that resulted in remedial legislation. Discusses effect of "scientific management" on women in various industries.

1029 Eastwood, Mary. FIGHTING JOB DISCRIMINATION: THREE FEDERAL APPROACHES. The Law and Women Series, no. 1 (LAW-L). Washington, D.C.: Today Publications & News Service, 1971. 27 p. Pamph.

Compares Title VII with Executive Orders 11246 and 11478. Available from Today Publications, a News Service which cosponsored the series with Human Rights for Women.

1030 "The Economic Status of Women." WOMEN'S LOBBY QUARTERLY 2 (October 1975): special issue.

Material on changing patterns of employment, welfare, and unemployment. Interviews with Congresswoman Martha Griffiths on taxes and social security and with economist Carolyn Bell on women's economic situation.

1031 Federal Reserve System. Board of Governors. EQUAL CREDIT OPPORTUNITY. Regulation B (12-CFR 202). Washington, D.C.: 1975. 14 p. Pamph.

Based on provision of section 703 of the Equal Credit Opportunities Act. Appendix lists federal enforcement agencies.

1032 Gilman, Charlotte Perkins. WOMEN AND ECONOMICS. Magnolia, Mass.: Peter Smith, 1898. vii, 340 p. Paper.

Major nineteenth-century feminist sociologist views the depressed status of women, particularly of American women, as a result of social conditioning.

1033 Hutchinson, Emilie J. WOMEN'S WAGES: A STUDY OF THE WAGES OF INDUSTRIAL WOMEN AND MEASURES SUGGESTED TO INCREASE THEM. Studies in History, Economics and Public Law, no. 89, 1. New York: Columbia University Press, 1919. Reprint. Columbia Studies in the Social Sciences. New York: AMS Press, 1968.

Studies various factors, including trade unionism and legislation, affecting women's wages during World War I.

1034 Kreps, Juanita W., ed. WOMEN AND THE AMERICAN ECONOMY: A LOOK AT THE 1980S. Englewood Cliffs, N.J.: Prentice-Hall, 1976. viii, 177 p. Figs.

Prepared for advanced reading by those attending the 1975 American Assembly, Columbia University. Papers review history of women's work in America, and discuss current and upcoming issues facing women.

1035 Lloyd, Cynthia B. SEX DISCRIMINATION, AND THE DIVISION OF LABOR. New York: Columbia University Press, 1975. xiv, 431 p. Bibliol

Presents material on employment, unemployment, wages, nonmarket activities (home, marriage, childraising), and governmental politics relating to women and women's liberation.

1036 McAdoo, Laura S. "Women's Economic Status in the South." ARENA 21 (June 1899): 741-56.

Reports ways in which southern attitudes toward women have affected their economic status.

1037 "Sex Discrimination in Employment." WOMEN'S LAW REPORTER 1 (Fall-Winter 1972-1973): 34-78.

Indexes over one-hundred cases, with Equal Employment Opportunity Commission decisions as well as bibliography of fifty-eight law review titles. Part 2 of the same article (Spring 1973, pp. 65-103) updates the above index and includes articles on discrimination, women in postgraduate education, unemployment benefits, and history of women in unions.

1038 Simmons, Adele, et al. EXPLOITATION FROM 9 TO 5: REPORT OF THE TWENTIETH CENTURY FUND TASK FORCE ON EMPLOYMENT. Lexington, Mass.: D.C. Heath & Co., 1975. xvi, 200 p. Tables, figs., biblio.

Includes material on affirmative action, Equal Employment Opportunity legislation and enforcement, labor unions, government employment, education, and child care. Detailed evidence supports conclusions.

1039 Tsuchigane, Robert, and Dodge, Norton. ECONOMIC DISCRIMINATION AGAINST WOMEN IN THE UNITED STATES: MEASURES AND CHANGES. Lexington Books. Lexington, Mass.: D.C. Heath & Co.,

1974. xiv, 152 p. Tables.

Presents "statistical examination of women's earnings and employment based on decennial census of Bureau of Labor Statistics data and other relevant materials." Includes information on factors affecting income, occupational and participation discrimination, age, marital status, and supply and demand of women in the labor force.

1040 U.S. Bureau of Labor. LAWS RELATING TO THE EMPLOYMENT OF WOMEN AND CHILDREN IN THE UNITED STATES, JULY 1907. Washington, D.C.: Government Printing Office, 1907. 150 p. Paper.

Lists laws state by state.

1041 U.S. Commission on Civil Rights. MINORITIES AND WOMEN AS GOVERNMENT CONTRACTORS, A REPORT. Washington, D.C.: 1975. xviii, 189 p. Tables.

Documents gross discrimination in assignment of government contracts (including the "Buy Indian" program) and subcontracts at federal, state, and local levels. Available from the Office of Information and Publications, U.S. Commission of Civil Rights.

1042 _____. MORTGAGE MONEY: WHO GETS IT? A CASE STUDY IN MORTGAGE LENDING DISCRIMINATION IN HARTFORD, CONNECTICUT. Clearinghouse Publication, no. 48. Washington, D.C.: 1974. 75 p. Tables. Offset, pamph.

Concludes that traditional banking procedures and standards cannot help but discriminate against women. Available from the commission.

1043 U.S. Congress. Joint Economic Committee. ECONOMIC PROBLEMS OF WOMEN: HEARINGS BEFORE THE JOINT ECONOMIC COMMITTEE. 93d Cong., 1st, 2d sess. Washington, D.C.: Government Printing Office, 1973-74. 634 p.

The first three sections report the 1973 hearings. The fourth, held in 1974, focuses on women who care for the home.

1044 U.S. Congress. Senate. REPORT ON THE CONDITION OF WOMEN AND CHILDREN WAGE-EARNERS, IN THE UNITED STATES. 19 vols. 61st Cong. 2d sess. Senate doc. nos. 86-104. Washington, D.C. Government Printing Office, 1912. Tables.

Reports on "industrial, social, moral, educational, and physical condition" of women and children. Begun in

1907. The nineteen volumes are entitled as follows:

1. THE COTTON TEXTILE INDUSTRY
2. MEN'S READY-MADE CLOTHING INDUSTRY
3. THE GLASS INDUSTRY
4. THE SILK INDUSTRY
5. WAGE-EARNING WOMEN IN STORES AND FACTORIES
6. THE BEGINNINGS OF CHILD LABOR LEGISLATION. Prepared by Elizabeth L. Otey.
7. CONDITIONS UNDER WHICH CHILDREN LEAVE SCHOOL TO GO TO WORK
8. JUVENILE DELINQUENCY AND ITS RELATION TO EMPLOYMENT
9. HISTORY OF WOMEN IN INDUSTRY IN THE UNITED STATES. Prepared by Helen L. Sumner.
10. HISTORY OF WOMEN IN TRADE UNIONS. Prepared by John B. Andrews and W.D.P. Bliss.
11. EMPLOYMENT OF WOMEN IN METAL TRADES. Prepared by Lucian W. Chaney.
12. EMPLOYMENT OF WOMEN IN LAUNDRIES. Prepared by Charles P. Neill.
13. INFANT MORTALITY AND ITS RELATION TO THE EMPLOYMENT OF MOTHERS
14. CAUSES OF DEATH AMONG WOMEN AND CHILD COTTONMILL OPERATIVES. Prepared by Arthur R. Perry.
15. RELATION BETWEEN OCCUPATION AND CRIMINALITY OF WOMEN. Prepared by Mary Conyngton.
16. FAMILY BUDGETS OF TYPICAL COTTON-MILL WORKERS. Prepared by Wood F. Worcester and Daisy W. Worcester.
17. HOOKWORM DISEASE AMONG COTTON-MILL OPERATORS. Prepared by Charles W. Styles.
18. EMPLOYMENT OF WOMEN AND CHILDREN IN SELECTED INDUSTRIES
19. LABOR LAWS AND FACTORY CONDITIONS

1045 U.S. Department of Housing and Urban Development. Office of Policy Development and Research. WOMEN IN THE MORTGAGE MARKET: STATISTICAL METHODS AND TABLES FOR WOMEN IN APPRAISING THE STABILITY OF WOMEN'S INCOME. Philadelphia: Kentron, 1976. viii, 110 p. Tables, charts, biblio.

Available from the Superintendent of Documents.

1046 U.S. Equal Employment Opportunity Commission. AFFIRMATIVE ACTION AND EQUAL EMPLOYMENT: A GUIDEBOOK FOR EMPLOYERS. 2 vols. Washington, D.C.: 1974. Biblio.

Gives legal basis for affirmative action programs with listing of specific references and resources. Available from the Superintendent of Documents.

1047 _____. AFFIRMATIVE ACTION PROGRAMS FOR WOMEN: A SURVEY OF INNOVATIVE PROGRAMS. Compiled by Jerolyn R. Lyle. Washington, D.C.: Government Printing Office, 1973. ii, 150 p. Biblio. Offset.

Discusses women in American economy, analyzes selected programs, and studies women in major corporations. Bibliography is annotated.

1048 _____. EEOC COMPLIANCE MANUAL. 3 vols. Washington, D.C.: Bureau of National Affairs, 1975-- . Looseleaf.

Issued to "guide personnel in processing of charges of discrimination under Title VII of the Civil Rights Act of 1964." Volume 1 deals with compliance procedures, volume 2 with interpretation, and volume 3 with conciliation standards. Each volume is revised and expanded when such becomes necessary.

1049 _____. EQUAL EMPLOYMENT OPPORTUNITY: JOB PATTERNS FOR MINORITIES AND WOMEN IN PRIVATE INDUSTRY. 10 vols. Washington, D.C.: 1971. Charts, tables.

Provides statistics on patterns in the country as a whole (volume 1) and by region (succeeding volumes).

1050 _____. WOMEN: PATH TO EQUAL EMPLOYMENT. Research Report, no. 2. Washington, D.C.: 1977. 211 p.

Studies women in private employment between 1966 and 1975.

1051 U.S. Social Security Administration. WOMEN AND SOCIAL SECURITY: LAW AND POLICY IN FIVE COUNTRIES. Prepared by Dalmer Hoskins and Lenore E. Bixby. Office of Research and Statistics Research Report, no. 42. Washington, D.C.: Government Printing Office, 1973. iv, 95 p.

"Purpose, evolution and general scope." Section 5 relates to the United States.

1052 Woodward, Helen B. THE LADY PERSUADERS. New York: Ivan

Obolensky, 1960. 189 p. Illus.

Relates the major role played by women's periodicals in elevating women's status from "legally dead" in the nineteenth century to that of financial control in the twentieth.

C. WOMEN IN INDUSTRY, TRADES, DOMESTIC WORK

1. Resources, Bibliographies

1053 Moser, Charlotte, and Johnson, Deborah, comps. RURAL WOMEN WORKERS IN THE TWENTIETH CENTURY: AN ANNOTATED BIBLIOGRAPHY. Central Rural Manpower and Public Affairs Special Paper, no. 15. East Lansing: Michigan State University, 1973. 70 p.

Includes material on immigration, education, full- and part-time employment, day care, organizing, women's liberation, and international trends.

1054 Soltow, Martha J., and Wery, Mary K. AMERICAN WOMEN AND THE LABOR MOVEMENT, 1825-1974: AN ANNOTATED BIBLIOGRAPHY. 2d rev. ed. Metuchen, N.J.: Scarecrow Press, 1976. 255 p.

See also 1101.

2. References

1055 Abbott, Edith. WOMEN IN INDUSTRY: A STUDY OF AMERICAN ECONOMIC HISTORY. New York: D. Appleton, 1910. xxii, 409 p. Tables, biblio. Reprint. American Labor: From Conspiracy to Collective Bargaining series. New York: Arno Press, 1969.

Pioneering work on women's place in American economy from colonial times to the twentieth century. Appendixes include material on child labor prior to 1870, women's wages in cotton mills, statistics on women in industry, and listing of occupations employing women in 1900.

1056 Ames, Azel. SEX IN INDUSTRY: A PLEA FOR THE WORKING GIRL. Boston: James R. Osgood, 1875. 158 p.

Argues against 534, supporting the view that industrial work is good for women's brains because it taxes them less. Seeks improved working conditions and elimination of child labor.

1057 Atherton, Sarah H. SURVEY OF WAGE-EARNING GIRLS BELOW SIXTEEN YEARS OF AGE IN WILKES-BARRE, PENNSYLVANIA, 1915. Women in Industry Series, no. 11. New York: National Consumers' League, n.d. 85 p. Tables, figs. Paper.

Pioneering study.

1058 Atkinson, Mary M. "Women in Farm Life and Rural Economy." ANNALS OF THE AMERICAN ACADEMY OF POLITICAL AND SOCIAL SCIENCES 143 (May 1929): 188-94.

1059 Baker, Elizabeth F. PROTECTIVE LABOR LEGISLATION WITH SPECIAL REFERENCE TO WOMEN IN THE STATE OF NEW YORK. Studies in History, Economics, and Public Law, 116, no. 2. New York: Columbia University, 1933. Reprint. New York: AMS Press, 1969. 467 p.

Discusses influences on and enforcement and effects of legislation on state and national levels.

1060 Barlow, Marjorie D., comp. NOTES ON WOMEN PRINTERS IN COLONIAL AMERICA AND THE UNITED STATES 1639-1975. Charlottesville: University of Virginia Press, 1976. 89 p. Biblio.

Largely unpublished material on 228 women.

1061 Beecher, Catharine E. LETTERS TO PERSONS WHO ARE ENGAGED IN DOMESTIC SERVICE. New York: Leavitt & Row, 1842. 235 p.

Offers instructions on how to conduct oneself socially and at work. To be read by mistresses to illiterate servants.

1062 Boone, Gladys. WOMEN'S TRADE UNION LEAGUES IN GREAT BRITAIN AND THE UNITED STATES OF AMERICA. Studies in History, Economics, and Public Law, no. 489. New York: Columbia University, 1942. Reprint. Columbia Studies in the Social Sciences, no. 483. New York: AMS Press, 1969. 283 p. Tables, diagrams, Biblio.

In context of larger labor movement. Appendixes include statistical material and constitution of organization in the United States.

1063 Brandeis, Louis D., and Goldmark, Josephine C. WOMEN IN INDUSTRY. DECISION OF THE SUPREME COURT IN CURT MULLER VS. STATE OF OREGON, UPHOLDING THE CONSTITUTIONALITY OF THE OREGON TEN-HOUR LAW FOR WOMEN AND BRIEF FOR THE STATE OF OREGON. New York: National Consumers' League, 1908. 113, 8 p. Biblio. Reprint. American Labor: From Conspiracy to Collective Bargaining series. New York: Arno Press, 1969.

1064 Bryner, Edna. THE GARMENT TRADES. Cleveland Foundation Publications, no. 19. Cleveland: Survey Committee of the Cleveland Foundation, 1916. 153 p. Illus.

1065 Butler, Elizabeth. WOMEN AND THE TRADES: PITTSBURGH, 1907-1908. Pittsburgh Survey of Russell Sage Foundation, vol. 1. New York: Charities Publication Committee, 1909. 440 p. Illus., tables, biblio. Reprint. American Labor: From Conspiracy to Collective Bargaining series. New York: Arno Press, 1969.

Pioneering study of working and social life of women in trades. Covers twenty-two thousand subjects in four-hundred establishments. Part of larger Sage project to diagnose economic and social conditions in industrial areas. Appendix includes 1909 Pennsylvania law on working hours and information on Margaret Morrison School of Women.

1066 Donovan, Frances R. THE WOMAN WHO WAITS. Boston: R.G. Badger, 1920. 228 p. Reprint. New York: Arno Press, 1974.

Difficulties of a waitress's life.

1067 Dublin, Thomas. "Women, Work and Protest in the Lowell Mills: 'The Oppressing Hand of Avarice Would Enslave Us.'" LABOR HISTORY 16 (Winter 1975): 99-116.

The dark side of the Lowell experiment.

1068 Eaton, Isabel. "Special Report on Negro Domestic Service in the Seventh Ward, Philadelphia." In THE PHILADELPHIA NEGRO: A SOCIAL STUDY, by W.E.B. Du Bois, pp. 427-509. Publications of the University of Pennsylvania Series in Political Economy and Public Law, no. 14. Philadelphia: for the University of Pennsylvania, 1899. Reprint. Millwood, N.Y.: Kraus Reprint Co., 1973. Tables.

Pioneering study which relates employment of black domestics to domestic employment generally and to the black population as a whole.

1069 Eisler, Benita, ed. THE LOWELL OFFERING: WRITINGS BY NEW ENGLAND MILL WOMEN (1840-1845). Philadelphia: J.B. Lippincott Co., 1977. 223 p. Illus., biblio.

Informative introduction. Selections from letters, stories, essays, and sketches.

1070 Foner, Philip S., ed. THE FACTORY GIRLS: A COLLECTION OF WRITINGS ON LIFE AND STRUGGLES IN THE NEW ENGLAND FACTORIES OF THE 1840S BY THE FACTORY GIRLS THEMSELVES, AND THE STORY, IN THEIR OWN WORDS, OF THE FIRST TRADE UNIONS

OF WOMEN WORKERS IN THE UNITED STATES. Urbana: University of Illinois Press, 1977. xxvii, 390 p.

Contains writings by the dissatisfied women who spearheaded formation of women's industrial unions. Includes essays, tracts, poems, and songs.

1071 Goldmark, Josephine C. FATIGUE AND EFFICIENCY: A STUDY IN INDUSTRY. Sponsored by the Russell Sage Foundation. New York: Charities Publications Committee, 1912. Part 1, xvii, 302 p.; Part 2, 591 p. Tables, figs.

Part 1 discusses kinds, effects, and economic aspects of fatigue in relation to particular industries; relation of overtime and scientific management to fatigue; enforcement of labor laws and courts. Part 2 discusses conditions which affect legislation relating to women.

1072 Hawes, Elizabeth. HURRY UP PLEASE, IT'S TIME. New York: Reynal & Hitchcock, 1946. 248 p.

Relates the experiences of the writer and other women with the United Auto Workers during and just after World War II.

1073 Haynes, Elizabeth R. "Negroes in Domestic Services in United States." JOURNAL OF NEGRO HISTORY 8 (October 1923): 384-442.

1074 Henry, Alice. THE TRADE UNION WOMAN. New York: D. Appleton, 1915. xxiv, 314 p. Illus., biblio.

1075 _____. WOMEN AND THE LABOR MOVEMENT. New York: George H. Doran, 1923. Reprint. American Labor: From Conspiracy to Collective Bargining series. New York: Arno Press, 1971.

Discusses women and the labor movement from the colonial period through the beginning of twentieth century. Material on immigrant women, problems of marriage and work, and so on.

1076 Hewes, Amy. WOMEN AS MUNITIONS MAKERS: A STUDY OF CONDITIONS IN BRIDGEPORT, CONNECTICUT. Pages 1-93 in volume bound with Henriette R. Walter's MUNITIONS WORKERS IN ENGLAND AND FRANCE. New York: Russell Sage Foundation, 1917. v, 158 p. Tables, biblio.

Studies working and home conditions, revealing social change in lives of uprooted women.

1077 Howe, Louise K. PINK COLLAR WORKERS: INSIDE THE WORLD OF WOMEN'S WORK. New York: G.P. Putnam's Sons, 1976.

301 p. Charts, tables, biblio.

Beautician, salesworker, waitress, office worker, and homemaker.

1078 Josephson, Hannah. GOLDEN THREADS: NEW ENGLAND MILL GIRLS AND MAGNATES. New York: Russell & Russell, 1949. ix, 325 p. Biblio.

Reconstructs life of mill girls and milieu in which they worked from the beginning of the Lowell project to its collapse.

1079 Kenneally, James J. WOMEN AND TRADE UNIONS. Monographs in Women's Studies. St. Albans, Vt.: Eden Press Women's Publications, 1978. ii, 240 p.

Focuses on women's involvement since the time of the Civil War. Considerable use of manuscript material.

1080 Lahne, Henry J. "Women and Children in the Mill." In his THE COTTON MILL WORKER, chap. 19. Labor in Twentieth Century American Series. New York: Farrar & Rinehart, 1944. xiii, 303 p. Biblio.

Some information on women, though more on children.

1081 Lobsenz, Johanna. THE OLDER WOMAN IN INDUSTRY. New York: Charles Scribner's Sons, 1929. xvi, 281 p. Tables, illus. Reprint. Women in America: From Colonial Times to the 20th Century series. New York: Arno Press, 1974.

Attitudes and problems between World War I and World War II.

1082 Lorwin, Lewis L. [Levine, Louis]. THE WOMEN'S GARMENT WORKERS: A HISTORY OF THE LADIES INTERNATIONAL GARMENT WORKERS UNION. New York: B.W. Heubsch, 1924. xxv, 608 p. Biblio. Reprint. American Labor: From Conspiracy to Collective Bargaining series. New York: Arno Press, 1969.

Exhaustive history from industrial beginnings in the early republic. Appendix includes statistics, descriptive analyses of occupations, information on wages and hours, and union activities. Bibliography cites much primary material.

1083 Lynd, Alice, and Lynd, Staughton, eds. RANK AND FILE: PERSONAL HISTORIES OF WORKING CLASS ORGANIZERS. Boston: Beacon Press, 1973. 296 p.

Includes women who are organizers in steel plants, airplane

parts factory, and an immigrant woman who was a war protester.

1084 MacLean, Annie M. "Factory Legislation for Women in the United States." AMERICAN JOURNAL OF SOCIOLOGY 3 (September 1867): 183-205.

Lists laws state by state.

1085 _____. "The Sweat Shop in Summer." AMERICAN JOURNAL OF SOCIOLOGY 9 (November 1903): 289-309.

First-hand account.

1086 _____. WAGE-EARNING WOMEN. The Citizen's Library of Economics, Politics and Society. New York: Macmillan Co., 1910. xiv, 202 p. Tables, charts. Reprint. New York: Arno Press, 1974.

Contains a 1907 survey of women workers in various industries in the East and parts of the Middle West as well as of pickers in Oregon and California and workers in Pennsylvania coal fields. Includes foldout of working women's population by state.

1087 Odencrantz, Louise C. ITALIAN WOMEN IN INDUSTRY: A STUDY OF THE CONDITIONS IN NEW YORK CITY. New York: Russell Sage Foundation, 1919. 345 p. Tables.

Study of interaction between immigrants and the industries that employ them.

1088 Pope, Jesse E. THE CLOTHING INDUSTRY IN NEW YORK. University of Missouri Studies, vol. 1, Social Science Series. Columbia: University of Missouri, 1905. Reprint. New York: Burt Franklin, 1970. xx, 339 p. Biblio.

From beginnings. Material on wages and conditions of employment, including sweating system and trade unions.

1089 Rhine, Alice H. "Women in Industry." In WOMAN'S WORK IN AMERICA, edited by Annie N. Meyer, chap. 11. American Women: Images and Realities series. New York: Arno Press, 1972.

History includes material on women's cooperatives and labor unions. Views socialism as the only system able to institute basic changes in the condition of women.

1090 Richardson, Dorothy. "The Long Day." In WOMEN AT WORK, edited by William L. O'Neill, pp. 3-303. Chicago: Quadrangle Books, 1972.

A "Saturday's child" on way to becoming a writer works as light housekeeper, box maker, artificial flower maker, and laundress. Intimate view larded with judgments about poor but respectable women.

1091 Robinson, Harriet J.H. EARLY FACTORY LABOR IN NEW ENGLAND. Reprint Edition. Boston: Wright & Potter, 1889. 26 p. Pamph.

From Fourteenth Annual Report of the Massachusetts Bureau of Statistics of Labor for 1883.

1092 _____. LOOM AND SPINDLE: OR, LIFE AMONG THE EARLY MILL GIRLS. New York: Thomas Y. Crowell Co., 1898. vii, 216 p. Reprint. New York: Arno Press, 1974.

Factory girl writes of life in Lowell and other New England mill towns. Includes sketch of LOWELL OFFERING and some of its contributors.

1093 Salmon, Lucy. DOMESTIC SERVICE. New York: Macmillan Co., 1897. xxiv, 307 p. Biblio. Reprint. American Women: Images and Realities series. New York: Arno Press, 1972.

Early statistical study and history of domestic employment in the United States written with view to improving conditions.

1094 Schipper, Agnes. "Measuring 30 Years by the Yard: Real Life in a 5 & 10 Store." MS. 2 (February 1974): 68-72, 99.

A lifetime spent at Woolworth's.

1095 Scoresby, William. AMERICAN FACTORIES AND THEIR FEMALE OPERATIVES. Boston: n.p., 1845. viii, 136 p. Tables. Reprint. Burt Franklin Research & Source Work Series, no. 184; American Classics in History and Social Sciences, no. 127. New York: Burt Franklin, 1968. viii, 136 p. Tables.

Lowell factory girls as paradigms.

1096 Seidman, Joel. THE NEEDLE TRADES. Labor in the Twentieth Century Series. New York: Farrar & Rinehart, 1942. xviii, 356 p.

Covers especially the history of the International Ladies Garment Workers Union, in broad context.

1097 Spradley, James P., and Mann, Brenda J. THE COCKTAIL WAITRESS: WOMAN'S WORK IN A MAN'S WORLD. New York: John Wiley, 1975. 154 p. Biblio., figs. Paper.

Sociological study.

1098 Stein, Leon. THE TRIANGLE FIRE. Philadelphia: J.B. Lippincott Co., 1962. 224 p. Illus.

Detailed account of fire and subsequent investigation.

1099 Stevens, George. "Women Printers." In his NEW YORK TYPOGRAPHICAL UNION NO. 6: STUDY OF A MODERN TRADE UNION AND ITS PREDECESSORS, chap. 21. Albany, N.Y.: J.B. Lyon, 1913. xix, 717 p. Illus.

History of women printers since colonial times records their rejection and then gradual acceptance by men's unions. Some references to Women's Trade Union League.

1100 Stone, Katherine. HANDBOOK FOR OCAW WOMEN. Denver, Colo.: Oil, Chemical and Atomic Workers International Union, 1973. xii, 82 p. Biblio. Pamph.

Problems facing women in industry and ways in which legislative and union action can help solve such problems.

1101 Tetrault, Jeanne, and Thomas, Sherry. COUNTRY WOMEN: A HANDBOOK FOR THE NEW FARMERS. Garden City, N.Y.: Doubleday & Co., Anchor Books, 1976. xvi, 306 p. Illus., biblio. Paper.

Issued by the group which established COUNTRY WOMEN. Includes resources listing.

1102 Tryon, Nolla M. HOUSEHOLD MANUFACTURES IN THE UNITED STATES, 1640-1860: A DISSERTATION OF THE GRADUATE SCHOOL OF ARTS AND LETTERS IN CANDIDACY FOR THE DEGREE OF DOCTOR OF PHILOSOPHY (DEPARTMENT OF EDUCATION). Library of Early American Industry and Business. Reprint. Economics Classics series. New York: Augustus M. Kelly, 1966. xii, 413 p. Tables, biblio.

Women as industrial workers in broad historical context.

1103 U.S. Congress. Senate. ABSTRACT OF THE STATISTICS OF MANUFACTURES, ACCORDING TO THE RETURNS OF THE SEVENTH CENSUS . . . 1858-59. Compiled by Joseph G. Kennedy. 35th Cong. 2d sess. Senate Executive Doc. no. 39. Washington, D.C.: n.p., 1895. 143 p. Tables. Reprint. Elmsford, N.Y.: Maxwell Reprint Co., 1974.

Tabulates the number of women employed in all industries in the United States and territories.

1104 U.S. Women's Bureau. CHRONOLOGICAL DEVELOPMENT OF LABOR LEGISLATION FOR WOMEN IN THE UNITED STATES. Bulletin no.

66-11. Washington, D.C.: 1931. 176 p.

1105 _____. THE NEW POSITION OF WOMEN IN AMERICAN INDUSTRY. Bulletin no. 12. Washington, D.C.: Government Printing Office, 1920. 158 p.

Employment during and after World War I, and the resulting change in status of women. Attitudes toward trade unions as evidenced in documents.

1106 Van Kleeck, Mary. ARTIFICIAL FLOWER MAKERS. New York: Survey Associates, 1913. xix, 261 p. Tables, illus.

Sponsored by the Russell Sage Foundation. Material on wages, working conditions, unemployment, training, and relevant legislation. Appendix includes text of state laws pertaining to women's employment.

1107 _____. A SEASONAL INDUSTRY: A STUDY OF THE MILLINERY TRADE IN NEW YORK. New York: Russell Sage Foundation, 1917. x, 276 p. Tables.

1108 _____. "Women and Machines." ATLANTIC MONTHLY 120 (February 1921): 250-60.

Women in industry in World War I.

1109 _____. WOMEN IN THE BOOKBINDING TRADES. New York: Survey Associates, 1913. xx, 270 p. Illus., tables.

Contains material similar to that in 1106. Sponsored by the Russell Sage Foundation.

1110 Van Vorst, Bessie, and Van Vorst, Marie. THE WOMAN WHO TOILS, BEING THE EXPERIENCES OF TWO LADIES AS FACTORY GIRLS. New York: Doubleday, Page, 1903. ix, 303 p. Illus.

Two upper-class women report their experiences in a Pittsburgh factory, a New York shirt factory, a Chicago theatrical costume factory, a Lynn, Massachusetts, shoe factory, and a Southern cotton mill.

1111 Wertheimer, Barbara M. WE WERE THERE: THE STORY OF WORKING WOMEN IN AMERICA. New York: Pantheon Books, 1977. xx, 427 p. Illus., biblio. Paper.

Readable, well-researched history through 1914. Published in cooperation with Trade Union Women's Studies, New York State School of Industrial and Labor Relations.

1112 Wertheimer, Barbara M., and Nelson, Anne H. TRADE UNION WOMEN: A STUDY OF THEIR PARTICIPATION IN NEW YORK CITY LOCALS. Praeger Special Studies in U.S. Economic, Social, and Political Issues. New York: Praeger Publishers, 1978. xviii, 178 p. Figs., tables. Offset.

Analyzes why women limited their union participation.

1113 Wetherby, Terry, ed. CONVERSATIONS: WORKING WOMEN TALK ABOUT DOING A "MAN'S JOB." Millbrae, Calif.: Les Femmes, 1977. xii, 269 p.

Contains twenty-two interviews with women in butchering, karate instruction, truck driving, driving race cars, and other occupations.

1114 Willett, Mabel H. THE EMPLOYMENT OF WOMEN IN THE CLOTHING TRADE. Columbia University Studies in History, Economics and Public Law, vol. 16, no. 2. New York: Columbia University, 1902. Reprint. Columbia University Studies in the Social Sciences, no. 42. New York: AMS Press, 1968. 206 p.

Includes historical background and information on factory conditions, immigrant women, labor legislation, and trade unions.

1115 Wolfe, French E. "Admission of Women." In his ADMISSION TO AMERICAN TRADE UNIONS, chap. 4. Johns Hopkins University, 1942. 181 p.

History of women in trade unionism. Analyzes what author considers weakness of women in unionism.

1116 Wolfson, Theresa. THE WOMAN WORKER AND THE TRADE UNIONS. New York: International Publishers Co., 1926. 224 p. Biblio.

Early study of women's potential in trade unions. Appendix includes statistics on women workers from 1910 to 1942, as well as union policies toward them.

1117 "Working Women." In CHINESE-AMERICAN WORKERS: PAST AND PRESENT, chap. 3. San Francisco: Getting Together, 1974.

Available from Getting Together, P.O. Box 26229, San Francisco, California 94126, or China Books and Periodicals, 125 Fifth Avenue, New York, New York.

1118 Working Women's Protective Union. THE WORKING WOMEN'S PROTECTIVE UNION. ITS CONDITION AND THE RESULTS . . . AFTER THIRTY-ONE YEARS OF ACTIVITY. New York: 1894. 25 p.

History of organization 1863-94.

1119 Wright, Carroll D. THE WORKING GIRLS OF BOSTON: FROM THE FIFTEENTH ANNUAL REPORT OF THE MASSACHUSETTS BUREAU OF STATISTICS OF LABOR FOR 1884. Boston: Wright & Potter, 1889. v, 133 p. Tables. Reprint. American Labor: From Conspiracy to Collective Bargaining series, no. 1. New York: Arno Press, 1969.

Pioneering work concerning itself with moral aspects of employment. Mirrors details of daily life.

See also 769, 771, 877.

D. WOMEN IN BUSINESS

1. Sources

The monthly BUSINESS WOMAN'S JOURNAL and the newsletters the EXECUTIVE WOMAN and 9 TO 5 provide current information on women in business.

1121 BUSINESS PERIODICALS INDEX. New York: H.W. Wilson Co., 1958-- . Monthly except July. Annual cumulation.

Indexed by subject. Succeeds INDUSTRIAL ARTS INDEX.

1122 Young, Margaret L., comp. BUSINESS AND LAW LIBRARIES, INCLUDING MILITARY AND TRANSPORTATION LIBRARIES. Vol. 1 of SUBJECT DIRECTORY OF SPECIAL LIBRARIES AND INFORMATION CENTERS. 5th ed. Detroit: Gale Research Co., 1979. xiii, 209 p.

For collections of manuscripts and related papers having to do with women in business see Ash and Calvert, page 3.

See also 1139.

2. Bibliographies

1123 Business and Professional Women's Foundation. A SELECTED ANNOTATED BIBLIOGRAPHY: WOMEN IN POSITIONS AT MANAGERIAL ADMINISTRATIVE AND EXECUTIVE LEVELS. Washington, D.C.: 1966. 19 p. Pamph.

Limited to publications 1955-65. Available from the foundation.

1124 _____. WOMEN EXECUTIVES: A SELECTED BIBLIOGRAPHY. Washington, D.C.: 1970. 26 p. Pamph.

Available from the foundation.

1125 Pask, Judith M., comp. THE EMERGING ROLE OF WOMEN IN MANAGEMENT: A BIBLIOGRAPHY. West Lafayette, Ind.: Krannert Graduate School of Industrial Administration, Purdue University, 1976. vii, 49 p.

Unannotated. Part 1 is organized around publication format, part 2 by subject. Available from the compiler, Library, Krannert Graduate School of Industrial Administration, Purdue University, West Lafayette, Indiana 47907.

See also 1141.

3. References

1126 American Women's Association. THE TRAINED WOMAN AND THE ECONOMIC CRISIS: EMPLOYMENT AND UNEMPLOYMENT AMONG A SELECTED GROUP OF BUSINESS AND PROFESSIONAL WOMEN IN NEW YORK CITY. Directed by Harriet Houghton. New York: 1931. vi, 102 p. Tables.

Studies effects of the depression of the 1930s on association members. Deals with age, education, resources, life-styles and so on. See also the sequel, 1127.

1127 _____. WOMEN WORKERS THROUGH THE DEPRESSION: A STUDY OF WHITE COLLAR EMPLOYMENT MADE BY THE WOMEN'S ASSOCIATION. Edited by Louise Pruett. New York: Macmillan Co., 1934. xvii, 164 p. Tables.

Extension of 1126 recording cumulative psychological and economic effects of the Great Depression on association members. Based on interviews.

1128 Basil, Douglas C. WOMEN IN MANAGEMENT. New York: Dunellen Publishing Co., 1972. xvi, 124 p. Biblio.

Studies barriers to promotion. Surveys status, attitudes, profiles, based on questionnaires.

1129 Benét, Mary K. THE SECRETARIAL GHETTO. New York: McGraw-Hill Book Co., 1973. v, 181 p.

History, role, and status of women office workers in Capitalist society.

1130 Business and Professional Women's Foundation. PROFILE OF BUSINESS AND PROFESSIONAL WOMEN. Washington, D.C.: 1970. 86 p.

Based on over fifty-three thousand responses.

1131 Donovan, Frances R. THE SALESLADY. University of Chicago Sociological Series. Chicago: University of Chicago Press, 1929. xi, 267 p. Illus. Reprint. Women in America: From Colonial Times to the 20th Century Series. New York: Arno Press, 1974.

Informal sociological study.

1132 Fenn, Margaret P., ed. "Women in Business: A New Look." JOURNAL OF CONTEMPORARY BUSINESS 5 (Winter 1976): 1-76.

Legal and social implications, and alternatives to the present system.

1133 Frank, Harold, ed. WOMEN IN THE ORGANIZATION. Philadelphia: University of Pennsylvania Press, 1977. xv, 310 p. Biblio. Paper.

Part 1 contains case studies to women in managerial and professional positions; part 2, nineteen readings that supply backgrounds for case studies.

1134 Ginzberg, Eli, and Yohalem, Alice M., eds. CORPORATE LIB: WOMAN'S CHALLENGE TO MANAGEMENT. Policy Studies in Employment and Welfare, no. 17. Baltimore: Johns Hopkins University, 1973. ix, 153 p. Figs., biblio. Paper.

Principal papers presented at 1971 Columbia University Conference comment on historical precedents, social implications, potentials for constructive action, importance of role models, discrimination in education and industry, life-styles, and change in employment patterns as they apply to women and minority groups.

1135 Hennig, Margaret, and Jardim, Anne. THE MANAGERIAL WOMAN. New York: Doubleday & Co., Anchor Books, 1977. xvii, 221 p.

Research study.

1136 Kanter, Rosabeth M. MEN AND WOMEN OF THE CORPORATION. New York: Basic Books, 1977. xv, 348 p. Tables, biblio.

Insights into corporate structure and methods by social psychologists.

1137 Killian, Ray A. THE WORKING WOMAN: A MALE MANAGER'S

VIEW. New York: American Management Association, 1971. x, 214 p.

Surveys of and interviews with both men and women aimed at revealing the "tremendous potential" of women.

1138 Lynch, Edith M. THE EXECUTIVE SUITE: FEMININE STYLE. New York: AMACOM, 1973. xiv, 258 p. Biblio.

Woman executive looks at usual and unusual jobs for women from inside, and at the relation of women's liberation and the law to the woman executive. Challenges the view of woman as victim.

1139 Rogalin, Wilma C., and Pell, Arthur R. WOMEN'S GUIDE TO MANAGEMENT POSITIONS. New York: Simon & Schuster, 1975. 149 p.

Deals with career potentials, legal implications of managerial positions, affirmative action, and promotion. Appendix includes case histories and lists career services.

1140 Simcich, Tina C. WOMEN AND MINORITIES IN BANKING: SHORTCHANGED/UPDATE. Edited by Wendy C. Schwartz. Praeger Special Studies in U.S. Economic, Social, and Political Issues. New York: Praeger, 1977. 173 p. Biblio., tables.

Reports study conducted for the Council on Economic Priorities in areas of general employment, employment of minority members, and women in the labor force. Includes profiles of individual banks as well as affirmative action and compliance reports.

1141 Stead, Bette Ann, ed. WOMEN IN MANAGEMENT. Englewood Cliffs, N.J.: Prentice-Hall, 1978. xv, 362 p. Biblio. Paper.

Thirty-eight articles having to do with stereotyping, equal opportunity, corporate wives, semantics, patterns of discrimination, styles of leadership among women, and future strategies. Appendix lists cases. Bibliography is annotated.

1142 Tepperman, Jean. NOT SERVANTS, NOT MACHINES: OFFICE WORKERS SPEAK OUT. Boston: Beacon Press, 1975. xiii, 188 p. Paper.

Much of the book is based on interviews with women involved in office workers' movement.

1143 U.S. Department of Commerce. Office of Minority Business Enterprise. WOMEN-OWNED BUSINESSES. Washington, D.C.: Government

Printing Office, 1976. 277, 7 p. Tables, charts, maps.

First comprehensive report to supply data on basic education, geographical divisions, and metropolitan areas.

1144 Valmeras, L. "Work in America: II, The Work Community." RADICAL AMERICA 5 (July-August 1971): 77-92.

Detailed first-hand account of working conditions and the working community by a female office worker in Detroit.

4. Videotape

1145 "The Executive Woman" -- (Video-cassettes). Ten cassettes. 3/4-inch videotapes.

Originally telecast over QPIX-TV. Tapes include interviews with women executives and editors. Material also on Womanschool (a school for women in Manhattan), divorce, and husbands and wives whose career demands separate them. Available from Sandra Brown, the EXECUTIVE WOMAN.

E. WOMEN IN THE PROFESSIONS

The word "profession" is used here in a broad sense to include materials about women who are peripherally involved in professional occupations and who could not properly be included elsewhere. See, for instance, 1326.

1. General

a. SOURCES, BIBLIOGRAPHIES

Most professional organizations now have women's caucuses or committees which provide data in their fields. More specialized information is available. For example, the American Association of University Women and the Project on the Status and Education of Women issue rosters of caucuses and committees in higher education. The Professional Women's Caucus and the Federation on Organizations for Professional Women have formed a coalition of women's caucuses and committees, the latter organization publishing an evaluation of women's registries.

Further general information may be secured from the following:

1146 Scientific Manpower Commission. PROFESSIONAL WOMEN AND MINORITIES: A MANPOWER DATA RESOURCE SERVICE. Prepared by Betty M. Vetter and Eleanor L. Babco. Washington, D.C.:

1975-- . Biblio. Looseleaf.

In four parts: (1) basic affirmative action information, (2) manpower data in all fields, (3) recruitment resources, and (4) bibliography with index. Subscription provides subscribers with semiannual updates and supplements containing accumulated news data.

For bibliographies in specific fields see each of the following sections of this chapter. For general bibliographies see this chapter, sections A.1, 2, and section B.

For collections of materials on the professions see Ash and Calvert, page 3.

b. REFERENCES

1147 Adams, Elizabeth K. WOMEN PROFESSIONAL WORKERS: A STUDY MADE FOR THE WOMEN'S EDUCATIONAL INDUSTRIAL UNION. New York: Macmillan Co., 1921. xiv, 467 p. Tables, biblio.

This study was the force in reshaping women's education and training for new professions. Early definition of term "professional."

1148 Dall, Caroline H. THE COLLEGE, THE MARKET, AND THE COURT: OR, WOMEN'S RELATIONS TO EDUCATION, LABOR, AND THE LAW. Boston: Lee & Shepard, 1867. 498 p. Reprint. American Women: Images and Realities series. New York: Arno Press, 1972.

Lectures delivered by author argue for freedom of choice by women in education and professions. Appendix updates to 1867 the earlier information on general medical education and on women in religion, art, labor, law, and suffrage work.

1149 Epstein, Cynthia F. WOMAN'S PLACE: OPTIONS AND LIMITS IN PROFESSIONAL CAREERS. Berkeley: University of California Press, 1970. x, 221 p. Tables, biblio. Paper.

Factors that keep women "in their place" despite the existence of statistical evidence that could be used to remedy injustice.

1150 Etzioni, Amitai, ed. THE SEMI-PROFESSIONS AND THEIR ORGANIZATION: TEACHERS, NURSES, SOCIAL WORKERS. Glencoe, Ill.: Free Press, 1969. xix, 328 p.

Relation to bureaucracy as well as theoretical considerations.

1151 Fogarty, Michael P., et al. SEX, CAREER AND FAMILY: INCLUDING AN INTERNATIONAL REVIEW OF WOMEN'S ROLES. Beverly Hills, Calif.: Sage Publications, 1971. 581 p. Figs., tables. Paper.

Focuses on top positions filled by married women and on "professional and managerial work at graduate level."

1152 Harris, Barbara J. BEYOND HER SPHERE: WOMEN AND THE PROFESSIONS IN AMERICAN HISTORY. Westport, Conn.: Greenwood Press, 1978. x, 212 p. Biblio.

Traces women's struggles to throw off views of them as intellectually unfit and home oriented. Discusses discriminations still facing women in professions.

1153 Meyer, Annie N., ed. WOMAN'S WORK IN AMERICA. New York: Henry Holt, 1891. viii, 457 p. Tables, biblio. Reprint. American Women: Images and Realities series. New York: Arno Press, 1972.

Eighteen articles by women on fields in which women were not welcome--education, journalism, law, medicine, social welfare, industry, nursing, and care of native Americans. Includes detailed information on women's and coeducational colleges.

1154 Ruddick, Sara, and Daniels, Pamela, eds. WORKING IT OUT: 23 WOMEN WRITERS, SCIENTISTS AND SCHOLARS TALK ABOUT THEIR LIVES AND WORK. New York: Pantheon Books, 1977. 349 p. Illus.

Interviews about dilemmas and satisfactions.

1155 Theodore, Athena, ed. THE PROFESSIONAL WOMAN. Cambridge, Mass.: Schenckman Publishing Co., 1971. xi, 769 p. Tables, biblio. Paper.

Anthology of articles includes material on sexual structure of professions, career choice processes, definition of female professional, career commitment and relation to marriage, the black woman professional, marginal professions, and problems of social work and social change. Excellent introduction. Distributed by General Learning, Morristown, New Jersey 07960.

See also 2144.

2. Education

a. SOURCES

Major sources of current information on the economic and legal status of women as educators may be secured from the Project on the Status and Education of

Women, Association of American Colleges (see page 99) and the Clearing House for Women's Studies (see page 89). Particularly helpful is the Project on Equal Education Rights, a project of the NOW Legal Defense and Education Fund. The project issues the newsletter PEER PERSPECTIVE which lists resources and other material spelling out remedies for discrimination in education. Delta Kappa Gamma Society International interests itself in matters educational both national and international. Other sources having to do solely with women include the American Association of University Women; the National Coalition for Research of Women's Education and Development; the National Association of Women Deans, Administrators and Counselors; and the National Council of Administrative Women in Education. Among the somewhat less specialized organizations are the National Education Association and the American Association of University Professors, whose national Committee W serves as a clearinghouse of information for its state and local chapters.

In addition, professional caucuses and caucuses of professional organizations distribute material. Ruth Oltmann has compiled a listing of women's caucuses and committees for the American Association of University Women, a reprint of which is available from the Project on the Status and Education of Women, which also issues updated listings in all academic areas.

Most of the organizations mentioned above issue monthly or quarterly journals and some, newsletters. Of these, the newsletter issued by the Project on the Status and Education of Women in particularly useful.

b. BIBLIOGRAPHIES

Many organizations listed above in section a. issued bibliographical material.

1156 Allen, John D., et al., comps. COLLECTIVE BARGAINING IN HIGHER EDUCATION: BIBLIOGRAPHY NO. 2. New York: CUNY Bernard Baruch College National Center for the Study of Collective Bargaining, 1974. 150 p.

Includes information on women faculty. Available from the center, 17 Lexington Avenue, New York, New York 10010.

1157 American Association of University Professors. "Bibliography of Studies on the Status of Women." Washington, D.C.: n.d. 10 p. Photocopy.

Available from the association.

See also 1171.

c. DIRECTORIES, BIOGRAPHICAL DICTIONARIES

1158 DIRECTORY OF AMERICAN SCHOLARS: A BIOGRAPHICAL DICTIONARY. New York: R.R. Bowker Co., 1942-- .

Lists scholars in history; English, speech, and drama; foreign languages, linguistics, and philology; philosophy, religion, and law. Updated every four or five years.

1159 LEADERS IN EDUCATION: A BIOGRAPHICAL DICTIONARY. Edited by Jacques Cattell Press. 5th ed. New York: R.R. Bowker Co., 1972-- . ix, 1,309 p.

1160 NATIONAL FACULTY DIRECTORY--1979: AN ALPHABETICAL LIST, WITH ADDRESSES, OF ABOUT 480,000 MEMBERS OF TEACHING FACULTIES AT JUNIOR COLLEGES, COLLEGES, AND UNIVERSITIES IN THE UNITED STATES AND AT SELECTED CANADIAN INSTITUTIONS. 2 vols. Detroit: Gale Research Co., 1978.

1161 Project on the Status and Education of Women. RECRUITING AIDS #3: ROSTERS, REGISTRIES AND DIRECTORIES OF WOMEN IN THE PROFESSIONS. Washington, D.C.: Association of American Colleges, 1974. 4 p. Offset.

Listings for thirty-five academic areas. Updates and supersedes RECRUITING AIDS 1 and 2. Available from the association.

1162 U.S. Office of Education. Division of Educational Statistics. EDUCATION DIRECTORY. Washington, D.C.: Government Printing Office, 1912-- . Annual.

In four parts: state governments, public school systems, higher education, and educational associations. General and statistical information on organizations and officials.

d. REFERENCES

1163 Abramson, Joan. THE INVISIBLE WOMAN: DISCRIMINATION IN THE ACADEMIC PROFESSION. Higher Education Series. San Francisco: Jossey-Bass, 1975. xiv, 248 p. Biblio.

Detailed discussion surveys channels inside and outside of institutions that may or may not be helpful in fighting discrimination.

1164 American Council on Education. WOMEN IN HIGHER EDUCATION. Edited by W. Todd Furniss, and Patricia A. Graham. Washington, D.C.: 1974. xiv, 336 p.

Contains papers prepared for the annual council meeting. Covers problems of women students and professionals, nepotism, academic programs, affirmative action, black liberation, and other topics. By Helen Astin, Leo Kanowitz, Juanita Kreps, McGeorge Bundy, Jacqueline Mattfield, Bernice Sandler, Sheila Tobias, and others.

1165 Beecher, Catharine E. THE DUTY OF AMERICAN WOMEN TO THEIR COUNTRY. New York: Harper, 1845. 164 p.

Urges achieving democratic future for country by becoming educators, by improving physical conditions of schoolrooms, by ending physical abuse, and by raising moral standards through religious instruction.

1166 _____. THE EVILS SUFFERED BY AMERICAN WOMEN AND THEIR CHILDREN: THE CAUSES AND REMEDY. New York: Harper, 1846. 36 p. Pamph.

Attacks low status of women as educators. Includes one of the few negative commentaries on the Lowell factory system.

1167 Bernard, Jessie S. ACADEMIC WOMEN. University Park: Pennsylvania State University Press, 1964. xxv, 331 p. Tables. Paper.

Chronicles the history of and discrimination against academic women discussed as well as their productivity, creativity, and family roles. Classic.

1168 _____. "My Four Revolutions: An Autobiographical History of the American Sociological Association." In THE AMERICAN WOMAN: HER CHANGING SOCIAL, ECONOMIC, AND POLITICAL ROLES, 1920-1970, edited by William H. Chafe, pp. 11-29. New York: Oxford University Press, 1972. Paper.

Describes how male bias has limited women's involvement in questions vital to our society.

1169 Carnegie Commission for Higher Education. OPPORTUNITIES FOR WOMEN IN HIGHER EDUCATION: THEIR CURRENT PARTICIPATION, PROSPECTS FOR THE FUTURE, AND RECOMMENDATIONS FOR ACTION. New York: McGraw-Hill Book Co., 1973. ix, 282 p. Tables, charts, biblio. Paper.

Studies women as students, faculty members, administrators, and nonacademic faculty employees. Discusses roles of college-educated women, affirmative action, continuing education, and child care centers.

1170 Donovan, Frances R. THE SCHOOLMA'AM. New York: Frederick A. Stokes, 1938. xii, 355 p. Biblios. Reprint. Women in America: from Colonial Times to the 20th Century series. New York: Arno Press, 1974.

Sociological study of types of teachers and professional problems they face.

1171 ERIC Clearinghouse on Higher Education. INSTITUTIONAL ANALYSIS OF SEX DISCRIMINATION: A REVIEW AND ANNOTATED BIBLIOGRAPHY. Compiled by Lora H. Robinson. Washington, D.C.: 1973. 10 p.

Summarizes reports and compilations having to do with sex discrimination related to salaries, status, and professional needs in seventeen selected colleges and universities. Copies available from the American Association of Higher Education. Bibliography reprint available also from the Project on the Status and Education of Women.

1172 Fishel, Andrew, and Pottker, Janice. NATIONAL POLITICS AND SEX DISCRIMINATION IN EDUCATION. Lexington, Mass.: D.C. Heath & Co., 1978. 176 p.

In collaboration with participants in the decision-making process, the authors analyze four major efforts to end discrimination.

1173 Gross, Neal, and Trask, Anne E. THE SEX FACTOR AND THE MANAGEMENT OF SCHOOL. New York: John Wiley & Sons, 1976. 279 p. Tables.

Study supported by the Office of Education focuses on career histories of men and women, reactions to sexual differences in education, and role performance and its effect on functioning and productivity.

1174 Hall, Samuel R. LECTURES TO FEMALE TEACHERS ON SCHOOL-KEEPING. Boston: Richardson, Lord & Holland, 1829. 179 p. Reprint. New York: Arno Press, 1969.

Pedagogical directions both practical and otherwise.

1175 Lester, Richard A. ANTIBIAS REGULATIONS OF UNIVERSITIES: FACULTY PROBLEMS AND THEIR SOLUTIONS. Prepared for the Carnegie Commission on Higher Education. New York: McGraw-Hill Book Co., 1974. xvi, 168 p. Biblio.

Includes analysis of discrimination in faculty appointment systems, cases, affirmative action guidelines, and administration. Also suggests ways to discrimination.

1176 National Association of College and University Business Officers, et al. FEDERAL REGULATIONS AND THE EMPLOYMENT PRACTICES OF COLLEGES AND UNIVERSITIES: A GUIDE TO THE INTERPRETATION OF FEDERAL REGULATIONS AFFECTING PERSONNEL ADMINISTRATION ON CAMPUS. Washington, D.C.: 1974-- . Looseleaf.

Subscription service updates information on sex discrimination.

1177 NOW Legal Defense and Education Fund. Project on Equal Education Rights. STALLED AT THE START: GOVERNMENT ACTION ON SEX BIAS IN THE SCHOOL. Washington, D.C.: 1978. 79 p. Charts, tables, biblio. Paper.

Reports on failure of government to enforce provisions of Title IX. Appendix includes material on government's complaint-handling process and listing of school districts charged with violations 1972-76.

1178 Project on the Status and Education of Women. American Association of Colleges. AFFIRMATIVE ACTION RESOURCES #2. Washington, D.C.: 1974. 3 p. Biblio. Offset.

In two parts: "Sources of General Information on Laws and Regulations" and "Availability Sources," which includes statistical material, summary reports, and so on. Available from the project.

1179 _____. "Black Women in Higher Education: A Review of Their Current Status." In MINORITY WOMEN & HIGHER EDUCATION, sec. 1. Washington, D.C.: n.d.

Combats myths with truths. Section 2 supersedes and updates 1 and lists studies, handbooks, directories, registries, placement agencies, national organizations and women's groups, and publications and directories of other media. Available from the project.

1180 Reuben, Elaine, and Hoffmann, Lenore, eds. "UNLADYLIKE AND UNPROFESSIONAL": ACADEMIC WOMEN AND ACADEMIC UNIONS. Commission on the Status of Women, pamphlet no. 2. New York: Modern Language Association, 1975. 54 p. Offset.

Experiences of academic women. Available from Modern Language Association, 62 Fifth Avenue, New York, New York 10011.

1181 Rossi, Alice S., and Calderwood, Ann, eds. ACADEMIC WOMEN ON ON THE MOVE. New York: Russell Sage Foundation, 1973. xv, 560 p. Tables, biblio.

Includes material on recruitment, institutional barriers, women dropouts, career profiles, black women, faculty wives, discrimination, political action, women's studies, and affirmative action.

1182 Sandler, Bernice. "Sex Discrimination, Educational Institutions, and the Law: A New Issue on Campus." JOURNAL OF LAW AND EDUCATION 2 (October 1975): 613-35.

Laws and legal issues and decisions relating to women on campus.

1183 Swint, Henry L. THE NORTHERN TEACHER IN THE SOUTH. 1862-1870. Nashville, Tenn.: Vanderbilt University Press, 1941. ix, 221 p. Biblio. Reprint. New York: Octagon Books, 1967.

1184 U.S. Commission on Civil Rights. AFFIRMATIVE ACTION IN EMPLOYMENT IN HIGHER EDUCATION: A CONSULTATION . . . SEPTEMBER 9-10, 1975. Washington, D.C.: 1975. vi, 239 p. Tables. Paper.

Includes historical background; material on laws, regulations, and guidelines; and reactions by representatives of colleges and universities.

1185 U.S. Equal Employment Opportunity Commission. Office of Planning, Research and Systems. EMPLOYMENT OPPORTUNITY IN THE SCHOOLS: JOB PATTERNS OF MINORITIES AND WOMEN IN PUBLIC ELEMENTARY AND SECONDARY SCHOOL, 1974. Prepared by Mary L. Froning. Research report no. 51. Washington, D.C.: 1977. 309 p.; various pagination.

Contains statistical information.

1186 "Women in the College." Edited by Susan McAllester. COLLEGE ENGLISH 32 (May 1971): special issue.

Contains articles on women in the education profession, children's literature, women and the literature curriculum, writing courses for women, feminist and radical criticism, images of American women, and law as it applies to women in higher education. Most material sponsored by the Commission on the Status of Women at the Modern Language Association meeting, December 1970.

3. Government Service

a. SOURCES, BIBLIOGRAPHIES

The U.S. Women's Bureau puts out material relating to women in federal employment. Federally Employed Women issues several publications, among them FEW'S NEWS AND VIEWS, a bimonthly newsletter, that includes legislation of interest, bibliographies, and chapter activities.

1187 Council of Planning Librarians. "Woman in Government and Politics: A Bibliography of American and Foreign Sources." Compiled by Rosalie Levenson. Exchange Bibliography no. 491. Monticello, Ill.: 1973. 80 p. Mimeo.

Unannotated. Focus is generally since 1940. Covers the military, foreign service, federal employment, judicial positions, municipal management, medicine, police, legislative branch, policy-making positions, and WASPS. Available from Mrs. Mary Vance, P.O. Box 229, Monticello, Illinois 61856.

See also 1194.

b. REFERENCES

1188 Addams, Jane. "Utilization of Women in City Government." In her NEWER IDEALS OF PEACE, chap. 7. The Citizens' Library of Economics, Politics and Sociology. New York: Macmillan Co., 1907. xviii, 243 p.

Points out women's responsibility for running of municipality, which the author views as an extension of the home.

1189 Beard, Mary R. WOMAN'S WORK IN MUNICIPALITIES. National Municipal League Series. New York: D. Appleton, 1915. xi, 344 p. Reprint. American Women: Images and Realities series. New York: Arno Press, 1972.

Presents overview of women's work in municipalities in areas of prostitution, housing, public safety, civic improvement, and recreation.

1190 Clemmer, Mary E. TEN YEARS IN WASHINGTON: OR, INSIDE LIFE AND SCENES IN OUR NATIONAL CAPITOL AS A WOMAN SEES THEM. EMBRACING A FULL ACCOUNT OF THE MANY MARVELS AND INTERESTING SIGHTS OF WASHINGTON: OF THE DAILY LIFE AT THE WHITE HOUSE, BOTH PAST AND PRESENT: OF THE WONDERS AND INSIDE WORKINGS OF OUR GOVERNMENT DEPARTMENTS, AND DESCRIPTIONS AND REVELATIONS OF EVERY

PHASE OF POLITICAL, PUBLIC AND SOCIAL LIFE AT THE NATION'S CAPITOL. . . . TO WHICH IS ADDED A FULL ACCOUNT OF THE LIFE AND DEATH OF PRESIDENT JAMES A. GARFIELD. Hartford, Conn.: Hartford Publishing, 1882. xxi, 608 p. Illus.

Unusual first-hand account of a newspaper woman about the place of women in the political life of the capital. Covers claimants and Civil War widows, women government workers working for disgraceful wages, and other topics.

1191 Federally Employed Women. THE ABC'S OF YOUR JOB: HANDBOOK OF PERSONNEL MANAGEMENT MATTERS. Washington, D.C.: 1971-- . Annual.

Series of fact sheets that interpret regulations.

1192 U.S. Civil Service Commission. 1976 DATA ON MINORITY GROUP AND WOMEN'S EMPLOYMENT IN THE FEDERAL GOVERNMENT. Washington, D.C.: 1976-- . Annual. Tables.

Statistics. Replaces STUDY OF EMPLOYMENT OF WOMEN IN THE FEDERAL GOVERNMENT. Available from the Superintendent of Documents.

1193 U.S. Equal Employment Opportunity Commission. MINORITIES AND WOMEN IN STATE AND LOCAL GOVERNMENT. Edited by Rosalind S. Reshad, et al. 6 vols. Research report no. 52. Washington, D.C.: 1977. Tables.

Material on women generally, and on black, Hispanic, Asian-American, and native American women. Information on distributions, salaries, job categories, participation rates, and so on supported by extensive statistical summaries. Volume 1 covers the nation, volume 2 states, volume 3 counties, volume 4 municipalities, volume 5 townships, and volume 6 special districts.

1194 Women's Action Alliance. THE FORGOTTEN FIVE MILLION: WOMEN IN PUBLIC EMPLOYMENT (A GUIDE TO ELIMINATING SEX DISCRIMINATION). Prepared by Catherine Samuels. New York: 1975. vi, 298 p. Appendix unpaged. Biblio. Offset, paper.

Document problems with remedies such as affirmative action, court suits, and union organizing. Lists resources, including organizations and training groups.

4. Health Careers

a. GENERAL

i. Sources, Bibliographies

Many professional organizations, such as the National Health Council, issue material on health careers.

1195 BULLETIN OF THE HISTORY OF MEDICINE. Baltimore: John Hopkins University Press, 1933-- . Quarterly.

Prints articles on the history of both medicine and nursing.

1196 Pennell, Maryland, and Showell, Shirlene, comps. WOMEN IN HEALTH CAREERS: CHART BOOK FOR INTERNATIONAL CONFERENCE ON WOMEN IN HEALTH. Washington, D.C.: American Public Health Association, 1976. xi, 147 p. Tables, figs.

Statistics on health careers in general, as well as on medicine and medical schools, dentistry, osteopathy, optometry, podiatry, pharmacy, veterinary medicine, nursing, and administration and medical technology. Address correspondence to International Programs Staff, Division of Medicine, Bureau of Health Manpower, Health Resources Administration, NIH Building 31, Room 3C-36, 9000 Rockville Pike, Bethesda, Maryland.

1197 U.S. Department of Labor and U.S. Department of Health, Education and Welfare. Health Resources Administration. MINORITIES AND WOMEN IN THE HEALTH FIELDS. APPLICANTS, STUDENTS, AND WORKERS. Washington, D.C.: 1975. vii, 101 p. Tables. Paper.

Part 2 offers statistics on male and female enrollments in professional schools, degrees conferred, and participation in occupations. Material relates to medicine, osteopathy, dentistry, optometry, pharmacy, podiatry, veterinary medicine, nursing and public health and allied fields, as well as preprofessional education. Updates the 1974 report.

1198 U.S. Department of Labor and U.S. Department of Health, Education and Welfare. Women's Action Program. AN EXPLORATORY STUDY OF WOMEN IN THE HEALTH PROFESSIONS SCHOOLS. 11 vols. Prepared by Urban and Rural Systems Association. San Francisco: Urban and Rural Systems Association, 1976-- . Illus., tables, charts, biblio.

Data analysis, findings, conclusions, and recommendations to eliminate barriers to women in medicine, osteopathic medicine, podiatry, pharmacy, and public health. An annotated bibliography comprises volume 10.

See also 1438, 1439.

b. DENTISTRY

i. Sources, Bibliography

The Association of American Women Dentists issues an annual directory of members and a biennial newsletter.

1199 Northwestern University Dental School Library. "Women in Dentistry: A Bibliography." Chicago: 1969. 2 p. Photocopy.

Unannotated listing of articles.

ii. References

1200 Austin, Grace B., et al. "Women in Dentistry and Medicine: Attitudinal Survey of Educational Experience." JOURNAL OF DENTAL EDUCATION 37 (November 1973): 11-17.

Subtle male prejudices make women feel "never quite accepted." Tally of questionnaires.

1201 Kingsley, Norman W. WOMAN: AN ORATION DELIVERED BEFORE THE AMERICAN ACADEMY OF DENTAL SCIENCE. Boston: Thomas Todd, 1883. 20 p. Pamph.

The author argues that "woman's sphere" fits her for being an assistant even though contemporary records indicate she was a successful practitioner in the 1890s.

1202 Kinsler, Miriam S. "The American Woman Dentist. A Brief Historical Review from 1855 through 1968." BULLETIN OF THE HISTORY OF DENTISTRY 17 (December 1969): 25-31.

1203 Linn, Erwin. "Women Dentists: Some Circumstances about Their Choice of a Career." JOURNAL OF THE CANADIAN DENTAL ASSOCIATION, no. 10 (1972), pp. 50-55.

See also 1155.

c. MEDICINE AND PSYCHIATRY

i. Sources

The American Medical Women's Association issues the monthly JOURNAL as well as material on medicine as a career for women and reports of its activities relating to abortion, drug abuse, day care centers, the Equal Rights Amendment, and other areas.

Professional organizations such as the American Psychological Association and the American Psychiatric Association maintain task forces on women and issue biographical directories of their members (see 1204 and 1205 below). Several of these, as well as the independent Association of Women in Psychology, issue newsletters.

1204 American Psychiatric Association. BIOGRAPHICAL DIRECTORY OF FELLOWS AND MEMBERS. 7th ed. New York: R.R. Bowker Co., 1977. Updated irregularly.

1205 American Psychological Association. BIOGRAPHICAL DIRECTORY. Washington, D.C.: 1948-- . Annual.

A who's who of psychology. Supersedes YEARBOOK.

For collections on women in medicine see Ash and Calvert, page 3.

ii. Bibliographies

1206 BIBLIOGRAPHY OF THE HISTORY OF MEDICINE. Bethesda, Md.: National Library of Medicine, 1965-- . Annual, with quinquennial cumulations.

1207 Chaff, Sandra L., et al., comps. WOMEN IN MEDICINE: A BIBLIOGRAPHY OF THE LITERATURE ON WOMEN PHYSICIANS. Metuchen, N.J.: Scarecrow Press, 1977. 1136 p.

International in scope. Covers statistical data as well as history of physicians in general and as individuals.

1208 Morais, Herbert M. "Bibliography: A Guide to the Literature." In his THE HISTORY OF THE NEGRO IN MEDICINE, pp. 281-304. Association for the Study of Negro Life and History. International Library of Negro Life and History Series. New York: Publishers Co., 1967. xiv, 317 p. Illus.

Some material on women.

1209 U.S. Library of Congress. Division of Bibliography. "Women as

Physicians in the United States." Compiled by Ann D. Brown. Washington, D.C.: Government Printing Office, 1940. 32 p. Typed.

iii. References

1210 Beshiri, Patricia. THE WOMAN DOCTOR: HER CONCERN IN MODERN MEDICINE. New York: Cowles Book, 1969. xiv, 240 p.

Study of women's current and future roles in medicine. Overview of medical schools, internship, residence and choice of specialty, with chapters on management of motherhood, postgraduate work, and continuing education.

1211 Blackwell, Elizabeth. ESSAY ON MEDICAL·SOCIOLOGY. 2 vols. London: Ernest Dell, 1892.

Presents the thinking of America's first woman doctor on a wide range of subjects related to medicine, such as medical responsibility, prostitution, and women's influence in the profession.

1212 Blake, John B. "Women and Medicine in Anti-Bellum America." BULLETIN OF THE HISTORY OF AMERICA 2 (1965): 99-123.

1213 Calhoun, M.L., et al. "Women in Veterinary Medicine." CORNELL VETERINARIAN 66 (October 1976): 455-75.

Deals with the history of women in veterinary medicine. A sequel by K.A. Haupt et al. (vol. 67 [January 1977], 1-23), deals with their current status and possible future.

1214 Dykman, Roscoe A., and Stalnaker, John M. "Survey of Women Physicians Graduating from Medical Schools 1925-1940." JOURNAL OF MEDICAL EDUCATION 32 (1957): 3-38.

1215 Ehrenreich, Barbara, and English, Deirdre. WITCHES, MIDWIVES AND NURSES: A HISTORY OF WOMEN HEALERS. Glass Mountain Pamphlet, no. 1. Old Westbury, N.Y.: Feminist Press, 1973. 48 p. Biblio.

Of particular interest is "Women and the Rise of the American Medical Profession," pages 21 ff. A condensed version is available from Feminist Press.

1216 Haseltine, Florence, and Yaw, Yvonne. WOMAN DOCTOR. Boston: Houghton Mifflin Co., 1976. 336 p.

Describes the struggle in a male-dominated profession.

1217 Howell, Mary [Campbell, Margaret A.] "WHY WOULD A GIRL GO INTO MEDICINE?" MEDICAL EDUCATION IN THE UNITED STATES: A GUIDE FOR WOMEN. 3d ed. Old Westbury, N.Y.: Feminist Press, 1973. 114 p.

Gives unpleasant facts about medical school education based on a survey of women medical students. Available from Clearinghouse for Women's Studies, Feminist Press.

1218 Hurd-Mead, Kate C. MEDICAL WOMEN OF AMERICA: A SHORT HISTORY OF THE PIONEER MEDICAL WOMEN OF AMERICA AND A FEW OF THEIR COLLEAGUES IN ENGLAND. New York: Froben, 1933. 95 p.

First integrated view of American women doctors. Provides material on their training and on their work as practitioners, teachers, and researchers in various specialities.

1219 Jacobi, Mary P. "Women in Medicine." In WOMAN'S WORK IN AMERICA, edited by Annie N. Meyer, chap. 7. New York: Henry Holt, 1891. Tables. Reprint. American Women: Images and Realities series. New York: Arno Press, 1972.

History of women in American medicine includes discussion of their education, discrimination practiced against them, and legislative support. Appendix lists medical scholarship produced by women 1872-90.

1220 Litoff, Judy B. AMERICAN MIDWIVES: 1860 TO THE PRESENT. Contributions in Medical History, no. 1. Westport, Conn.: Greenwood Press, 1978. xi, 197 p.

1221 Lopate, Carol. WOMEN IN MEDICINE. Josiah Macy Foundation Series. Baltimore: Johns Hopkins University Press, 1968. xvii, 204 p. Tables.

Inquires into aspects of women doctors' training and life. Deals with counseling, dropouts, specialization, marriage, and so on. Appendix contains statistics through 1965.

1222 THE MALE MIDWIFE AND THE FEMALE DOCTOR: THE GYNECOLOGY CONTROVERSY IN NINETEENTH-CENTURY AMERICA. New York: Arno Press, 1974. Variously paged. Illus.

Anthology of addresses, essays, and lectures during the period 1820-53.

1223 Noall, Clair. GUARDIANS OF THE HEARTH: UTAH'S PIONEER MIDWIVES AND WOMEN DOCTORS. Bountiful, Utah: Horizon, 1974. 189 p.

1224 Smith, Elizabeth C. "Heirs to Trotula: Early Women Physicians in the United States." NEW YORK STATE JOURNAL OF MEDICINE 77 (June 1977): 1142-65.

Material on regional hospitals and medical colleges accepting and training women doctors.

1225 Spieler, Carolyn, ed. WOMEN IN MEDICINE, 1976. New York: Josiah Macy, Jr., Foundation, 1977. viii, 127 p. Tables, biblio.

Report of the Macy conference indicates that the increasing numbers of women in medicine are viewed as a force for radical change.

1226 Walsh, Mary R. DOCTORS WANTED: NO WOMEN NEED APPLY: SEXUAL BARRIERS IN THE MEDICAL PROFESSION, 1835-1975. New Haven, Conn.: Yale University Press, 1977. 303 p. Illus.

1227 "Women in Psychiatry and Medicine." AMERICAN JOURNAL OF PSYCHIATRY 43 (October 1973): special section.

Data on, and training of, women psychiatrists, and sources of conflict in the woman medical student. Reprints are available from the JOURNAL.

1228 Wrenn, Marie-Claude. "YOU'RE THE ONLY ONE HERE WHO DOESN'T LOOK LIKE A DOCTOR": PORTRAIT OF A WOMAN SURGEON. New York: Thomas Y. Crowell, 1977. 240 p.

Composite study.

See also 1155; chapter 8, section C.I.b.

d. NURSING

i. Sources, Bibliographies

The National League for Nursing is a primary source for information on nursing and nursing education, as well as health planning and action. It issues an annual catalog of its publications and a monthly newsletter that includes information on employment, education, and legislation. The American Nurses Association is another source of information.

1229 American Nurses Association. THE NATION'S NURSES: 1972. INVENTORY OF REGISTERED NURSES. Prepared by Aleda V. Roth, and Alice R. Walden. Kansas City, Mo.: 1974. 125 p. Illus., charts, tables. Paper.

Comprehensive statistical information. Ongoing updates.

1230 CUMULATIVE INDEX TO NURSING LITERATURE AND ALLIED HEALTH LITERATURE: INCLUDING A LIST OF SUBJECT HEADINGS. Glendale, Calif.: Seventh Day Adventist Hospital Association, 1956-- . 5 bimonthly issues, annual cumulation.

Indexes all English-language periodicals related to nursing. Includes a special section on book reviews, pamphlets, and audiovisual materials.

1231 INTERNATIONAL NURSING INDEX. New York: American Journal of Nursing Co. in cooperation with the National Library of Medicine, 1966-- . Quarterly, annual cumulations.

Computer-produced international listing includes a wide variety of published materials, among them books, articles, and doctoral dissertations. Indexes periodical articles.

1232 NURSING STUDIES INDEX: AN ANNOTATED GUIDE TO REPORTED STUDIES, RESEARCH IN PROGRESS: RESEARCH METHODS AND HISTORICAL MATERIALS IN PERIODICALS, BOOKS AND PAMPHLETS, PUBLISHED IN ENGLISH. Prepared by Yale School of Nursing Index Staff. 4 vols. Philadelphia: J.B. Lippincott Co., 1963-72.

By subject.

1233 Thompson, Alice McC., comp. A BIBLIOGRAPHY OF NURSING LITERATURE, 1859-1960, WITH AN HISTORICAL INTRODUCTION. London: Library Association for the Royal College of Nursing and National Council of Nurses of the United Kingdom in Association with King Edward's Hospital Fund for London, 1968. xx, 132 p.

Guide to periodicals and monographs. Though British-produced, it includes many items relating to the profession in America.

1234 U.S. Health Resources Development Bureau. Division of Nursing. SOURCEBOOK, NURSING PERSONNEL WITH BIBLIOGRAPHY. Compiled by Helen H. Hudson and Margaret D. McCarthy. Washington, D.C.: 1975. vi, 239 p. Illus.

Available from the National Technical Information Service, Springfield, Virginia 22151.

For a further listing of nursing organizations see 403.

ii. References

1235 American Nurses Association. FACTS ABOUT NURSING. Kansas City, Mo.: 1976. 237 p. Illus., charts, tables. Paper.

Valuable source of statistics pertaining to distribution of

registered nurses, nursing education, economic status, allied nursing personnel and information on organizations. Includes only new and updated material.

1236 Ashkenas, Thais L. AIDS AND DETERRENTS TO THE PERFORMANCE OF ASSOCIATE DEGREE CANDIDATES IN NURSING. League Exchange, no. 99. New York: National League for Nursing, 1975. 168 p.

Available from the league.

1237 Ashley, Jo Ann. HOSPITALS, PATERNALISM, AND THE ROLE OF THE NURSE. New York: Teachers College Press, Columbia University, 1976. xi, 158 p. Biblio. Paper.

Views nursing as a profession rooted in exploitation.

1238 Barton, Clara. "Woman in Philanthropy: Work of the Red Cross Society." In WOMEN'S WORK IN AMERICA, edited by Annie N. Meyer, chap 18. New York: Henry Holt, 1891. Reprint. American Women: Images and Realities series. New York: Arno Press, 1972.

Founder of the Red Cross recounts her work with the organization. Includes articles formulated at the Geneva Conference of 1863.

1239 Boganno, M.F., et al. "The Short-run Supply of Nurses' Time." JOURNAL OF HUMAN RESOURCES 9 (Winter 1974): 80-94.

Employment of married nurses depends upon the ratio of husband's earnings to nurses' wage rate.

1240 Bullough, Bonnie, and Bullough, Vern. THE EMERGENCE OF MODERN NURSING. 2d ed. New York: Macmillan Co., 1969. vii, 277 p. Illus., biblio.

Gives background from primitive times and details the development of nursing in America.

1241 Cheney, Ednah D. "Woman in Philanthropy--Care of the Sick." In WOMEN'S WORK IN AMERICA, edited by Annie N. Meyer, chap. 13. New York: Henry Holt, 1891. Reprint. American Women: Images and Realities series. New York: Arno Press, 1972.

Discusses training schools for nurses from colonial times through the nineteenth century. Sketchy.

1242 Dulles, Foster R. THE AMERICAN RED CROSS: A HISTORY. New York: Harper & Brothers, 1950. ix, 554 p.

Chapters 2 and 3 deal with Clara Barton's work. Role of women is implicit throughout.

1243 Flanagan, Lydia, comp. ONE STRONG VOICE: THE STORY OF THE AMERICAN NURSES ASSOCIATION. Kansas City, Mo.: American Nurses Association, 1976. xiii, 692 p. Illus., biblio.

History of nursing in America 1776-1976. Includes speeches by association presidents which reflect contemporary nursing issues. The appendix reviews association activities and significant events 1896-1976, biographical sketches of executive directors, and association stand on National Health Insurance and related issues.

1244 Grissum, Marlene, and Spengler, Carol. WOMAN POWER AND HEALTH CARE. Boston: Little, Brown and Co., 1976. xv, 314 p.

Focuses on similarity between nurse's status and that of women in general, and need for change for both.

1245 Holland, Mary A.G., comp. OUR ARMY NURSES: INTERESTING SKETCHES AND PHOTOGRAPHS OF OVER 100 OF THE NOBLE WOMEN WHO SERVED IN HOSPITALS AND BATTLEFIELDS DURING THE LATE CIVIL WAR, 1861-1865. Boston: Lounsberry, Nichols & Worth, 1897. 600 p. Illus.

Sentimentally framed, but much primary material in first-person narratives.

1246 Hott, Jacqueline R. "Nursing and Politics: The Struggle Inside the Nursing Body Politic." NURSING FORUM 15 (1976): 325-40.

This article and the following one by Diane J. Powell--"The Struggle Outside Nursing's Body Politic" (pp. 341-62)--focus on major issues currently facing the nursing profession.

1247 Hughes, Everett C., et al. TWENTY THOUSAND NURSES TELL THEIR STORY. A Report on Studies of Nursing Functions Sponsored by the American Nurses Association. Philadelphia: J.B. Lippincott Co., 1958. xi, 280 p. Biblio.

Professional and personal considerations at mid-century.

1248 Knopf, Lucille, comp. RN'S ONE AND FIVE YEARS AFTER GRADUATION. New York: National League for Nursing, 1975. 113 p. Tables.

Presents material on employment patterns, marriage, professional fields, and education. The appendix includes relevant data from earlier study. Available from the league.

1249 Knopf, Lucille, et al., comps. PRACTICAL NURSES FIVE YEARS AFTER GRADUATION: NURSE CAREER-PATTERN STUDY. New York: National League for Nursing, 1970. 76 p.

Employment, education follow-up of three thousand nurses. Available from the league.

1250 Lewis, Edith P., comp. CHANGING PATTERNS OF NURSING PRACTICE. Contemporary Nursing Series. New York: American Journal of Nursing, 1971. x, 332 p. Tables, biblio. Paper.

Anthology deals with the need for changing roles and relationships, and for new roles in a profession dominated traditionally by women.

1251 Livermore, Mary A. MY STORY OF THE WAR: A WOMAN'S NARRATIVE OF FOUR YEARS PERSONAL EXPERIENCE AS NURSE IN THE UNION ARMY, AND IN RELIEF WORK AT HOME, CAMPS, AND AT THE FRONT DURING THE WAR OF THE REBELLION. Hartford, Conn.: A.D. Worthington, 1889. 700 p. Illus. Reprint. American Women: Images and Realities series. New York: Arno, 1972.

1252 National League for Nursing. CURRENT ISSUES IN NURSING EDUCATION. New York: 1974. 51 p. Pamph.

Contains papers presented at eleventh conference of Council of Baccalaureate and Higher Degree Programs, 1974. Topics deal with preparation of nurses and health nurse clinicians as well as minority women in nursing.

1253 Poole, Ernest. NURSES ON HORSEBACK. New York: Macmillan Co., 1933. viii, 168 p.

Frontier nursing service.

1254 Roberts, Mary M. AMERICAN NURSING: HISTORY AND INTERPRETATION. New York: Macmillan Co., 1954. 688 p. Illus.

Standard twentieth-century history.

1255 Safier, Gwendolyn. CONTEMPORARY AMERICAN LEADERS IN NURSING: AN ORAL HISTORY. New York: McGraw-Hill Book Co., 1977. vii, 392 p. Biblio.

Seventeen interviews with leaders in nursing education, administration, research, pediatrics, and public health.

1256 Shoemaker, Sister M. THE HISTORY OF NURSE MIDWIFERY IN THE UNITED STATES. Master's thesis, Catholic University of America, 1947.

1257 Staupers, Mabel K. NO TIME FOR PREJUDICE: A STORY OF INTEGRATION OF NEGROES IN NURSING IN UNITED STATES. New York: Macmillan Co., 1961. xiii, 206 p. Biblio.

Short history of black women as nurses precedes history of National Association of Colored Graduate Nurses. Account of struggles for integration within armed forces and American Nurses Association.

1258 Stewart, Isabel M., and Austin, Anne L. A HISTORY OF NURSING FROM ANCIENT TO MODERN TIMES. 5th ed. New York: G.P. Putnam's Sons, 1962. 516 p. Illus., biblio.

See especially chapter 8, "Nursing in the New World from Early to Modern Times," and chapter 11, "The United States of America."

1259 Thoms, Adah B., comp. PATHFINDERS: A HISTORY OF THE PROGRESS OF COLORED GRADUATE NURSES . . . AND THE BIOGRAPHIES OF MANY NURSES. New York: Kay Printing, 1929. xiv, 240 p.

A short history of black women in nursing precedes a listing of hospitals and biographies of graduates, black nurses in World War I, development of black health centers, missionary nurses, and founding of the National Association of Colored Graduate Nurses.

5. Law

a. SOURCES, BIBLIOGRAPHIES

Various associations serve as sources of information on women in the legal profession. Women in the Legal Profession, American Association of Law Schools; Women's Caucus, Law Students Division, American Bar Association; the Committee on Women in Legal Education, of the Association of American Law Schools; the National Association of Women Lawyers; and the Women's Caucus of the National Lawyers Guild are among them.

1260 DIRECTORY OF WOMEN LAW GRADUATES AND ATTORNEYS IN THE UNITED STATES. Edited by Lee Ellen Ford. Butler, Ind.: Ford Associates, 1977-- . Biennial.

1261 INDEX TO LEGAL PERIODICALS. New York: H.W. Wilson Co.,

American Association of Law Libraries, 1908-- . Monthly. Triennial cumulations.

b. REFERENCES

1262 Bittenbender, Ida M. "Woman and the Law." In WOMEN'S WORK IN AMERICA, edited by Annie N. Meyer, chap. 9. New York: Henry Holt, 1891. Reprint. American Women: Images and Realities series. New York: Arno Press, 1972.

Nineteenth-century legal practice by women.

1263 Epstein, Cynthia F. "Women Lawyers and Their Professions: Inconsistency of Social Controls and Their Consequences for Professional Performances." Paper presented to the 64th Annual Meeting of the Sociological Association, September 4, 1969, at San Francisco, California. Mimeo. Reprinted in THE PROFESSIONAL WOMAN, edited by Athena Theodore, pp. 669-89. Cambridge, Mass.: Schenckman Publishing Co., 1971. Paper.

Institutional norms applied to women run counter to official male norms, making for ease in both communities but diminishing women's ambition to succeed.

1264 Fenten, D.X. MS-ATTORNEY. Philadelphia: Westminster, 1974. 160 p. Illus.

Examines discrimination against women, and training and qualifications for a career in law. Lists American law schools.

1265 Gelsincan, James, et al. "Women Attorneys and the Judiciary." DENVER LAW JOURNAL 52 (1975): 881-909.

Interactions during trials.

1266 Knight, H. "Women and the Legal Profession." CONTEMPORARY 103 (May 1913): 689-96.

1267 "Locked Out?" STUDENT LAWYER JOURNAL 16 (November 1970): special issue.

1268 Schwartz, Helene E. LAWYERING. New York: Farrar, Straus & Giroux, 1976. x, 308 p.

Personal narrative reveals prejudices of man-dominated profession.

1269 Timothy, Mary. JURY WOMAN. San Francisco: Glide, Emty, 1975.

276 p. Paper.

Report of a jurist during the trial of Angela Davis.

1270 "Women in the Law." JURIS DOCTOR: MAGAZINE FOR THE NEW LAWYER 2 (March 1972): special issue.

Articles on sexism in the law profession.

See also chapter 2, section C.2.c.

6. Library Sciences

a. BIBLIOGRAPHY, SOURCES

1271 American Library Association. ALA YEARBOOK. Chicago: 1975-- . Annual.

Includes some information on historical but more on current status of women librarians.

1272 ______. A BIOGRAPHICAL DIRECTORY OF LIBRARIANS IN THE UNITED STATES AND CANADA. Edited by Lee Ash, and B.A. Uhlendorf. 5th ed. Chicago: 1970. xviii, 1250 p.

Formerly WHO'S WHO IN LIBRARY SERVICE.

1273 AMERICAN LIBRARY DIRECTORY: A CLASSIFIED LIST OF LIBRARIES IN THE UNITED STATES AND CANADA WITH PERSONNEL AND STATISTICAL DATA. New York: R.R. Bowker Co., 1923-- . Biennial.

1274 LIBRARY LITERATURE: AN ANNOTATED INDEX OF CURRENT BOOKS, PAMPHLETS AND PERIODICAL LITERATURE RELATING TO THE LIBRARY PROFESSION. New York: H.W. Wilson Co., 1933-35-- .

Continuation of LIBRARY LITERATURE, 1921-32. By author and subject. Currently lists accessions of Educational Resources Information Center Clearinghouse.

See also 1278, 1282.

b. REFERENCES

Information on women librarians may be obtained from the Women's National Book Association.

1275 Frary, Carlyle J., and Learmont, Carol L. "Placements and Salaries;

1974: Promise or Illusion?" LIBRARY JOURNAL 100 (1 October 1975): 1767-74.

Based on statistical information.

1276 Guyton, Theodore L. UNIONIZATION: THE VIEWPOINT OF LIBRARIANS. Chicago: American Library Association, 1975. xiii, 204 p. Tables, biblio. Paper.

See especially chapter 4, "Sex and Marital Status."

1277 Josey, E.J. "Can Library Affirmative Action Succeed?" LIBRARY JOURNAL 100 (1 January 1975): 28-31.

Discusses minority groups in library work.

1278 LIBRARY JOURNAL 96 (September 1971): special issue. Biblio.

Presents material on women in academic libraries, including their legal status. Bibliography is annotated.

1279 Myers, Margaret, and Scarborough, Mayra, eds. WOMEN IN LIBRARIANSHIP: MELVIL'S RIB SYMPOSIUM. Proceedings of the Eleventh Annual Symposium Sponsored by the Alumni and the Faculty of Rutgers University Graduate School of Library Science. New Brunswick, N.J.: Bureau of Library and Information Science Research, Rutgers University Graduate School of Library Service, 1975. x, 112 p. Biblio.

Problems of discrimination facing librarians. Appendix includes federal laws and regulations having to do with discrimination in educational institutions.

1280 Schiller, Anita R. "The Disadvantaged Majority: Women Employed in Libraries." AMERICAN LIBRARIES 1 (April 1970): 345-49.

Discusses patterns of discrimination in administrative posts and wage levels and what can be done about them.

1281 Sellen, Betty-Carol, and Marshall, Joan K., eds. WOMEN IN A WOMAN'S PROFESSION: STRATEGIES & PROCEEDINGS OF THE PRECONFERENCE ON THE STATUS OF WOMEN IN LIBRARIANSHIP SPONSORED BY THE AMERICAN LIBRARY ASSOCIATION SOCIAL RESPONSIBILITIES ROUND TABLE TASK FORCE ON THE STATUS OF WOMEN. DOUGLASS COLLEGE, RUTGERS UNIVERSITY, JULY, 1974. New Brunswick, N.J.: American Library Association, 1974. 90 p. Biblio. Offset.

Contains material on discrimination; on workshops on self-image, education, and affirmative action, on career development; and on union organizing and tactics. Appends film listing.

1282 U.S. Bureau of Labor Statistics. LIBRARY MANPOWER: A STUDY OF SUPPLY AND DEMAND WITH SELECTED BIBLIOGRAPHY. Prepared by Anne S. Kahl and Mary I. Dela Vergue. Bulletin no. 1,852. Washington, D.C.: Government Printing Office, 1975. xi, 94 p. Tables, charts, biblio.

See especially chapter 1, "Current Manpower Situation." Available from the Superintendent of Documents.

7. Media

a. GENERAL

i. Sources

Professional organizations that may be helpful sources of information are Women in Communications, Media Women, Women on Words and Images, Women's Media Alliance, and Feminists on Children's Media. They variously issue monthly publications, newsletters, membership directories, statistical rundowns, and informational pamphlets.

1283 Beasley, Maurine, and Silver, Sheila, comps. WOMEN IN MEDIA: A DOCUMENTARY SOURCE BOOK. Washington, D.C.: Women's Institute for Freedom of the Press, 1977. viii, 198 p. Biblio. Paper.

Contains chapters on individual journalists, feminist publishers, and problems with monitoring of the media. Includes also guidelines, statement by Women's Institute regarding freedom of the press.

1284 MEDIA REPORT TO WOMEN INDEX/DIRECTORY. Washington, D.C.: Women's Institute for Freedom of the Press, 1972/73-- . Annual.

Annotated index to MEDIA REPORT TO WOMEN cumulates annually. Directory covers all feminist media including television, radio, periodicals, music, theater, art, women's collections, and so on. In addition, it lists texts of relevant laws, court decisions, and the like. It is updated completely each year.

1285 MEDIA-REVIEW DIGEST-MRD, PART I. Edited by Cynthia Rigg. Ann Arbor, Mich.: Pierian Press, 1974.

Subject index to film, filmstrip, and miscellaneous media includes some women. Lists also producers and distributors.

1286 National Organization for Women. Images of Women Committee. MEDIA REPORT TO WOMEN: A MONTHLY REPORT ON WHAT WOMEN ARE DOING AND THINKING ABOUT THE COMMUNICATIONS MEDIA AND RELATED MEDIA INFORMATION. Washington, D.C.: 1972/73-- . Monthly.

Volume 1 (1972-73) deals with discrimination in relation to radio license renewal, in press services, at the WASHINGTON POST, and in the status of women in book publishing; volume 2 (1974) deals with discrimination in advertising, the NEW YORK TIMES, in film, and with the possibilities of cable TV as a feminist communications medium; volume 2 contains first-person experiences of TV women and women in managerial positions, and material on feminist radio networks and video letters and the image of women in films.

ii. Bibliographies

1287 Blum, Eleanor. BASIC BOOKS IN THE MASS MEDIA: AN ANNOTATED SELECTED BOOKLIST COVERING BOOK PUBLISHERS, BROADCASTING, FILMS, NEWSPAPERS, MAGAZINES AND ADVERTISING. Urbana: University of Illinois Press, 1962. vi, 103 p.

Lists many primary sources, anthologies, and leads to further research for the "layman." Useful though dated.

1288 Love, Barbara J., ed. FOREMOST WOMEN IN COMMUNICATIONS: A BIBLIOGRAPHICAL REFERENCE WORK ON ACCOMPLISHED WOMEN IN BROADCASTING, PUBLISHING, ADVERTISING, PUBLIC RELATIONS, AND ALLIED PROFESSIONS. New York: Foremost Americans Publishing, in association with R.R. Bowker Co., 1970. xvii, 788 p.

Contains nearly eight thousand entries. Includes geographical and subject index.

iii. References

1289 Hole, Judith, and Levine, Ellen. "Media." In their REBIRTH OF FEMINISM, chap. 6. New York: Quadrangle, 1971.

Presents material on the image and status of women in the media, coverage of the women's movement, and feminist media.

1290 Strainchamps, Ethel R., ed. ROOMS WITH NO VIEW: A WOMAN'S GUIDE TO THE MAN'S WORLD OF THE MEDIA. New York: Harper & Row, 1974. xxvii, 333 p. Paper.

Controversial anthology on discrimination in publishing and television. For Media Women's Association.

See also 127.

b. JOURNALISM, BOOK PUBLISHING, ARCHIVES

i. Sources

Professional organizations that may be helpful are the National League of American Pen Women, American Newspaper Women's Club, National Federation of Press Women, and Women's National Press Club.

ii. References

1291 Boughner, Genevieve J. WOMEN IN JOURNALISM: A GUIDE TO THE OPPORTUNITIES AND A MANUAL OF THE TECHNIQUES OF WOMEN'S WORK FOR NEWSPAPERS AND MAGAZINES. New York: D. Appleton, 1926. xxi, 348 p. Biblio.

Analyzes historical role of women in certain positions only.

1292 Dickinson, Susan E. "Women in Journalism." In WOMAN'S WORK IN AMERICA, edited by Annie N. Meyer, chap. 6. New York: Henry Holt, 1891. Reprint. American Women: Images and Realities series. New York: Arno Press, 1972.

Woman journalist surveys women in the field from the Revolution to the end of the nineteenth century.

1293 Hudak, Leona M. EARLY AMERICAN WOMEN PRINTERS AND PUBLISHERS, 1639-1820. Metuchen, N.J.: Scarecrow Press, 1978. 835 p.

Includes bio-bibliographies of twenty-five women and appends a list about whom there is little information.

1294 Marzoff, Marion. UP FROM THE FOOTNOTE: A HISTORY OF WOMEN JOURNALISTS. New York: Hastings House, Publishers, 1977. x, 310 p.

Chronicles women journalists from before the Revolution to the present. Includes women in the media and women teachers of journalism.

1295 Penn, I. Garland. "Afro-American Women in Journalism." In his THE AFRO-AMERICAN PRESS AND ITS EDITORS, chap. 21. Springfield, Mass.: Willey, 1891. 565 p. Illus.

Biographical sketches of nineteenth-century black women editors.

1296 Ross, Ishbel. LADIES OF THE PRESS. New York: Harper, 1936.

622 p.

History of women in American journalism since colonial times. Part 4 discusses individual women in journalism in eleven cities and regions.

1297 Royall, Anne N. LETTERS FROM ALABAMA, 1817-1822. Biographical notes by Lucille Griffith. Southern Historical Publications, no. 14. University: University of Alabama Press, 1969. 292 p.

The letters of an early nineteenth-century journalist who began a successful career in her fifties.

1298 "Women in Archives." AMERICAN ARCHIVIST 36 (April 1973): special issue. Tables.

Status of woman as archivists, and the relation of the field to women's history and to the feminist movement.

c. RADIO, TELEVISION

American Women in Radio and Television issues information on women in these media.

1299 Gelfman, Judith S. WOMEN IN TELEVISION NEWS. New ed. New York: Columbia University Press, 1976. x, 186 p. Illus., tables, biblio.

Discusses problems of discrimination and how some women have overcome them. Based on interviews.

1300 Maple, Jessie. HOW TO BECOME A UNION CAMERAWOMAN: FILM-VIDEOTAPE. New York: L.J. Film Productions, 1977. 86 p. Biblio. Paper..

By the first black woman to join the union.

1301 U.S. Commission on Civil Rights. WINDOW DRESSING ON THE SET: WOMEN AND MINORITIES IN TELEVISION. A REPORT. Washington, D.C.: 1977. ix, 181 p. Tables, figs., biblio. Paper.

Includes material on the portrayal and employment of women and minorities; Federal Communication Commission regulations; and the commission's findings and recommendations.

See also 2070; chapter 9, section F.

8. Police Work, Military Service

a. POLICE WORK

The International Association of Women Police and the Police Foundation issue material on women in police work.

i. Bibliography

1302 Sherman, Marion, and Sherman, Lewis J., comps. "Bibliography on Policewomen: 1945-1972." LAW & ORDER 21 (March 1973): 80-83.

See also 1308.

ii. References

1303 Abrecht, Mary Ellen, with Stern, Barbara L. THE MAKING OF A WOMAN COP. New ed. New York: William Morrow & Co., 1976. 275 p.

First-person narrative.

1304 Bloch, Peter B., and Anderson, Deborah. POLICEWOMEN ON PATROL: FINAL REPORT. Washington, D.C.: Police Foundation, 1974. 76 p.

Compares assignments, performances and attitudes of policewomen with those of policemen. Available from the foundation.

1305 Cirile, Marie. DETECTIVE MARIE CIRILE: MEMOIRS OF A POLICE OFFICER. Garden City, N.Y.: Doubleday & Co., 1975. Illus. 222 p.

1306 Fleming, Alice. NEWS ON THE BEAT: WOMAN POWER IN THE POLICE FORCE. New York: Coward, McCann & Geoghegan, 1975. 224 p.

Reports experiences of women in the New York Police Department.

1307 Hamilton, Mary E. THE POLICEWOMAN: HER SERVICE AND IDEALS. New York: Frederick A. Stokes, 1924. xviii, 200 p. Reprint. Police in America series. New York: Arno Press, 1971.

1308 Hutzel, Eleonore L., assisted by MacGregor, Madeline L. THE POLICE WOMAN'S HANDBOOK. New York: Columbia University Press, 1933. vii, 303 p. Biblio.

1309 Milton, Catherine. WOMEN IN POLICING. Police Foundation Study. Washington, D.C.: Police Foundation, 1972. 96 p. Illus.

Available from the foundation.

1310 Owings, Chloe. WOMEN POLICE: A STUDY OF THE DEVELOPMENT AND STATUS OF THE WOMEN POLICE MOVEMENT. Montclair, N.J.: Patterson Smith, 1969. 337 p.

Details history of women in police work and discusses training for a police career.

1311 POLICE CHIEF 42 (April 1975): special issue.

Discusses female officers at work, their adjustment and status.

1312 Sullivan, Mary. MY DOUBLE LIFE. New York: Farrar & Rinehart, 1938. 302 p. Illus.

b. MILITARY SERVICE

1313 Binkin, Martin, and Bach, Shirley J. WOMEN AND THE MILITARY. Washington, D.C.: Brookings Institute, 1977. xii, 134 p. Tables, figs.

Includes historical overview and material on current polices, institutional attitudes, economic and social implications, military effectiveness, and proposals for optimum utilization of women.

1314 Goldman, Nancy. "The Changing Role of Women in the Armed Forces." In CHANGING WOMEN IN A CHANGING SOCIETY, edited by Joan Huber, pp. 130-49. Chicago: University of Chicago Press, 1973. Biblio.

1315 Heiman, Grover, Jr., and Myers, Virginia H. CAREERS FOR WOMEN IN UNIFORM. Philadelphia: J.B. Lippincott Co., 1971. 224 p.

Discusses training and opportunities.

1316 Hinton, Addie W., and Johnson, Kathryn M. TWO COLORED WOMEN WITH THE AMERICAN EXPEDITIONARY FORCES. Brooklyn: Brooklyn-Eagle, 1920. 256 p. Illus. Reprint. New York: AMS Press, 1971.

Welfare workers assigned by the YWCA to black troops in World War I observe a wide range of discriminatory practices.

1317 Treadwell, Mattie E. THE WOMAN'S ARMY CORPS. United States Army in World War II Special Studies. Washington, D.C.: Office of the Chief of Military History, Department of the Army, 1954. 841 p. Illus., charts.

Includes history of women in the military from 1776 through World War II, organization, growth in numbers, War Department policies relating to women, leadership of women. Appendix includes statistics on Women's Army Corps and bibliographical notes.

1318 "Women: The Recruiter's Last Resort." RECON 2 (September 1974): special issue.

Four case histories of one single and one married marine, and members of the U.S. Women's Army Corps and the U.S. Women's Air Force.

For collections having holdings relating to women in military service see Ash and Calvert, page 3.

9. Politics

a. SOURCES

Among the organizations that issue material on women's involvement in political activities are the Woman's Party; the Center for American Women and Politics; the League of Women Voters; the National Women's Political Caucus, which publishes also a newsletter; the Women's Lobby, which publishes the newsletter ALERT; and the major political parties.

1319 Theis, Paul A., and Henshaw, Edmund L., Jr., eds. WHO'S WHO IN AMERICAN POLITICS: A BIOGRAPHICAL DIRECTORY OF UNITED STATES POLITICAL LEADERS. New York: R.R. Bowker Co., 1967/68-- . Biennial.

See also 1328.

b. BIBLIOGRAPHIES

1320 Rutgers University. Eagleton Institute of Politics. Center for the American Woman and Politics. WOMEN IN PUBLIC OFFICE: A BIBLIOGRAPHICAL DIRECTORY AND STATISTICAL ANALYSIS. 2d ed. Project director, Kathy Stanwick. Metuchen, N.J.: Scarecrow Press, 1978. 600 p. Tables, biblio. Offset.

See also 1187, 1328.

c. REFERENCES

1321 Amundsen, Kirsten. A NEW LOOK AT THE SILENT MAJORITY: WOMEN AND AMERICAN DEMOCRACY. Englewood Cliffs, N.J.: Prentice-Hall, 1977. xiii, 172 p. Paper.

"New findings reveal . . . the superficiality and the token nature of the changes that have come about in recent years" since the writing of THE SILENCED MAJORITY (see 1322).

1322 ______. THE SILENCED MAJORITY: WOMEN AND AMERICAN DEMOCRACY. Englewood Cliffs, N.J.: Prentice-Hall, 1971. viii, 184 p. Tables. Paper.

Analyzes myths and ideologies that make American women politically ineffectual and seriously weaken our democracy.

1323 Beecher, Henry W. WOMAN'S INFLUENCE IN POLITICS. Boston: R.F. Wallcut, 1860. 18 p. Pamph.

Negative appraisal.

1324 Chamberlain, Hope. A MINORITY OF MEMBERS: WOMEN IN THE UNITED STATES CONGRESS. New York: Praeger Publishers, 1973. ix, 374 p.

Contains biographical sketches. The appendix includes a list of women in Congress 1917-73.

1325 Diamond, Irene. SEX ROLES IN THE STATE HOUSE: New Haven, Conn.: Yale University Press, 1977. xii, 214 p. Tables, figs.

Claims that "sex differentiation decreases as competition for political office increases."

1326 Evans, Ernestine. "Women in the Washington Scene." CENTURY MAGAZINE 106 (August 1923): 507-17.

Presents biographical sketches of women active in Washington in the early twenties.

1327 Githens, Marianna, and Prestage, Jewel C., eds. A PORTRAIT OF MARGINALITY: THE POLITICAL BEHAVIOR OF THE AMERICAN WOMAN. New York: David McKay Co., 1977. xvii, 428 p. Tables. Paper.

Includes material on problems involved, characteristics of women active in politics, and black women in politics.

1328 Gruberg, Marion. WOMEN IN AMERICAN POLITICS: AN ASSESSMENT AND SOURCE-BOOK. Oshkosh, Wis.: Academia, 1968. viii, 336 p. Illus., tables, biblio.

Author traces and explains women's role in politics since 1920. Provides statistics.

1329 Jaquette, Jane S., ed. WOMEN IN POLITICS. New York: John Wiley & Sons, 1974. xxxvii, 367 p. Illus.

Anthology. Part 1 deals with American women, part 2 with women of other countries.

1330 Kerber, Linda. "The Republican Mother: Women and the Enlightenment--An American Perspective." AMERICAN QUARTERLY 28 (Summer 1976): 187-205.

Mothers of the early republic, though not citizens, filled a political role.

1331 Kirkpatrick, Jeane J. THE NEW PRESIDENTIAL ELITE: MEN AND WOMEN IN NATIONAL POLITICS. New York: Russell Sage Foundation and The Twentieth Century Fund, 1976. xix, 605 p. Tables, figs.

Part 2 deals with the personal and political characteristics of women and their problems in the power structure.

1332 _____. POLITICAL WOMAN. New York: Basic Books, 1974, xiii, 274 p.

Major study of women holding congressional office. Sponsored by Center for the American Woman and Politics of the Eagleton Institute of Politics at Rutgers.

1333 McCourt, Kathleen. WORKING CLASS WOMEN AND GRASS-ROOTS POLITICS. Bloomington: Indiana University Press, 1977. v, 256 p. Tables, biblio. Offset.

Based on studies made of a previously neglected segment of women living in Chicago's southwest side.

1334 Martin, George M. "American Women and Paternalism." ATLANTIC MONTHLY 133 (June 1924): 744-53.

Libertarian maintains that action groups at national level, though effective politically, serve to maintain herd (paternalistic) attitudes more among women than among men because of historical conditioning.

1335 Parker, J.A. ANGELA DAVIS: THE MAKING OF A REVOLUTIONARY. New Rochelle, N.Y.: Arlington House, 1973. 272 p.

Discusses Davis's role in the contemporary black movement as a symbol and heroine.

1336 Republican Party. National Committee, 1960-1964. THE HISTORY OF WOMEN IN REPUBLICAN CONVENTIONS AND WOMEN IN THE REPUBLICAN NATIONAL COMMITTEE. Compiled by Josephine L. Good. Washington, D.C.: 1963. 58 p.

1337 Roosevelt, Eleanor, and Hickok, Lorena B. LADIES OF COURAGE. New York: E.P. Putnam's Sons, 1954. vii, 512 p.

Gives an account of women's political activities after the passage of Nineteenth Amendment, focusing on the Roosevelt administration. Contains a political profile of Eleanor Roosevelt by coauthor Hickok. Includes "How to Break into Politics."

1338 Tolchin, Susan J. WOMEN IN CONGRESS, 1917-1977. Washington, D.C.: Government Printing Office, 1976. iii, 112 p. Illus.

1339 Tolchin, Susan J., and Tolchin, Martin. CLOUT: WOMANPOWER AND POLITICS. New York: Coward, McCann & Geoghegan, 1974. 320 p.

Relates interviews with women who have succeeded in politics. The appendix contains suggestions on how to do the same.

1340 Young, Louise M. "Women's Place in American Politics: The Historical Perspective." JOURNAL OF POLITICS 30 (August 1976): 295-335.

d. ORAL HISTORY

1341 Bancroft Library. Regional Oral History Office. CALIFORNIA POLITICAL LEADERS, 1920-1970. In WOMEN IN POLITICS ORAL HISTORY PROJECT, unit 2.

Partially completed project based on interviews with women active in politics between the passage of the Nineteenth Amendment and the current women's movement. Two interviews presently bound and available in manuscript repositories are:

Number 58. Bernice H. May. A NATIVE DAUGHTER'S LEADERSHIP IN PUBLIC AFFAIRS. 2 vols. paged consecutively. Berkeley: Regional

History Office, Bancroft Library, University of California, 1975. xiii, 540 p.

Number 69. Malca Chall. CLARA SHIRPSER: ONE WOMAN'S ROLE IN DEMOCRATIC PARTY POLITICS: NATIONAL, CALIFORNIA, AND LOCAL, 1950-1973. 2 vols. paged consecutively. Berkeley: Regional History Office, Bancroft Library, University of California, 1975. vii, 671 p.

10. Religion and Related Fields

a. SOURCES

Many sources of information on the status of the women in church and in church-related activities exist. Among them are yearbooks and journals issued by various denominations. Women's caucuses within denominations frequently issue newsletters relating to general issues that affect them, as well as to their activities. For a partial listing of these groups see entry 417. Among nonsectarian organizations that issue material specifically concerned with women in religion are the American Academy of Religion's Task Force on the Status of Women, Church Employed Women, the International Association of Ministers, the joint Committee of Organizations Concerned about the Status of Women in the Church, and the National Assembly of Women Religious. The Working Conference of Women in Theology and National Organization of Women issue packets on religion.

Historical material relating to women in religious activities may be gleaned from church histories and histories of religious-utopian societies, such as the Church of the Latter Day Saints and the Shakers, and from missionary records.

Some current periodicals on the subject of women in religion are the WOMAN'S PULPIT, LILITH and EXPONENT II.

For a listing of manuscript collections see Ash and Calvert, page 3.

See also 1343.

b. BIBLIOGRAPHIES

Bibliographical material is available from the Women's History Research Center.

1342 Bass, Dorothy, comp. "American Women in Church and Society: 1607-1920." Auburn Studies in Education, publication no. 2, Auburn Program. New York: Union Theological Seminary, 1973. 36 p. Mimeo.

Partially annotated. Focuses on the history of women in religion, chiefly Protestantism, but covers a wide range in general categories as well.

1343 Farians, Elizabeth, comp. "Selected Bibliography of Women and Religion, 1965-1972." Cincinnati: 1973. 29 p. Mimeo.

Includes printed matter, films, and organizations. Available from Farians, 6125 Webbland Place, Cincinnati, Ohio 42513.

1344 Fischer, Clare B. "Woman: A Theological Perspective." Berkeley, Calif.: Center for Women and Religion of the Graduate Theological Union, 1975. 70 p. Mimeo.

Wide-ranging collection extends theology to include witchcraft, goddess worship, and other areas. Being updated and revised. Write Center for Women and Religion, Graduate Theological Union, 2465 LeConte Avenue, Berkeley, California 94709.

See also 5, 314, 1369.

c. REFERENCES

1345 Borromeo, Sister Charles. THE NEW NUNS. New York: New American Library, 1967. vi, 216 p.

Catholic sisters dealing with changes in their life-styles and community relations.

1346 Bowles, Ada C. "Woman in the Ministry." In WOMAN'S WORK IN AMERICA, edited by Annie N. Meyer, chap. 8. New York: Henry Holt, 1891. Reprint. American Women: Images and Realities series. New York: Arno Press, 1972.

Traces women in American ministries since Anne Hutchinson. Argues their "special fitness."

1347 Calvo, Janis. "Quaker Women Ministers in Nineteenth-Century America." QUAKER HISTORY 63 (Autumn 1974): 75-93.

1348 Cavert, Inez M. WOMEN IN AMERICAN CHURCH LIFE. New York: Friendship, 1947. 93 p.

1349 "The Church and Women's Liberation." DIALOG 10 (Spring 1971): 93-139.

1350 Cooke, George W. UNITARIANISM IN AMERICA: A HISTORY OF ITS ORIGIN AND DEVELOPMENT. Boston: American Unitarian Association, 1902. xi, 463 p. Illus. Reprint. St. Clair Shores, Mich.: Scholarly Press, 1969.

Note chapter 13, "The Woman's Alliance and Its Predecessors"; chapter 16 includes "The Enfranchisement of Women"; and chapter 18 "Work of Unitarian Women in Education."

1351 Culver, Elsie T. WOMEN IN THE WORLD OF RELIGION. New York: Doubleday & Co., 1967. xx, 340 p. Biblio.

Good background. Considerable material on American women. Note chapter 10 on witches.

1352 Desroches, Henri. THE AMERICAN SHAKERS: FROM NEO-CHRISTIANITY TO PRESOCIALISM. Amherst: University of Massachusetts Press, 1971. 357 p. Charts.

Scholarly study underlines the lack of sexism in the sect which produced the document "The Motherhood of God."

1353 Ebaugh, Helen R.F. OUT OF THE CLOISTER: A STUDY OF ORGANIZATIONAL DILEMMAS. Austin: University of Texas Press, 1977. 208 p. Tables, illus.

Sociological analysis of Catholic orders for women by one-time religious.

1354 Elliott, Errol T. QUAKERS ON THE AMERICAN FRONTIER: A HISTORY OF THE WESTWARD MISSIONS, SETTLEMENTS, AND DEVELOPMENT OF FRIENDS ON THE AMERICAN CONTINENT. Richmond, Ind.: Friends United, 1969. 434 p. Illus., charts, biblio.

Notes women's contributions throughout.

1355 Ermarth, Margaret S. ADAM'S FRACTURED RIB. Philadelphia: Fortress Press, 1970. xvi, 159 p.

Discusses women's role and status principally in the Lutheran Church.

1356 Farians, Elizabeth. THE DOUBLE CROSS: WRITINGS ON WOMEN AND RELIGION. Cincinnati: 1973. Variously paged.

Collection of writings by woman who has been head of NOW's Ecumenical Task Force on Women and Religion and also of the Joint Committees of Organizations Concerned About the Status of Women in the Church.

1357 Fischer, Clare B., et al., eds. WOMEN IN A STRANGE LAND: SEARCH FOR A NEW IMAGE. Philadelphia: Fortress Press, 1975. x, 133 p. Biblio.

Discusses feminists' attempts to modify sexist attitudes in the church.

1358 Gearhart, Sally, and Johnson, William R. LOVING WOMEN, LOVING MEN: GAY LIBERATION AND THE CHURCH. San Francisco: Glide, 1975.

Anthology. Largely by males but perceptive discussions of church policies in relation to homosexuality.

1359 Gillard, John T. COLORED CATHOLICS IN THE UNITED STATES. Baltimore: Josphite Press, 1941. x, 298 p. Tables, biblio.

Presents scattered information on black sisters.

1360 Gilman, Charlotte P. HIS RELIGION AND HERS: A STUDY OF OUR FATHERS AND THE WORK OF OUR MOTHERS. New York: Century, 1923. xi, 300 p.

Concludes that men's negative characteristics will inhibit development of true religion until woman effects changes within herself.

1361 Hageman, Alice L., ed. SEXIST RELIGION AND WOMEN IN THE CHURCH: NO MORE SILENCE! New York: Association Press, 1974. 221 p.

Written in collaboration with the Women's Caucus of Harvard Divintiy School.

Discusses black, Jewish, and subculture women in religion, women in missions, and general topics.

1362 Hunter, Fannie MacD. WOMEN PREACHERS. Dallas: Berarach Printing, 1905. 100 p.

1363 Lee, Luther. WOMEN'S RIGHT TO PREACH THE GOSPEL: A SERMON PREACHED AT THE ORDINATION OF REV. MISS ANTOINETTE L. BROWN, AT SOUTH BUTTE, WAYNE COUNTRY, NEW YORK, SEPT. 15, 1853. Syracuse, N.Y.: 1853. 22 p. Pamph.

Argues that the Bible supports ordination of women.

1364 Moore, R. Lawrence. "The Spiritualist Medium: A Study of Female Professionalism in Victorian America." AMERICAN QUARTERLY 27 (May 1975): 200-21.

Views the spiritualist medium's profession as a socially acceptable form of female passivity and frailty.

1365 Proctor, Priscilla, and Proctor, William. WOMEN IN THE PULPIT: IS GOD AN EQUAL OPPORTUNITY EMPLOYER? Garden City, N.Y.: Doubleday & Co., 1976. 176 p.

Presents points of view of thirty feminist spiritual leaders.

1366 Ruether, Rosemary. "Women's Liberation in Historical and Theological Perspective." SOUNDINGS 53 (Winter 1970): 363-73.

1367 Verdesi, Elizabeth H. IN BUT STILL OUT: WOMEN IN THE CHURCH. Philadelphia: Westminster Press, 1976. 218 p. Biblio.

Focuses on the Presbyterian Church.

1368 Willard, Frances E. WOMEN IN THE PULPIT. Chicago: Women's Temperance Publication Association, 1888. 173 p.

Head of the Women's Christian Temperance Union believes there should be more women in ministry.

1369 "Woman: New Dimensions." THEOLOGICAL STUDIES 36 (December 1975): special issue.

International in scope. Includes a bibliographical essay on recent literature.

See also 768.

11. Sciences, Engineering, and Aeronautics

a. SOURCES

Most professional and academic organizations relating to the sciences have established women's caucuses from which information on status and activities may be obtained. A selected listing of professional organizations is available in 403 and 417. A fairly complete listing of academic caucuses is available from the Project on the Status and Education of Women.

The Association of Women in Science issues a newsletter and a registry of its members. The Society of Women Engineers sends out printed material on statistics relating to employment and educational issues, and reprints of articles in a variety of publications upon request.

1370 AMERICAN MEN AND WOMEN OF SCIENCE: A BIOGRAPHICAL

DIRECTORY. Edited by Jacques Cattell Press. New York: R.R. Bowker Co., 1906-- . Irregular.

To 1970 this was entitled AMERICAN MEN OF SCIENCE. . . .Since 1970 (12th ed.) issued in two sections: one on biological and physical sciences, the other on behavioral sciences.

1371 Young, Margaret L., et al., eds. SCIENCE AND TECHNOLOGY LIBRARIES. Vol. 5 of SUBJECT DIRECTORY OF SPECIALIZED LIBRARIES AND INFORMATION CENTERS. Detroit: Gale Research Co., 1975. xiv, 364 p.

See also sources in section E.4 of this chapter; and 1382.

b. BIBLIOGRAPHIES

1372 American Association for the Advancement of Science. WOMEN IN DEVELOPMENT: PRELIMINARY ANNOTATED BIBLIOGRAPHY. Washington, D.C.: 1975. 62 p.

Available from the association, 1776 Massachusetts Avenue, N.W., Washington, D.C. 20061.

1373 Council of Planning Librarians. WOMEN AND GEOGRAPHY: AN ANNOTATED BIBLIOGRAPHY AND GUIDE TO SOURCES OF INFORMATION. Comp. by Bonnie Loyd. Exchange Bibliography no. 1159. Washington, D.C.: 1976. 8 p.

Partially annotated. Available from Mrs. Mary Vance, P.O. Box 229, Monticello, Illinois 61856.

1374 _____. WOMEN IN ENGINEERING: A BIBLIOGRAPHY ON THEIR PROGRESS AND PROSPECTS. Compiled by Christy Roysdon. Exchange Bibliography no. 878. Washington, D.C.: 1975. 22 p.

Partially annotated. Includes a listing of organizations, their publications and activities. Available from Mrs. Mary Vance, P.O. Box 229, Monticello, Illinois 61856.

1375 Davis, Audrey B. BIBLIOGRAPHY ON WOMEN, WITH SPECIAL EMPHASIS ON THEIR ROLES IN SCIENCE AND SOCIETY. New York: Science History Publications, 1974. 50 p. Paper.

See also section E.4, a.i., of this chapter.

c. REFERENCES

1376 Bell, Carolyn S. "Women in Science: Definitions and Data for Economic Analysis." ANNALS OF THE NEW YORK ACADEMY OF SCIENCES 208 (15 March 1973): 134-42.

Opportunities reflect the ability to cope with conventional responsibilities.

1377 Bugliarello, George, et al., eds. WOMEN IN ENGINEERING: BRIDGING THE GAP BETWEEN SOCIETY AND TECHNOLOGY. PROCEEDINGS OF AN ENGINEERING FOUNDATION CONFERENCE, JULY 12-16, 1971, NEW ENGLAND COLLEGE, HENNIKER, NEW HAMPSHIRE. Chicago: University of Illinois at Chicago Circle, 1972. 110 p. Offset, paper.

Considers how to increase participation of women in technology. Available from Vivian H. Cardwell, Assistant to the Dean, College of Engineering, University of Illinois at Chicago Circle, Box 4348, Chicago, Illinois, 60680.

1378 Heeman, Kathleen. "Fighting the 'Fly-Me' Airlines." CIVIL RIGHTS DIGEST 3 (December 1976): 48-59.

1379 Kane, Paula, and Chandler, Christopher. SEX OBJECTS IN THE SKY: A PERSONAL ACCOUNT OF A STEWARDESS REBELLION. Chicago: Follett Publishing Co., 1974. 159 p.

By a woman who became a union representative.

1380 Keil, Sally V.W. THOSE WONDERFUL WOMEN IN THEIR FLYING MACHINES: THE UNKNOWN HEROINES OF WORLD WAR II. New York: Rawson, Wade, 1969. x, 334. Illus.

1381 Kotel, Janet. "The MS Factor in ASME." MECHANICAL ENGINEERING 95 (July 1973): 9-21. Illus., figs., tables.

Presents overview of women's status in the American Society of Mechanical Engineers.

1382 Kreinberg, Nancy, ed. I'M MADLY IN LOVE WITH ELECTRICITY AND OTHER COMMENTS ABOUT THEIR WORK BY WOMEN IN SCIENCE AND ENGINEERING. Berkeley: Lawrence Hall of Engineering, University of California, 1978. 37 p. Illus.

Reports on questionnaire sent out to women in engineering, mathematics, physics, astronomy, chemistry, and the life sciences. Includes listing of resource people, publications, and organizations. Available from the Lawrence Hall of Science, University of California, Berkeley, California 94420, attention Careers.

1383 McCullough, Joan. "13 Who Were Left Behind." MS. 2 (September 1973): 41-45.

Reports on America's women astronauts.

1384 Mattfield, Jacquelyn A., and Van Aken, Carol G., eds. WOMEN AND THE SCIENTIFIC PROFESSIONS: THE M.I.T. SYMPOSIUM ON AMERICAN WOMEN IN SCIENCE AND ENGINEERING. Cambridge: M.I.T. Press, 1965. Reprint. Westfield, Conn.: Greenwood Press, 1976. xviii, 250 p.

Uses a cross-disciplinary approach to the understanding of woman's status in scientific professions. Discusses difficulties facing women, pros and cons of employing women, government employment of women scientists. Participants include Bruno Bettelheim, Alice Rossi, Mary Bunting, Jessie Bernard, and Erik Erikson.

1385 May, Charles P. WOMEN IN AERONAUTICS. New York: Thomas Nelson, 1962. 259 p. Biblio.

Covers the topic of women in aeronautics to the space age. Undocumented.

1386 Perrucci, Carolyn C. "Minority Status and the Pursuit of Professional Careers." WOMEN IN SCIENCE AND ENGINEERING 49 (December 1970): 245-59. Biblio.

1387 Rossiter, Margaret W. "Women Scientists in America before 1920." AMERICAN SCIENTIST 62 (May-June 1974): 312-22. Tables.

Offers commentary on and statistical analysis of patterns of discrimination, with some remedies.

1388 Salembier, Olive, and Ingersoll, Alfred C., eds. WOMEN IN ENGINEERING AND MANAGEMENT: PROCEEDINGS OF AN ENGINEERING FOUNDATION CONFERENCE, JULY 16-21, 1972, NEW ENGLAND COLLEGE, HENNIKER, NEW HAMPSHIRE. 138 p. Offset, paper.

Focuses on ways for women to achieve executive status. Available from the College of Engineering, University of Illinois at Chicago Circle, Box 4348, Chicago, Illinois 60680.

1389 Schilling, Gerhard F., and Hunt, M. Kathleen. WOMEN IN SCIENCE AND TECHNOLOGY: U.S./U.S.S.R. COMPARISONS. Santa Monica, Calif.: RAND Corp., 1974. 67 p. Biblio.

In lower echelons, Russian women far outnumber American women, but in upper levels, men predominate in both countries.

1390 Scientific Manpower Commission. SCIENTIFIC, ENGINEERING, TECHNICAL MANPOWER COMMENTS. Washington, D.C.: 1963-- . Monthly.

Digest of reports. Contains a special section on the latest developments in recruiting, training, and utilization of women and minorities. Available from Scientific Manpower Commission.

1391 Society of Women Engineers. Statistical and Publications Committee. REPORT ON WOMEN UNDERGRADUATE ENGINEERING STUDENTS, BIENNIAL DURING 1959-1974. New York: 1974. 16 p. Offset. Pamph.

Chronicles firsts by years, enrollments, and fields. Appendix lists enrollments in schools by state.

1392 "Successful Women in the Sciences: An Analysis of Determinants." ANNALS OF THE NEW YORK ACADEMY OF SCIENCES 208 (15 March 1973): special issue.

Contains nearly fifty articles and papers coming out of conferences. Discusses the individual, family relationships, and educational and economic matters. Participants include Mary Calderone, Esther Peterson, Cynthia Epstein, Lotte Bailyn, and Patricia Albjerg Graham.

1393 "Women, Science, and Society." SIGNS 4 (Autumn 1978): special issue.

Contains material on American women in science, 1830 to 1880, as well as more general information on women in medicine and science, and listing of women's caucuses.

1394 Yost, Edna. AMERICAN WOMEN IN SCIENCE AND TECHNOLOGY. New York: Dodd, Mead & Co., 1959. xiv, 176 p. Illus.

Includes zoologists, biochemists, physicists, a meteorologist, and an embryologist.

1395 Zahm, John A. WOMEN IN SCIENCE: WITH AN INTRODUCTORY CHAPTER ON WOMAN'S LONG STRUGGLE FOR THINGS OF THE

MIND. New York: D. Appleton, 1913. 452 p.

12. Social Work, Philanthropy

a. SOURCES, BIBLIOGRAPHIES

Among the many organizations that issue information on volunteer work are Call for Action, the Commission on Voluntary Service and Action, and the National Center for Voluntary Action. For a fuller listing of such organizations see 403.

The University of Minnesota Libraries maintains the Social Welfare History Archives, in which private papers of many women active in philanthropic and welfare activities are deposited.

1396 ENCYCLOPEDIA OF SOCIAL WORK. New York: National Association of Social Workers, 1965-- . Irregular.

Supersedes SOCIAL WORK YEAR BOOK. Includes the history of social work and welfare, articles, biographies with bibliographies, statistics, and a directory of agencies.

1397 U.S. Public Health Service. Division of Community Health Services. DIRECTORY OF HOMEMAKER SERVICES: HOMEMAKER AGENCIES IN THE UNITED STATES WITH SELECTED DATA. Washington, D.C.: Government Printing Office, 1958-- . Irregular.

Title varies. Listings by state. Available from the Superintendent of Documents.

For further sources see 1409.

For further bibliographical reference see 1404.

b. REFERENCES

1398 Addams, Jane. THE SECOND TWENTY YEARS AT HULL HOUSE, SEPTEMBER 1909 TO SEPTEMBER 1929, WITH A RECORD OF A GROWING WORLD CONSCIOUSNESS. New York: Macmillan Co., 1930. xiii, 413 p.

Contains material on the Progressive Party, the women's movement between 1909 and 1929, peace efforts 1914-19, domestic and international postwar problems, prohibition, immigration, the courts, and the arts at Hull House.

1399 ______. THE SOCIAL THOUGHT OF JANE ADDAMS. Edited by

Christopher Lasch. American Heritage Series. Indianapolis: Bobbs-Merrill, 1965. viii, 266 p. Biblio. Paper.

Contains selections from Addams's writings on social settlements, cities and immigrants, and political and social reform including suffrage, education, and peace activities.

1400 ______. TWENTY YEARS AT HULL HOUSE. New York: Macmillan Co., 1910. xvii, 462 p. Illus. Paper.

Classic on founding of Chicago Settlement House.

1401 Barney, Susan H. "Women in Philanthropy -- Care of the Criminal." In WOMAN'S WORK IN AMERICA, edited by Annie N. Meyer, chap. 14. New York: Henry Holt, 1891. Reprint. American Women: Images and Realities series. New York: Arno Press, 1972.

Discusses women in prison reform in late nineteenth-century America.

1402 Clarke, Ida C. AMERICAN WOMEN AND THE WORLD WAR. New York: D. Appleton, 1918. 545 p.

Includes information on the Red Cross, women in industry, contributions to state organizations, and a directory of women's organizations aiding defense effort.

1403 Daniels, Arlene K. "The Place of Volunteerism in the Lives of Women: Analysis of Four Types of Volunteer Experience." San Francisco: Scientific Analysis Corp., 1975. 38 p., plus unnumbered section. Tables. Mimeo.

Two subjects work in an institutional setting, two in a loosely organized network. Available from the Program on Women, Northwestern University, 619 Emerson Street, Evanston, Illinois 60201.

1404 Davis, Allen F. SPEARHEADS FOR REFORM: THE SOCIAL SETTLEMENTS AND THE PROGRESSIVE MOVEMENT, 1890-1914. Urban Life in America Series. New York: Oxford University Press, 1967. xviii, 322 p. Biblio. Paper.

Presents material on Jane Addams, Lillian Wald, Mary Simkovitch, Mary Kelley, and others in a broad social context. Note especially "Working Women and Children." Helpful bibliographical essay.

1405 Davis, Allen F., and McCree, Mary L., eds. EIGHTY YEARS AT HULL HOUSE. Chicago: Quadrangle Books, 1969. 256 p. Illus.

Comprised of selections about Hull House by women involved in its founding. From beginnings to present day.

1406 Fletty, Valborg E. "Public Service of Women's Organizations." Unpublished Ph.D. dissertation, Syracuse University, 1952.

1407 Goodale, Frances A. THE LITERATURE OF PHILANTHROPY. Distaff Series. New York: Harpers, 1893. ix, 210 p.

Anthology of articles by New York women. Topics deal with criminal reform, tenement life, nursing, work with Red Cross, blacks, American natives, abolitionism, and education of the blind.

1408 Greenbie, Marjorie B. LINCOLN'S DAUGHTERS OF MERCY. New York: G.P. Putnam's Sons, 1944. 211 p.

Relates beginning of women's humanitarian war work in America.

1409 Loeser, Herta. WOMEN, WORK AND VOLUNTEERING. Boston: Beacon Press, 1974. xvi, 254 p. Biblio. Paper.

The work and people who do it. Lists resources.

1410 Lowell, Josephine S. "Women in Philanthropy--Charity." In WOMAN'S WORK IN AMERICA, edited by Annie N. Meyer, chap. 12. New York: Henry Holt, 1891. Reprint. American Women: Images and Realities series. New York: Arno Press, 1972.

Lists fields of charity work open to women of the 1890s and also social agencies of the period.

1411 Lutz, Alma, ed. WITH LOVE, JANE: LETTERS FROM AMERICAN WOMEN WRITTEN ON WAR FRONTS. New York: John Day Co., 1945. xiv, 199 p.

During World War II.

1412 Melder, Keith. "Ladies Bountiful: Organized Women's Benevolence in Early 19th Century America." NEW YORK HISTORY 48 (July 1967): 231-54.

Background, development, and consequences of volunteer organizations to 1840.

1413 Quinton, Amelia S. "Women in Philanthropy--Care of the Indian." In WOMAN'S WORK IN AMERICA, edited by Annie N. Meyer, chap. 15. New York: Henry Holt, 1891. Reprint. American Women: Images and Realities series. New York: Arno Press, 1972.

Traces efforts to gain legislative recognition of native Americans. Includes texts of petitions.

1414 Scudder, Vida D. THE RELATION OF COLLEGE WOMEN TO SOCIAL NEED. Series 2, no. 30. N.p.: Association of College Alumni, 1890. No pagination. Pamph.

Early plea for trained personnel especially for settlement work.

1415 Spencer, Anna G. WOMAN'S SHARE IN SOCIAL CULTURE. New York: M. Kennerly, 1913. xi, 331 p. Reprint. American Women: Images and Realities series. New York: Arno Press, 1972.

Collected articles by a woman preacher involved with problems of child labor and prostitution.

1416 "Volunteerism: Your Money or Your Life." MS. 3 (February 1975): special section.

Three articles on the pros and cons of volunteer work for women.

1417 Wald, Lillian. THE HOUSE ON HENRY STREET. New York: Henry Holt, 1915. xx, 417 p. Reprint. New York: Dover Publications, 1971.

Recounts the founding of settlement house.

See also chapter 4, section G; and 705, 768, 1155.

13. Sports

a. SOURCES, BIBLIOGRAPHIES

Information on all aspects of women in sports, including employment and competition, is available from the Association for Intercollegiate Athletics for Women; from the International Association for Physical Education and Sports for Girls and Women; and from the American Association for Health, Physical Education and Recreation. The Task Force on Women in Sports of the National Organization for Women issues brochures on legal guidelines set forth by Title IX, performance records of women athletes, and various bibliographies having to do with women in sports. The Women's Sports Foundation serves as an information center and issues a newsletter to members.

Packets are issued on the legal aspects of women's employment and competition by the Women's Rights Project of the American Civil Liberties Union and by the Women's Equity Action League. The WOMEN'S RIGHTS LAW REPORTER prints information on legal cases having to do with women in sports.

Two periodicals that deal with women in all aspects of sports are WOMENSPORTS and the SPORTSWOMAN. Many serials, both in periodical and in newsletter form, are devoted to individual sports, such as WOMEN'S TRACK & FIELD WORLD, the WOMAN BOWLER, the WOMAN GOLFER, and WOMEN IN TENNIS.

For items on physical education as a health activity see chapter 8, section A.

1418 Glab, Kathi. "'Sporting Women': A Bibliography." BOOTLEGGER 6 (September-October 1974): 9-12.

Annotated. Includes a listing of women's sports associations.

See also 1430, 1431, 1432.

b. REFERENCES

1419 American Association for Health, Physical Education and Recreation. DGWS RESEARCH REPORTS: WOMEN IN SPORTS. 2 vols. Edited by Dorothy V. Harris. Washington, D.C.: 1971-73. Biblio.

Available from the association.

1420 _____. WOMEN'S ATHLETICS: COPING WITH CONTROVERSY. Edited by Barbara J. Hoepner. Washington, D.C.: 1974. 120 p. Biblio.

Presents material on intercollegiate athletics, women in the Olympics, and sociological and psychological aspects of women in sports. Available from the association.

1421 Breslin, Catherine. "The Female Jocks Go to Washington." NEW YORK 6 (7 December 1973): 67-82.

Tells how efforts of two Olympics winners produced the 1973 Amateur Athletic Act and helped reduce discrimination against women in sports.

1422 Gerber, Ellen W., et al. THE AMERICAN WOMEN IN SPORT. The Social Significance of Sport Series. Reading, Mass.: Addison-Wesley Publishing Co., 1974. xi, 562 p. Biblio.

Section 1 deals with participation, section 2 with social views of sports, section 3 with the nature of the woman athlete, and section 4 with biophysical perspectives.

1423 Halsey, Elizabeth. WOMEN IN PHYSICAL EDUCATION: THEIR ROLE IN WORK, HOME, AND HISTORY. New York: G.P. Putnam's, 1961. xi, 247 p. Illus.

1424 Haney, Lynn. THE LADY IS A JOCK. New York: Dodd, Mead & Co., 1973. 180 p. Illus.

Discusses women who are jockeys.

1425 Huey, Linda. A RUNNING START: AN ATHLETE, A WOMAN. New York: Quadrangle, New York Times, 1976. xiv, 240 p. Illus.

Top-ranking athlete attacks the stereotype of woman as unathletic.

1426 Klafs, Carl E., and Lyon, M. Joan. THE FEMALE ATHLETE: CONDITIONING, COMPETITION AND CULTURE. St. Louis, Mo.: C.V. Mosby Co., 1973. x, 216 p. Illus.

Discusses historical, physiological, psychological, and cultural aspects of female athletes.

1427 Leepson, Marc. "Women in Sports." EDITORIAL RESEARCH REPORT, 26 May 1977, pp. 331-48. Biblio.

1428 Lichtenstein, Grace. A LONG WAY, BABY: BEHIND THE SCENES IN WOMEN'S PRO TENNIS. New York: William Morrow & Co., 1974. 239 p. Illus.

Close-up personal view.

1429 Pennsylvania. State University. College of Health, Physical Education and Recreation. WOMEN AND SPORT: A NATIONAL RESEARCH CONFERENCE. Edited by Dorothy V. Harris. Pennsylvania State Health, Physical Education and Recreation Series, no. 2. University Park, Pa.: 1972. 416 p.

Compendium of articles having to do with professional, social, and biological aspects of women in athletics.

1430 Pratt, John L., and Benagh, Jim. THE OFFICIAL ENCYCLOPEDIA OF SPORTS. New York: Franklin Watts, 1965. viii, 344, R1-R90 p. Illus., biblio.

Main text gives history of each sport and its stars. R section lists records and individual bibliographies.

1431 Project on the Status and Education of Women. WHAT CONSTITUTES EQUALITY FOR WOMEN IN SPORT?--FEDERAL LAW PUTS WOMEN

IN THE RUNNING. Washington, D.C.: Association of American Colleges, 1974. 21 p. Biblio. Offset.

Includes information on funding and administration of programs. Lists resources.

1432 "Revolution in Women's Sports." WOMENSPORTS (September 1974): special issue.

Articles deal with financial discrimination against women in sports, federal acts and orders as they pertain to athletics, and women on men's varsity teams. Includes a manual on discriminatory practices, a list of women's athletic scholarships, and a resource listing.

1433 "Sex Discrimination and Intercollegiate Athletics." IOWA LAW REVIEW 61 (December 1975): special issue.

1434 U.S. Lawn Tennis Association. OFFICIAL ENCYCLOPEDIA OF TENNIS. Edited by the association staff. New York: Harper & Row, 1972. viii, 472 p. Illus.

Includes a listing of women greats and champions.

Chapter 8

HEALTH, MENTAL HEALTH, AND SEXUALITY

Since matters of physical and mental health and sexuality know no political boundaries, the limited number of items in this chapter in no way reflects the abundance of general material available on these subjects. Most, though not all, of the items that follow have been chosen because they have been shaped by conditions peculiar to the United States. Distinctions between what is "national" in nature and what is not are, of course, not always easy to make. Included among the titles are references that, while not directly relevant to the subject at hand, have implications for research on American women in the four areas with which this chapter is concerned.

A. PHYSICAL HEALTH

1. Sources

Major sources of printed material relating to the subject of women's health are the U.S. Department of Health, Education and Welfare and the U.S. Public Health Service. The National Women's Health Network addresses itself to women's health concerns on the federal level, runs the National Women's Health Information Clearinghouse and issues NETWORK NEWSLETTER, a bi-monthly news alert. The Health Research Group interests itself in the drugs that have been prescribed for women, and issues various kinds of information on the drugs and related issues. The National Organization of Women maintains a task force on women and health. HEALTHRIGHT, a woman's health education and advocacy organization, publishes both pamphlets and a quarterly newsletter. HERSELF is a periodical that deals specifically with matters pertaining to the health of women.

1435 Cowan, Belita H., comp. WOMEN'S HEALTH CARE: RESOURCES, WRITINGS, BIBLIOGRAPHIES. Ann Arbor, Mich.: Anshen, 1978. Illus. Paper.

> Essays on a wide range of health issues relating to women. Includes a directory of women's health groups. To be updated biennially. Available from the compiler, 556

Second Street, Ann Arbor, Michigan 48103.

1436 Source Collective. WOMEN'S HEALTH: ORGANIZING FOR HEALTH CARE: A TOOL FOR CHANGE. Source Catalog 3. Boston: Beacon Press, 1974. 248 p. Paper.

Includes material on women's clinics, birth control, abortion, and childbirth. Lists centers, organizations, and audiovisual sources.

1437 U.S. Maternal and Child Health Service. MATERNAL AND CHILD HEALTH SERVICES OF STATE AND LOCAL HEALTH DEPARTMENTS, 1971. MCHS Statistical Series, no. 4. Washington, D.C.: 1971. No pagination. Tables.

Provides statistical material on family planning, maternity nursing, child health services, clinics, and midwives. Available from the U.S. Department of Health, Education and Welfare and the Mental Health Administration, Rockville, Maryland 20852.

1438 Wasserman, Paul, and Giesecke, Joan, comps. HEALTH ORGANIZATIONS OF THE UNITED STATES AND CANADA: A DIRECTORY OF VOLUNTARY ASSOCIATIONS, PROFESSIONAL SOCIETIES AND OTHER GROUPS RELATED TO HEALTH AND OTHER FIELDS. 3d ed. Washington, D.C.: McGrath Publishing Co., 1974. v, 249 p.

Gives summary information for each organization.

1439 WHO'S WHO IN HEALTH CARE. New York: Hanover, 1977. xiv, 764 p.

Contains over eight thousand biographical sketches. Includes a geographical index.

1440 Young, Margaret L., et al., eds. HEALTH SERVICES LIBRARIES. Vol. 39 of SERVICE DIRECTORY OF SPECIAL LIBRARIES AND INFORMATION CENTERS. Detroit: Gale Research Co., 1975. xiv, 176 p.

U.S. section, pages 1-158.

2. Bibliographies

Bibliographies are available from the government agencies mentioned at the head of this chapter, from the U.S. Maternal and Child Health Service, and from the U.S. Office of Statistical Analysis. The National Organization of Women Task Force on Older Women also issues a bibliography having to do with health.

1441 Hunt, Vilma R., comp. THE HEALTH OF WOMEN AT WORK: A BIBLIOGRAPHY. Program on Women, Occasional Papers, no. 2, Northwestern University. Evanston, Ill.: Northwestern University, 1977. 173 p. Offset, stapled.

Unannotated. Available from the Program on Women, Northwestern University, 619 Emerson Street, Evanston, Illinois 60201.

1442 Northwestern University. Program on Women. WOMEN AND HEALTH: A BIBLIOGRAPHY WITH SELECTED ANNOTATIONS. Compiled by Sheryl K. Ruzek. Occasional Papers, no. 1. Evanston, Ill.: n.d. 76 p. Offset.

Available from the Program on Women, Northwestern University, 619 Emerson Street, Evanston, Illinois 60201.

1443 Spirduso, Waneen W., comp. BIBLIOGRAPHY OF RESEARCH INVOLVING FEMALE SUBJECTS. Washington, D.C.: American Alliance for Health, Physical Education and Recreation, 1976. 212 p.

Available from Louise Lyle, Coordinator, Publications Sales, American Alliance for Health, Physical Education and Recreation, 1201 16 Street, Washington, D.C. 20036.

1444 U.S. Department of Health, Education and Welfare. National Center for Health Statistics. ANNOTATED BIBLIOGRAPHY ON VITAL AND HEALTH STATISTICS. Washington, D.C.: Government Printing Office, 1970. ix, 143 p. Paper.

Presents data on fertility, maternal mortality, and outcomes of pregnancy other than birth. Available from the Superintendent of Documents.

1445 U.S. Department of Health, Education and Welfare. National Clearinghouse for Drug Abuse Information. WOMEN AND DRUGS: ANNOTATED BIBLIOGRAPHY. Prepared in cooperation with Student Association for Study of Hallucinogens (STASH). Madison, Wis.: 1975. iii, 62 p.

See also 1435, 1468.

3. References

1446 Alcott, William A. THE YOUNG WOMAN'S BOOK OF HEALTH. New York: Miller & Orton, Mulligan, 1855. 311 p.

How to be healthy though conventional in mid-nineteenth century America.

1447 Arms, Suzanne. IMMACULATE DECEPTION: A NEW LOOK AT WOMEN AND CHILDBIRTH IN AMERICA. Boston: Houghton-Mifflin Co., 1975. xv, 398 p. Illus., biblio.

Criticizes hospitals' treatment of childbirth as an illness. Pleads for a return to midwifery.

1448 Association of College Alumnae. Special Committee. Annie G. Howes, chairman. HEALTH STATISTICS OF WOMEN COLLEGE GRADUATES. Boston: Wright & Potter, 1885. 78 p. Tables, questionnaire foldout. Pamph.

Pioneering study based on Massachusetts Bureau of Labor statistics surveys conditions of childhood, pre- and post-graduate health, and individual health of subjects. Concludes that college education is "in harmony with that vast law of survival of the fittest."

1449 Austin, George L. A DOCTOR'S TALK WITH MAIDEN, WIFE, AND MOTHER. Boston: Lee & Shepard, 1882. 240 p.

Responding to the question "What is the matter with the American woman?" the author expresses contemporary attitudes toward intercourse, abortion, and so on.

1450 Beecher, Catharine E. LETTERS TO THE PEOPLE ON HEALTH AND HAPPINESS. New York: Harper, 1855. vi, 192 p. Illus. Excerpted in PIONEERS OF WOMEN'S EDUCATION IN THE UNITED STATES: EMMA WILLARD, CATHERINE [sic] BEECHER, MARY LYON, edited by Willystine Goodwell, pp. 215-26. New York: McGraw-Hill Book Co., 1951. Reprint. New York: AMS Press, 1970.

Exemplifies rising interest in mid-nineteenth century in healthy rather than in genteelly languishing women.

1451 Boston Women's Health Book Collective. OUR BODIES, OURSELVES: A BOOK BY AND FOR WOMEN. Rev. and enl. ed. New York: Simon & Schuster, 1976. 383 p. Illus., biblio. Oversize, paper.

Offers material on sexuality, human relationships, homosexuality, nutrition, lesbianism, rape and self-defense, venereal disease, birth control, abortion, childbearing, menopause, and political aspects of American health care as it applies to women. Available also in Spanish translation.

1452 Corea, Gena. WOMEN'S HEALTH CARE: THE HIDDEN MALPRACTICE, HOW AMERICAN MEDICINE TREATS WOMEN AS PATIENTS AND PROFESSIONALS. New York: William Morrow & Co., 1977. 308 p. Biblio.

Investigative account of the devastating effects of the male-dominated medical profession on women.

1453 Dreifus, Claudia, ed. SEIZING OUR BODIES: THE POLITICS OF WOMEN'S HEALTH. New York: Vintage Books, Random House, 1978. xxxi, 320 p. Biblio. Paper.

Includes twenty-two articles on women's health and health movement in the United States. Contains material on childbirth, abortion, medicine as a male-dominated profession, and women in the health business.

1454 Drinker, Cecil K. "Childbearing in 1790." In his NOT SO LONG AGO: A CHRONICLE OF MEDICINE AND DOCTORS IN COLONIAL PHILADELPHIA, chap. 3. New York: Oxford University Press, 1937. xii, 183 p.

Based largely on women's journals.

1455 Ehrenreich, Barbara, and English, Deirdre. COMPLAINTS AND DISORDERS: THE SEXUAL POLITICS OF SICKNESS. Glass Mountain Pamphlet, no. 2. Old Westbury, N.Y.: Feminist Press, 1975. 96 p. Biblio. Paper.

Discusses medicine as a political force in the treatment of lower-, middle- and upper-class women.

1456 Frankfurt, Ellen. VAGINAL POLITICS. New York: Quadrangle, New York Times, 1972. xxxviii, 250 p. Illus. Paper.

Attacks the male medical establishment. Includes material on self-examination, abortion, drugs and consumer rights, cancer and venereal disease, democratic medical care, therapy, and self-help groups.

1457 Jennings, Samuel K. THE MARRIED LADIES COMPANION; OR THE POOR MAN'S FRIEND. 2d ed., rev. New York: L. Dow, 1808. iv, 304 p. Reprint. New York: Medicine and Society in America series. Arno Press, 1972.

Offers advice to the new wife and the mother of daughters. Includes information on midwifery.

1458 Kerr, Barbara. STRONG AT THE BROKEN PLACES: WOMEN WHO HAVE SURVIVED DRUGS. Chicago: Follett Publishing Co., 1974. 333 p. Illus.

1459 Kushner, Rose. BREAST CANCER: A PERSONAL HISTORY AND AN INVESTIGATIVE REPORT. New York: Harcourt, Brace, Jovanovich,

1975. xiii, 400 p.

Discusses social, economic, psychological, and personal aspects of mastectomies in America.

1460 Napheys, George H. THE PHYSICAL LIFE OF WOMEN: ADVICE TO THE MAIDEN, WIFE, AND MOTHER. Philadelphia: G. MacLean, 1869. 252 p.

Best seller.

1461 Project on the Status and Education of Women. HEALTH SERVICES FOR WOMEN: WHAT SHOULD THE UNIVERSITY PROVIDE? Washington, D.C.: 1972. 11 p. Biblio. Offset.

Section 1 deals with services women are demanding, section 2 with what institutions are doing toward establishing programs and using already existing resources.

1462 Seaman, Barbara, and Seaman, Gideon. WOMEN AND THE CRISIS IN SEX HORMONES. New York: Rawson Associates, 1977. xiv, 502 p.

Investigative study of a major health threat to the health of American woman.

1463 Stage, Sarah. FEMALE COMPLAINTS: LYDIA PINKHAM AND THE BUSINESS OF WOMEN'S MEDICINE. New York: W.W. Norton, 1979. 304 p. Illus.

Illuminates success of multimillion dollar business in biographical-sociological context.

1464 Stockham, Alice B. TOKOLOGY: A BOOK FOR EVERY WOMAN. Chicago: Progress, 1883. xiv, 373 p.

Nineteenth-century text on midwifery which notes special sufferings of American women. Views active life, sensible dress, fresh air, and diet control as healthful for pregnant women. Material also on sexual mores, birth control, and abortion.

1465 U.S. Congress. Senate. ALCOHOLIC ABUSE AMONG WOMEN, SPECIAL PROBLEMS AND UNMET NEEDS. HEARING BEFORE THE SUBCOMMITTEE ON ALCOHOLISM AND NARCOTICS OF THE COMMITTEE ON LABOR AND PUBLIC WELFARE . . . SEPTEMBER 29, 1976. 94th Cong. 2d sess. Washington, D.C.: Government Printing Office, 1976. iv, 421 p. Illus., biblio.

1466 U.S. Department of Health, Education and Welfare. THE REPORT OF

THE WOMEN'S ACTION PROGRAM. Washington, D.C.: Government Printing Office, 1972. 116 p.

Points out the double standard of health care for men and women in America. (The department did not wish to distribute this report.)

1467 U.S. Maternal and Child Health Service. HEALTH OF THE AMERICAN INDIAN: REPORT OF A REGIONAL TASK FORCE. DHEW Publication no. (HS) 73-5118. Washington, D.C.: Government Printing Office, 1973. 31 p. Pamph.

Includes some material on maternal health services and family planning. Available from the Superintendent of Documents.

1468 Wertz, Richard W., and Wertz, Dorothy C. LYING-IN: A HISTORY OF CHILDBIRTH IN AMERICA. New York: Free Press; London: Collier-Macmillan, 1977. xii, 260 p. Illus., biblio.

Well-researched study.

1469 Woolfolk, William, and Woolfolk, Joann. THE GREAT AMERICAN BIRTH RITE: BABIES AS BIG BUSINESS. New York: Dial Press, 1975. 294 p.

Surveys economic aspects of childbirth. Based on interviews.

4. In Microform

1470 Women's History Research Center. WOMEN'S HEALTH/MENTAL HEALTH. Berkeley, Calif.: 1975.

This microform series reproduces nearly all that has been published on women's health and mental health by the women's movement in pamphlets, flyers, position papers, and press clippings. Material falls into the following categories: 1, physical and mental health of women; 2, physical and mental illnesses of women; 3, biology, women and the life cycle; 4, birth control and population control; 5, sex and sexuality; black and Third World women; 7, appendix: special issues of magazines pertaining to women's health. Available with reel guides and annotated catalogs from the center.

5. Oral History

See chapter 6, section D.2.e.

B. PHYSICAL EDUCATION

1. References

1471 Griffin, Patricia S. PERCEPTION OF WOMEN'S ROLES AND FEMALE SPORT INVOLVEMENT AMONG A SELECTED SAMPLE OF COLLEGE STUDENTS. Washington, D.C.: Educational Resources Information Center, 1972. 16 p. Biblio.

Statistical analysis.

1472 Hackensmith, C.W. A HISTORY OF PHYSICAL EDUCATION. New York: Harper & Row, 1966. viii, 566 p.

Contains sections on American women. Appendix lists professional organizations.

1473 Miller, Donna Mae, and Russell, Kathryn R.E. "Sport and Women." In their SPORT: A CONTEMPORARY VIEW, chap. 7. Health Education, Physical Education and Recreation Series. Philadelphia: Lea & Febiger, 1971. xv, 202 p. Biblio.

Discusses sociological considerations.

1474 Park, Roberta J. "Harmony and Cooperation: Attitudes toward Physical Education and Recreation in Utopian Social Thought and American Communitarian Experiments, 1825-1865." RESEARCH QUARTERLY 45 (October 1974): 276-92.

Important contributions to an enlightened understanding of, and attitudes toward, physical education for women.

1475 "Research Studies on the Female Athlete." JOURNAL OF PHYSICAL EDUCATION AND RECREATION 46 (January 1975): special issue.

Articles on the capacity of women as against men and the relation of menstruation to athletics.

1476 Schwenden, Norman. THE HISTORY OF PHYSICAL EDUCATION IN THE UNITED STATES. New York: A.S. Barnes Co., 1942. xv, 237 p. Biblio.

Chronicles physical education from the colonial period to date of publication. Note chapter 5, "Education and Exercise for Girls and Women" and chapter 13, "Dance as an Integral Part of Physical Education."

1477 Willard, Frances E. A WHEEL WITHIN A WHEEL: HOW I LEARNED

TO RIDE A BICYCLE. London: Hutchison, 1895. xi, 75 p. Illus.

Delightful recounting of temperance leader's mastering of bicycle named Gladys; includes remarks on women's health and clothing.

2. In Microform

1478 Health, Physical Education and Recreation Microform. HEALTH, PHYSICAL EDUCATION AND RECREATION MICROFORM PUBLICATIONS BULLETIN. Eugene, Oreg.: 1965-- . Semiannual. Cumulated index, 1949-72.

Index of American publications in the fields of health, physical education, and recreation.

C. SEXUALITY

1. General

a. RESOURCES, SOURCES, BIBLIOGRAPHIES

The Multi-Media Resource Center issues three times a year a RESOURCE GUIDE that contains articles as well as book and film reviews relating to human sexuality. It distributes films, slides, tapes, and educational guides issued by the National Sex Forum, as well as independently produced films, to professionals in the field.

1479 Carey, Emily A., comp. "Women: Sexuality, Psychology & Psychotherapy (A Bibliography)." Boston: Womanspace, 1976. 29 p. Mimeo., stapled.

Unannotated. Available from Womanspace.

1480 Ellis, Albert, and Abarbanel, Albert, eds. THE ENCYCLOPEDIA OF SEXUAL BEHAVIOR. 2 vols. New York: Hawthorn Books, 1967.

b. REFERENCES

1481 Acton, William. FUNCTIONS AND DISORDERS OF THE REPRODUCTIVE ORGANS IN YOUTH, IN ADULT AGE, AND IN ADVANCED LIFE, CONSIDERED IN THEIR PHYSIOLOGICAL, SOCIAL, AND PSYCHOLOGICAL RELATIONS. Philadelphia: Lindsay & Blakiston, 1865. 269 p.

Influential volume that shaped Victorian attitudes toward women's sexuality.

1482 Barker-Benfield, G.A. THE HORRORS OF THE HALF-KNOWN LIFE: MALE ATTITUDES TOWARD WOMEN AND SEXUALITY IN NINETEENTH CENTURY AMERICA. New York: Harper & Row, Colophon Books, 1976. xiv, 352 p. Paper.

Includes detailed studies of the Reverend John Todd and Augustus Gardner as representatives of prevailing attitudes.

1483 Bartell, Gilbert. GROUP SEX: A SWINGER'S EYEWITNESS REPORT ON THE AMERICAN WAY OF SWINGING. New York: Peter Wyden, 1971. x, 298 p.

Anthropologist's view.

1484 Bode, Janet. VIEW FROM ANOTHER CLOSET: EXPLORING BISEXUALITY IN WOMEN. New York: Hawthorn Books, 1976. 223 p. Biblio. Paper.

Interviews on experiences and attitudes.

1485 Breasted, Mary. OH! SEX EDUCATION. New York: Frederick S. Praeger, 1970. vii, 345 p.

Investigation of sex programs in the United States. Informal but incisive.

1486 Bullough, Vern, and Bullough, Bonnie. SIN, SICKNESS AND SANITY: A HISTORY OF SEXUAL ATTITUDES. New York: New American Library, 1977. vii, 276 p. Paper.

Gives backgrounds of attitudes and their influences to date.

1487 Cleaver, Eldridge. "White Woman, Black Man." In his SOUL ON ICE, chap. 4. New York: McGraw-Hill Book Co., 1968.

Provides sociopsychological insights.

1488 Collier, John. THE HYPOCRITICAL AMERICAN: AN ESSAY ON SEX ATTITUDES IN AMERICA. Indianapolis: Bobbs-Merrill Co., 1964. viii, 210 p. Biblio.

Discusses historical determinants of American attitudes toward chastity, adultery, noncoital sex acts, homosexuality, incest, prostitution, and pornography.

1489 Davis, Katherine B. FACTORS IN THE SEX LIFE OF TWENTY-TWO HUNDRED WOMEN. Publications of the Bureau of Social Hygiene. New York: Harper, 1929. xx, 430 p. Tables, biblio. Reprint. Family in America series. New York: Arno Press, 1972.

Early statistical study.

1490 Day, Beth. SEXUAL LIFE BETWEEN BLACKS AND WHITES: THE ROOTS OF RACISM. New York: World Publishing Co., 1972. xv, 376 p. Biblio.

Discusses relationships between blacks and whites before the Civil War and the ways in which they have been written about. Includes case studies of "mixed" marriages.

1491 Degler, Carl N. "What Ought to Be and What Was: Women's Sexuality in the Nineteenth Century." AMERICAN HISTORICAL REVIEW 79 (December 1974): 1467-90.

The resilience of women in the face of repressive sexual ideologies.

1492 DeMartino, Manfred F. THE NEW FEMALE SEXUALITY. New York: Julian Press, 1969. xv, 236 p. Biblio.

Uses Maslow tests to explore sexual attitudes of Canadian and U.S. nudists.

1493 Ditzion, Sidney. MARRIAGE, MORALS, AND SEX IN AMERICA: A HISTORY OF IDEAS. New York: Bookman Associates, 1953. 440 p.

Author maintains that the history of sexual reform movements from colonial times spells out the "complete history of the woman's rights movement."

1494 Ellis, Albert. THE AMERICAN SEXUAL TRAGEDY. Rev. ed. New York: Grove Press, Black Cat Book, 1962. 320 p. Biblio. Paper.

Studies American sexual mores based on attitudes expressed in mass media.

1495 Haller, John S., Jr., and Haller, Robin M. THE PHYSICIAN AND SEXUALITY IN VICTORIAN AMERICA. Urbana: University of Illinois Press, 1974. xv, 331 p. Illus., biblio.

Discusses sexism in the practice of medicine, with implications for morals and mores.

1496 Halsell, Grace. BLACK/WHITE SEX. New York: William Morrow & Co., 1972. 222 p. Paper.

Views interracial sex as "central to race relations in this country." Based on interviews.

1497 Hammer, Signe, ed. WOMEN, BODY AND CULTURE: ESSAYS ON THE SEXUALITY OF WOMEN IN A CHANGING SOCIETY. New York: Harper & Row, Perennial Books, 1975. 342 p. Biblio.

Contains articles on sexual identity and other aspects of sexuality by Karen Horney, Clara Thompson, Joyce McDougall, Margaret Mead, and others.

1498 Hernton, Calvin C. COMING TOGETHER: BLACK POWER, WHITE HATRED AND SEXUAL HANGUPS. New York: Random House, 1971. 181 p.

1499 ______. SEX AND RACISM IN AMERICA. Garden City, N.Y.: Doubleday & Co., 1965. 180 p. Paper.

Note chapter 2, "The White Woman," and chapter 5, "The Negro Woman."

1500 Himelhock, Jerome, and Fava, Sylvia F., eds. SEXUAL BEHAVIOR IN AMERICAN SOCIETY: AN APPRAISAL OF THE FIRST TWO KINSEY REPORTS. New York: W.W. Norton & Co., 1955. xvii, 446 p. Biblio.

Discusses implications of the Kinsey reports for marriage, class structure, religion, law, psychiatry, social attitudes, and behavior. Prepared for the Society of the Study of Social Problems.

1501 Hirsch, Arthur H. THE LOVE ELITE: THE STORY OF WOMAN'S EMANCIPATION AND HER DESIRE FOR SEXUAL FULFILLMENT. New York: Julian Press, 1963. 281 p.

Shows how the implementing of new sexual attitudes affects society. Based on interviews.

1502 Hite, Shere. THE HITE REPORT: A NATIONWIDE SURVEY OF FEMALE SEXUALITY. New York: Macmillan Co.; London: Collier-Macmillan, 1976. xl, 438 p. Paper.

Analyzes results of a questionnaire distributed, with the cooperation of the New York chapter of National Organization of Women, to three-thousand American women. Indicates need for a new definition of female sexuality. The appendix contains questionnaires and a statistical breakdown of findings.

1503 Hunt, Morton M. SEXUAL BEHAVIOR IN THE 70'S. Chicago: Playboy Press, 1974. xiii, 395 p. Biblio.

1504 Kinsey, Alfred C., et al. SEXUAL BEHAVIOR IN THE HUMAN FEMALE. Philadelphia: W.B. Saunders, 1953. xxx, 842 p. Figs., tables, biblio.

Major study.

1505 Mellen, Joan. WOMEN AND THEIR SEXUALITY IN THE NEW FILM. New York: Horizon Press, 1973. 255 p. Illus. Paper.

Asserts that old assumptions dominate new films. International in scope but many American films are included. Note Chapter 2, "The Mae West Nobody Knows."

1506 Reiss, Ira L. PREMARITAL SEX STANDARDS IN AMERICA. New York: Free Press, 1960. 286 p. Biblio.

Cultural origins.

1507 Rosenberg, Charles E. "Sexuality, Class and Role in 19th Century America." AMERICAN QUARTERLY 25 (May 1973): 131-53.

Describes characteristics of and paradoxes in attitudes toward sexuality, and how they served their society.

1508 Rugoff, Milton. PRUDERY & PASSION: SEXUALITY IN VICTORIAN AMERICA. New York: G.P. Putnam's Sons, 1971. 413 p. Biblio.

The influence of Mrs. Grundy and various figures and movements on manners and morals between 1789 and 1900. Touches on birth control, prostitution, homosexuality, temperance, religious cults, literature, and polygamy.

1509 Schaefer, Leah C. WOMEN AND SEX: SEXUAL EXPERIENCES AND REACTIONS OF A GROUP OF THIRTY WOMEN AS TOLD TO A FEMALE PSYCHOTHERAPIST. New York: Pantheon Books, 1973. xiv, 269 p. Biblio.

1510 Seaman, Barbara. FREE AND FEMALE: THE SEX LIFE OF THE CONTEMPORARY WOMAN. New York: Coward, McCann & Geoghegan, 1972. 288 p.

1511 Sherfy, Mary Jane. THE NATURE AND EVOLUTION OF FEMALE SEXUALITY. New York: Random House, 1972. xii, 188 p. Paper.

Biological approach to female sexuality in light of recent research.

1512 Shiloh, Ailon, and Gebhard, Paul H., eds. STUDIES IN HUMAN SEXUAL BEHAVIOR. Springfield, Ill.: Charles C Thomas, Publisher, 1970. xxviii, 460 p. Tables, charts, biblio.

Anthology includes women-related material on premarital sex, delinquency and prostitution, homosexuality, and venereal disease.

1513 Smith-Rosenberg, Carroll. "The Hysterical Woman: Sex Roles and Sex Conflicts in Nineteenth-Century America." SOCIAL RESEARCH 39 (1972): 652-78.

1514 Smith-Rosenberg, Carroll, and Rosenberg, Charles. "The Female Animal: Medical and Biological Views of Woman and Her Roles in Nineteenth-Century America." JOURNAL OF AMERICAN HISTORY 60 (September 1973): 332-56.

1515 Sonenschein, David, and Ross, Mark J.M. "Sex Information in the 'Romance' 'Confessions' Magazines." MEDICAL ASPECTS OF HUMAN SEXUALITY 5 (August 1971): 136-57.

Contains "reflections of sociosexual experiences of a number of people."

1516 Sorensen, R.C. ADOLESCENT SEXUALITY IN OUR CONTEMPORARY AMERICA: PERSONAL VALUES AND SEXUAL BEHAVIOR AGES THIRTEEN TO NINETEEN. The Sorensen Report. New York: World Publishing Co., 1973. xix, 549 p.

Includes material on sex roles, birth control, parental relationships, and statistics.

1517 Tyler, Parker. A PICTORIAL HISTORY OF SEX IN FILMS. Secaucus, N.J.: Citadel Press, 1974. 252 p. Illus.

Covers mostly American films.

1518 Wolfe, Linda. PLAYING AROUND: WOMEN AND EXTRA-MARITAL SEX. New York: William Morrow & Co., 1975. xi, 248 p. Biblio.

Based on interviews.

See also 673.

c. IN MICROFORM

See 1470.

2. Lesbianism

a. RESOURCES, SOURCES

Some publishers of books by and about lesbians are the Lavender Press, the

Diana Press, and the Violet Press. Lesbian periodicals include the LADDER and the 13TH MOON.

1519 A GAY CHRONOLOGY, JANUARY 1969-MAY 1975: INDEX AND ABSTRACTS FROM THE NEW YORK TIMES. Homosexuality: Lesbians and Gay Men in Society, History and Literature series. New York: Arno Press, 1975.

Computer printout of all articles over a period of seventeen months from the NEW YORK TIMES Information Bank.

For additional material see also 1527, 1535.

b. BIBLIOGRAPHIES

The Women's History Research Center issues a list of gay women's periodicals, compiled in 1973, which may be secured from the center.

The Arno Press issues the Homosexuality: Lesbians and Gay Man in Society, History and Literature series, which contains fifty-four titles and two periodicals. The publisher will send a list of titles on request.

1520 Sharma, Umesh D., and Rudy, Wilfred C., comps. HOMOSEXUALITY: A SELECT BIBLIOGRAPHY. Waterloo, Ont.: 1970. 114 p.

1521 Weinberg, Martin S., and Bell, Paul P., comps. HOMOSEXUALITY: AN ANNOTATED BIBLIOGRAPHY. New York: Harper & Row, 1972. xiii, 550 p.

Includes bibliography of bibliographies and dictionaries on lesbianism.

See also 1650, 1654.

c. REFERENCES

1522 Abbott, Sidney, and Love, Barbara. SAPPHO WAS A RIGHT ON WOMAN. New York: Stein & Day Publishers, 1972. 251 p. Biblio. Paper.

Recounts lesbians' successful struggle for recognition by the National Organization of Women.

1523 Birkby, Phyllis, et al., eds. AMAZON EXPEDITION: A LESBIAN FEMINIST ANTHOLOGY. New York: Times Change, 1973. 93 p. Paper.

Ten articles include material on family relationships, Emily

Dickinson, and the relation of lesbianism to feminism.

1524 Boggan, E. Carrington, et al. THE RIGHTS OF GAYS: THE BASIC ACLU GUIDE TO A GAY PERSON'S RIGHTS. New York: Avon Books, 1975. xii, 268 p.

Question-answer format deals with all legal aspects of homosexuality. The appendix tabulates laws applying to homosexuals, antidiscrimination laws in Minnesota and Michigan, and lists resources.

1525 Falk, Ruth. WOMEN LOVING: A JOURNEY TOWARD BECOMING AN INDEPENDENT WOMAN. New York: Random House, Bookworks, 1975. xxiii, 550 p. Illus., biblio. Paper.

Lesbian women in Washington, D.C., and California discuss core issues and individual experiences of sharing.

1526 Jay, Karla, and Young, Allen, eds. AFTER YOU'RE OUT: PERSONAL EXPERIENCES OF GAY MEN AND LESBIAN WOMEN. New York: Links, 1975. xii, 296 p. Paper.

Articles on identity, survival, and self-reliance in the community and as individuals.

1527 _____. OUT OF THE CLOSETS: VOICES OF GAY LIBERATION. New York: Jove; Harcourt Brace Javonovich, 1977. 429 p. Biblio. Paper.

Material on the relation of gay liberation to women's liberation, the media, law, and psychotherapy; and on role and consciousness raising. Includes gay manifestos and a resource listing.

1528 Johnston, Jill. LESBIAN NATION: THE FEMINIST SOLUTION. New York: Simon & Schuster, 1973. 283 p. Biblio. Paper.

Personal experience in a large social context.

1529 Katz, Jonathan. GAY AMERICAN HISTORY: LESBIANS AND GAY MEN IN THE U.S.A. New York: Thomas Y. Crowell Co., 1976. xiv, 690 p. Illus., biblio. Paper.

Pioneering work. Gives history from 1566 to the present.

1530 Klaitch, Dolores. WOMAN & WOMAN: ATTITUDES TOWARD LESBIANISM. New York: William Morrow & Co., 1975. 287 p. Biblio. Paper.

Note especially part 1, chapter 4, "Post-Freud American

Confusion," and material on Gertrude Stein in part 2, chapter 8.

1531 Krich, A.M., ed. THE HOMOSEXUALS SEEN BY THEMSELVES AND AUTHORITIES. New York: Citadel Press, 1954. 346 p.

Ten female homosexuals view themselves. Psychoanalytical approach.

1532 Martin, Del, and Lyon, Phyllis. LESBIAN/WOMAN. San Francisco: Glide, 1972. 283 p.

Presents "the everyday life experience of the Lesbian." Goes on to recount the founding of the Daughters of Bilitis.

1533 Simpson, Ruth. FROM THE CLOSET TO THE COURTS: THE LESBIAN TRANSITION. New York: Viking Press, 1976. xi, 180 p. Paper.

Challenges mechanisms that exclude lesbians from various social institutions.

1534 Tobin, Kay, and Wicker, Randy. THE GAY CRUSADERS. New York: Paperback Library, 1972. 283 p. Biblio. Paper.

Includes interviews with four lesbians, among them the founders of the Daughters of Bilitis.

1535 Vida, Ginny, ed. OUR RIGHT TO LOVE: A LESBIAN RESOURCE BOOK. Englewood Cliffs, N.J.: Prentice-Hall, 1978. 318 p. Illus., biblio.

Articles are grouped in sections covering social, economic, legal, sexual, and personal aspects of lesbianism. Includes resources listing.

See also 1488, 1684.

D. MENTAL HEALTH

1. Resources, Sources

The JOURNAL OF THE PSYCHOLOGY OF WOMEN issued by the Division of the Psychology of Women of the American Psychological Association focuses on articles that integrate the biological and sociocultural with current psychological knowledge about women. Among the journals of broader scope within the field that print material on women's psychology are the AMERICAN JOURNAL OF PSYCHOLOGY, the JOURNAL OF GENERAL PSYCHOLOGY, the

JOURNAL OF SOCIAL ISSUES, the JOURNAL OF COUNSELING PSYCHOLOGY, and STATE AND MIND: PEOPLE LOOK AT PSYCHOLOGY (formerly the RADICAL THERAPIST, ROUGH TIMES, and RT: A JOURNAL OF RADICAL THERAPY). A mental health kit, which includes thirty reprints of both general and specialized articles, is available from KNOW.

Womanspace Feminist Therapy Collective issues resource listings and bibliographies on therapy, counseling, and related subjects.

1536 Council on Research in Bibliography. MENTAL HEALTH BOOK REVIEW INDEX. 17 vols. New York: Research Center for Mental Health, New York University, 1956-72.

Includes reviews of over two hundred journals.

1537 PSYCHOLOGICAL ABSTRACTS. Lancaster, Pa.: American Psychological Association, 1927-- . Monthly.

Abstracts new books and articles; grouped by subject.

1538 PSYCHOSOURCES: A PSYCHOLOGY RESOURCE CATALOG. New York: Bantam Books, 1973. 215 p. Paper.

Pages 40-53 are devoted to material on women, much of it general. Includes listing of film sources and tape libraries.

See also 1540.

2. Bibliographies

1539 Cambridge-Goddard Graduate School for Social Change. Feminist Studies Program. WOMEN AND PSYCHOLOGY. Cambridge, Mass.: 1972. 36 p. Paper.

Annotated. Based on feminist challenges to traditional assumptions underlying psychological research. Includes bibliography of bibliographies. Available from the school, 5 Upland Road, Cambridge, Massachusetts 02140.

1540 Midlarsky, Elizabeth. WOMEN, PSYCHOPATHOLOGY, AND PSYCHOTHERAPY: A PARTIALLY ANNOTATED BIBLIOGRAPHY. Ms. no. 1472. New York: American Psychological Association, 1977. 120 p. Paper. Available also in microfiche.

Includes items dealing with mental problems associated with women's sex roles, as well as references relating to women in mental health practice and female clients. Available from the association, 1200 Seventeenth Street, New York, New York 20036.

1541 U.S. Department of Health, Education and Welfare. National Institute of Mental Health. WOMAN AND MENTAL HEALTH: SELECTED ANNOTATED REFERENCES 1970-1973. Compiled by Phyllis E. Cromwell. Washington, D.C.: Government Printing Office, 1975. viii, 247 p.

Over eight hundred items on social, economic, and psychological pressures on women demonstrating "diversity of, or lack of, expert opinion on female psychological and sociocultural processes."

1542 Walstedt, Joyce J. THE PSYCHOLOGY OF WOMEN: A PARTIALLY ANNOTATED BIBLIOGRAPHY. Spokane, Wash.: Past-Time Feminist Book Center, 1972. iii, 76 p. Offset, paper.

Lists items on sex role, adolescence, young adulthood, middle and old age, minority women, sexuality, and other topics. Available from KNOW.

See also 2, 3, 5, 1559, 1560.

3. References

1543 Bardwick, Judith, ed. READINGS IN THE PSYCHOLOGY OF WOMEN. New York: Harper & Row, 1972. xi, 335 p. Tables, biblio.

Overview based on thesis that biology determines psychology.

1544 Bayes, M., et al. "The Mental Health Center and the Women's Liberation Group: An Intergroup Encounter." PSYCHIATRY 40 (February 1977): 66-78.

1545 Chesler, Phyllis. WOMEN AND MADNESS. Garden City, N.Y.: Doubleday & Co., 1972. xxiii, 359 p. Illus., tables.

Sex-role stereotyping and therapeutic double standards underlie much of women's mental illness.

1546 Deutsch, Helene. THE PSYCHOLOGY OF WOMEN: A PSYCHOLOGICAL INTERPRETATION. 2 vols. New York: Grune & Stratton, 1944-45. Biblio. Paper.

Volume 1 deals with all aspects of women's psychology except motherhood, the subject of volume 2.

1547 Franks, Violet, and Burtle, Vasanti, eds. WOMEN IN THERAPY: NEW PSYCHOTHERAPIES FOR A CHANGING SOCIETY. New York: Brunner/Mazel, 1974. xiii, 441 p. Biblio.

Anthology of selections on historical considerations, biological and cultural influences, problematic behaviors, current therapies, agency listings, and new directions.

1548 Freud, Sigmund. "Female Sexuality." In his COLLECTED PAPERS, vol. 1, pp. 252-72, supervisor of translators, Joan Rivière. The International Psycho-Analytical Library, no. 27. London: Hogarth, Institute of Psycho-Analysis, 1952.

Analyzes the roots of female "deficiency."

1549 Gordon, Richard E., et al. THE SPLIT-LEVEL TRAP. New York: Bernard Geis, 1960. 348 p.

Probes emotional problems coming out of suburban life. Based on case histories.

1550 Gotkin, Janet, and Gotkin, Paul. TOO MUCH ANGER, TOO MANY TEARS. New York: Quadrangle Books, 1975. 416 p.

Gives account of a woman's traumatic experience with mental hospitalizations.

1551 Hall, G. Stanley. "Adolescent Girls and Their Education." In his ADOLESCENCE: ITS PSYCHOLOGY AND ITS RELATION TO PHYSIOLOGY, ANTHROPOLOGY, SOCIOLOGY, SEX, CRIME, RELIGIONS AND EDUCATION, vol. 2, pp. 561-647. New York: D. Appleton, 1904. Tables.

Psychologist-educator theorizes that "we study women" as "we study children." Widely used textbook.

1552 Harding, M. Esther. WOMAN'S MYSTERIES, ANCIENT AND MODERN. New York: Longmans, Green, 1935. xvi, 342 p.

Jungian analyst links moon myths with woman's experience.

1553 Horney, Karen. FEMININE PSYCHOLOGY. New York: W.W. Norton & Co., 1973. 269 p.

Previously uncollected essays demonstrate Horney's divergence from Freud's theories regarding women.

1554 Jefferson, Lara. THESE ARE MY SISTERS: A SCHIZOPHRENIC WOMAN'S ACCOUNT OF HER EXPERIENCE IN A MIDWEST MENTAL HOSPITAL. Garden City, N.Y.: Doubleday & Co., Anchor Books, 1975. 196 p. Paper.

1555 Maccoby, Eleanor E., ed. THE DEVELOPMENT OF SEX DIFFERENCES. Stanford Studies in Sex Differences, no. 5. Stanford, Calif.: Stanford University Press, 1966. 351 p. Illus., biblio.

Collected papers coming out of work group discussion.

1556 Mander, Anica V., and Rush, Anne K. FEMINISM AS THERAPY. New York: Random House, 1974. 127 p. Paper.

Defines feminism and feminist therapy, and suggests techniques for self-help.

1557 Miller, Jean B., ed. PSYCHOANALYSIS AND WOMEN. New York: Brunner/Mazel, 1973. xv, 415 p. Biblio. Paper.

Historical survey includes selections by Karen Horney, Alfred Adler, Clara Thompson, Mary Jane Sherfey, Mabel Cohen, Robert Stoller, Robert Seidenberg, and Lester Gelb.

1558 Mitchell, Juliet. PSYCHOANALYSIS AND FEMINISM. New York: Pantheon Books, 1971. 182 p.

Part 1 deals with the women's liberation movement here and abroad, part 2 with production, reproduction, sexuality, and socialization of children, as well as a reevaluation of Freud's theories on women.

1559 Rawlings, Edna I., and Carter, Dianne, eds. PSYCHOTHERAPY FOR WOMEN: TREATMENT TOWARD EQUALITY. Springfield, Ill.: Charles C Thomas, Publisher, 1977. xix, 477 p. Tables, illus., biblio.

Nineteen articles on feminist and nonsexist therapy, assertion training, career counseling, and psychotherapy for lesbians. Discusses social activism and radical feminism as therapy and as challenges to psychotherapy.

1560 Sherman, Julia A. ON THE PSYCHOLOGY OF WOMEN: A SURVEY OF EMPIRICAL STUDIES. Springfield, Ill.: Charles C Thomas, Publisher, 1971. ix, 304 p. Biblio. Paper.

Material on role, adolescence, pregnancy, motherhood, and later years.

1561 Steiner, Claude, et al. READINGS IN RADICAL PSYCHIATRY. New York: Grove Press, 1975. vi, 202 p. Paper.

Members of Radical Psychiatry Center discuss theory, special therapies and community organizing for treatment relating to women in broad context.

1562 Stoloff, Carolyn. "Who Joins Women's Liberation?" PSYCHIATRY: JOURNAL FOR THE STUDY OF INTERPERSONAL PROCESSES 36 (August 1973): 325-40.

Contradicts popular view of women in women's liberation as frustrated and aggressive.

1563 Storer, H.R. CAUSATION, COURSE AND TREATMENT OF INSANITY IN WOMEN. Boston: Lee & Shepard, 1871. 236 p. Reprint. Medicine and Society in America series. New York: Arno Press, 1972.

1564 Strouse, Jean, ed. WOMEN AND ANALYSIS: DIALOGUES ON PSYCHOANALYSIS VIEWS OF FEMININITY. New York: Grossman Publishers, 1974. 429 p. Paper.

Arguments of Helen Deutsch, Karen Horney, Marie Bonaparte, Clara Thomson, and others are countered by those of Juliet Mitchell, Elizabeth Janeway, Margaret Mead, Robert Coles, and others.

1565 Tennov, Dorothy. PSYCHOTHERAPY: THE HAZARDOUS CURE. New York: Abelard-Schuman, 1975. xviii, 314 p. Biblio.

Dangers of therapy, particularly to women.

1566 Thompson, Clara M. ON WOMEN: SELECTED FROM INTERPERSONAL PSYCHOANALYSIS. Ed. by Maurice R. Green. New York: Basic Books, 1964. xv, 192 p. Biblio. Paper.

1567 Unger, Rhoda K., and Denmark, Florence L., eds. WOMAN: DEPENDENT OR INDEPENDENT VARIABLE? New York: Psychological Dimensions, 1975. 828 p. Figs., tables, biblio.

Articles on sex-role stereotyping and development, psychoanalysis and women, sex differences in cognitive functions, psychosexuality, and female achievement.

4. In Microform; Audiovisual Material. See 1470.

Chapter 9

WOMEN IN THE ARTS

A. GENERAL

1. Resources, Bibliographies

1568 Navaretta, Cynthia, comp. GUIDE TO WOMEN'S ART ORGANIZATIONS: GROUPS, ACTIVITIES, NETWORKS, PUBLICATIONS. New York: Midmarch Associates, 1979. 84 p. Illus., biblio. Pamph.

Partially annotated. Includes painting, sculpture, photography, architecture, design, film and radio, dance, music, theater, and writing.

1569 Williams, Ora, comp. AMERICAN BLACK WOMEN IN THE ARTS AND SOCIAL SCIENCES: A BIBLIOGRAPHIC SURVEY. Metuchen, N.J.: Scarecrow Press, 1973. xix, 141 p. Illus. Offset.

Lists works by and about black women artists and contributors to social sciences. The appendix includes a listing of black periodicals, publishing houses, and audiovisual materials.

For specialized bibliographies in the arts, see particular arts sections following.

2. References

Women in the Performing Arts issues a useful newsletter, available from Susan Stone, 3524 North Broadway, Chicago, Illinois 60657. Ongoing review of women's activities in the arts appears regularly in the "On the Arts" section of MS. magazine.

1570 Butcher, Margaret J. THE NEGRO IN AMERICAN CULTURE. 2d ed. New York: Alfred A. Knopf, 1972. x, 313 p.

Discusses women in all arts in the context of the total

contribution of blacks to American culture.

1571 "Women and the Arts." ARTS IN SOCIETY 11 (Spring-Summer 1974): special issue.

Overview of women in the arts includes material on image, cultural institutions, feminism in the arts and in social change, poetry, and book reviews. Reports are from the National Conference on Women and the Arts held at Wingspread, The Johnson Foundation Conference Center, Racine, Wisconsin.

B. ART, ARCHITECTURE, PHOTOGRAPHY, AND CRAFTS

1. Sources

Organizations that supply information on women in the visual and spatial arts are the National Association of Women Artists, the Women's Caucus for Art, National Women in the Arts, and the Women and Arts Task Force of the National Organization for Women. For women in architecture there are Women Architects, Landscape Architects and Planners, and the Alliance of Women in Architecture. There are many regional organizations as well, such as Wisconsin Women in the Arts and Organization of Women in Architecture, San Francisco Bay Area.

Among the periodicals devoted to women in the arts are the FEMINIST ART JOURNAL, SOJOURNER, and WOMEN AND ART. Some periodicals of more general nature are ARTFORUM, ARTS MAGAZINE, and ART NEWS: NEW YORK.

1572 AMERICAN ART DIRECTORY. New York: R.R. Bowker Co., 1898-- . Irregular.

Covers museums, exhibitions, art literature, art education, and other subjects.

1573 McCoy, Garnett. ARCHIVES OF AMERICAN ART: A DIRECTORY OF RESOURCES. New York: R.R. Bowker Co., 1972. ix, 163 p.

Locates collections of artists' personal papers as well as records of exhibitions. Available in microform at listed regional repositories. Moderate representation of nineteenth- and twentieth-century women.

1574 Wasserman, Paul, et al., eds. MUSEUM MEDIA. Detroit: Gale Research Co., 1973-- . Biennial.

See also 1578.

2. Bibliographies

1575 ARTBIBLIOGRAPHIES: MODERN. Santa Barbara, Calif.: American Bibliographical Center, Clio, 1973-- . Semiannual.

The 1969, 1970, and 1971 edition were issued annually under the title of LOMA: LITERATURE ON MODERN ART. Covers artists and movements since 1800. International in scope.

1576 THE ART INDEX. New York: H.W. Wilson Co., 1929-- . Quarterly. Annual and triennial cumulations.

Author-subject index to a selected list of fine arts periodicals.

1577 Council of Planning Librarians. "Women in Architecture: An Annotated Bibliography, and Guide to Sources of Information." Compiled by Carolyn R. Johnson. Exchange Bibliography no. 549. Monticello, Ill.: 1974. 25 p. Mimeo.

Unannotated. Material on architecture and related professions. Available from Mrs. Mary Vance, P.O. Box 229, Monticello, Illinois 61856.

1578 Sims, Lowery S. "Black Americans in the Visual Arts: A Survey of Bibliographic Material and Research Sources." ARTFORUM 11 (April 1973): 66-70.

Includes special section on women artists as well as some relevant general sources.

1579 Sokol, David M., ed. AMERICAN ARCHITECTURE AND ART: A GUIDE TO INFORMATION SOURCES. American Studies Information Guide Series, no. 2. Detroit: Gale Research Co., 1976. xii, 341 p.

Some women in painting, sculpture, and the decorative arts.

See also 1600, 1604.

3. Biographical Indexes, Directories

1580 Cederholm, Theresa D. AFRO-AMERICAN ARTISTS: A BIO-BIBLIOGRAPHICAL DIRECTORY. Boston: Boston Public Library, 1973.

345 p. Illus., biblio.

Brief sketches of Meta Fuller, Lois Jones, Alma Thomas, Marie Johnson, Kay Brown, Norma Morgan, Betty Blayton, and Barbara Chase-Riboud.

1581 Collins, Jimmie L. WOMEN ARTISTS IN AMERICA: EIGHTEENTH CENTURY TO THE PRESENT. Chattanooga, Tenn.: n.p., 1971. Illus. Offset.

Lists, with biographical sketches, four thousand artists including painters, sculptors, printmakers, and ceramists.

1582 ______. WOMEN ARTISTS IN AMERICA II. Chattanooga, Tenn.: n.p., 1975. Illus. Offset.

Focuses on contemporary women.

1583 Cummings, Paul. A DICTIONARY OF CONTEMPORARY AMERICAN ARTISTS. 2d ed. New York: St. Martin's, 1971. 368 p. Biblio.

Gives personal and bibliographical material on artists since 1940. Limited on women.

1584 Smith, Ralph C. A BIOGRAPHICAL INDEX OF AMERICAN ARTISTS. Baltimore: Williams & Wilkins, 1930. 102 p.

From colonial times. Includes "lost" women.

1585 Waters, C.E.C. WOMEN IN THE FINE ARTS, FROM THE SEVENTH CENTURY B.C. TO THE TWENTIETH CENTURY A.D. Boston: Houghton Mifflin Co., 1904. li, 395 p. Illus.

Includes some obscure American women artists.

1586 WHO'S WHO IN AMERICAN ART: A BIOGRAPHICAL DIRECTORY OF CONTEMPORARY ARTISTS, EDITORS, CRITICS, EXECUTIVES, ETC. New York: R.R. Bowker, 1936-37-- . Irregular.

1587 Women's History Research Center. FEMALE ARTISTS PAST AND PRESENT. Berkeley, Calif.: 1974. 150 p.

Directory.

4. References

a. GENERAL REFERENCES

The Woman's Art Club of New York issued catalogs of shows of women's art at the turn of the century.

1588 Cole, Doris. FROM TIPI TO SKYSCRAPER: A HISTORY OF WOMEN IN ARCHITECTURE. Press Series on the Human Environment. Boston: i press, 1974. xi, 136 p. Illus., biblio. Paper.

Discusses a wide variety of contributions by American women.

1589 Cooper, Patricia, and Bufferd, Norma P. THE QUILTERS: WOMEN AND DOMESTIC ART. Garden City, N.Y.: Doubleday & Co., 1977. 157 p. Illus.

Includes interviews with quilters in Texas and New Mexico.

1590 Dewhurst, C. Kurt, et al. ARTISTS IN APRONS: FOLK ART BY AMERICAN WOMEN. New York: E.P. Dutton in association with the Museum of American Folk Art, 1979. xviii, 202 p. Illus., biblio. Paper.

Focuses on women without formal art training. Includes brief biographies.

1591 Elliott, Maud H., ed. ART AND HANDICRAFT IN THE WOMEN'S BUILDING OF THE WORLD'S COLUMBIAN EXPOSITION. CHICAGO, 1873. Chicago: Rand, McNally, 1894. 320 p. Illus.

In addition to articles on women in art and handicrafts, fifteen articles include those on women in science, literature, education, music, and organizations.

1592 Frost, Henry A., and Sears, William R. WOMEN IN ARCHITECTURE AND LANDSCAPE ARCHITECTURE. Institute for Co-ordination of Women's Interests, publication no. 7. Northampton, Mass.: Smith College, 1928. 28 p.

Encourages women to combine a professional life with wife and motherhood.

1593 Janis, Sidney. THEY TAUGHT THEMSELVES: AMERICAN PRIMITIVES OF THE 20TH CENTURY. New York: Dial Press, 1942. 236 p. Illus.

Contains brief materials on Anna Mary Moses, Ella Southworth, Hazel Knapp, Josephine Joy, Flora Lewis, and Jessie Predmore.

1594 Kohlman, Rena T. "America's Women Sculptors." INTERNATIONAL STUDIOS 76 (December 1922): 225-35.

Reports on twenty women working in the 1920s.

1595 Lippard, Lucy R. FROM THE CENTER: FEMINIST ESSAYS ON WOMEN'S ART. New York: E.P. Dutton & Co., 1976. vi, 314 p. Illus.

Contains essays on general topics, monographs on individual artists, and fiction.

1596 ______. "The Pains and Pleasures of Rebirth: Women's Body Art." ART IN AMERICA 64 (May-June 1976): 73-81.

Points out differences between body art of male and female artists.

1597 McSpadden, Joseph W. FAMOUS SCULPTORS OF AMERICA. New York: Dodd, Mead & Co., 1924. xv, 377 p. Illus., biblio.

Includes group of women sculptors.

1598 Moore, Julia G. HISTORY OF THE DETROIT SOCIETY OF WOMEN PAINTERS AND SCULPTORS, 1903-1953. Detroit: published with the approval of the Detroit Society of Women Painters and Sculptors by private subscription, 1953. 96 p. Illus.

Discusses training and professional achievements of a group of Michigan artists.

1599 Munsterberg, Hugo. A HISTORY OF WOMEN ARTISTS. New York: Clarkson N. Potter, 1975. ix, 150 p. Illus.

Provides good general background history in all visual arts from prehistoric times.

1600 Torre, Susan, ed. WOMEN IN AMERICAN ARCHITECTURE: A HISTORIC AND CONTEMPORARY PERSPECTIVE. New York: Watson-Guptill Publications, 1977. 224 p. Illus., biblio.

Presents material on domestic design for and by women, symbolic implications of design, and women as critics. Bibliography lists works on related professions, organizations, and statistical sources.

1601 Tucker, Anne, ed. THE WOMAN'S EYE. Collins Associates Book. New York: Alfred A. Knopf, 1976. 169 p. Illus., biblio. Paper.

Introduction discusses the role, status, and image of women. Ten American women photographers are represented in the text.

1602 Tufts, Eleanor. OUR HIDDEN HERITAGE: FIVE CENTURIES OF WOMEN ARTISTS. New York: Paddington, Two Continents Publishing Group, 1974. xix, 256 p. Illus., biblio.

Offers material on Sarah Peale, Edmonia Lewis and I. Rice Periera, in an international context.

1603 Vanderpoel, Emily N. AMERICAN LACE AND LACEMAKERS. New Haven, Conn.: Yale University Press, 1924. xx, 14 p. (text) 110 p. (pls.) Illus.

Contains an informational introduction followed by plates.

1604 WOMEN OF PHOTOGRAPHY: AN HISTORICAL SURVEY. San Francisco: San Francisco Museum of Art, 1975. Unpaged. Illus., biblio.

Exhibition catalog. Contains informative introduction and a bibliography on each artist. International, but stresses American women.

b. ART PRODUCTION AND REPRODUCTION

1605 College Art Association Women's Caucus. SLIDES OF WORKS BY WOMEN ARTISTS: A SOURCE BOOK. Compiled by Mary D. Garrard. New York: 1974. iii, 94 p. Offset.

Half of text is devoted to listings by museums and commercial sources, the other half is given to individual artists from the seventeenth to twentieth centuries. Emphasis is on American artists. Updates are planned.

1606 Gerdts, William H. "Marble and Nudity." ART IN AMERICA 59 (May-June 1971): 60-67.

Asserts that nudity of the female in nineteenth-century American sculpture served as an outlet for continuing repressed Puritan sexuality.

1607 Kahlenberg, Mary H., and Berlant, Anthony. THE NAVAJO BLANKET. New York: Frederick A. Praeger, 1972. 112 p. 97 p. Illus., biblio.

Catalog includes a history of earlier techniques used by native American women, as well as more recent innovations.

1608 Little, Frances. EARLY AMERICAN TEXTILES. New York: Century, 1931. xvi, 267 p. Illus., biblio.

Chronicle textiles from colonial times through the rise of industrial production.

1609 Munro, Isabel S., and Munro, Kate M., comps. INDEX TO RE-

PRODUCTIONS OF AMERICAN PAINTINGS: A GUIDE TO PICTURES OCCURRING IN MORE THAN EIGHT HUNDRED BOOKS. New York: H.W. Wilson Co., 1948. 731 p.

See also the supplement, item 1610.

1610 _____. INDEX TO REPRODUCTIONS OF AMERICAN PAINTINGS: FIRST SUPPLEMENT. New York: H.W. Wilson Co., 1964. 480 p.

More useful than item 1609.

1611 Safford, Carleton L., and Bishop, Robert. AMERICA'S QUILTS AND COVERLETS. New York: Weathervane Books, 1974. 313 p. Illus., biblio.

c. INDIVIDUAL ARTISTS

1612 Cortissoz, Royal. EXHIBITION OF SCULPTURE BY ANNA HYATT HUNTINGTON. New York: American Academy of Arts and Letters, 1936. 38 p. Illus.

An essay introduces a chronological listing of Huntington's work.

1613 Dannett, Sylvia G.L. "Mary Edmonia Lewis, 1846-1890: The First Negro to Achieve Active Recognition in the Field of Sculpture." In PROFILES OF NEGRO WOMANHOOD, by Sylvia G.L. Dannett, pp. 118-23. Negro Heritage Library. Yonkers, N.Y.: Educational Heritage, 1964.

Includes biographical and historical material.

1614 Iskin, Ruth E. "Toward a Feminist Imperative: The Art of Joan Snyder." CHRYSALIS 1 (1977): 101-15.

Aesthetic and personal considerations.

1615 Lesley, E.P. "Patience Lovell Wright, America's First Sculptor." ART IN AMERICA 24 (October 1936): 148-54.

Relates life of an eighteenth-century wax modeler.

1616 Lippard, Lucy R. EVA HESSE. New York: New York University Press, 1976. 249 p. Illus., biblio. Paper.

Includes chronology and catalog raisonné.

1617 McLanathan, Richard B.K. THE ART OF MARGUERITE STIX. New York: Harry N. Abrams, 1977. 191 p. Illus.

1618 Nemser, Cindy. ART TALK. CONVERSATIONS WITH 12 WOMEN ARTISTS. New York: Charles Scribner's Sons, 1975. xiv, 367 p. Illus., biblio.

Americans include Louise Nevelson, Lee Krasner, Alice Neel, Grace Hartigan, Marisol, Eva Hesse, Lila Katzen, Eleanor Antin, Audrey Flack, and Nancy Grossman.

1619 Nevelson, Louise, with McKown, Diana. DAWNS + DUSKS. New York: Charles Scribner's Sons, 1976. 190 p. Illus.

Contains taped conversations.

1620 Novotny, Ann. ALICE'S WORLD: THE LIFE AND PHOTOGRAPHY OF AN AMERICAN ORIGINAL. ALICE AUSTIN 1866-1952. Old Greenwich, Conn.: Chatham Press, 1976. 221 p. Illus.

Biographical commentary accompanies a wealth of photographs.

1621 Payne, Elizabeth R. "Anne Whitney: Sculptor." ART QUARTERLY 25 (Autumn 1962): 244-61.

Criticism of Whitney's work includes biographical information.

1622 Rose, Barbara. FRANKENTHALER. New York: Harry N. Abrams, 1972. 272 p. Illus., biblio.

Includes excellent reproductions of the abstractionist's work.

1623 Willis, Eda. "The First Woman Painter in America." INTERNATIONAL STUDIO 87 (July 1927): 13-20, 84.

Henrietta Johnston began painting portraits in 1708 in the Carolina territory.

d. CURRENT ISSUES

1624 Alloway, Lawrence. "Women's Art in the 70's." ART IN AMERICA 64 (May-June 1976): 64-72.

Summarizes exhibitions, critical approaches and writing, and avant-garde activities. Has useful notes.

1625 Dinerman, Beatrice. "Women in Architecture." ARCHITECTURAL FORUM 131 (December 1969): 50-51. Reprinted in 1155.

Claims that women are at the bottom of the professional pool. Backs up its claims with statistical evidence.

1626 A DOCUMENTARY HISTORY OF WOMEN ARTISTS IN REVOLUTION. 2d ed. New York: W.A.R., c/o Women's Interart Center, 1973. v, 74 p. Paper.

Documents the struggle of women artists over their exclusion from the Whitney Museum over up to the time of the founding of the Women's Interart Center. Available from KNOW.

1627 Dreyfus, Patricia A. "Women's Liberation and Women Designers." PRINT 24 (May-June 1970): 29-35, 74, 79.

Points out that opportunity for women designers exists, along with economic and psychological barriers to it.

1628 Hess, Thomas B., and Baker, Elizabeth C., eds. ART AND SEXUAL POLITICS: WOMEN'S LIBERATION, WOMEN ARTISTS, AND ART HISTORY. Art News Series. New York: Collier-Macmillan, 1973. ix, 150 p. Illus. Paper.

Elaine de Kooning, Louise Nevelson, and others debate the question "Why have there been no great women artists?" Reprint of "Women's Liberation: Women Artists and Art History," ARTNEWS 69 (January 1971): special issue.

For a listing of organizations of women in the arts and women's art galleries see 402, 417.

For information on women's studies in art and art history see 473.

C. DANCE

1. Sources, Bibliographies

The periodicals DANCE MAGAZINE and DANCE NEWS report current activities in dance. DANCE PERSPECTIVES deals with historical material in addition.

1629 Belknap, Yancey S., comp. GUIDE TO DANCE PERIODICALS. New York: Scarecrow Press, 1931-50, quinquennial; biennial since 1952.

Not published between 1936 and 1945.

1630 Chujoy, Anatole, and Manchester, P.W., comps. THE DANCE ENCYCLOPEDIA. Rev. and enl. ed. New York: Simon & Schuster, 1967. xii, 992 p. Illus.

Includes general and specialized articles on American and

international dance and dancers.

1631 DANCE WORLD. New York: Crown, 1966-- . Annual.

1632 DICTIONARY CATALOG OF THE DANCE COLLECTION: A LIST OF AUTHORS, TITLES AND SUBJECTS OF MULTI-MEDIA MATERIALS IN THE DANCE COLLECTION OF THE PERFORMING ARTS RESEARCH CENTER OF THE NEW YORK PUBLIC LIBRARY. 10 vols. New York: New York Public Library, Astor, Lenox and Tilden Foundations; Boston: G.K. Hall, 1974.

Lists books, periodicals, articles, manuscripts, visual materials, tape recordings, and films of major U.S. collections.

1633 Magriel, Paul D., comp. A BIBLIOGRAPHY OF DANCING: A LIST OF BOOKS AND ARTICLES ON DANCE AND RELATED SUBJECTS. New York: H.W. Wilson Co., 1936. 229 p. Reprint. New York: Benjamin Blom, 1966.

Note especially material on Isadora Duncan and Martha Graham.

See also 2070, 2081, 2084.

2. References

1634 Berman, Susan K. "Four Breakaway Choreographers." MS. 3 (April 1975): 39-45.

Information on Elaine Summers, Yvonne Ranier, Trisha Brown, and Lucinda Child.

1635 Duncan, Isadora. THE ART OF THE DANCE. Edited by Sheldon Cheney. New York: Theatre Arts Books, 1928. 147 p.

Foreword includes tributes, text of the essays by Isadora Duncan on Greek dance and her aesthetic principles.

1636 [Ellington, George]. "Ballet Girls in New York a Century Ago: Virtues and Vices." DANCE MAGAZINE 48 (January 1974): 31-33, 62, 65. Reprinted from his THE WOMEN OF NEW YORK, OR THE UNDERWORLD OF THE GREAT CITY. ILLUSTRATING THE LIFE OF THE WOMEN OF FASHION, WOMEN OF PLEASURE, ACTRESSES AND BALLET GIRLS, PICKPOCKETS AND SHOPLIFTERS, ARTISTS' FEMALE MODELS, WOMEN OF THE TOWN, ETC., ETC. New York: New York Book, 1869. Reprint. New York: Arno Press, 1972.

1637 Freedley, George. "The Black Crook and the White Fawn." DANCE INDEX 4 (June 1945): 4-16. Illus.

Describes mid-nineteenth-century extravaganza that ran for over forty years and had substantial support from "American ladies" as performers.

1638 Graham, Martha. THE NOTEBOOKS OF MARTHA GRAHAM. New York: Harcourt Brace Jovanovich, 1973. xvi, 464 p. Illus.

Reveals range and depth of dancer's vision in extensive notations over a creative lifetime. Listings of first performances.

1639 Kurath, Gertrude P. IROQUOIS MUSIC AND DANCE. Smithsonian Institution, Bureau of American Ethnology, no. 187. Washington, D.C.: Government Printing Office, 1964. xv, 268 p.

Contains songs and directions for dances for women.

1640 Lloyd, Margaret. BORZOI BOOK OF MODERN DANCE. New York: Alfred A. Knopf, 1949. xxiii, 356, xxvi p. Illus., biblio. Reprint. Brooklyn: Dance Horizons, 1969.

History includes sections on Isadora Duncan, Ruth St. Denis, Martha Graham, Doris Humphrey, and others.

1641 Martin, John J. AMERICA DANCING: THE BACKGROUND AND PERSONALITIES OF THE MODERN DANCE. Brooklyn: Thomas Barnhard, 1936. vi, 320 p. Plates. Reprint. Brooklyn: Dance Horizons, 1968.

Gives overview of American dance. Includes chapters on Isadora Duncan, Martha Graham, Doris Humphrey, and passages on many lesser figures.

1642 _____. BOOK OF THE DANCE. New York: Tudor Publishing Co., 1963. 192 p. Illus.

Discusses American female dancers in the context of general history of the dance.

1643 Mazo, Joseph H. PRIME MOVERS: THE MASTERS OF MODERN DANCE. New York: W.W. Norton & Co., 1977. 322 p. Illus., biblio.

Has chapters on Loie Fuller, Isadora Duncan, Ruth St. Denis, Martha Graham, and Twyla Tharp.

1644 Sorrell, Walter, ed. THE DANCE HAS MANY FACES. New York: World Publishing Co., 1951. xvi, 288 p. Illus.

Contains articles on sources of the dance, its relation to other arts, and other topics by Agna Enters, Ruth St. Denis, Hanya Holm, Ruth Page, Pearl Primus, Helen Tamiris, and others.

D. LITERATURE

1. General

a. BIBLIOGRAPHIES, BIBLIOGRAPHICAL GUIDES

Many publishers will send upon request specialized catalogs of the books they issue by and about women.

1645 "Belles Lettres: Criticism, Literary History, Essays, Novels, Tales, Dramas, etc." In TRÜBNER'S GUIDE TO AMERICAN LITERATURE, compiled by Nicolas Trübner. London: 1859. cxlix, 554 p. Reprint. Detroit: Gale Research Co., 1966.

Reflects mid-nineteenth-century attitudes toward women's writing.

1646 Blanck, Jacob N., comp. BIBLIOGRAPHY OF AMERICAN LITERATURE. 6 vols. New Haven, Conn.: Yale University Press, 1955-- .

Selective. Scholarly. Includes authors known and read "in their own time," while excluding some best-selling women writers. Presently published are five volumes, A through Thomas W. Parsons. Unannotated.

1647 Boos, Florence, comp. "1974 Bibliography of Women in British and American Literature: 1660-1900." WOMEN AND LITERATURE 3 (Fall 1975): 33-64.

1648 Burke, W.J., and Howe, Will D., eds. AMERICAN AUTHORS AND BOOKS, 1640 TO THE PRESENT DAY. 3d ed., rev. New York: Crown Publishers, 1962. 719 p.

Lists books by and about authors, listed by author.

1649 CONTEMPORARY AUTHORS: A BIO-BIBLIOGRAPHICAL GUIDE TO CURRENT AUTHORS AND THEIR WORKS. Detroit: Gale Research Co., 1962-- . Frequency varies.

Complete bibliographical, personal, and professional information on each author as well as listings of work in progress. Cumulative index.

1650 Damon, Gene, et al., comps. THE LESBIAN IN LITERATURE: A BIBLIOGRAPHY. 2d ed. Reno, Nev.: 1975. 96 p. Paper.

Available from THE LADDER (see appendix H).

1651 Foley, Patrick K., comp. AMERICAN AUTHORS, 1795-1895: A BIBLIOGRAPHY OF FIRST AND NOTABLE EDITIONS CHRONOLOGICALLY ARRANGED WITH NOTES. Boston: n.p., 1897. xvi, 350 p. Reprint. New York: Milford House, 1969.

Includes numerous women writers as well as listings of initials and pseudonyms used.

1652 Havlice, Patricia P., comp. INDEX TO AMERICAN AUTHOR BIBLIOGRAPHIES. Metuchen, N.J.: Scarecrow Press, 1971. vii, 294 p.

Not so inclusive as 1660 but lists some authors which 1660 omits.

1653 Hirschfelder, Arlene B., comp. AMERICAN INDIAN AUTHORS: A REPRESENTATIVE BIBLIOGRAPHY. New York: Association of Indian Affairs, 1970. 45 p. Pamph.

Annotated. Includes women. Available from the association, 432 Park Avenue, New York, New York 10016.

1654 HOMOSEXUALITY IN LITERATURE. Catalog no. 6. Elmhurst, N.Y.: Elysian Fields, Booksellers, n.d. 42 p. Offset, pamph.

Wide ranging list includes bibliography, film, and photo essays. Available from Elysian Fields, 81-13 Broadway, Elmhurst, New York 11373.

1655 Kuda, Marie J., comp. WOMEN LOVING WOMEN: A SELECT AND ANNOTATED BIBLIOGRAPHY OF WOMEN LOVING WOMEN IN LITERATURE. Chicago: Womanpress, 1975. 28 p. Pamph.

Fiction, poetry, biography, and autobiography by and about lesbian experience, much of it American. Appends a short listing of reference works.

1656 Matthews, Geraldine O., and the Afro-American Materials Project Staff of Library Science, North Carolina Central University, comps. BLACK AMERICAN WRITERS, 1773-1949: A BIBLIOGRAPHY & UNION LIST. Boston: G.K. Hall & Co., 1975. xv, 271 p.

1657 Modern Language Association. MLA INTERNATIONAL BIBLIOGRAPHY OF BOOKS AND ARTICLES ON MODERN LANGUAGES AND LITERATURE. 1956-- . Annual.

Succeeds MLA AMERICAN BIBLIOGRAPHY (1919-55).

1658 National Council of Women of the United States. THE ONE HUNDRED BEST BOOKS BY AMERICAN WOMEN DURING THE PAST ONE HUNDRED YEARS 1833-1933 AS CHOSEN BY THE NATIONAL COUNCIL OF WOMEN. Edited by Anita Browne. Chicago: Associated Authors Service, 1933. 128 p.

1659 "Neglected Women Writers: A Collection of Bibliographies." Bloomington: University of Indiana, 1972. Each author paged separately. Dittoed.

Includes twenty-two writers of prose and poetry.

1660 Nilon, Charles H., comp. BIBLIOGRAPHY OF BIBLIOGRAPHIES IN AMERICAN LITERATURE. New York: R.R. Bowker Co., 1970. xi, 483 p.

Excellent guide to individual authors.

1661 Rubin, Louis D., Jr., comp. A BIBLIOGRAPHICAL GUIDE TO THE STUDY OF SOUTHERN LITERATURE. Southern Literature Studies Series. Baton Rouge: Louisiana State University Press, 1969. xxiv, 351 p. Paper.

Provides bibliography and essays on twenty-five women writers.

1662 Schwartz, Narda C. ARTICLES ON WOMEN WRITERS, 1960-1975: A BIBLIOGRAPHY. Santa Barbara, Calif.: American Bibliographical Center--Clio Press, 1977. xx, 336 p.

Although international in scope, a number of items relate to American novelists, poets, diarists, and other.

1663 Swisher, Robert, comp. BLACK AMERICAN LITERATURE. Archer, Jill A., comp. BLACK AMERICAN FOLKLORE. Focus: Black American Bibliographical Series, vol. 4. Bloomington: Indiana University Libraries and Focus: Black America, 1969. 25 p. Paper.

1664 Turner, Darwin, comp. AFRO-AMERICAN WRITERS. Goldenbook Bibliographies in Language and Literature Series. New York: Appleton-Century-Crofts, 1970. xvii, 117 p. Paper.

Includes listings of books by both well-known and obscure women writers since Phillis Wheatley. The appendix focuses on criticisms of African and Afro-American characters. A supplement expands all categories.

1665 Wednesday Afternoon Club of New York City. LIST OF BOOKS BY THE WOMEN NATIVES OR RESIDENTS OF THE STATE OF NEW YORK. New York: 1893. 218 p.

Issued on behalf of women managers of New York World's Columbian Exposition to draw attention to women's work in literature.

See also 1679, 1681; sections D2a, D3a, and D4a of this chapter.

b. BIOGRAPHICAL DICTIONARIES, MISCELLANEOUS SOURCES

1666 Adams, Oscar F., ed. A DICTIONARY OF AMERICAN AUTHORS. Boston: Houghton Mifflin Co., 1904. viii, 587 p. Reprint. Detroit: Gale Research Co., 1969.

Includes many women authors, with information on each author and her work.

1667 AMERICAN LITERARY MANUSCRIPTS: A CHECKLIST OF HOLDINGS IN ACADEMIC, HISTORICAL AND PUBLIC LIBRARIES, MUSEUMS, AND AUTHORS' HOMES. 2d ed. Athens: University of Georgia Press, 1977. liii, 387 p.

Lists many women. Updates 1961 volume. Sponsored by Modern Language Association of America, American Literature Section.

1668 Atherton, Lawrence, comp. WHO'S WHO AMONG NORTH AMERICAN AUTHORS. 7 vols. Los Angeles: Golden Syndicate, 1921-34. Reprint. WHO WAS WHO AMONG NORTH AMERICAN AUTHORS 1921-1939. 2 vols. Gale Composite Biographical Dictionary Series, no. 1. Detroit: Gale Research Co., 1976.

Includes journalists difficult to find elsewhere. Reprint includes all names and pseudonyms found in all original editions.

1669 Chesman, Adrean, and Joan, Polly, comps. DIRECTORY OF WOMEN WRITING. Newfield, N.Y.: Women Writing, 1977. 91 p. Offset, pamph.

Includes addresses. Available from Women Writing Press, R.D. 3, Newfield, New York 14867.

1670 Fulton, Len, ed. INTERNATIONAL DIRECTORY OF LITTLE MAGAZINES AND SMALL PRESSES. 13th ed. Paradise, Calif.: Dustbooks, 1977-78. 440 p. Paper.

Contains subject heading listing of over one hundred women's periodicals and presses, with annotations on each entry. Updated annually.

1671 Kunitz, Stanley J., and Haycraft, Howard, eds. AMERICAN AUTHORS, 1600-1900: A BIOGRAPHICAL DICTIONARY OF AMERICAN AUTHORS. New York: H.W. Wilson Co., 1938. 846 p. Illus., biblio.

Lists a considerable number of women writers, with bibliography and photograph of each.

1672 _____. TWENTIETH CENTURY AUTHORS. New York: H.W. Wilson Co., 1942. viii, 1577 p. Illus., biblio.

Includes some American women hard to find elsewhere. International in scope.

1673 Levi, Doris J., and Milton, Nerissa L., comps. DIRECTORY OF BLACK LITERARY MAGAZINES. Focus Series, no. 1. Washington, D.C.: Negro Bibliographic and Research Center, 1970. 19 p. Pamph.

Annotated. Available from the center, 117 R Street, N.E., Washington, D.C. 20002.

1674 Rush, Theresa G., et al., comps. BLACK AMERICAN WRITERS PAST AND PRESENT: A BIOGRAPHICAL AND BIBLIOGRAPHICAL DICTIONARY. 2 vols. Metuchen, N.J.: Scarecrow Press, 1975. Illus.

Lists over two thousand writers, many of them women, from the early eighteenth century on.

1675 Shockley, Anna A., and Chandler, Sue P., comps. LIVING BLACK AMERICAN AUTHORS: A BIOGRAPHICAL DICTIONARY. New York: R.R. Bowker Co., 1973. xv, 220 p.

Includes many women.

Reviews of books by and about women appear in WOMEN'S STUDIES ABSTRACTS (see 467) and BOOK REVIEW DIGEST (see page 4).

For periodicals focusing on critical issues having to do with women in literature refer to WOMEN AND LITERATURE and SIGNS.

For listings of various contemporary titles in fiction and science fiction, and women's comics, see 417; for listings of contemporary poetry, 1887-1927.

For a listing of collections having manuscript holdings, see Ash and Calvert, page 3 above.

c. CRITICISM

1676 Bruere, Martha B., and Beard, Mary R. LAUGHING THEIR WAY: WOMEN'S HUMOR IN AMERICA. New York: Macmillan Co., 1934. xv, 295 p.

Discusses a wide range of humorist writing, with some graphics, by women from the Revolution into the twentieth century, drawn from fiction, poetry, and other literary media.

1677 Cantrow, Ellen. "The Radicalizing of the Teaching of Literature." CHANGE: THE MAGAZINE OF HIGHER LEARNING 4 (May 1972): 50-61. Abridged version reprinted in THE POLITICS OF LITERATURE, edited by Louis Kampf and Paul Lauter, pp. 57-100. New York: Pantheon Books, 1970.

1678 Cone, Helen G. "Women in Literature." In WOMEN'S WORK IN AMERICA, edited by Annie N. Meyer, chap. 5. New York: Henry Holt, 1891. Reprint. American Women: Images and Realities series. New York: Arno Press, 1972.

Presents a historical view. Cone was an end-of-the-century poet.

1679 Curley, Dorothy N., et al. LIBRARY OF CRITICISM: MODERN AMERICAN LITERATURE. 4th enl. ed. 3 vols. New York: Frederick Ungar, 1969. xviii, 470 p.

Excerpts criticisms of major writers through the 1950s and includes bibliography of each author's works. Cumulative. Expanded editions issued irregularly.

1680 Diamond, Arlyn, and Edwards, Lee J., eds. THE AUTHORITY OF EXPERIENCE: ESSAYS IN FEMINIST CRITICISM. Amherst: University of Massachusetts Press, 1977. xiv, 366 p.

Contains five essays on American literature about frontier women, and women in Herman Melville, Kate Chopin, Katherine Anne Porter, and Ernest Hemingway.

1681 Donovan, Josephine, ed. FEMINIST LITERARY CRITICISM: EXPLORATIONS IN THEORY. Lexington: University Press of Kentucky, 1975. 81 p.

Contains five essays coming out of a University of Kentucky symposium. Note especially Cheri Register's "American Feminist Criticism: A Bibliographical Introduction."

1682 Earnest, Ernest P. THE AMERICAN EVE: IN FACT AND FICTION,

1775-1914. Urbana: University of Illinois Press, 1974. 280 p. Biblio.

Analyzes stereotypical attitudes toward women that shaped fictional and actual views of women before World War I.

1683 Ehrlich, Carol. "The Woman Book Industry." In CHANGING WOMEN IN A CHANGING SOCIETY, edited by Joan Huber, pp. 268-82. Chicago: University of Chicago Press, 1973.

Reviewing seventeen books of 1971-72 by women in accordance with conventional criteria, the author accuses publishers of exploiting women writers.

1684 Foster, Jeannette. SEX VARIANT WOMEN IN LITERATURE: A HISTORICAL AND QUANTITATIVE SURVEY. New York: Vantage, 1965. 412 p.

Gives background from classical times. Includes material on Margaret Fuller, Adah Mencken, Emily Dickinson, "Michael Field," Amy Lowell, and Edna St. Vincent Millay as well as on works of Henry James, Sherwood Anderson, and others.

1685 Freeman, Julia D. [Forrest, Mary]. WOMEN OF THE SOUTH DISTINGUISHED IN LITERATURE. New York: Charles B. Richardson, 1866. 511 p. Illus.

Contains biographies and selections of thirty-five women, among whom are Anna Mowatt (Ritchie) and Emma D.E.N. Southworth.

1686 Griswold, Rufus W. THE PROSE WRITERS OF AMERICA. Philadelphia: Carey & Hart, 1847. 552 p.

Includes some women.

1687 Hart, John S. THE FEMALE PROSE WRITERS OF AMERICA, AND SPECIMENS OF THEIR WRITING. Philadelphia: E.H. Butler, 1855. vii, 536 p. Illus.

Covers both well-known and obscure writers.

1688 Hiatt, Mary. THE WAY WOMEN WRITE. New York: Teachers College, Columbia University, 1977. vii, 152 p. Tables, biblio.

Presents a close stylistic analysis of women's and men's writing. Focuses on American writers.

1689 Maglin, Nan B. "Rebel Women Writers, 1894-1925." Ph.D. dissertation, Union Graduate School, 1975.

1690 Mason, Bobbie Ann. THE GIRL SLEUTH: A FEMINIST GUIDE. Old Westbury, N.Y.: Feminist Press, 1975. xi, 144 p. Biblio. Paper.

Discusses "heroines," mostly of girls' series books but including LITTLE WOMEN.

1691 Myers, Carol. WOMEN IN LITERATURE: CRITICISM OF THE SEVENTIES. Metuchen, N.J.: Scarecrow Press, 1976. vii, 256 p. Biblio.

International in scope. Includes material on women as writers and as fictional characters; feminist criticism; reviews and interviews.

1692 Olsen, Tillie. "Silences--When Writers Don't Write." HARPER'S 231 (October 1965): 153-61. Reprinted in 132.

Focuses chiefly on women writers.

1693 Porter, Dorothy B. "Organized Educational Activities of Negro Literary Societies, 1828-1846." JOURNAL OF NEGRO EDUCATION 5 (October 1936): 555-76.

1694 Rogers, Katherine M. THE TROUBLESOME HELPMATE: A HISTORY OF MISOGYNY IN LITERATURE. Seattle: University of Washington Press, 1966. xvi, 288 p. Paper.

Provides excellent background. Some American women writers are mentioned.

1695 Showalter, Elaine. WOMEN'S LIBERATION AND LITERATURE. New York: Harcourt Brace, 1971. lx, 338 p. Paper.

Contains criticism of poetry, fiction, and drama by and about women, with selections from other disciplines for perspective.

1696 Springer, Marlene, ed. WHAT MANNER OF WOMEN: ESSAYS ON ENGLISH AND AMERICAN LIFE AND LITERATURE. New York: New York University Press, 1977. xx, 357 p. Paper.

Contains six essays on women in literature--in early America (1790-1870), in the nineteenth and twentieth centuries, in novels between World Wars I and II, in contemporary writing, and in black American literature.

1697 Stearns, Bertha-Monica. "Early Western Magazines for Ladies." MISSISSIPPI VALLEY HISTORICAL REVIEW 18 (1931): 319-30.

1698 Thompson, Ralph. AMERICAN LITERARY ANNUALS AND GIFT

BOOKS, 1825-1865. New York: H.W. Wilson Co., 1936. 183 p.

Reveals women's literary tastes.

1699 Wasserstrom, William. HEIRESS OF ALL THE AGES: SEX AND SENTIMENT IN THE GENTEEL TRADITION. Minneapolis: University of Minnesota Press, 1959. 157 p.

Views the role of women in genteel literature as transcending conflicts within society in order to save society from itself. Contains useful notes.

1700 White, Cynthia L. WOMEN'S MAGAZINES, 1963-1968. London: Michael Joseph, 1970. 348 p. Biblio.

Discusses and lists American and British periodicals.

1701 "Women Writing and Teaching." Edited by Elaine Hedges. COLLEGE ENGLISH 34 (October 1972): special issue.

Includes material on women writers by Tillie Olsen and Adrienne Rich. Also discusses Emily Dickinson, women's role in producing texts, and women's political effectiveness.

See also chapter 2B1c passim.

d. ANTHOLOGIES

General anthologies of women's writings are constantly being issued. Also, many women's general literary magazines, such as APHRA, BLACK MARIA, CHOMO-URI, FOCUS, LIBERA, MATRIX, and 13TH MOON, may serve as anthologies. General literary magazines, such as LITTLE REVIEW and the UNIVERSITY OF MASSACHUSETTS REVIEW, issue special numbers on and by women.

1702 Berg, Stephen, and Marks, S.J., eds. ABOUT WOMEN. Greenwich, Conn.: Fawcett World Library, 1973. 400 p. Paper.

Contains short fiction, poetry, and essays by and about women.

1703 Cade, Toni, [Bambara], ed. THE BLACK WOMAN: AN ANTHOLOGY. New York: Signet, Mentor, et al., 1970. 256 p. Paper.

Includes poems, essays, and fiction which reflect a range of black women's lives.

1704 Covina, Gina, and Galina, Laurel, eds. THE LESBIAN READER: AN

AMAZON QUARTERLY ANTHOLOGY. Guerneville, Calif.: Amazon Press, 1975. 247 p. Biblio.

Available from Book People, 2940 Seventh Street, Berkeley, California 94710.

1705 Folsom, Marcia McC., and Kirschner, Linda H., eds. BY WOMEN: AN ANTHOLOGY OF LITERATURE. Boston: Houghton Mifflin Co., 1976. ix, 478 p. Illus.

Largely by American women. Appends biographical notes.

1706 Greer, Barbara, and Reid, Coletta, eds. THE LAVENDAR READER: LESBIAN ESSAYS FROM THE LADDER. Baltimore: Diana Press, 1976. 356 p. Illus.

Includes essays on life-style, feminism, sexuality, and images in art.

1707 Kominski, Margaret, ed. MOVING TO ANTARCTICA: AN ANTHOLOGY OF WOMEN'S WRITING. American Dust Series, no. 2. Paradise, Calif.: Dustbooks, 1975. x, 165 p. Paper.

Poetry, fiction, drama.

1708 Murray, Michele, ed. A HOUSE OF GOOD PROPORTION: IMAGES OF WOMEN IN LITERATURE. New York: Simon & Schuster, 1973. 379 p. Paper.

Poems, stories, and excerpts from novels grouped around traditional roles played by women.

1709 Watkins, Mel, and David, Jay, eds. TO BE A BLACK WOMAN: PORTRAITS IN FACT AND FICTION. New York: William Morrow & Co., 1971. 285 p.

Anthology of fiction, nonfiction, and poetry organized around themes of black woman as slave, as exploitee of white society, as family protector, and as fighter for human rights.

2. Fiction

a. BIBLIOGRAPHIES, SOURCES

1711 AMERICAN LITERARY REALISM: 1870-1910. Arlington, Tex.: 1967-- . Quarterly.

Primarily bibliographical, although it includes some book reviews. Among women on whom bibliographies have been issued are Sara Orne Jewett, Louisa May Alcott, Helen

Hunt Jackson, Constance Fenimore Woolson, Rose Terry Cooke, Kate Chopin, Alice Brown, Zona Gale, Susan Glaspell, and Gertrude Atherton.

1712 Coan, Otis W., and Lillard, Richard G., comps. AMERICA IN FICTION: AN ANNOTATED LIST OF NOVELS THAT INTERPRET ASPECTS OF LIFE IN THE UNITED STATES, CANADA, AND MEXICO. 5th ed. Palo Alto, Calif.: Pacific Books, 1967. viii, 232 p. Offset.

Lists many regional books by and about women.

1713 Cook, Dorothy E., and Monro, Isabel S., comps. SHORT STORY INDEX. New York: H.W. Wilson Co., 1953. 1,553 p.

With supplements through 1969.

1714 Deodene, Frank, and French, William P., comps. BLACK AMERICAN FICTION SINCE 1952: A PRELIMINARY CHECKLIST. Chatham, N.J.: Chatham Bookseller, 1970. 25 p. Offset, pamph.

1715 Wegelin, Oscar, ed. EARLY AMERICAN FICTION, 1774-1830: A COMPILATION OF THE TITLES OF FICTION BY WRITERS BORN OR RESIDING IN NORTH AMERICA, NORTH OF THE MEXICAN BORDER AND PRINTED PRIOR TO 1831. 3d ed. New York: Peter Smith, 1929. 37 p.

1716 WOMEN AND LITERATURE: AN ANNOTATED BIBLIOGRAPHY OF WOMEN WRITERS. 3d ed. Cambridge, Mass.: Sense & Sensibility Collective, 1976. vi, 212 p. Illus. Offset, paper.

International in scope. Lists 386 works by period by American women, as well as anthologies and critical works relating to them.

1717 Wright, Lyle, ed. AMERICAN FICTION, 1774-1850: A CONTRIBUTION TOWARD BIBLIOGRAPHY. 2d rev. ed. San Marino, Calif.: Huntington Library, 1969. xviii, 411 p.

See annotation for 1719.

1718 _____. AMERICAN FICTION, 1851-1875: A CONTRIBUTION TOWARD BIBLIOGRAPHY. San Marino, Calif.: Huntington Library, 1965. xviii, 438 p.

See annotation for 1719.

1719 _____. AMERICAN FICTION, 1876-1900: A CONTRIBUTION TOWARD BIBLIOGRAPHY. San Marino, Calif.: Huntington Library,

1966. xix, 683 p.

The three bibliographies above list works of women writers, many of whom are little known.

See also 1733.

b. ANTHOLOGIES

1720 Cahill, Susan, ed. WOMEN AND FICTION. New York: New American Library, 1975. xix, 379 p.

Twenty-six stories, mostly from the twentieth century.

1721 Edwards, Lee R., and Diamond, Carolyn, eds. AMERICAN VOICES, AMERICAN WOMEN: A COLLECTION OF FICTION EXPLORING LIFE ON THE PRAIRIES, IN CITIES, AND IN NEW ENGLAND VILLAGES--AND THE VARIED INDIVIDUAL WOMEN WHO LOVED IT. New York: Avon Books, 1973. 432 p. Paper.

Fourteen stories by Harriet Spofford, Elizabeth Phelps, Mary Wilkins Freeman, Kate Chopin, Mary Austin, Dorothy Canfield Fisher, Susan Glaspell, and Jessie Fauset.

1722 Greer, Barbara, and Reid, Coletta. THE LESBIANS HOME JOURNAL: STORIES FROM THE LADDER. Baltimore: Diana Press, 1976. 326 p. Illus.

1723 Hamalian, Linda, and Hamalian, Leo, eds. SOLO: WOMEN ON WOMEN ALONE. New York: Dee, 1977. 367 p. Paper.

Twenty-seven stories. Biographical notes on authors.

1724 Parker, Jeri, ed. UNEASY SURVIVORS: FIVE WOMEN WRITERS. Santa Barbara, Calif.: Peregrine Smith, 1975. 219 p. Biblio. Paper.

Selections by Sarah Orne Jewett, Mary Wilkins Freeman, Willa Cather, Ellen Glasgow, and Edith Wharton, each preceded by a biographical headnote.

1725 Reit, Ann, ed. THE WORLD OUTSIDE: COLLECTED STORIES BY WOMEN AT WORK. Englewood Cliffs, N.J.: Prentice-Hall, 1977. 224 p. Illus. Paper.

Includes six stories by American authors.

1726 Rotter, Pat, ed. BITCHES AND SAD LADIES: AN ANTHOLOGY OF FICTION BY AND ABOUT WOMEN. New York: Harpers Magazine, Harper & Row, 1975. 445 p. Paper.

Thirty-six stories about "new women."

1727 Schneiderman, Beth K., ed. BY AND ABOUT WOMEN: AN ANTHOLOGY OF SHORT FICTION. New York: Harcourt, Brace, Jovanovich, 1975. 337 p. Biblio. Paper.

Twenty stories grouped around the themes of girlhood, marriage, fulfillment, and age. Provides headnotes to each story and a bibliography for each grouping.

1728 Stadler, Quandra P. OUT OF OUR LIVES: A SELECTION OF CONTEMPORARY BLACK FICTION. Washington, D.C.: Howard University Press, 1975. xvi, 298 p.

Seventeen stories include those by Imamu Baraka, Ann Petry, Alice Walker, and Ann Shockley.

1729 Washington, Mary H., ed. BLACK-EYED SUSANS: CLASSIC STORIES BY & ABOUT BLACK WOMEN. Garden City, N.Y.: Doubleday & Co., Anchor Books, 1975. xxxii, 163 p.

Authors of the ten stories that attack stereotyping include Alice Walker, Toni Cade Bambara, Toni Morrison, and Gwendolyn Brooks.

1730 WOMEN: FEMINIST STORIES BY NINE AUTHORS. New York: Eakin, 1972. 146 p.

Many of the stories were published originally in APHRA.

c. CRITICISM

1731 Allen, Mary. THE NECESSARY BLANKNESS: WOMEN IN MAJOR AMERICAN FICTION OF THE SIXTIES. Urbana: University of Illinois Press, 1976. 226 p.

Comments on works by John Barth, Thomas Pynchon, Ken Kesey, Philip Roth, John Updike, Joyce Carol Oates, and Sylvia Plath.

1732 Auchincloss, Louis. PIONEERS AND CARETAKERS: A STUDY OF NINE AMERICAN WOMEN NOVELISTS. Minneapolis: University of Minnesota Press, 1961. 202 p. Paper.

Biographical approach to Sara Orne Jewett, Edith Wharton, Ellen Glasgow, Elizabeth Madox Roberts, Katherine Ann Porter, Jean Stafford, Carson McCullers, Mary McCarthy, and Willa Cather. Chapters on Wharton and Glasgow were printed also as numbers 12 and 33 of the University of Minnesota Pamphlets on American Writers series.

1733 Brown, Herbert R. THE SENTIMENTAL NOVEL IN AMERICA, 1780-1860. Durham, N.C.: Duke University Press, 1940. ix, 407 p. Biblio. Reprint. New York: Octagon Books, 1975.

Discusses many popular women writers. Excellent bibliography.

1734 Fiedler, Leslie. LOVE AND DEATH IN THE AMERICAN NOVEL. New York: Criterion, 1960. 603 p. Reprint. Cleveland: World Publishing Co., 1962. Paper.

Discussion of the "fair maiden" and the "dark lady" as they appear in American fiction as well as extensive commentary on the asexual nature of American fiction and the reason for it.

1735 Gloster, Hugh M. NEGRO VOICES IN AMERICAN FICTION. Chapel Hill: University of North Carolina Press, 1948. Reprint. New York: Russell & Russell, 1965. xiv, 295 p. Biblio.

Some books by black women and some books about black women by men in social and political context.

1736 Hart, James D. THE POPULAR BOOK: A HISTORY OF AMERICA'S LITERARY TASTE. New York: Oxford University Press, 1950. Reprint. Westport, Conn.: Greenwood Press, 1976. xii, 351 p. Biblio. Paper.

Discusses women as writers and readers. See especially chapter 4, "The Power of Sympathy"; chapter 6, "Home Influence"; and chapter 7, "The Gates Ajar."

1737 Jessup, Josephine. FAITH OF OUR FEMINISTS: A STUDY IN THE NOVELS OF EDITH WHARTON, ELLEN GLASGOW, WILLA CATHER. New York: A.R. Smith, 1950. 128 p. Biblio. Reprint. New York: Biblo & Tanner, 1965.

Notes similarities in attitudes and life-styles of the three women mentioned in the title.

1738 Lawrence, Margaret. THE SCHOOL OF FEMININITY: A BOOK FOR AND ABOUT WOMEN AS THEY ARE INTERPRETED THROUGH FEMININE WRITERS OF YESTERDAY AND TODAY. New York: Frederick A. Stokes, 1936. xii, 382 p. Illus. Reprint. Port Washington, N.Y.: Kennikat Press, 1966.

Freudian approach to English and American writers of the earlier twentieth century. American writers include Anita Loos, Dorothy Parker, Katherine Brush, Edna Ferber, Fannie Hurst, Dorothy Canfield, Djuna Barnes, Phyllis Bentley, Ruth Suckow, Evelyn Scott, Edith Wharton, Kay Boyle,

Ellen Glasgow, Pearl Buck, and Willa Cather.

1739 Maglin, Nan B. "Early Feminist Fiction: The Dilemma of Personal Life." PROSPECTS 2 (1976): 167-91.

Maintains that despite certain observed conventions, much early feminist fiction deals with the struggle toward selfhood and the view of marriage as problematic.

1740 Page, Sally. FAULKNER'S WOMEN/CHARACTERIZATION AND MEANING. Deland, Fla.: Everett/ Edwards, 1973. 260 p.

1741 Pannill, Linda S. "The Artist-Heroine in American Fiction, 1890-1920." Unpublished Ph.D. thesis, University of North Carolina at Chapel Hill, 1975.

Discusses the female protagonists in the novels of Ellen Glasgow, Willa Cather, and Mary Austin.

1742 Weil, Dorothy. IN DEFENSE OF WOMEN: SUSANNA ROWSON (1792-1824). University Park: Pennsylvania State University Press, 1976. 204 p. Biblio.

Popular novelist as observer and supporter of women's cause.

1743 Wood, Anne D. "The 'Scribbling Women and Fanny Fern: Why Women Wrote." AMERICAN QUARTERLY 23 (Spring 1971): 3-24.

Points out that Fern's novel RUTH HALL, admired by Hawthorne, urges women to "Write! Write!" as means of surviving and escape from home.

d. SELECTED WORKS BY INDIVIDUAL AUTHORS

An asterisk (*) indicates that biographical or autobiographical material on the author is listed in chapter 10. Except for those titles followed by SS, which are short stories, all titles are novels.

i. Fiction by Women

(a). EIGHTEENTH CENTURY

1744 *Foster, Hannah W.
THE COQUETTE: A NOVEL FOUNDED ON FACT (1797). Best seller.

1745 *Rowson, Susannah R.
CHARLOTTE TEMPLE: A TALE OF TRUTH (1791). Best seller; paper.

LUCY TEMPLE (1828). Best seller.

(b). NINETEENTH CENTURY

1746 Aguilar, Grace.
HOME INFLUENCE: A TALE FOR MOTHERS AND DAUGHTERS (1847). Best seller.

1747 *Alcott, Louisa May.
LITTLE WOMEN (1868). Best seller; paper. WORK (1873).

1748 *Blake, Lillie D.
FETTERRED FOR LIFE; OR, LORD AND MASTER, A STORY OF TODAY (1874).

1749 Campbell, Helen S.
MISS MELINDA'S OPPORTUNITY: A STORY (1886).
MRS. HERNDON'S INCOME (1866).

1750 Chopin, Kate.
THE COMPLETE WORKS OF KATE CHOPIN. Edited by Per Seyersted. Baton Rouge: Louisiana State University, 1967. Includes THE AWAKENING (1899).
See also 1829.

1751 Cooke, Rose Terry.
HUCKLEBERRIES GATHERED FROM NEW ENGLAND HILLS (1891). SS.

Craddock, Charles Egbert (pseud.). See Murfree, Mary Noailles.

1752 Cummins, Maria S.
THE LAMPLIGHTER (1854). Best seller.

1753 Davis, Rebecca Harding. "Life in the Iron Mills." ATLANTIC MONTHLY 7 (April 1861): 430-35. Available from the Feminist Press. Paper.

Fern, Fanny (pseud.). See Parton, Susan P.W.

1754 *Freeman, Mary E. Wilkins.
A HUMBLE ROMANCE AND OTHER STORIES (1887). SS. Paper.
A NEW ENGLAND NUN AND OTHER STORIES (1891). SS. Paper.

1755 *French, Alice [Thanet, Octave].
KNITTERS IN THE SUN (1887).
STORIES OF A WESTERN TOWN, 1893. SS.

1756 Gilman, Charlotte Perkins.
"The Yellow Wallpaper (1892)." SS. Available from the Feminist Press. Paper.

1757 Green, Anna K.
THE LEAVENWORTH CASE (1878). Best seller.

1758 *Jackson, Helen M.F. Hunt [H.H.]
RAMONA (1884). Best seller; paper.

1759 *Jewett, Sarah Orne.
TALES OF NEW ENGLAND (1890). SS. Paper.
THE COUNTRY OF THE POINTED FIRS (1896). SS.

1760 *King, Grace E.
TALES OF A TIME AND PLACE (1892). SS. Paper.
BALCONY STORIES (1893). SS. Paper.

1761 Monk, Maria.
AWFUL DISCLOSURES OF MARIA MONK, AS EXHIBITED IN A NARRATIVE OF HER SUFFERINGS DURING A RESIDENCE OF FIVE YEARS AS A NOVICE, AND TWO YEARS AS A BLACK NUN, WITH THE HOTEL DIEU NUNNERY IN MONTREAL (1896).

1762 *Murfree, Mary Noailles [Craddock, Charles Egbert].
IN THE TENNESSEE MOUNTAINS (1884). SS. Paper.

1763 Parton, Sara P.W. [Fern, Fanny].
FERN LEAVES FROM FANNY'S PORTFOLIO (1853).
RUTH HALL (1855).

1764 Pemberton, Caroline C.
THE CHARITY GIRL (1901).

Phelps, Elizabeth Stuart. See Ward, Elizabeth Stuart Phelps.

1765 *Sedgwick, Catharine M.
A NEW-ENGLAND TALE (1822). Best seller.
REDWOOD (1824). Best seller.

1766 Slosson, Annie T.
DUMB FOXGLOVE AND OTHER STORIES (1898). SS.

1767 Southworth, Emma D.E.N.
THE FATAL MARRIAGE (1863). Best seller.
SELF-RAISED (1876). Best seller.

1768 Stephens, Anna S.
MALESKA, OR THE INDIAN WIFE OF THE WHITE HUNTER (1860). Best seller.

1769 *Stowe, Harriet Beecher.
UNCLE TOM'S CABIN; OR, LIFE AMONG THE LOWLY (1852). Best seller; paper.
A KEY TO UNCLE TOM'S CABIN (research), 1853. Best seller.

1770 Tenney, Tabitha G.
FEMALE QUIXOTISM (1801).

Thanet, Octave (pseud.). See French, Alice.

1771 *Ward, Elizabeth Stuart Phelps.
THE SUNNYSIDE: OR THE COUNTRY MINISTER'S WIFE (1851). Best seller.
THE GATES AJAR (1851). Best seller.

1772 Warren, Caroline.
THE GAMESTERS (1805).

1773 Watkins, Francis E.
IOLA LEROY; OR, THE SHADOWS UPLIFTED (1892).

1774 Whitcher, Frances M.B.
WIDOW BEDOTT PAPERS (1834).

1775 Wilson, Augusta J. [Evans, Augusta J.].
ELMO (1853). Best seller.
BEULAH (1859). Best seller.

1776 Wood, Mrs. Henry.
EAST LYNNE (1861). Novel and play; best seller.

1777 *Woolson, Constance Fenimore.
ANNE (1882).
FOR THE MAJOR (1883). Paper.
THE FRONT YARD, AND OTHER ITALIAN STORIES (1894). SS.

(c). TWENTIETH CENTURY

1778 *Angelou, Maya.
I KNOW WHY THE CAGED BIRD SINGS (1970). Paper.

1779 Arnow, Harriet.
THE DOLLMAKER (1972). Paper.

1780 *Atherton, Gertrude.
BLACK OXEN (1923).

1781 Bambara, Toni [Cade].
THE SEA BIRDS ARE STILL ALIVE: COLLECTED STORIES (1977). SS.

1782 Barnes, Djuna.
NIGHTWOOD (1937). Paper.

1783 Calisher, Hortense.
TEXTURE OF LIFE, 1963; ON KEEPING WOMEN, 1977.

1784 *Cather, Willa.
O PIONEERS! (1913). Paper.
THE SONG OF THE LARK (1915). Paper.
MY ÁNTONIA (1918). Paper.
A LOST LADY (1923). Paper.

1785 Chase, Mary Ellen.
MARY PETERS (1934).

1786 Didion, Joan.
PLAY IT AS IT LAYS (1970). Paper.

1787 Ferber, Edna.
DAWN O'HARA, THE GIRL WHO LAUGHED (1911).
SHOW BOAT (1926). Paper.

1788 Fisher, Dorothy Canfield.
THE BENT TWIG (1915).

1789 *Fitzgerald, Zelda.
SAVE ME THE WALTZ (1932). Paper.

1790 *Gale, Zona.
MISS LULU BETT (1921).

1791 *Glasgow, Ellen.
BARREN GROUND (1925). Paper.

1792 Glyn, Elinor.
THREE WEEKS (1907).

1793 Gould, Lois.
SUCH GOOD FRIENDS (1970). Paper.

1794 Grau, Shirley Ann.
THE BLACK PRINCE AND OTHER STORIES (1955). Paper. SS.
THE KEEPERS OF THE HOUSE (1971). Paper.

1795 *Hurst, Fanny.
LUMMOX (1923).
ANY WOMAN (1950).

1796 *Hurston, Zora Neale.
SERAPH IN THE SUWANEE (1948).
THEIR EYES WERE WATCHING GOD (1965). Paper.

1797 Jackson, Shirley.
THE LOTTERY (1949). SS. Paper.
WE HAVE ALWAYS LIVED IN THE CENTER (1962).

1798 Jong, Erica.
FEAR OF FLYING (1973). Paper.

1799 *McCarthy, Mary.
THE COMPANY SHE KEEPS (1942). SS. Paper.
THE GROUP (1954). Paper.

1800 McCullers, Carson.
THE HEART IS A LONELY HUNTER (1940). Paper.
THE MEMBER OF THE WEDDING (1946). Paper.

1801 Marshall, Paule.
BROWN GIRL, BROWNSTONES (1959).

1802 Mitchell, Margaret.
GONE WITH THE WIND (1836). Best seller; paper.

1803 Norris, Kathleen.
MOTHER (1911).

1804 Oates, Joyce Carol.
THEM (1969). Paper.
THE WHEEL OF LOVE (1970). SS. Paper.

1805 O'Connor, Flannery.
COMPLETE STORIES (1971). SS.

1806 Olsen, Tillie.
TELL ME A RIDDLE (1960). Paper.
YONNANDIO (1973). Paper.

1807 Paley, Grace.
THE LITTLE DISTRUBANCES OF MAN (1958). SS. Paper.

1808 Peterkin, Julia.
SCARLET SISTER MARY (1928).

1809 Petry, Ann.
THE STREET (1946). Paper.
MISS MURIEL AND OTHER STORIES (1971). SS.

1810 *Plath, Sylvia.
THE BELL JAR (1971). Paper.

1811 Porter, Eleanor H.
POLLYANNA (1913). Best seller.

1812 Porter, Katherine Anne.
PALE HORSE, PALE RIDER (1970). Paper. Includes OLD MORTALITY, NOON WINE, and title story.

Waldrip, Louise, and Bauer, Shirely A. A BIBLIOGRAPHY OF THE WORKS OF KATHERINE ANNE PORTER, and A BIBLIOGRAPHY OF THE CRITICISM OF THE WORKS OF KATHERINE ANNE PORTER. Metuchen, N.J.: Scarecrow Press, 1969. 219 p.

1813 Rawlings, Marjorie Kinnan.
THE YEARLING (1938). Paper.

1814 Rice, Alice C. Hegan.
MRS. WIGGS OF THE CABBAGE PATCH (1901).

1815 Rinehart, Mary Roberts.
THE CIRCULAR STAIRCASE (1908).

1816 Roiphe, Anne H.
UP THE SANDBOX (1971).

1817 Sarton, May.
MRS. STEVENS HEARS THE MERMAIDS SINGING (1975). Paper.

1818 Shulman, Alix K.
MEMOIRS OF AN EX-PROM QUEEN (1972). Paper.

1819 Smith, Lillian.
STRANGE FRUIT (1944).

1820 Sontag, Susan.
I ETCETERA (1978). SS. Paper.

1821 Stafford, Jean.
THE INTERIOR CASTE (1953). Includes BOSTON ADVENTURE, THE MOUNTAIN LION, novels, and CHILDREN ARE BORED ON SUNDAYS (SS).

1822 Stead, Christina.
THE MAN WHO LOVED CHILDREN (1940). Paper.

1823 *Stein, Gertrude.
THREE LIVES (1909). Paper.

1824 Stratton-Porter, Gene.
A GIRL OF THE LIMBERLOST (1909).

1825 Stuart, Ruth McEnery.
A GOLDEN WEDDING, AND OTHER TALES (1893).
AUNT AMITY'S SILVER WEDDING, AND OTHER STORIES (1909). SS.

1826 Suckow, Ruth.
IOWA INTERIORS (1926). SS.

1827 Walker, Alice.
IN LOVE & TROUBLE (1973). SS.
MERIDIAN (1976). SS.

1828 Welty, Eudora.
THIRTEEN STORIES (1965). SS.
THE OPTIMIST'S DAUGHTER (1972). Paper.

1829 *Wharton, Edith.
THE HOUSE OF MIRTH (1905). Paper.
THE AGE OF INNOCENCE (1920). Paper.
THE OLD MAID (1924).

Springer, Marlene. EDITH WHARTON AND KATE CHOPIN: A REFERENCE GUIDE. Series Seventy. Boston: G.K. Hall & Co., 1976. 305 p.

1830 Wiggin, Kate Douglas.
REBECCA OF SUNNYBROOK FARM (1903). Paper.

1831 Yezierska, Anzia.
BREAD GIVERS (1925).

ii. Fiction About Women by Men

1832 Brown, Charles Brockden.
CLARA HOWARD (1801).

1833 Cooper, James Fenimore.
JACK TIER (1848).

1834 Crane, Stephen.
MAGGIE, A GIRL OF THE STREETS (1893). Paper.

1835 Cummings, A[riel] I.
THE FACTORY GIRL: OR, GARDEZ LE COEUR (1847).

1836 Dreiser, Theodore.
SISTER CARRIE (1900). Paper.
JENNIE GERHARDT (1911).

1837 Gaines, Ernest J.
THE AUTOBIOGRAPHY OF (MISS) JANE PITTMAN (1971). Paper.

1838 Garland, Hamlin.
ROSE OF DUTCHER'S COOLLY (1859). Paper.

1839 Hawthorne, Nathaniel.
THE SCARLET LETTER (1850). Paper.
THE BLITHEDALE ROMANCE (1852). Paper.

1840 Herrick, Robert.
ONE WOMAN'S LIFE (1913).
TOGETHER (1908).

1841 Howells, William Dean.
THE LADY OF THE AROOSTOOK (1879).
A MODERN INSTANCE (1881). Paper.

1842 James, Henry.
DAISY MILLER (1897). Paper.
PORTRAIT OF A LADY (1881). Paper.
THE BOSTONIANS (1886). Paper.

1843 Lewis, Sinclair.
MAIN STREET (1920). Paper.
ANN VICKERS (1933).

1844 Melville, Herman.
"The Tartarus of Maids." PIAZZA TALES (1856).

1845 Roth, Philip.
WHEN SHE WAS GOOD (1967). Paper.

1846 Toomer, Jean.
CANE (1923). Paper.

3. Poetry

a. BIBLIOGRAPHIES, INDEXES

For a listing of little magazines and small presses printing current poetry by women see 1670. KNOW issues an American Women's Poetry Series. For titles of poetry books, many of them printed by small feminist presses, see 417.

1847 Chapman, Dorothy H. INDEX TO BLACK POETRY. Boston: G.K. Hall & Co., 1974. xxii, 541 p.

Includes some women. Based on Dorothy Porter's partially annotated THE NEGRO IN THE UNITED STATES: A SELECTED BIBLIOGRAPHY (Washington, D.C.: Library of Congress, 1970. x, 313 p.) and her NORTH AMERICAN NEGRO POETS: A BIBLIOGRAPHICAL CHECKLIST OF THEIR WRITINGS 1760-1944 (1945).

1848 Davis, Lloyd M., and Irwin, Robert, comps. CONTEMPORARY

AMERICAN POETRY: A CHECKLIST. Metuchen, N.J.: Scarecrow Press, 1975. iv, 183 p.

Lists over eleven hundred volumes of poetry, many of them small-press publications.

1849 Granger, Edith, comp. GRANGER'S INDEX TO POETRY. Edited by William James Smith. 6th ed. New York: Columbia University Press, 1973. xxxvii, 2223 p.

Indexes 514 anthologies from 1904 on by title, first line, author, and subject of poems. International in scope. Update in 1978 drops some entries of earlier edition but adds others.

1850 Zulauf, Sander W., and Weiser, Irwin H. INDEX OF AMERICAN PERIODICAL VERSE. Metuchen, N.J.: Scarecrow Press, 1971-- . Annual.

By author, title.

See also 1870.

b. CRITICISM

1851 Kindilien, Carlin T. AMERICAN POETRY IN THE EIGHTEEN NINETIES. Providence, R.I.: Brown University Press, 1956. xv, 223 p.

Discusses Emily Dickinson as an end-of-the-century influence. Contains scattered information on Martha Bianchi, Alice Brown, Charlotte Gilman, Louise Guiney, Helen Jackson, Harriet Monroe, Josephine Peabody, Lizette Reese, and others.

1852 Malkoff, Karl. CROWELL'S BOOK OF CONTEMPORY AMERICAN POETRY. New York: Thomas Y. Crowell Co., 1973. 338 p.

Includes critical assessments and bio-bibliographies of Elizabeth Bishop, Gwendolyn Brooks, Mari Evans, Isabel Gardner, Nikki Giovanni, Louise Gluck, Erica Jong, Carolyn Kizer, Denise Levertov, Sylvia Plath, Adrienne Rich, Sonia Sanchez, Anne Sexton, Mary Swenson, and Alice Walker.

1853 Shouse, Elaine M. "An Analysis of the Poetry of Three Revolutionary Poets: Don L. Lee Nikki Giovanni, and Sonia Sanchez." Ph.D. thesis, University of Illinois at Urbana-Champagne, 1976.

Discusses audience, message, and style.

1854 Sprague, Rosemary. IMAGINARY GARDENS: A STUDY OF FIVE AMERICAN POETS. Philadelphia: Chilton Book Co., 1969. xviii, 237 p. Illus.

Contains studies of Emily Dickinson, Amy Lowell, Sara Teasdale, Edna St. Vincent Millay, and Marianne Moore. Includes poems of each.

1855 Watts, Emily S. THE POETRY OF AMERICAN WOMEN FROM 1632 TO 1945. Austin: University of Texas Press, 1977. xvi, 218. Biblio.

Claims that an understanding of women's poetry, which is possibly no different from that of men, is necessary to an understanding of the development of American poetry.

1856 Williams, Ellen. HARRIET MONROE AND THE POETRY RENAISSANCE: THE FIRST TEN YEARS OF POETRY, 1912-1922. Urbana: University of Illinois Press, 1977. xiv, 312 p.

Editor whose efforts opened the modern era in American poetry.

c. ANTHOLOGIES

1857 "American Women Poets." WEID: THE SENSIBILITY REVIEW 12 (December 1976): special issue. Bicentennial Issue 2.

1858 Bernikov, Louise, ed. THE WORLD SPLIT OPEN: FOUR CENTURIES OF WOMEN POETS IN ENGLAND AND AMERICA, 1552-1950. New York: Random House, Vintage Books, 1974. xxix. 346 p. Paper.

Comprises an excellent introduction. Short biography precedes each group of selections.

1859 Chester, Laura, and Barba, Sharon, eds. RISING TIDES: 20TH-CENTURY AMERICAN WOMEN POETS. New York: Washington Square Press, 1973. 410 p. Illus. Paper.

Discusses twentieth-century poets beginning with Gertrude Stein. Photograph and short biography precedes each group of selections.

1860 Griswold, Rufus W., ed. THE FEMALE POETS OF AMERICA. 2d ed. Philadelphia: Carey & Hart, 1849. 486 p. Reprint. New York: MSS Information Corp., 1972.

Begins with Anne Bradstreet. Includes biographical and critical notes.

1861 Herringshaw, Thomas W., ed. LOCAL AND NATIONAL POETS OF AMERICA, WITH BIOGRAPHICAL SKETCHES AND CHOICE SELECTIONS FROM OVER ONE THOUSAND LIVING AMERICAN POETS. Chicago: American, 1890. iv, x, 1036 p. Illus.

Includes many hard-to-find minor figures.

1862 Howe, Florence, and Bass, Ellen, eds. NO MORE MASKS: AN ANTHOLOGY OF POEMS BY WOMEN. Garden City, N.Y.: Doubleday & Co., Anchor Books, 1973. 396 p. Paper.

Covers twentieth-century poets beginning with Amy Lowell. Includes brief biographical sketches.

1863 Iverson, Lucille, and Ruby, Kathryn, eds. WOMEN BECOME NEW: POEMS BY CONTEMPORARY AMERICAN WOMEN. New York: Bantam Books, 1975. xxi, 234 p. Paper.

Includes forty-three poets.

1864 Juhasz, Suzanne. NAKED AND FIERY FORMS: MODERN AMERICAN POETRY BY WOMEN, A NEW TRADITION. New York: Harper & Row, 1976. 214 p.

1865 Konek, Carol, and Walters, Dorothy. I HEAR MY SISTERS SINGING: POEMS BY TWENTIETH CENTURY WOMEN. New York: Thomas Y. Crowell Co., 1976. xiv, 295 p. Paper.

1866 May, Caroline, ed. THE AMERICAN FEMALE POETS: WITH CRITICAL AND BIOGRAPHICAL NOTICES. Philadelphia: Lindsay & Blakiston, 1848. viii, 559 p. Illus.

Covers eighty women poets, beginning with Anne Bradstreet.

1867 Miles, Sara, et al., eds. ORDINARY WOMEN. MUJERES COMUNES: AN ANTHOLOGY OF POEMS BY NEW YORK WOMEN. New York: Ordinary Women, 1976. 136 p. Illus. Paper.

Includes poems mostly by black and Third World women. Available from P.O. Box 664, Old Chelsea Station, New York, New York 10011.

1868 Reit, Ann, ed. ALONE AMID ALL THIS NOISE: A COLLECTION OF WOMEN'S POETRY. Englewood Cliffs, N.J.: Prentice-Hall, 1977. 218 p.

1869 Stanford, Ann. THE WOMEN POETS IN ENGLISH: AN ANTHOLOGY. New York: McGraw-Hill Book Co., 1972. xlix, 374 p.

Covers American women in historical context.

1870 Stedman, Edmund C., ed. AN AMERICAN ANTHOLOGY, 1787-1900: SELECTIONS ILLUSTRATING THE EDITOR'S CRITICAL REVIEW OF AMERICAN POETRY IN THE NINETEENTH CENTURY. Boston: Houghton Mifflin Co., 1900. lxvii, 878 p. Reprint. New York: Greenwood Press, 1968.

Includes many women. Biographical sketches with bibliographical listings conclude text.

d. SELECTED WORKS BY INDIVIDUAL AUTHORS

An asterisk (*) indicates that biographical or autobiographical material on the author is listed in chapter 10.

i. Seventeenth and Eighteenth Centuries

1871 *Bradstreet, Anne.
THE WORKS OF ANNE BRADSTREET. Edited by Jeannine Hinsley. 1967.

1872 Warren, Mercy Otis.
POEMS, DRAMATIC AND MISCELLANEOUS (1790).

1873 *Wheatley, Phillis.
LIFE AND WORKS OF PHILLIS WHEATLEY, CONTAINING HER COMPLETE POETICAL WORKS, NUMEROUS LETTERS, CENTURY AND A HALF AGO. Edited by G. Herbert Renfro. n.p., 1916. Reprint. Black Heritage Library Collection. Freeport, N.Y.: Books for Libraries, 1972. Paper.

ii. Nineteenth Century

1874 Cary, Alice, and Cary, Phebe.
POEMS BY ALICE AND PHEBE CARY (1850).

1875 Coolbrith, Ina.
SONGS FROM THE GOLDEN GATE (1895).

1876 *Dickinson, Emily.
THE POEMS OF EMILY DICKINSON, INCLUDING VARIANT READINGS CRITICALLY COMPARED WITH ALL KNOWN MANUSCRIPTS. Edited by Thomas H. Johnson. 3 vols. Cambridge, Mass.: Harvard University Press/Belknap Press, 1958.
THE LETTERS OF EMILY DICKINSON. Edited by Thomas H. Johnson, and Theodora Ward. 3 vols. Cambridge, Mass.: Harvard University Press/Belknap Press, 1958.

1877 *Gilman, Charlotte Perkins.
IN THIS OUR WORLD (1889).

1878 Guiney, Louise Imogene.
A ROADSIDE HARP (1893).

1879 *Howe, Julia Ward.
FROM SUNSET RIDGE: POEMS OLD AND NEW 1898.

1880 *Jackson, Helen Hunt.
VERSES BY H.H. (1870).
SONNETS AND LYRICS (1876).

1881 *Lazarus, Emma.
COMPLETE WORKS OF EMMA LAZARUS (1888). 2 vols.

1882 Moulton, Louise Chandler.
SWALLOW FLIGHTS AND OTHER POEMS (1878).

1883 Reese, Lizette Woodworth.
A BRANCH OF MAY (1887).

1884 *Sigourney, Lydia Huntley.
MORAL PIECES IN PROSE AND VERSE (1815).
WATER DROPS, A PLEA FOR TEMPERANCE (1847).

1885 *Wilcox, Ella Wheeler.
POEMS OF PASSION (1883).
POEMS OF PLEASURE (1888).

1886 *Woolson, Constance Fenimore.
TWO WOMEN (1862).

iii. Twentieth Century

1887 Ai.
KILLING FLOOR (1979). Paper.

1888 Alta.
I AM NOT A PRACTICING ANGEL (1975). Paper.

1889 Bishop, Elizabeth.
THE COMPLETE POEMS (1969). Paper.

1890 *Bogan, Louise.
THE BLUE ESTUARIES: POEMS 1923-1968 (1968).

1891 Branch, Anne Hempstead.
SONNETS FROM A LOCKED BOX, AND OTHER POEMS (1929).

1892 Brooks, Gwendolyn.
THE WORLD OF GWENDOLYN BROOKS (1971).

1893 Clifton, Lucille.
GOOD NEWS ABOUT THE EARTH (1972).
AN ORDINARY WOMAN (1974). Paper.

1894 Crapsey, Adelaide.
VERSE (1915).

1895 DiPrima, Diane.
DINNERS AND NIGHTMARES (1974). Paper.

1896 Doolittle, Hilda [H.D.].
COLLECTED POEMS (1925).
SELECTED POEMS (1957). Paper.

1897 Evans, Mari.
I AM A BLACK WOMAN (1970). Paper.

1898 *Giovanni, Nikki.
BLACK FEELING, BLACK TALK, BLACK JUDGEMENT (1968).
MY HOUSE (1972). Paper.

1899 Johnson, Georgia.
THE HEART OF A WOMAN (1918).
BRONZE (1922).

1900 Jong, Erica.
HERE COMES. Originally published as FRUITS AND VEGETABLES and HALF-LIVES (1975). Paper.

1901 Jordan, June.
SOME CHANGES (1971). Paper.

1902 Kumin, Maxine.
THE NIGHTMARE FACTORY (1970). Paper.

1903 Levertov, Denise.
THE FREEING OF THE DUST (1975).
LIFE IN THE FORESTS (1978). Paper.
Wilson, Robert A.J. A BIBLIOGRAPHY OF DENISE LEVERTOV. New York: Phoenix Book Shop, 1972. i, 98 p.

1904 Lifshin, Lynn.
UPSTATE MADONNA . . . POEMS--1970-1974 (1975). Paper.

1905 Lorde, Audre.
FROM A LAND WHERE OTHER PEOPLE LIVE (1973).

1906 *Lowell, Amy.
COMPLETE POETICAL WORKS (1955).

1907 Loy, Minna.
LUNAR BAEDEKER (1923).

1908 McGinley, Phyllis.
SIXPENCE IN HER SHOE (1964).

1909 Merriam, Eve.
FAMILY CIRCLE (1946).
OUT LOUD (1973).

1910 *Millay, Edna St. Vincent.
COLLECTED POEMS (1956). Paper.

1911 Moore, Marianne.
THE COMPLETE POEMS OF MARIANNE MOORE (1968).

1912 Owens, Rochelle.
I AM THE BABE OF JOSEPH STALIN'S DAUGHTER (1972).
THE JOE 82 CREATION POEMS (1974). Paper.

1913 Parker, Dorothy.
THE COLLECTED POETRY OF DOROTHY PARKER (1944).

1914 Piercy, Marge.
BREAKING CAMP (1968).
HARD LOVING (1969). Paper.

1915 *Plath, Sylvia.
THE COLOSSUS (1961).
ARIEL (1965). Paper.

1916 Rich, Adrienne.
POEMS SELECTED AND NEW 1950-1974 (1975). Paper.

1917 Riding, Laura.
SELECTED POEMS: IN FIVE SETS (1970). Paper.

1918 Rukeyser, Muriel.
THE COLLECTED POEMS OF MURIEL RUKEYSER, 1978.

1919 Sanchez, Sonia.
WE A BADDDDD PEOPLE (1968). Paper.

1920 Sexton, Anne.
ALL MY PRETTY ONES (1961).
LOVE POEMS (1967). Paper.

1921 Stein, Gertrude.
TENDER BUTTONS (1914).
BEE TIME VINE AND OTHER PIECES (1913-1927) (1953).

1922 Swenson, May.
TO MIX WITH TIME (1963).
NEW AND SELECTED: THINGS TAKING PLACE (1978).

1923 *Teasdale, Sara.
THE COLLECTED POEMS OF SARA TEASDALE (1937). Paper.

1924 Wakoski, Diane.
THE GEORGE WASHINGTON POEMS (1967).
THE MOTORCYCLE BETRAYAL POEMS (1971).
VIRTUOSO LITERATURE FOR TWO AND FOUR HANDS (1975).

1925 Walker, Alice.
REVOLUTIONARY PETUNIAS (1973).

1926 Walker, Margaret.
FOR MY PEOPLE (1942).
PROPHETS FOR A NEW DAY (1970).

1927 Wylie, Eleanor.
THE COLLECTED POEMS OF ELEANOR WYLIE (1923).
LAST POEMS (1943).

e. TAPES

BLACK BOX distributes commercial and noncommercial cassettes of women reading their poems. Poets include Denise Levertov, Adrienne Rich, Muriel Rukeyser, Sylvia Plath, Sonia Sanchez, Marilyn Hacker, and many others.

1928 Modern American Poetry Criticism Series. Deland, Fla.: Everett Edwards, 1975-- .

Lectures on Marianne Moore, Louise Bogan, Sylvia Plath, Emily Dickinson, Denise Levertov, and Muriel Rukeyser.

4. Drama

a. BIBLIOGRAPHIES

Many feminist theater companies write their own plays and may supply texts upon request.

1929 Arata, Esther S., and Rotoli, Nicholas J. BLACK AMERICAN PLAYWRIGHTS, 1801 TO THE PRESENT: A BIBLIOGRAPHY. Metuchen, N.J.: Scarecrow Press, 1976. vii, 295 p. Biblio. Offset.

1930 Batchelder, Eleanor, comp. PLAYS BY WOMEN: A BIBLIOGRAPHY. New York: Womanbooks, 1977. 41 p.

From before the nineteenth century to the present. Lists works by individual playwrights and subject as well as anthologies.

1931 Ireland, Norma. INDEX TO FULL-LENGTH PLAYS, 1944-64. Useful Reference Series, no. 92. Boston: F.W. Faxon Co., 1965. xxii, 296 p.

By subject. International in scope.

1932 PLAY INDEX. 3 vols. New York: H.W. Wilson Co., 1953-68.

Three volumes--1949-1952, 1953-1960, 1961-1967--list all types of plays by author, title, and subject. They include also information on collections and cast directory.

1933 Weingarten, Joseph A. MODERN AMERICAN PLAYWRIGHTS, 1918-1945: A BIBLIOGRAPHY. 2 vols. in 1. New York: 1946-47.

Includes thirty-five hundred titles.

b. ANTHOLOGIES

1934 Hatch, James, ed. BLACK THEATER, USA: FORTY PLAYS BY BLACK AMERICANS, 1847-1974. New York: Macmillan Co., Free Press, 1974. x, 886 p. Biblio.

Contains seven plays from 1925 to 1928 and four from 1960 to 1970 by women.

1935 Moore, Honor, ed. THE NEW WOMEN'S THEATRE: TEN PLAYS BY CONTEMPORARY AMERICAN WOMEN. New York: Random House, Vintage Books, 1977. xxxvii, 537 p.

Authors include Ntozake Shange, Tina Howe, Ursula Molinaro, Ruth Wolff and Honor Moore. The introduction gives a brief history of women's theater.

1936 Owens, Rochelle, ed. SPONTANEOUS COMBUSTION: EIGHT NEW AMERICAN PLAYS. The Winter Repertory, no. 6. New York: Winter House, 1972. 224 p.

Includes plays by Adrienne Kennedy, Megan Terry, Julie Bovasso, and Rochelle Owens. Also supplies biographical material on playwrights.

1937 Sullivan, Gloria, and Hatch, James, eds. PLAYS BY AND ABOUT WOMEN: AN ANTHOLOGY. New York: Random House, 1973.

xv, 425 p.

Includes plays by Lillian Hellman, Alice Gerstenberg, Clare Boothe, Megan Terry, and Alice Childress.

c. WORKS BY INDIVIDUAL AUTHORS

i. Plays by Women

An asterisk (*) before an entry indicates that biographical or autobiographical material on the author is listed in chapter 10. The listing is necessarily a selected one.

(a). EIGHTEENTH CENTURY

1938 *Rowson, Susanna R.
SLAVES IN ALGIERS; OR, A STRUGGLE FOR FREEDOM (1794).
THE FEMALE PATRIOT (1795).

1939 *Warren, Mercy Otis.
THE ADULATEUR (1773).
THE GROUP (1775).

See also 2095.

(b). NINETEENTH CENTURY

1940 Bateman, Mrs. Sidney.
SELF (1856).

1941 *Howe, Julia Ward.
LEONORA; OR, THE WORLD'S OWN (1857).
HIPPOLYTUS (1864).

1942 Ritchie, Anna C. Mowatt.
FASHION; OR, LIFE IN NEW YORK (1845).

1943 Robinson, Harriet J.H.
THE NEW PANDORA: A DRAMA (1889).

1944 *Stowe, Harriet Beecher.
UNCLE TOM'S CABIN (1852).

See also 1776. For reviews of some of the aforementioned plays, see 2099.

(c). TWENTIETH CENTURY

1945 Akin, Zoe.
DECLASSÉ! (1919).
DADDY'S GONE A HUNTING (1921).

1946 Austin, Mary.
THE ARROW MAKER (1911).

1947 Boothe, Clare.
THE WOMEN (1936).
KISS THE BOYS GOOD-BYE (1938).

1948 Bovasso, Julie.
SCHUBERT'S LAST SERENADE (1971).

1949 Chase, Marry Ellen.
HARVEY (1944).
MRS. McTHING (1952).

1950 Childress, Alice.
A WINE IN THE WILDERNESS (1969).

1951 Crothers, Rachel.
A MAN'S WORLD (1909).
HE AND SHE (1911).
OURSELVES (1913).
THE OLD LADY (1916).
EXPRESSING WILLIE (1924).
WHEN LADIES MEET (1932).
SUSAN AND GOD (1937).

1952 Dayton, Katherine, and Kaufman, George.
FIRST LADY (1935).

1953 Drexler, Rosalyn.
THE LINE OF LEAST RESISTANCE AND OTHER PLAYS (1967).

1954 Ferber, Edna, and Kaufman, George.
THE ROYAL FAMILY (1927).
DINNER AT EIGHT (1932).

1955 Fletcher, Julia C. [Fleming, George].
A MAN AND HIS WIFE (1900).

1956 Glaspell, Susan.
SUPPRESSED DESIRES (1914).
WOMAN'S HONOR (1918).
THE VERGE (1921).
ALISON'S HOUSE (1930).

1957 Hansberry, Lorraine.
A RAISIN IN THE SUN (1959).
TO BE YOUNG, GIFTED, AND BLACK (1969).

1958 *Hellman, Lillian.
THE LITTLE FOXES (1939).

WATCH ON THE RHINE (1941).
THE AUTUMN GARDEN (1951).
TOYS IN THE ATTIC (1960).

1959 Heywood, Dorothy, and Heywood, DuBose.
PORGY (1927).

1960 International Ladies' Garment Workers Union.
PINS AND NEEDLES (1936).

1961 Kummer, Clare.
GOOD GRACIOUS, ANNABELLE (1916).

1962 Lamb, Myra.
THE MOD DONNA AND SCYKLON Z (1971).

1963 McNaid, Irene Taylor.
THE COLOR LINE (1928).

1964 Millay, Edna St. Vincent.
THE KING'S HENCHMAN (1926).

1965 Owen, Rochelle.
THE KARL MARX PLAYS AND OTHERS (1974).

1966 Peabody, Josephine Prescott.
THE PIPER (1910).
THE PORTRAIT OF MRS. W. (1922).

1967 Rinehart, Mary Roberts, and Hopwood, Avery.
THE BAT (1920).

1968 Stein, Gertrude.
FOUR SAINTS IN THREE ACTS (1934).

1969 Terry, Megan.
VIET ROCK, COMINGS AND GOINGS, KEEP TIGHTLY CLOSED IN A COOL DRY PLACE AND THE GLOAMING OH MY DARLING: FOUR PLAYS. New York: Simon & Schuster, 1967.

See also 2099.

ii. Selected Plays About Women by Men

(a). EIGHTEENTH CENTURY

1970 THE BETTER SORT; OR, A GIRL OF SPIRIT (1789).

1971 Bidwell, Barnabas.
THE MERCENARY MATCH (1784).

(b). NINETEENTH CENTURY

1972 Arthur, Joseph.
MIZZOURA (1893).

1973 Barker, James Nelson.
THE INDIAN PRINCESS; OR, LA BELLE SAUVAGE (1808).

1974 Belasco, David.
THE GIRL I LEFT BEHIND ME (1894).
THE GIRL OF THE GOLDEN WEST (1910).

1975 Boucicault, Dion.
THE OCTAROON; OR, LIFE IN LOUISIANA (1859).

1976 Custis, George Washington Parker.
POCOHANTAS; OR, THE SETTLERS OF VIRGINIA (1830).

1977 Daly, Augustin.
DIVORCE (1871).

1978 Foster, Charles.
BERTHA, THE SEWING MACHINE GIRL (1871).

1979 Herne, James A.
DRIFTING APART; titled also MARY, THE FISHERMAN'S CHILD (1888).
MARGARET FLEMING (1890).

1980 Howard, Bronson.
YOUNG MRS. WINTHROP (1882).
ONE OF OUR GIRLS (1885).

1981 Howells, William Dean.
THE MOUSETRAP (1889).

1982 A LIVE WOMAN IN THE MINES (1857).

1983 MacKaye, Steele.
WON AT LAST (1877).
HAZEL KIRKE (1880).

1984 Noah, Mordecai.
SHE WOULD BE A SOLDIER; OR, THE PLAINS OF CHIPPEWA (1819).
THE FRONTIER MAID (1840).

1985 Owen, Robert Dale.
POCOHANTAS (1837).

(c). TWENTIETH CENTURY

1986 Albee, Edward.
WHO'S AFRAID OF VIRGINIA WOOLF (1962).
TINY ALICE (1964).

1987 Barry, Philip.
PARIS BOUND (1929).
THE PHILADELPHIA STORY (1939).

1988 Behrman, S.N.
DUNNIGAN'S DAUGHTER (1945).

1989 Davis, Owen.
NELLIE, THE BEAUTIFUL CLOAK MODEL (1906).

1990 De Mille, William C.
IN 1999 (1914).

1991 Hart, Moss.
LADY IN THE DARK (1941).

1992 Howard, Sidney.
THE SILVER CORD (1926).

1993 Inge, William.
COME BACK, LITTLE SHEBA (1950).

1994 Kanin, Garson.
BORN YESTERDAY (1946).

1995 Kelly, George.
CRAIG'S WIFE (1925).
THE DEEP MRS. SYKES (1945).

1996 Marcus, Frank.
THE KILLING OF SISTER GEORGE (1965).

1997 Middleton, George.
NOWADAYS (1914).

1998 O'Neill, Eugene.
ANNA CHRISTIE (1921).
DESIRE UNDER THE ELMS (1921).
MOURNING BECOMES ELECTRA (1931).
LONG DAY'S JOURNEY INTO NIGHT (1956).

1999 Rice, Elmer.
DREAM GIRL (1945).

2000 Sheldon, Edward.
THE HIGH ROAD (1922).

2001 Walter, Eugene.
THE EASIEST WAY (1908).

2002 Wilder, Thornton.
THE SKIN OF OUR TEETH (1942).

2003 Williams, Tennessee.
THE GLASS MENAGERIE (1945).
A STREETCAR NAMED DESIRE (1947).

E. FILM

1. Sources, Bibliographies, Guides

Many women's film festivals now issue catalogs which may serve as guides and indexes to films by and about women.

The Women's History Research Center issues a listing of films, filmmakers, and filmographies.

2004 Betancourt, Jeanne. WOMEN IN FOCUS. Dayton, Ohio: Pflaum, 1974. 186 p. Biblio. Paper.

Guide to 16 mm films. Includes reviews, biographical sketches of filmmakers and their filmographies, distributors, and suggestions for programs. General bibliography annotated.

2005 Chicago Art Institute. Film Center. FILMS BY WOMEN/CHICAGO '74. Chicago: 1974. 39 p. Illus.

Report on the first women's film festival includes biographies of directors.

2006 Chicorel, Marietta, ed. CHICOREL INDEX TO FILM LITERATURE. Chicorel Index Series, vols. 22, 22A. New York: Chicorel Library, 1975.

Lists more available items.

2007 Dawson, Bonnie, comp. WOMEN'S FILMS IN PRINT: AN ANNOTATED GUIDE TO 800 FILMS BY WOMEN. San Francisco: Bootlegger, 1975. 165 p. Biblio. Offset, paper.

Lists 16mm films, as well as distributors and film festivals.

2008 Halliwell, Leslie. THE FILMGOER'S COMPANION. 4th ed., rev. New York: Hill & Wang, 1974. xi, 873 p. Illus.

Comprises an encyclopedia of films, film stars, terms, and so on. Filmography lists basic books; the subject of some relate to women.

2009 Kowalski, Rosemary R. WOMEN AND FILM: A BIBLIOGRAPHY. Metuchen, N.J.: Scarecrow Press, 1976. 278 p. Offset.

Partially annotated. Lists items on women as performers, filmmakers, and commentators, as well as on images of women in film.

2010 INTERNATIONAL MOTION PICTURE ALMANAC. New York: Quigley, 1929-- . Annual.

Title varies. Lists awards, who's who, pictures with leads, journals, and periodicals.

2011 Michael, Paul, et al., eds. THE AMERICAN MOVIES REFERENCE BOOK: THE SOUND ERA. Englewood Cliffs, N.J.: Prentice-Hall, 1969. 629 p. Illus., biblio.

2012 Powers, Anne, comp. BLACKS IN AMERICAN MOVIES: A BIBLIOGRAPHY. Metuchen, N.J.: Scarecrow Press, 1974. x, 197 p.

Lists periodicals only. See "Black Image: Women" and "Actors and Actresses."

2013 Project on the Status and Education of Women. WOMEN AND FILM: A RESOURCE HANDBOOK. Washington, D.C.: n.d. 26 p. Offset.

Includes information on the way to plan a film festival, and lists long and short films and slides for programs, as well as other resource materials.

2014 Wetmore, Patricia C., ed. WOMEN'S FILMS: A CRITICAL GUIDE. Bloomington: Audio-Visual Center, Indiana University, 1975. 121 p.

Part 1 is a critical guide; part 2 is a reprint of the center's supplement on women's films; part 3 lists films distributed by the university.

See also 2018, 2030, 2070, 2081, 2084.

2. References

Biographies (see 2264), autobiographies (see 2397), and commentaries on the films of a single star (see 2024) continue to be published. Scattered material on women in film may be available in FILM QUARTERLY, FILM COMMENT, and FILM CULTURE.

2015 Gish, Lillian, with Pinchot, Ann. THE MOVIES, MR. GRIFFITH AND ME. Englewood Cliffs, N.J.: Prentice-Hall, 1964. xii, 388 p. Illus.

Growing up with the motion picture industry.

2016 Griffith, Richard, and Mayer, Arthur. THE MOVIES. Rev. ed. New York: Simon & Schuster, 1970. xv, 494 p. Illus., biblio.

Overview of women stars. How female stars have reinforced conventional roles is particularly clear in "The Movie Family," "The Greatest Show on Earth," and "Stars of the Twenties."

2017 Johnston, Claire. THE WORK OF DOROTHY ARZNOR: TOWARDS A FEMINIST CINEMA. London: British Film Institute, 1975. 34 p. Illus. Pamph.

Includes interview, filmography.

2018 Kay, Karyn, and Peary, Gerald, eds. WOMEN AND THE CINEMA: A CRITICAL ANTHOLOGY. New York: E.P. Dutton & Co., 1977. xvi, 464 p. Illus., biblio.

International in scope. Contains material on feminist perspectives and theory, actresses, filmmakers, and women and political films. Bibliographies and selected filmographies accompany each section.

2019 Lahne, Kalton C. LADIES IN DISTRESS. South Brunswick, N.J.: A.S. Barnes; London: Thomas Yoseloff, 1971. 334 p. Illus.

Short film history of forty film stars of the silent screen from Greta Garbo to Barbara LaMarr and including Geraldine Farrar.

2020 Parish, James H. GOOD DAMES. South Brunswick, N.J.: A.S. Barnes; London: Thomas Yoseloff, 1974. 277 p. Illus.

Contains biographical data and other information on Eve Arden, Agnes Moorhead, Angela Lansbury, Thelma Ritter, and Eileen Heckart. Includes filmography.

2021 ______. THE PARAMOUNT PRETTIES. New Rochelle, N.Y.: Arlington House, 1972. 587 p. Illus.

Material similar to that in 2020 on Gloria Swanson, Clara

Bow, Claudette Colbert, Carole Lombard, Marlene Dietrich, Miriam Hopkins, Sylvia Sidney, Mae West, Dorothy Lamour, Paulette Goddard, Veronica Lake, Diana Lynn, Betty Hutton, Lisbeth Scott, and Shirley MacLaine.

2022 _____. THE RKO GALS. New Rochelle, N.Y.: Arlington House, 1974. 896 p. Illus.

Material similar to that in 2020 on Ann Harding, Constance Bennett, Irene Dunne, Ginger Rogers, Katherine Hepburn, Ann Shirley, Lucille Ball, Joan Fontaine, Wendy Barrie, Lupe Velez, Maureen O'Hara, Jane Russell, Barbara Hale, and Greer Garson.

2023 _____. THE SLAPSTICK QUEENS. South Brunswick, N.J.: A.S. Barnes, 1973. 297 p. Illus.

Material similar to that in 2020 on Marjorie Main, Joan Davis, Judy Canova, and Phyllis Diller.

2024 Raymond, Lee. THE FILMS OF MARY PICKFORD. South Brunswick, N.J.: A.S. Barnes; London: Thomas Yoseloff, 1970. 175 p. Illus.

2025 Rosen, Marjorie. POPCORN VENUS: WOMEN, MOVIES & THE AMERICAN DREAM. New York: Coward, McCann & Geoghegan, 1973. 416 p. Illus., biblio.

First serious social study of interaction between American society and women actresses and technicians in film.

2026 "Sexual Politics and Film." VELVET LIGHT TRAP 6 (Fall 1972): special issue.

Material on Alice Blaché, women directors, images of women in film, feminist criticism. Available from the VELVET LIGHT TRAP, Old Hope Schoolhouse, Cottage Grove, Wisconsin 53527.

2027 Slide, Anthony. EARLY AMERICAN CINEMA. International Film Guide Series. New York: A.S. Barnes, 1970. 192 p. Illus., biblio.

Early female stars in general historical context according to company affiliation. Note especially chapter 8, "Pearl White and the Serial Queens."

2028 _____. EARLY WOMEN DIRECTORS: THEIR ROLE IN THE DEVELOPMENT OF THE SILENT CINEMA. South Brunswick, N.J.: A.S. Barnes; London: Thomas Yoseloff, 1977. 119 p. Illus., biblio.

Discusses thirty pioneers.

2029 _____. GRIFFITH ACTRESSES. New York: A.S. Barnes, 1973. 181 p. Illus., biblio.

Relates the history of the early American cinema.

2030 Smith, Sharon. WOMEN WHO MAKE MOVIES. Cinema Study Series. New York: Hopkinson & Blake, 1975. 307 p. Illus., biblio. Paper.

Part 1 is an international overview of women who have made movies since 1896; part 2 covers women who work outside of Hollywood; and part 3 is a directory of women filmmakers in the United States. Includes a listing of organizations making films by and about women, and distributors.

2031 Spears, Jack. HOLLYWOOD: THE GOLDEN ERA. South Brunswick, N.J.: A.S. Barnes; London: Thomas Yoseloff, 1971. 440 p. Illus.

Discusses women in context of film history from the time of the silents to Cinerama. See especially the chapters on Norma Talmadge, Mary Pickford, and Colleen Moore. Documented.

2032 "Women in Film." FILM LIBRARY 5 (Winter 1971-72): special issue.

Includes reviews of films by and about women, interviews, and commentary. Available from Film Library Information Council, Box 348, Radio City Station, New York, New York 10019.

See also 139, 144, 1505, 1517.

F. MUSIC

1. Resources, Sources

PAID MY DUES: A JOURNAL OF WOMEN IN MUSIC covers articles on discrimination against women in music, on women in the media and related subjects, lists of compositions by women composers, and much else. The newsletter MUSICA publishes information on means by which women can record their music and reach a variety of audiences.

2033 Armstrong, Toni, comp. WE SHALL GO FORTH. 1977 LISTING: RESOURCES IN WOMEN'S MUSIC. Crestwood, Ill.: 1977. 28 p. Offset, stapled.

Regional listings of production and recording companies; facilities, distributors, and coffeehouses; individual technicians, songwriters and songbooks; publications and publishers, and feminist radio networks, stations, and programs. Updating planned. Available from the compiler, 12751 Park Place, #H-1, Crestwood, Illinois 60445.

2034 International Association of Music Libraries. Commission on Research Libraries. DIRECTORY OF MUSIC RESEARCH LIBRARIES. Part I: CANADA AND THE UNITED STATES. Edited by Rita Benton. Iowa City: University of Iowa Press, 1967. ix, 70 p.

2035 Pool, Jeannie G., ed. WOMEN IN MUSIC HISTORY: A RESEARCH GUIDE. New York: 1977. 42 p. Pamph.

International in scope. Includes printed sources, listings of organizations, discography of women composers. Available from the editor, Box 436, Ansonia Station, New York, New York 10023.

See also 2045, 2050, 2055.

2. Bibliographies, Discographies, Abstracts

THE SCHWANN RECORD AND TAPE GUIDE, available at any record store, is regularly updated and covers all fields of recorded music.

2036 Ashley, Patricia, and Handley, Donna. "Here They Are--On a Plastic Platter: A Complete Discography of Women Composers." MS. 4 (November 1975): 111-14.

Lists works of forty-six women whose works are available on professional recordings. Reviews accompany some items.

2037 International Repertory of Music Literature. FILM ABSTRACTS OF MUSICAL LITERATURE. Flushing, N.Y.: 1967-- . Quarterly.

Service abstracts and indexes literature since January 1971.

2038 MUSIC INDEX. Detroit: Coordinators, 1949-- . Monthly, annual cumulations.

Service abstracting and indexing over three hundred periodicals in English. International in scope.

2039 Skowronski, JoAnn. WOMEN IN AMERICAN MUSIC: A BIBLIOGRAPHY. Metuchen, N.J.: 1978. viii, 183 p.

Partially annotated. Includes sources, bibliography and

general history, as well as history of specialized periods--1776 to 1834, 1835 to 1868, 1869 to 1938, and 1939 to 1976.

See also 2070, 2081, 2084.

3. Biographical Dictionaries, Who's Whos, Directories

2040 American Society of Composers, Authors and Publishers. BIOGRAPHICAL DICTIONARY OF COMPOSERS, AUTHORS AND PUBLISHERS. New York: 1966. 845 p.

2041 Anderson, E. Ruth, comp. CONTEMPORARY AMERICAN COMPOSERS: A BIOGRAPHICAL DICTIONARY. Boston: G.K. Hall & Co., 1976. v, 513 p. Offset.

Appends special listing of about five hundred women.

2042 Bull, Storm. INDEX TO BIOGRAPHIES OF CONTEMPORARY COMPOSERS. Vol. 2. New York: Scarecrow Press, 1974. xxiv, 567 p.

Supersedes volume 1. International in scope.

2043 Claghorn, Charles E. BIOGRAPHICAL DICTIONARY OF AMERICAN MUSIC. West Nyack, N.Y.: Parker Publishing Co., 1973. 491 p.

From the seventeenth century to the present. Includes some women.

2044 Ebel, Otto. WOMEN COMPOSERS: A BIOGRAPHICAL HANDBOOK OF WOMEN'S WORK IN AMERICA. Brooklyn: F.H. Chandler, 1902. viii, 151 p.

2045 Galt, Martha C. "To the Ladies." In her KNOW YOUR AMERICAN MUSIC, pp. 42-45. Augusta, Maine: Kennebec Journal Print Shop, 1943. 72 p. Biblio.

Lists women as composers in nine categories, with references to sources.

2046 Grove, George, comp. DICTIONARY OF MUSIC AND MUSICIANS. 5th ed. Edited by Eric Blom. 9 vols. New York: St. Martin's Press, 1973. Illus., biblio. Paper.

2047 INTERNATIONAL WHO'S WHO IN MUSIC AND MUSICIANS' DIRECTORY. Cambridge, Engl.: International Who's Who in Music, 1935-- . Irregular.

Titled WHO'S WHO IN MUSIC AND MUSICIANS INTERNATIONAL DIRECTORY from 1935 to 1972.

2048 Smith, Julia F., comp. DIRECTORY OF AMERICAN WOMEN COMPOSERS. Chicago: National Federation of Women's Clubs, 1970. iv, 51 p.

Lists over six hundred composers, their genre of composition, and publishers. Selected listings of compositions by musical genre with their publishers and publishers' addresses. Available from federation headquarters, Suite 1215, 600 South Michigan Avenue, Chicago, Illinois 60605.

4. References

2049 Barnes, Edwin N.C. AMERICAN WOMEN IN CREATIVE MUSIC. Tuning in on American Music Series. Washington, D.C.: Musical Education Publications, 1936. 44 p. Pamph.

Suggestive for further research.

2050 Cheney, Joyce, et al., comps. ALL OUR LIVES: A WOMEN'S SONGBOOK. Baltimore: Diana Press, 1976. 200 p. Illus., biblio. Paper.

Traditional and new songs. Includes listing of resources.

2051 Dew, Joan. SINGERS & SWEETHEARTS: THE WOMEN OF COUNTRY MUSIC. Garden City, N.Y.: Doubleday & Co., 1977. 148 p. Illus.

Chapters on Loretta Lynn, Tammy Wynette, June Carter, Dolly Parton, and Tanya Tucker.

2052 Drinker, Sophie. MUSIC AND WOMEN: THE STORY OF WOMEN IN THEIR RELATION TO MUSIC. New York: Coward, McCann, 1948. xv, 323 p. Illus., biblio.

Traces women's contributions from prehistoric times to the twentieth century. Written to "compensate" women for lack of mention in histories of music.

2053 Elson, Arthur. "America." In his WOMAN'S WORK IN MUSIC, chap. 9. Boston: L.C. Page, 1903.

Composers of instrumental, operatic, and chamber music, and songs. Includes piano and opera performers.

2054 Ewen, David. NEW COMPLETE BOOK OF AMERICAN MUSICAL THEATER. New York: Holt, Rinehart & Winston, 1970. xxv, 800 p. Illus.

Women in the context of theater history.

2055 Howard, John T. OUR AMERICAN MUSIC: A COMPREHENSIVE HISTORY FROM 1620 TO THE PRESENT. New York: Thomas Y. Crowell Co., 1965. xxii, 944 p. Biblio.

Has some information on women. Useful contemporary periodical listing.

2056 Kolodin, Irving. THE STORY OF THE METROPOLITAN OPERA, 1883-1966: A CANDID HISTORY. 4th ed. New York: Alfred A. Knopf, 1966. xxi, 762 p.

Opera singers in context of general history.

2057 Ladd, George T. "Why Women Cannot Compose Music." YALE REVIEW 8 (July 1917): 789-806.

Claims that lacking "creative imagination," women "have not," therefore "cannot."

2058 Orloff, Katherine. ROCK 'N ROLL WOMAN. Los Angeles: Nash Publishing Corp., 1974. 199 p. Illus. Paper.

Interviews with twelve artists.

2059 Smith, Cecil M. MUSICAL COMEDY IN AMERICA. New York: Theatre Arts Books, 1950. x, 374 p. Illus.

From 1864.

2060 Smith, Eva N. [Mrs. G.C.S.], comp. WOMEN IN SACRED SONG: A LIBRARY OF HYMNS, RELIGIOUS POEMS AND SACRED MUSIC. Boston: D. Lothrop, 1885. xxviii, 883 p.

Includes missionary, temperance, and patriotic songs as well as songs on motherhood.

2061 Sonneck, O.G. EARLY OPERA IN AMERICA. New York: G. Schirmer, 1915. viii, 230 p. Reprint. New York: Benjamin Blom, 1963.

Women in opera from prerevolutionary times to 1800.

2062 Sutro, Florence S. WOMEN IN MUSIC AND LAW. New York: Author's Publishing Co., 1895. 48 p. Illus. Pamph.

Lists compositions by American women.

2063 Thompson, Oscar. THE AMERICAN SINGER: A HUNDRED YEARS OF SUCCESS IN OPERA. New York: Dial Press, 1937. 426 p. Illus.

Includes chapters on many individual singers since the early nineteenth century. The appendix lists appearances and debuts.

2064 Towers, John. WOMEN IN MUSIC. Winchester, Va.: Enterprise Printing Co., 1897. 30 p.

Lists individual composers with works dated.

2065 Trotter, James M. MUSIC AND SOME HIGHLY MUSICAL PEOPLE: CONTAINING BRIEF CHAPTERS ON . . . REMARKABLE MUSICIANS OF THE COLORED RACE. Boston: Lee & Shepard, 1878. 353 p. Illus. Reprint. Basic Afro-American Reprint Library Series. New York: Johnson Reprint Corp., 1968.

Includes black female vocal and instrumental musicians.

2066 WOMEN IN MUSIC. New York: Orchestrate Classique, July 1, 1935-December 1940.

Newsletter whose main object was to "present facts and news pertaining to women conductors and women's orchestras here and abroad."

G. STAGE

1. Resources, Sources, Directories

A newsletter, WOMEN IN PERFORMING ARTS, issued irregularly by the Theater Department of Northwestern University, lists women's theater groups and networks, and sources of information for both.

2067 Boston Public Library. THE ALLEN A. BROWN COLLECTION RELATING TO THE STAGE. Boston: 1919. 952 p.

Stage history and drama listing.

2068 Gilder, Rosamond, and Freedley, George, comps. THEATRE COLLECTIONS IN LIBRARIES AND MUSEUMS: AN INTERNATIONAL HANDBOOK. New York: Theatre Arts Books, 1936. 182 p. Reprint. New York: Johnson Reprint Corp., 1970.

Arranged geographically.

2069 Guernsy, Otis L., Jr., comp. DIRECTORY OF THE AMERICAN THEATER 1894-1941. New York: Dodd, Mead & Co., 1971. 343 p.

Part 1 lists playwrights, librettists, composers, and lyricists; part 2 the plays by title.

2070 GUIDE TO PERFORMING ARTS, 1957-- . New York: Scarecrow Press, 1960-- . Annual.

Main sections are followed by sections on television arts.

2071 New York Public Library. Research Libraries. CATALOG OF THE THEATRE AND DRAMA COLLECTIONS. 21 vols. Boston: G.K. Hall & Co., 1967.

International in scope. The twelve volumes of part 1 cover the drama collection and include listings of anthologies and periodicals; part 2, the remaining nine volumes, covers aspects of theater including history, biography, and criticism.

2072 NEW YORK TIMES DIRECTORY OF THE THEATER. New York: Arno Press, 1973. 1,009 p. Illus.

Indexes reviews in volumes 9 and 10 of 2087. Includes additional material drawn from volume 1 of 2087, as well as some new text.

2073 Sharp, Harold S., and Sharp, Marjorie Z. INDEX TO CHARACTERS IN THE PERFORMING ARTS. 5 vols. New York: Scarecrow Press, 1966-72.

Lists characters in musicals, operas, nonmusical theater, and other performing media.

2074 THE THEATER BOOK OF THE YEAR . . . A RECORD AND AN INTERPRETATION. New York: Alfred A. Knopf, 1942/43-- . Irregular.

2075 THEATRE ARTS MONTHLY. New York: Theatre Arts Monthly, 1939-64.

2076 THEATRE MAGAZINE INDEX 1900-1930. Compiled by H. Cornyn. New York: Scarecrow Press, 1964. 289 p.

2077 THEATRE WORLD. New York: Theatre World, 1945-- . Annual.

Surveys American theater, including biographical sketches of those in most areas of theater.

2078 Young, William C., comp. AMERICAN THEATRICAL ARTS: A GUIDE TO MANUSCRIPTS IN THE UNITED STATES AND CANADA. Chicago: American Library Association, 1971. 166 p.

2. Bibliographies

2079 ANNOTATED BIBLIOGRAPHY OF NEW PUBLICATIONS IN THE PERFORMING ARTS. New York: Drama Book Shop, 1970-- . Quarterly.

Categorized though not indexed. International in scope.

2080 Baker, Blanche M., comp. THEATRE AND ALLIED ARTS: A GUIDE TO BOOKS DEALING WITH THE HISTORY, CRITICISM, AND TECHNIC OF DRAMA AND THE THEATRE, AND RELATED ARTS AND CRAFTS. New York: H.W. Wilson Co., 1952. xiii, 536 p. Reprint. New York: Benjamin Blom, 1967.

2081 Chicorel, Marietta. CHICOREL BIBLIOGRAPHY ON THE PERFORMING ARTS. Chicorel Index Series, vol. 3A. New York: Chicorel Library Publishing Corp., 1972. 486 p.

Lists popular sources of theater, dance, motion pictures, opera, and television. Includes performers and writers.

2082 Hatch, James, ed. BLACK IMAGE ON THE AMERICAN STAGE: A BIBLIOGRAPHY OF PLAYS & MUSICALS 1770-1970. New York: Drama Book Specialists, 1970. xiii, 162 p.

Unannotated.

2083 Litto, Frederic M. AMERICAN DISSERTATIONS ON THE DRAMA AND THE THEATRE: A BIBLIOGRAPHY. Kent, Ohio: Kent State University Press, 1969. 519 p.

2084 Schoolcraft, Ralph N. PERFORMING ARTS IN PRINT: AN ANNOTATED BIBLIOGRAPHY. New York: Drama Book Specialists, 1973. 761 p.

Covers theater, drama, television, radio, mass media, popular arts, and other media.

2085 Stratman, Carl J. AMERICAN THEATRICAL PERIODICALS, 1798-1967: A BIBLIOGRAPHICAL GUIDE. Riverside, Ill.: Duke Press, 1970. 133 p.

2086 THEATRE ARTS PUBLICATIONS AVAILABLE IN THE UNITED STATES. Washington, D.C.: American Educational Theatre Association, 1959-64.

The section covering 1947-52 is edited by William W. Melnitz, 91 pages; the section covering 1953-57 is edited by Roger M. Busfield, 188 pages.

See also 2088, 2104.

3. Reviews

2087 NEW YORK TIMES THEATRE REVIEWS, 1920-1970. 10 vols. New York: New York Times, 1971. Illus.

Chronologically arranged. The appendix lists awards, prizes, productions, and runs.

4. Biographical References

2088 Rigdon, Walter, ed. THE BIOGRAPHICAL ENCYCLOPEDIA & WHO'S WHO OF THE AMERICAN THEATRE. New York: James H. Heineman, 1966. xiv, 1,101 p.

Includes biographical bibliography.

2089 WHO'S WHO IN THE THEATRE: A BIOGRAPHICAL RECORD OF THE CONTEMPORARY STAGE. London: Pitman, 1912-- . Irregular.

Fifteenth edition (1972) gives good coverage to New York theater.

5. References

2090 Blum, Daniel. GREAT STARS OF THE AMERICAN STAGE: A PICTORIAL RECORD. New York: Greenberg, 1952. Illus.

Short profiles of actresses from Lillian Russell to Joan McCracken.

2091 Brown, Thomas A. A HISTORY OF THE AMERICAN STAGE; CONTAINING BIOGRAPHICAL SKETCHES OF NEARLY EVERY MEMBER OF THE PROFESSION THAT HAS APPEARED ON THE AMERICAN STAGE, FROM 1733 TO 1870. New York: Pick & Fitzgerald, 1870. 421 p. Illus. Reprint. American Culture Series. New York: Benjamin Blom, 1968.

First complete history contains both biographical and professional detail on hundreds of stage personalities.

2092 Clapp, John B., and Edget, Edwin F. PLAYERS OF THE PRESENT. 3 vols. in 1. Publications of the Dunlap Society, n.s. 9, 11, and 13. New York: Dunlap Society, 1899-1901. 331 p. Reprint. New York: Benjamin Blom, 1970.

Sketches of stage personalities from the Civil War to 1900.

2093 Dalrymple, Jean. CAREERS AND OPPORTUNITIES IN THE THEATRE. New York: E.P. Dutton & Co., 1969. 256 p. Illus.

By actress-director-producer. The appendix lists schools, theaters, and other useful information.

2094 Dell 'Olio, Anselma. "The Founding of the New Feminist Theatre." In NOTES FROM THE SECOND YEAR, MAJOR WRITINGS OF THE RADICAL FEMINISTS, edited by Shulamith Firestone, p. 101. New York: Radical Feminism, 1969.

2095 Dunlap, William. HISTORY OF THE AMERICAN THEATRE AND ANECDOTES OF THE PRINCIPAL ACTORS. 2d ed. New York: J. Oram, 1797. xii, 387 p. Reprint. Burt Franklin Resource & Research Works Series, no. 36. New York: Burt Franklin, 1963.

Includes many women. Appendix lists women playwrights.

2096 Hughes, Langston, and Meltzer, Milton. BLACK MAGIC: A PICTORIAL HISTORY OF THE NEGRO IN AMERICAN ENTERTAINMENT. Englewood Cliffs, N.J.: Prentice-Hall, 1967. 375 p. Illus.

Half of the text is devoted to women.

2097 Isaacs, Edith J. THE NEGRO IN THE AMERICAN THEATRE. College Park, Md.: McGrath Publishing, 1947. 143 p. Biblio.

Women in the larger context of black theater.

2098 Marks, Edward B. THEY ALL HAD GLAMOUR: FROM THE SWEDISH NIGHTINGALE TO THE NAKED LADY. New York: Julian Messner, 1944. xviii, 448 p. Illus. Reprint. Westport, Conn.: Greenwood Press, 1972.

Beginning with "The Black Crook" through nineteenth-century theater and opera. Includes material on Jennie Lind, Marie Piccolomini, Adelina Patti, Lola Montez, and Adah Mencken. Also lists singers, songs, singing teachers, casts, musical programs--and more.

2099 Moses, Montrose J., and Brown, John Mason. AMERICAN THEATRE 1752-1934. New York: W.W. Norton & Co., 1934. 391 p.

Includes contemporary reviews of actresses, singers, and women playwrights from the early nineteenth century on.

2100 Rea, Charlotte. "Women's Theatre Groups." DRAMA REVIEW 18 (June 1972): 79-89.

Overview. Points out differences between traditional theater and women's groups, and between the groups themselves. Lists many plays written by women.

2101 Seilhamer, George O. HISTORY OF THE AMERICAN THEATRE. 3 vols. Philadelphia: Globe Printing, 1888-91. Reprint. Grosse Pointe, Mich.: Scholarly Press, 1968.

Gossipy eighteenth-century history refers to many actresses.

2102 Strang, Lewis C. FAMOUS ACTRESSES OF THE DAY IN AMERICA. 2 vols. Stage Lovers Series. Boston: L.C. Page, 1899-1902. x, 360 p.

Describes thirty-one eminent actresses of the turn of the century.

2103 ______. FAMOUS STARS OF LIGHT OPERA. Boston: L.C. Page, 1906. 293 p. Illus.

2104 TDR: THE DRAMA REVIEW 12 (Summer 1968): special issue.

Prints plays by Sonia Sanchez and Dorothy Ahmad. Includes a directory of black theaters and a selected bibliography on black theater between 1960 and 1968.

2105 Wilson, Garff B. THREE HUNDRED YEARS OF AMERICAN DRAMA AND THEATER: FROM YE BEAR AND YE CUBBE TO HAIR. Englewood Cliffs, N.J.: Prentice-Hall, 1973. viii, 536 p. Illus., biblio.

Good general background.

2106 Ziegfeld, Florenz, Jr. "Picking Pretty Girls for the Stage." AMERICAN MAGAZINE 88 (December 1919): 34, 119-22, 125. Reprinted in THE CALL OF THE WILD, edited by Roderick Nash, pp. 256-65. The American Culture Series. New York: George Braziller, 1970.

Chapter 10

BIOGRAPHIES, AUTOBIOGRAPHIES

A. BIBLIOGRAPHIES OF BIBLIOGRAPHIES

2107 Le Beau, Dennis, and Tarbert, Gary, comps. BIOGRAPHICAL DICTIONARIES MASTER INDEX 1975-76: A GUIDE TO MORE THAN 725,000 LISTINGS IN OVER 500 CURRENT WHO'S WHOS AND OTHER WORKS OF COLLECTIVE BIOGRAPHY. 3 vols. Detroit: Gale Research Co., 1975.

To be issued biennially.

2108 Slocum, Robert B., comp. BIOGRAPHICAL DICTIONARIES AND RELATED WORKS. Detroit: Gale Research Co., 1967. xvi, 1,156 p.

Annotated. Lists 4,829 collections. Supplement issued in 1972.

B. BIBLIOGRAPHIES

2109 Brignano, Russell C. BLACK AMERICANS IN AUTOBIOGRAPHY: AN ANNOTATED BIBLIOGRAPHY OF AUTOBIOGRAPHIES AND AUTOBIOGRAPHICAL BOOKS WRITTEN SINCE THE CIVIL WAR. Riverside, Ill.: Duke Press, 1974. ix, 118 p.

2110 Dargan, Marion, comp. GUIDE TO AMERICAN BIOGRAPHY. 2 vols. Albuquerque: University of New Mexico Press, 1949-52. Reprint. 2 vols. in 1. Westport, Conn.: Greenwood Press, 1973. 510 p.

Part 1, 1607-1815; part 2, 1815-1933. Moderate number of well- and little-known women.

2111 Kaplan, Louis, et al., comps. A BIBLIOGRAPHY OF AMERICAN AUTOBIOGRAPHIES. Madison: University of Wisconsin Press, 1961. xii, 372 p. Offset.

To 1945. Annotated.

2112 Lillard, Richard G. AMERICAN LIFE IN AUTOBIOGRAPHY: A DESCRIPTIVE GUIDE. Stanford, Calif.: Stanford University Press, 1956. v, 140 p.

Annotated. Some women in almost every occupation.

2113 O'Neill, Edward H. BIOGRAPHY BY AMERICANS, 1658-1936: A SUBJECT BIBLIOGRAPHY. Philadelphia: University of Pennsylvania; London: Milford, 1939. 465 p.

See also 850, 2122, 2179.

C. WHO'S WHOS, INDEXES, ENCYCLOPEDIAS, DICTIONARIES, MISCELLANEOUS SOURCES

2114 AMERICAN WOMEN: THE OFFICIAL WHO'S WHO AMONG THE WOMEN OF THE NATION, 1935-36. Los Angeles: American, 1935-39.

Volume 2, 1937-38; volume 3, 1939-40. Ceased publication after volume 3 but resumed in 1958. See 2129.

2115 Bair, Frank, and Nykoruk, Barbara, eds. BIOGRAPHY NEWS: A BIMONTHLY COMPILATION OF NEWS STORIES AND FEATURE ARTICLES FROM AMERICAN NEWSPAPERS COVERING PERSONALITIES OF NATIONAL INTEREST IN ALL FIELDS. Detroit: Gale Research Co., 1974-76.

2116 BIOGRAPHICAL CYCLOPEDIA OF AMERICAN WOMEN. Vol. 1 edited by Mabel W. Cameron. New York: Halvord, 1924. 400 p. Vol. 2 edited by Erma C. Lee. New York: Franklin W. Lee, 1925. 304 p. Vol. 3 edited by Erma C. Lee and Henry C. Wiley. New York: Williams-Wiley, 1928. 282 p.

Informative, though somewhat sentimental and disorganized.

2117 BIOGRAPHY INDEX: A CUMULATIVE INDEX OF BIOGRAPHICAL MATERIAL IN BOOKS AND MAGAZINES. New York: H.W. Wilson Co., 1947-- . Quarterly. Cumulated annually and triannually.

Covers seventeen hundred periodicals. Alphabetical. Indexed by profession and occupation. International in scope.

2118 Boris, Joseph J., ed. WHO'S WHO IN COLORED AMERICA: A BIOGRAPHICAL DICTIONARY OF NOTABLE LIVING PERSONS OF NEGRO DESCENT IN AMERICA. 7 vols. New York: Who's Who in Colored America, 1927-50.

2119 CURRENT BIOGRAPHY. New York: H.W. Wilson Co., 1940-- . Monthly.

International in scope. Updated, and annually cumulated as CURRENT BIOGRAPHY YEARBOOK, which includes cumulated index for preceding ten-year periods. The 1946-54 issues are entitled CURRENT BIOGRAPHY: WHO'S NEW AND WHY.

2120 Howes, Durward, ed. AMERICAN WOMEN: THE STANDARDIZED BIOGRAPHICAL DICTIONARY OF NOTABLE WOMEN, 1939-1940. Vol. 3. Los Angeles: American Publications, 1939. cliv, 1,083 p. Reprint. Teaneck, N.J.: Zephyrus, 1974.

Who's who format. End matter includes index to women's organizations with data on each.

2121 Ireland, Norma O., comp. INDEX TO WOMEN OF THE WORLD FROM ANCIENT TO MODERN TIMES: BIOGRAPHIES AND PORTRAITS. Useful Reference Series. Westwood, Mass.: F.W. Faxon, 1970. xxcviii, 573 p. Biblio.

Although international in scope, stress is on American women pioneers, intellectual as well as historical. Lists general compilations and collections in specialized fields relating to women.

2122 James, Edward T., et al., eds. NOTABLE AMERICAN WOMEN, 1607-1950, A BIOGRAPHICAL DICTIONARY. 3 vols. Cambridge, Mass.: Harvard University Press, Belknap Press, 1971.

Includes 1,359 entries of women who died between 1607 and 1950, and bibliography of primary and secondary works of each. Excellent historical introduction. The appendix lists women by activities and affiliations. Supplement for the years 1951-75 is in process.

2123 Johnson, Allen, et al., eds. DICTIONARY OF AMERICAN BIOGRAPHY. 20 vols. New York: Scribner's, 1928-36.

Seven hundred of fifteen thousand entries are of women. Supplements since issued contain an increasing number of women.

2124 Johnson, Rossiter, ed. THE TWENTIETH CENTURY BIOGRAPHICAL DICTIONARY OF NOTABLE AMERICANS. 10 vols. Boston: Biographical Society, 1904.

Includes women who are difficult to find in other sources.

2125 Leonard, John W., comp. WOMAN'S WHO'S WHO OF AMERICA:

A BIOGRAPHICAL DICTIONARY OF CONTEMPORARY WOMEN IN THE UNITED STATES AND CANADA, 1914-1915. New York: American Commonwealth, 1914. 961 p.

Interrogates each subject on the question of suffrage.

2126 McGRAW-HILL ENCYCLOPEDIA OF WORLD BIOGRAPHY. 12 vols. New York: McGraw-Hill Book Co., 1973.

Includes photographs and listing of works by and about some American women.

2127 Outstanding Young Women of America. OUTSTANDING YOUNG WOMEN OF AMERICA. Washington, D.C.: 1966-73. Annual.

Lists young women between the ages of twenty-one and thirty-five who have distinguished themselves in accordance with community standards.

2128 WHO'S WHO IN AMERICA. Chicago: Marquis Who's Who, 1899-- . Biennial.

Check also more specialized Who's Who volumes, covering American history, government, finance and industry, religion, law, and other areas, as well as regional listings issued by the same publisher. See also 2114, 2130.

2129 WHO'S WHO OF AMERICAN WOMEN: A BIOGRAPHICAL DICTIONARY OF NOTABLE LIVING AMERICAN WOMEN. Chicago: A.N. Marquis, 1958-- . Biennial.

2130 WHO WAS WHO IN AMERICA: A COMPANION BIOGRAPHICAL REFERENCE TO WHO'S WHO IN AMERICA. Chicago: Marquis Who's Who, 1942-1973.

Volume covering 1607-1896 is called the historical volume and was revised in 1967. Volume 1 covers 1897-1942, volume 2 1945-50, volume 3 1951-60, volume 4 1961-68, volume 5 1969-73.

See also 87.

D. COLLECTED BIOGRAPHIES

2131 Aikman, Duncan. CALAMITY JANE AND THE LADY WILDCATS. New York: H. Holt and Co., 1927. xii, 347 p. Reprint. New York: Ballantine, 1973. Paper.

Includes chapters on Belle Starr, Lola Montez, and Carrie Nation.

2132 Bacon, Martha L. PURITAN PROMENADE. Boston: Houghton Mifflin Co., 1964. 160 p. Illus., biblio.

Contains biographical sketches of Phillis Wheatley, Lydia Sigourney, Catharine Beecher, Delia Bacon, and the Yale "Gallinippers."

2133 Bradford, Gamaliel. PORTRAITS OF AMERICAN WOMEN. Boston: Houghton Mifflin Co., 1917. x, 276 p. Illus., biblio. Reprint. Essay Index Reprint Series. Freeport, N.Y.: Books for Libraries, 1969.

Includes lives of Abigail Adams, Sarah Ripley, Mary Lyon, Harriet Beecher Stowe, Margaret Fuller Ossoli, Frances Willard, and Emily Dickinson. A sentimental, inaccurate source, but popular for many years.

2134 _____. WIVES. New York: Harper, 1925. 298 p. Illus. Reprint. American Women: Images and Realities series. New York: Arno Press, 1972.

Presents "psychographs" of wives of Abraham Lincoln, Benedict Arnold, Aaron Burr, James Madison, Jefferson Davis, Benjamin Butler, and James Blaine.

2135 Brawley, Benjamin. WOMEN OF ACHIEVEMENT WITHIN THE FIRE-SIDE SCHOOLS. Chicago: Woman's American Baptist Home Missionary Society, 1919. 92 p. Illus.

Provides a general introduction to the place of black women in American life. Includes sketches of Harriet Tubman, Nora Gordon, Meta Fuller, Mary Bethune, and Mary Terrell.

2136 Brown, Hallie Q., comp. HOMESPUN HEROINES AND OTHER WOMEN OF DISTINCTION. The Black Heritage Library Collection. Xenia, Ohio: Aldine, 1926. Reprint. Freeport, N.Y.: Books for Libraries, 1971. vii, 248 p.

Contains sketches and testimonials of over fifty black women from colonial times on. Includes an extract on black women pioneers in California.

2137 Burnett, Constance B. FIVE FOR FREEDOM. New York: Abelard-Schumann, 1953. 317 p. Biblio. Reprint. Westport, Conn.: Greenwood Press, 1968.

Consists of popular sketches of Lucretia Mott, Elizabeth Cady Stanton, Lucy Stone, Susan B. Anthony, and Carrie Chapman Catt.

2138 Chace, Elizabeth B., and Lowell, Lucy B. TWO QUAKER SISTERS: FROM THE ORIGINAL DIARIES OF ELIZABETH BUFFUM CHACE AND LUCY BUFFUM LOWELL. New York: Liveright, 1937. 183 p. Illus.

Details the personal lives of Chace and Lowell, as well as presenting material on antislavery, temperance, and other causes.

2139 Clement, J., ed. NOBLE DEEDS OF AMERICAN WOMEN, WITH BIOGRAPHICAL SKETCHES OF SOME OF THE MORE PROMINENT. Buffalo, N.Y.: George H. Derby, 1851. xviii, 480 p.

Describes deeds as noble because they are within the "proper sphere of women." Anecdotal.

2140 Daniel, Sadie I. WOMEN BUILDERS. Revised and enl. by Charles H. Wesley, and Thelma D. Perry. Washington, D.C.: Associated Publishers, 1931. xvii, 308 p. Illus.

Contains biographical essays on Lucy Laney, Maggie Walker, Jane Barrett, Mary Bethune, Nannie Burroughs, Charlotte Brown, Jane Hunter, Harriet Tubman, Fannie Coppin, Maria Baldwin, Ida Barnett, and Hallie Brown.

2141 Dannett, Sylvia G.L. PROFILES OF NEGRO WOMANHOOD. 2 vols. Negro Heritage Library. Yonkers, N.Y.: Educational Heritage, 1964. Illus., biblio.

Volume 1, 1619 to 1900; volume 2, 1900 on.

2142 Dash, Joan. A LIFE OF ONE'S OWN: THREE GIFTED WOMEN AND THE MEN THEY MARRIED. New York: Harper & Row, 1973. xx, 388 p. Biblio.

Includes two Americans, Margaret Sanger and Edna St. Vincent Millay.

2143 Dexter, Elizabeth A. CAREER WOMEN OF AMERICA. Francestown, N.H.: Marshall Jones, 1950. xiii, 254 p. Biblio.

Chronicles lesser-known women, from colonial times on, who were teachers, doctors, entertainers, writers, tavern-keepers, businesswomen, and so forth.

2144 _____. COLONIAL WOMEN OF AFFAIRS: WOMEN IN BUSINESS AND THE PROFESSIONS IN AMERICA BEFORE 1776. Boston: Houghton Mifflin Co., 1924. xiii, 213 p. Illus., biblio.

Includes accounts of a tavern manager, merchant, dressmaker, nurse, teacher, landed proprietor, writer, religious leader, actress, printer.

2145 Donovan, Frank R. THE WOMEN IN THEIR LIVES: THE DISTAFF SIDE OF THE FOUNDING FATHERS. New York: Dodd, Mead & Co., 1966. 339 p. Illus.

Describes the mothers, wives, and other women in the lives of Benjamin Franklin, George Washington, John Adams, Thomas Jefferson, Alexander Hamilton, and James Madison.

2146 Drotning, Phillip T., and South, Wesley W. UP FROM THE GHETTO. New York: Cowles Book, 1970. xii, 207 p. Paper.

Includes biographical and other information on Anne Langford, Shirley Chisholm, and Gwendolyn Brooks.

2147 Ellet, Elizabeth F. THE QUEENS OF AMERICAN SOCIETY. 6th ed. Philadelphia: Porter & Coates, 1867. ii, 464 p. Illus.

Discusses the "flowers of the sex" from colonial times to mid-nineteenth century, including Martha Washington, Mercy Warren, the Adams women, and Dolly Madison, through Sarah Polk, Jessie Fremont, and Mrs. Auguste Belmont.

2148 _____. THE WOMEN OF THE AMERICAN REVOLUTION. 3 vols. New York: Baker & Haskell, 1848. Reprint. American History and Americana Series, no. 47. New York: Haskell House, 1969. Illus.

Attempts, through anecdotal sketches of women, famous and obscure, to define woman's place in American history.

2149 Engle, Paul. WOMEN IN THE AMERICAN REVOLUTION. Chicago: Follett Publishing Co., 1976. xvii, 299 p. Illus., biblio.

Eighteen biographies of women who fought, who wrote, who sympathized with the British, who were unique individuals, and who involved themselves primarily in family life.

2150 Foreman, Carolyn. INDIAN WOMEN CHIEFS. Muskogee, Okla.: Oklahoma Star, 1954. Reprint. Muskogee, Okla.: Hoffman, 1966. 86 p.

Provides general information on Indian women in positions of power, as well as information on specific individuals.

2151 Gallagher, Dorothy. HANNAH'S DAUGHTERS: SIX GENERATIONS

OF AN AMERICAN FAMILY, 1876-1976. New York: Thomas Y. Crowell Co., 1976. 343 p. Illus.

Points out that each generation repeats the patterns of the preceding one against backgrounds of social change and crisis.

2152 Ginzberg, Eli, and Yohalem, Marie. EDUCATED AMERICAN WOMEN: SELF PORTRAITS. Conservation of Human Resources Project, no. 3. New York: Columbia University Press, 1966. xii, 198 p. Paper.

Gives life histories of twenty-six of the women described in LIFE STYLES OF EDUCATED WOMEN (see 591). Analyzes factors making for their diversity as planners, recasters, adapters, and the unsettled.

2153 Gish, Lillian. DOROTHY AND LILLIAN GISH. New York: Charles Scribner's Sons, 1973. 312 p. Illus.

2154 Gray, Dorothy. WOMEN OF THE WEST. Millbrae, Calif.: Les Femmes, 1976. 179 p.

Biographies of twenty women from Sacajawea to Willa Cather.

2155 Gridley, Marion E. AMERICAN INDIAN WOMEN. New York: Hawthorn Books, 1974. vi, 178 p. Biblio.

Describes sixteen women from colonial times on who have made contributions.

2156 Halsey, Frances W. WOMEN AUTHORS OF OUR DAY IN THEIR HOMES. New York: James Pott, 1898. xvi, 300 p. Illus.

Describes twenty-seven authors of the 1890s.

2157 Hanaford, Phebe A. DAUGHTERS OF AMERICA: OR, WOMEN OF THE CENTURY. Augusta, Me.: True, 1882. 750 p. Illus.

Sketches historical figures grouped as social leaders, philanthropic workers, writers and artists, scientists, lecturers, preachers and missionaries, educators, physicians, businesswomen, inventors, lawyers, printers, librarians, agriculturalists, historians, and travelers.

2158 Hays, Elinor R. THOSE EXTRAORDINARY BLACKWELLS. New York: Harcourt Brace, World, 1967. x, 349 p. Illus., biblio.

Discusses the Blackwell family which contributed seven activists to the mid-nineteenth-century women's movement.

2159 Kisner, Arlene, ed. WOODHULL AND CLAFLIN'S WEEKLY: THE LIVES AND WRITINGS OF VICTORIA WOODHULL AND TENNESSEE CLAFLIN. New York: Times Change, 1974. 64 p. Pamph.

Presents selections from the WEEKLY 1870-76.

2160 Kramer, Sydelle, and Masur, Jenny, eds. JEWISH GRANDMOTHERS. Boston: Beacon Press, 1976. 174 p. Illus. Paper.

Contains the remarks of ten immigrant women speaking of their lives.

2161 Kunitz, Stanley J. [Tante, Dilly], ed. LIVING AUTHORS: A BOOK OF BIOGRAPHIES. New York: H.W. Wilson Co., 1931. vii, 466 p. Illus., biblio.

Includes some hard-to-get material on women authors of the earlier twentieth century.

2162 Lamson, Peggy. FEW ARE CHOSEN: AMERICAN WOMEN IN POLITICAL LIFE TODAY. Boston: Houghton Mifflin, 1968. xxxii, 240 p. Illus.

Sketches of Frances Bolton, Esther Peterson, Martha Griffiths, Patsy Mink, Margaret Heckle, Constance Motley, Eugenie Anderson, Ann Mallo, and Ella Grasso.

2163 Langford, Laura C.H. [Holloway]. THE LADIES OF THE WHITE HOUSE; OR, IN THE HOME OF THE PRESIDENTS FROM WASHINGTON TO CLEVELAND, 1789-1886. 2 vols. New York: Funk & Wagnalls, 1886. Illus.

Claims to be the first such biography. Covers first ladies through Mrs. Garfield.

2164 Longwell, Marjorie R. AMERICA AND WOMEN: FICTIONIZED BIOGRAPHY. Philadelphia: Dorrance, 1961. ix, 205 p.

Contains chapters on Eliza Lucas Pinckney, an eighteenth-century South Carolina businesswoman, and Maggie Walker, the first black woman bank president.

2165 Majors, Monroe A. NOTED NEGRO WOMEN: THEIR TRIUMPHS AND ACTIVITIES. Chicago: Donohue & Henneberry, 1893. xvi, 365 p. Illus. Reprint. Freeport, N.Y.: Books for Libraries, 1971.

Consists of biographical sketches, articles, letters, and poems relating to both well- and little-known black women from colonial times through the nineteenth century. Available in microform from University Microfilms, Ann Arbor, Michigan.

2166 Marble, Annie R. THE WOMEN WHO CAME ON THE MAYFLOWER. Boston: Pilgrim, 1920. 110 p.

Focuses on women as members of the community rather than as individuals.

2167 Merriam, Eve, comp. GROWING UP FEMALE IN AMERICA: TEN LIVES. Garden City, N.Y.: Doubleday & Co., 1971. 308 p. Illus. Paper.

Contains the autobiographical writings of Eliza Southgate (schoolgirl), Elizabeth Cady Stanton, Maria Mitchell (astronomer), Maria Loughlin (Confederate officer's wife) Arvazine Copper (Western pioneer), Anna Shaw (minister and doctor), Susie King (freed slave), Gertrude Stein, and Mountain Wolf Woman (Winnebago Indian).

2168 Mott, Abigail F., comp. BIOGRAPHICAL SKETCHES AND INTERESTING ANECDOTES OF PERSONS OF COLOR, TO WHICH IS ADDED A SELECTION OF PIECES IN POETRY. 2d ed. New York: Mahlon Day, 1837. iv, 260 p.

Contains biographical sketches by an abolitionist of colonial black and native American women, and the humiliations of both.

2169 Nies, Judith. SEVEN WOMEN: PORTRAITS FROM THE AMERICAN RADICAL TRADITION. New York: Viking Press, 1977. xvi, 236 p. Biblio.

Includes chapters on Sarah Grimké, Harriet Tubman, Elizabeth Cady Stanton, Mother Jones, Charlotte Perkins Gilman, Anna Louise Strong, and Doris Day.

2170 OUR FAMOUS WOMEN: AN AUTHORIZED RECORD OF THE LIVES AND DEEDS OF DISTINGUISHED WOMEN OF OUR TIMES. Hartford, Conn.: A.D. Worthington, 1884. xxvii, 815 p. Illus.

Subscription book of sentimental biographies of thirty famous women by thirty well-known writers.

2171 Parton, James. DAUGHTERS OF GENIUS: A SERIES OF SKETCHES OF AUTHORS, ARTISTS, REFORMERS, AND HEROINES, QUEENS, PRINCESSES AND WOMEN OF SOCIETY, WOMEN SCIENTIFIC AND PECULIAR. Philadelphia: Hubbard, 1888. 563 p. Illus.

Offers a feminist-pacifist approach to American women--Harriet Beecher Stowe, Louisa May Alcott, Mrs. Benedict Arnold, Laura Bridgman, Maria Mitchell, and others--and to English women travelers in America--Mrs. Trollope and Harriet Martineau.

2172 Peacock, Virginia T. FAMOUS AMERICAN BELLES. Philadelphia: J.B. Lippincott Co., 1901. 297 p. Illus.

Describes leaders in American society.

2173 Rawick, George P., ed. THE AMERICAN SLAVE: A COMPOSITE AUTOBIOGRAPHY. 19 vols. Contributions to Afro-American and African Studies Series, no. 11. Westport, Conn.: Greenwood Press, 1941-74.

2174 Ray, L.P., and Ray, Emma J. TWICE SOLD, TWICE RANSOMED: AUTOBIOGRAPHY OF MR. AND MRS. L.P. RAY. N.p.: 1926. 320 p. Illus. Reprint. Black Heritage Library Collection. Freeport, N.Y.: Books for Libraries, 1970.

Describes the lives and works in slums, jails, missions, and temperance groups of a couple born in slavery.

2175 Ross, Ishbel. CHARMERS AND CRANKS: TWELVE FAMOUS AMERICAN WOMEN WHO DEFIED CONVENTION. New York: Harper & Row, 1965. xii, 306 p. Illus., biblio.

Reports on Madame Jumel, Hetty Green, Mrs. Frank Leslie, the Fox sisters, the Claflin sisters, Mrs. Jack Gardner, Carrie Nation, Nellie Bly, Isadora Duncan, and Aimee Semple McPherson.

2176 Scruggs, Lawson A. WOMEN OF DISTINCTION: REMARKABLE IN WORKS AND INVINCIBLE IN CHARACTER. Raleigh, N.C.: 1893. xxiii, 382 p.

One of the earliest black biographical collections.

2177 Showalter, Elaine, ed. THESE MODERN WOMEN: AUTOBIOGRAPHICAL ESSAYS FROM THE TWENTIES. Old Westbury, N.Y.: Feminist Press, 1978. 147 p. Paper.

Reproduces twenty articles in which the NATION commissioned seventeen women to examine the feminist foundations of their lives and three psychologists of different schools to comment on the autobiographies.

2178 Stein, Leo, ed. FRAGMENTS OF AUTOBIOGRAPHY. Women in America from Colonial Times to the Twentieth Century series. New York: Arno Press, 1974. Variously paged.

Describes women who led unique lives on the frontier, in prison, as lawyer, as scholar in foreign university, presidential candidate, and horse thief. Pieces by Southern, native American, and black women. Includes short articles about women printed in the NATION in 1926.

2179 Stoddard, Hope. FAMOUS AMERICAN WOMEN. New York: Thomas Y. Crowell Co., 1970. viii, 461 p. Illus., biblio.

Consists of short biographies, with bibliographies, of forty-two American women of the nineteenth and twentieth centuries in professions and arts.

2180 Stokes, Olivia E. LETTERS AND MEMORIES OF SUSAN AND ANNA BARTLETT WARNER. New York: G.P. Putnam's Sons, 1925. x, 229 p. Illus.

Susan was a popular writer. Anna wrote hymns.

2181 Stowe, Lyman B. SAINTS, SINNERS AND BEECHERS. Indianapolis: Bobbs-Merrill Co., 1934. 450 p. Reprint. Freeport, N.Y.: Books for Libraries, 1970.

Describes Catharine, Harriet, Mary, and Isabella Beecher in family context.

2182 Teitz, Joyce. WHAT'S A NICE GIRL LIKE YOU DOING IN A PLACE LIKE THIS? New York: Coward, McCann & Geoghegan, 1974. 285 p.

Contains biographical essays on the rewarding professional-personal lives of several women. Includes a lawyer, physician, oceanographer, physicist, company president, campaign committee chairperson, economist, foreign service officer, systems analyst, and writer.

2183 Tharp, Louise H. THE PEABODY SISTERS OF SALEM. Boston: Little, Brown and Co., 1950. x, 392 p. Illus.

Sophia married Nathaniel Hawthorne; Mary married Horace Mann; Elizabeth ran the Transcendental Bookshop in Boston. Undocumented.

2184 Thomson, Mortimer N. [Doesticks, P.B., Q.K. Philander]. THE WITCHES OF NEW YORK, AS ENCOUNTERED BY Q.K. PHILANDER DOESTICKS, P.B. New York: Literature House. Rudd & Carleton, 1859. xiii, 493 p. Reprint. American Humorists Series. Saddle River, N.J.: Gregg Press, 1969.

Muckraking satire of sixteen women of nineteenth-century New York City.

2185 Thorp, Margaret. FEMALE PERSUASION: SIX STRONG-MINDED WOMEN. New Haven, Conn.: Yale University Press, 1949. x, 253 p. Illus., biblio.

Sketches of Catharine Beecher, Jane Swisshelm, Amelia

Bloomer, Sara J. [Grace Greenwood] Lippincott, Louisa McCord, and Lydia Maria Child.

2186 Truax, Rhoda. THE DOCTORS JACOBI. Boston: Little, Brown and Co., 1952. 270 p.

Fictionalized biography of woman physician and her husband.

2187 Willard, Frances E. A WOMAN OF THE CENTURY: FOURTEEN HUNDRED-SEVENTY BIOGRAPHICAL SKETCHES ACCOMPANIED BY PORTRAITS OF LEADING WOMEN IN ALL WALKS OF LIFE. Buffalo: Charles Wells Moulton, 1893. 812 p. Illus. Reprint. Detroit: Gale Research Co., 1967.

2188 Willard, Frances E., and Livermore, Mary A., comps. AMERICAN WOMEN: FIVE HUNDRED BIOGRAPHIES WITH OVER 1,400 PORTRAITS. A COMPREHENSIVE ENCYCLOPEDIA OF THE LIVES AND ACHIEVEMENTS OF AMERICAN WOMEN DURING THE NINETEENTH CENTURY. 2 vols. New York: Most, Crowell & Kirk Patrick, 1897. Reprint. Detroit: Gale Research Co., 1973.

Two outstanding feminists compile a useful and interesting volume.

2189 Woodward, Helen B. THE BOLD WOMEN. New York: Farrar, Straus & Young, 1953. 373 p. Biblio.

Among the better-known women are Anne Royall, Jane Swisshelm, and Harriet Tubman. Among the lesser known are Kate Field and Adah Isaacs Mencken.

2190 Wright, Richardson. FORGOTTEN LADIES: NINE PORTRAITS FROM THE AMERICAN FAMILY ALBUM. Philadelphia: J.B. Lippincott Co., 1928. 307 p. Illus., biblio.

Sketches of the Indian woman "the Savage Maid," the Storer sisters (theater), Sophy Haphy (beloved of George Wesley), Deborah Sampson (revolutionary war soldier), Maria Mark (contributor to Know-Nothingism), Anne Royall (journalist), Sara J. Hale (editor), the Fox sisters (mediums) and Belle Boyd (Confederate spy). Writing poor but material unique.

2191 Yost, Edna. AMERICAN WOMEN OF NURSING. Philadelphia: J.B. Lippincott Co., 1955. xiii, 197 p.

Biographies of women who contributed to American nursing include Adelaide Nutting, Lillian Wald, Anne Goodrich, Estelle Osborne, and Lucile Leone.

2192 _____. AMERICAN WOMEN OF SCIENCE. Philadelphia: J.B. Lippincott Co., 1952. xviii, 233 p.

Sketches of Ellen Richards, Annie Cannon, Alice Hamilton, Florence Sabin, Mary Pennington, Lillian Gilbreth, Libbie Hyman, Wanda Farr, Hazel Stiebling, Florence Seibert, Katherine Blodgett, and Margaret Mead.

See also chapter 3, section B; and chapter 9, section G.5.

E. INDIVIDUAL BIOGRAPHIES, AUTOBIOGRAPHIES

Adams, Abigail

2193 Adams, Abigail. NEW LETTERS OF ABIGAIL ADAMS: 1788-1801. Edited by Stewart Mitchell. Boston: Houghton Mifflin Co., 1947. xlii, 281 p. Illus., biblio.

2194 Whitney, Janet. ABIGAIL ADAMS. Boston: Little, Brown and Co., 1947. xii, 357 p. Illus., biblio.

Adams, Hannah

2195 Adams, Hannah. A MEMOIR OF HANNAH ADAMS: WRITTEN BY HERSELF, WITH ADDITIONAL NOTES BY A FRIEND. Boston: Gray & Bower, 1832. iv, 110 p.

First American woman to support herself by writing.

Adams, Maude

2196 Robbins, Phyllis. MAUDE ADAMS: AN INTIMATE PORTRAIT. New York: Pitman, 1952. vi, 308 p. Illus.

Actress.

Addams, Jane

2197 Addams, Jane. JANE ADDAMS: A CENTENNIAL READER. Edited by Emily C. Johnson. New York: Macmillan Co., 1960. xix, 330 p.

Peace worker and social reformer.

2198 Davis, Allen F. AMERICAN HEROINE: THE LIFE AND LEGEND OF JANE ADDAMS. New York: Oxford University Press, 1975. 339 p. Paper.

2199 Perkins, M. Helen, comp. A PRELIMINARY CHECKLIST FOR A BIBLIOGRAPHY ON JANE ADDAMS. Rockford, Ill.: 30 April 1960. 43 p. Offset.

Compiled under the direction of the Rockford Area Jane Addams Center and Committee. Ample though not complete. Lists of primary and secondary sources.

See also 1398, 1399, 1400, 1405.

Adler, Polly

2200 Adler, Polly. A HOUSE IS NOT A HOME. New York: Rinehart, 1953. 374 p.

Agassiz, Elizabeth Cary

2201 Paton, Lucy A. ELIZABETH CARY AGASSIZ. Boston: Houghton Mifflin Co., 1919. viii, 423 p. Illus.

Activist and wife of scientist.

Alcott, Louisa May

2202 Alcott, Louisa May. HER LIFE, LETTERS AND JOURNALS. Edited by Edna D. Cheney. Boston: Roberts Brothers, 1881. v, 404 p. Illus. Reprint. New York: Burt Franklin, 1973. Paper.

Writer.

2203 Gulliver, Lucile, comp. LOUISA MAY ALCOTT: A BIBLIOGRAPHY. Boston: Little, Brown and Co., 1932. 71 p. Reprint. Burt Franklin Bibliographical and Reference Series, no. 292. New York: Burt Franklin, 1973.

2204 Saxton, Martha. LOUISA MAY: A MODERN BIOGRAPHY OF LOUISA MAY ALCOTT. Boston: Houghton Mifflin Co., 1977. viii, 428 p. Illus., biblio.

Alda, Frances

2205 Alda, Frances. MEN, WOMEN AND TENORS. Boston: Houghton Mifflin Co., 1937. 307 p.

Opera singer.

Alderson, Nannie

2206 Alderson, Nannie, and Smith, Helena H. A BRIDE GOES WEST. Lincoln: University of Nebraska Press, 1969. ii, 273 p. Paper.

Wife of an early Montana rancher.

Aldrich, Darragh

2207 Aldrich, Darragh. LADY IN LAW. Chicago: Ralph Fletcher Seymour, 1950. 347 p. Illus.

Minnesota lawyer-senator, suffragist, and humanitarian.

Allen, Florence E.

2208 Allen, Florence E. TO DO JUSTLY. Forest Grove, Oreg.: International School Book Services, 1965. ix, 201 p. Illus.

U.S. circuit judge involved in suffrage, peace activities, and in Tennessee Valley Authority decision.

Ames, Mary

2209 Ames, Mary. FROM A NEW ENGLAND WOMAN'S DIARY IN DIXIE IN 1865. New York: Negro Universities Press, 1969. vi, 125 p.

White teacher in Freedman's school.

Anderson, Marian

2210 Anderson, Marian. MY LORD, WHAT A MORNING: AN AUTOBIOGRAPHY. New York: Viking Press, 1956. viii, 312 p. Illus.

Singer.

Anderson, Mary

2211 Anderson, Mary. WOMAN AT WORK: THE AUTOBIOGRAPHY OF MARY ANDERSON AS TOLD TO MARY N. WINSLOW. Minneapolis: University of Minnesota Press; London: Oxford, 1951. Reprint. Westport, Conn.: Greenwood Press, 1973. x, 266 p. Illus.

First head of Women's Bureau.

Angelou, Maya

2212 Angelou, Maya. SINGIN' AND SWINGIN' AND GETTIN' MERRY LIKE CHRISTMAS. New York: Random House, 1976. 242 p. Paper.

Writer.

Anna Katharina

2213 Fries, Adelaide L. THE ROAD TO SALEM. Chapel Hill: University of North Carolina Press, 1944. x, 316 p. Illus.

Eighteenth-century Moravian woman.

Anonymous

2214 Anonymous. THE AUTOBIOGRAPHY OF A HAPPY WOMAN. New York: Moffat, Yard, 1914. xiii, 373 p. Reprint. New York: Arno Press, 1974.

The random thoughts of a "woman who is happy because she works" . . . outside the home.

Anthony, Susan B.

2215 Harper, Ida H. THE LIFE AND WORK OF SUSAN B. ANTHONY, INCLUDING THE TRIUMPHS OF HER LAST YEARS, ACCOUNT OF HER DEATH AND FUNERAL AND COMMENTS OF THE PRESS: A STUDY OF THE EVOLUTION OF THE STATUS OF WOMEN. 3 vols. Indianapolis: Hollenbeck; Kansas City, Mo.: Bowen-Merrill, 1898-1908. Illus. Reprint. Women's Rights and Liberation: Essential Documents series. New York: Arno Press, 1969.

Feminist.

2216 Lutz, Alma. SUSAN B. ANTHONY: REBEL, CRUSADER, HUMANITARIAN. Boston: Beacon Press, 1959. xii, 340 p. Illus., biblio.

Arapaho Woman

2217 Michelson, Truman. "Narrative of an Arapaho Woman." AMERICAN ANTHROPOLOGIST, n.s. 35 (October-December 1933): 595-610. Biblio.

Atherton, Gertrude

2218 Atherton, Gertrude. ADVENTURES OF A NOVELIST. New York:

Blue Ribbon, 1932. 598 p.

Novelist.

2219 McClure, Charlotte S. "A Checklist of Writings of and about Gertrude Atherton." AMERICAN LITERARY REVIEW 9 (Spring 1976): 103-62.

Bacon, Delia

2220 Hopkins, Vivian. PRODIGAL PURITAN: A LIFE OF DELIA BACON. Cambridge, Mass.: Harvard University Press, Belknap Press, 1959. 362 p. Illus., biblio.

Originator of the theory that Francis Bacon wrote Shakespeare's plays.

Baez, Joan

2221 Baez, Joan. DAYBREAK. New York: Dial Press, 1968. 159 p. Paper.

Singer.

Bailey, Pearl

2222 Bailey, Pearl. THE RAW PEARL. New York: Harcourt, Brace, 1968. 206 p. Paper.

Singer.

Balch, Emily Greene

2223 Randall, Mercedes M. IMPROPER BOSTONIAN: EMILY GREENE BALCH. New York: Twayne Publishers, 1964. 475 p. Illus.

Founder of Women's Trade Union League and head of Women's International League for Peace and Freedom.

Barton, Clara

2224 Barton, Clara. THE STORY OF MY CHILDHOOD. New York: Baker & Taylor, 1907. 125 p. Illus.

Founder of the Red Cross.

2225 Ross, Ishbel. ANGEL OF THE BATTLEFIELD: THE LIFE OF CLARA BARTON. New York: Harpers, 1956. xi, 305 p. Illus., biblio.

Beard, Mary Ritter

2226 Lane, Ann J., ed. MARY RITTER BEARD: A SOURCEBOOK. Studies in the Life of Women. New York: Schocken Books, 1977. x, 252 p. Biblio. Paper.

Feminist-historian. Part 1 of book discusses life and work; part 2 includes selections from writings and speeches.

Beecher, Catharine E.

2227 Harveson, Mae E. CATHARINE ESTHER BEECHER (PIONEER EDUCATOR). Philadelphia: University of Pennsylvania, 1932. x, 295 p. Illus., biblio. Reprint. American Education: People, Ideas and Institutions series. New York: Arno Press, 1969.

Educator. The appendix includes the constitution of the American Women's Education Association.

2228 Sklar, Kathryn K. CATHARINE BEECHER: A STUDY IN AMERICAN DOMESTICITY. New Haven, Conn.: Yale University Press, 1973. Reprint. New York. W.W. Norton, 1976. 373 p. Illus. Paper.

Bethune, Mary McCleod

2229 Holt, Rockham. MARY McCLEOD BETHUNE. Garden City, N.Y.: Doubleday & Co., 1964. 306 p. Illus.

Educator.

Bickerdyke, Mary Ann

2230 Baker, Nina B. CYCLONE IN CALICO: THE STORY OF MARY ANN BICKERDYKE. Boston: Little, Brown and Co., 1952. 278 p.

Humanitarian worker on the Civil War front.

Blackwell, Elizabeth

2231 Blackwell, Elizabeth. PIONEER WORK IN OPENING THE MEDICAL PROFESSION TO WOMEN: AUTOBIOGRAPHICAL SKETCHES. New York: Longmans, Green, 1895. ix, 264 p. Reprint. New York: Schocken Books, 1977.

Founder of the New York Dispensary.

2232 Wilson, Dorothy C. LONE WOMAN: THE STORY OF ELIZABETH BLACKWELL, THE FIRST WOMAN DOCTOR. Boston: Little, Brown and Co., 1970. 469 p. Illus., biblio.

Appends primary sources to the bibliography.

See also 2158.

Blake, Lillie Devereux

2233 Blake, Katherine, and Wallace, Margaret L. CHAMPION OF WOMEN: THE LIFE OF LILLIE DEVEREUX BLAKE. New York: Fleming H. Revell, 1943. 224 p. Illus.

Suffragist writer.

Blatch, Harriot Stanton

2234 Blatch, Harriot S., and Lutz, Alma. CHALLENGING YEARS: THE MEMOIRS OF HARRIOT STANTON BLATCH. New York: G.P. Putnam's Sons, 1940. Reprint. Washington, D.C.: Zenger Publishing Co., 1976. xvi, 347 p. Illus.

Reports the public rather than the private events in the life of this feminist and pacifist.

Bloomer, Amelia

2235 Bloomer, Dexter C. THE LIFE AND WRITINGS OF AMELIA BLOOMER. Boston: Arena, 1895. 387 p.

Feminist.

Bloor, Ella

2236 Bloor, Ella R. WE ARE MANY: AN AUTOBIOGRAPHY OF ELLA REEVE BLOOR. New York: International Publishers Co., 1940. 320 p. Illus.

"America's leading labor agitator."

Bly, Nellie

2237 Noble, Iris. NELLIE BLY: FIRST WOMAN REPORTER. (1867-1922). New York: Julian Messner, 1956. 192 p. Biblio.

Bogan, Louise

2238 Bogan, Louise. WHAT THE WOMAN LIVED: SELECTED LETTERS OF LOUISE BOGAN, 1920-1970. Edited by Ruth Limmer. New York: Harcourt Brace Jovanovich, 1973. ixv, 401 p.

Poet and critic.

2239 Couchman, Jane. "Louise Bogan: A Bibliography of Primary and Secondary Materials, 1915-1975." BULLETIN OF BIBLIOGRAPHY 33 (1976): 73-77, 104, 111-26, 178-81.

Bolton, Frances P.

2240 Loth, David. THE LONG WAY FORWARD: THE BIOGRAPHY OF CONGRESSWOMAN FRANCES P. BOLTON. New York: Longmans, Green, 1957. 302 p.

Bowne, Eliza S.

2241 Bowne, Eliza S. A GIRL'S LIFE EIGHTY YEARS AGO: SELECTIONS FROM THE LETTERS OF ELIZA SOUTHGATE BOWNE. New York: Scribner's, 1887. xii, 239 p.

Young educated woman who lived first in New England, then in South Carolina.

Box-Car Bertha

2242 Box-Car Bertha, as told to Rutman, Ben L. SISTER OF THE ROAD. New York: Gold Label, 1937. 314 p.

A hobo-prostitute.

Bradstreet, Anne

2243 Berryman, John. HOMAGE TO MISTRESS BRADSTREET. New York: Farrar, Straus & Cudahy, 1956. Unpaged. Illus.

Poet.

2244 Piercy, Josephine K. ANNE BRADSTREET. Twayne's United States Authors Series, no. 73. New York: Twayne Publishers, 144 p. Biblio. Paper.

Brown, Catharine

2245 Anderson, Rufus. MEMOIR OF CATHARINE BROWN, A CHRISTIAN INDIAN OF THE CHEROKEE NATION. 2d ed. Boston: Croker & Brewster, 1825. viii, 180 p.

Brown, Charlotte

2246 Brown, Charlotte. "The Journal of Charlotte Brown, Matron of the General Hospital with the English Forces in America, 1754-1756." In COLONIAL CAPTIVITIES, MARCHES AND JOURNEYS, edited by Isabel Calder, pp. 169-98, under the auspices of the National Society of Colonial Dames of America. New York: Macmillan Co., 1935. Reprint. Port Washington, N.Y.: Kennikat Press, 1967.

Carroll, Anna Ella

2247 Greenbie, Marjorie B. MY DEAR LADY: THE STORY OF ANN ELLA CARROLL, THE "GREAT UNRECOGNIZED MEMBER OF LINCOLN'S CABINET." New York: Whittlesey House, 1940. xx, 316 p. Illus., biblio. Reprint. Women in America: From Colonial Times to the 20th Century series. New York: Arno Press, 1974.

Strategist of Civil War battles.

Casal, Mary

2248 Casal, Mary. THE STONE WALL: AN AUTOBIOGRAPHY. Chicago: Eyncourt, 1930. 227 p. Reprint. Homosexuality: Lesbians and Gay Men in Society, History and Literature series. New York: Arno Press, 1975.

Lesbian post-Civil War experience.

Cassatt, Mary

2249 Sweet, Frederick A. MISS MARY CASSATT: IMPRESSIONIST FROM PENNSYLVANIA. Norman: University of Oklahoma, 1966. xx, 242 p. Illus., biblio.

Cather, Willa

2250 Lathrop, JoAnna, comp. WILLA CATHER: A CHECKLIST OF HER PUBLISHED WRITING. Lincoln: University of Nebraska Press, 1975. xiii, 118 p. Paper.

Author.

2251 Woodress, James L. WILLA CATHER: HER LIFE AND WORK. Lincoln: University of Nebraska Press, 1975. 288 p. Biblio.

Catt, Carrie Chapman

2252 Peck, Mary G. CARRIE CHAPMAN CATT: A BIOGRAPHY. New York: H.W. Wilson Co., 1944. 495 p. Illus.

Suffragist.

Clare, Adah

2253 Parry, Albert. "The Rise of the Queen of Bohemia" and "The Fall of the Queen of Bohemia." In his GARRETS AND PRETENDERS: A HISTORY OF BOHEMIANISM IN AMERICA, chaps. 2 and 3. Enl. ed. New York: Dover Publications, 1960. xviii, 422 p. Illus., biblio. Paper.

Actress.

Clay, Laura

2254 Fuller, Paul E. LAURA CLAY AND THE WOMAN'S RIGHTS MOVEMENT. Lexington: University Press of Kentucky, 1975. x, 217 p. Illus., biblio.

Officer of the National American Woman's Suffrage Association.

Coleman, Ann Raney

2255 King, Richard C., ed. THE VICTORIAN LADY ON THE TEXAS FRONTIER: THE JOURNAL OF ANN RANEY COLEMAN. London: Foulsham, 1972. 190 p. Biblio., illus.

Coolidge, Grace

2256 Ross, Ishbel. GRACE COOLIDGE AND HER ERA: THE STORY OF A PRESIDENT'S WIFE. New York: Dodd, Mead & Co., 1962. ix, 370 p. Illus., biblio.

Crandall, Prudence

2257 Fuller, Edmund. PRUDENCE CRANDALL: AN INCIDENT OF RACISM IN NINETEENTH CENTURY CONNECTICUT. Middletown, Conn.: Wesleyan University Press, 1971. 113 p. Illus., biblio.

Educator.

Cushman, Charlotte

2258 Leach, Joseph. BRIGHT PARTICULAR STAR: THE LIFE AND TIMES OF CHARLOTTE CUSHMAN. New Haven, Conn.: Yale University Press, 1970. xvi, 453 p. Illus.

Nineteenth-century actress.

Dalrymple, Jean

2259 Dalrymple, Jean. SEPTEMBER CHILD: THE STORY OF JEAN DALRYMPLE BY HERSELF. New York: Dodd, Mead & Co., 1963. xvi, 318 p. Illus.

Producer, director, and playwright.

Daly, Maria L.

2260 Daly, Maria L. DIARY OF A UNION LADY. Edited by Harold E. Hammond. New York: Funk & Wagnalls, 1962. xlvii, 396 p.

Wife of a New York judge.

Dandridge, Dorothy

2261 Dandridge, Dorothy, and Conrad, Earl. EVERYTHING AND NOTHING: THE DOROTHY DANDRIDGE TRAGEDY. New York: Abelard & Schumann, 1970. viii, 215 p.

Actress.

D'Arusmont, Frances (Wright)

2262 D'Arusmont, Frances [Wright]. LIFE, LETTERS, AND LECTURES: 1834-1844. New York: n.p., 1844. Reprint. American Women: Images and Realities series. New York: Arno Press, 1972.

Social reformer. Includes A COURSE OF POPULAR LECTURES; WITH THREE ADDRESSES, ON VARIOUS PUBLIC OCCASIONS, AND A REPLY TO THE CHARGES AGAINST THE FRENCH REFORMERS OF 1789 (London, 1834); SUPPLEMENT COURSE OF LECTURES, CONTAINING THE LAST FOUR LECTURES DELIVERED IN THE UNITED STATES (London, 1834); and BIOGRAPHY, NOTES. AND POLITICAL LETTERS OF FRANCES WRIGHT D'ARUSMONT NOS. 1 AND 2 (New York, 1844).

2263 Perkins, Alice G., and Wolfson, Theresa. FRANCES WRIGHT, FREE ENQUIRER: THE STUDY OF A TEMPERMENT. New York: Harper, 1939. 393 p. Illus., biblio.

Davies, Marion

2264 Guiles, Fred L. MARION DAVIES: A BIOGRAPHY. New York: McGraw-Hill Book Co., 1972. xii, 419 p. Illus., biblio.

Screen actress.

Davis, Angela

2265 Davis, Angela. AUTOBIOGRAPHY. New York: Random House, 1974. 400 p. Paper.

Author and teacher.

Davis, Mrs. Jefferson

2266 Ross, Ishbel. FIRST LADY OF THE SOUTH: THE LIFE OF MRS. JEFFERSON DAVIS. New York: Harper, 1958. xii, 475 p. Biblio.

Day, Dorothy

2267 Day, Dorothy. THE LONG LONELINESS. New York: Harper, 1952. 288 p.

Catholic social activist.

De Mille, Agnes

2268 De Mille, Agnes. AND PROMENADE HOME. Boston: Little, Brown and Co., 1958. 301 p. Illus.

Dancer.

Demorest, Ellen Curtis

2269 Ross, Ishbel. CRUSADERS AND CRINOLINES: THE LIFE AND TIMES OF ELLEN CURTIS DEMOREST AND WILLIAM JENNINGS DEMOREST. New York: Harper & Row, 1963. x, 290 p. Illus., biblio.

A fashion designer-businesswoman and her husband and partner.

Dezba

2270 Reichard, Gladys A. DEZBA: WOMAN OF THE DESERT. New York: J.J. Augustin, 1939. xxvi, 161 p. Illus.

Navajo woman.

Dickinson, Anna

2271 Chester, Giraud. EMBATTLED MAIDEN: THE LIFE OF ANNA DICKINSON. New York: G.P. Putnam's Sons, 1951. xi, 307 p. Illus., biblio.

Civil War orator and lecturer.

Dickinson, Emily

2272 Buckingham, Willis J. EMILY DICKINSON: AN ANNOTATED BIBLIOGRAPHY. Bloomington: Indiana University Press, 1970. xii, 322 p.

Poet.

2273 Sewall, Richard B. THE LIFE OF EMILY DICKINSON. 2 vols. New York: Farrar, Straus & Giroux, 1974. Illus., biblio.

Dix, Dorothea

2274 Marshall, Helen E. DOROTHEA DIX: FORGOTTEN SAMARITAN. Chapel Hill: University of North Carolina Press, 1937. Reprint. New York: Russell & Russell, 1967. x, 298 p. Illus., biblio.

Reformer.

Dodge, Grace H.

2275 Graham, Abbie. GRACE H. DODGE: MERCHANT OF DREAMS. New York: Woman's Press, 1926. 329 p.

Social welfare worker.

Dorr, Rheta L.C.

2276 Dorr, Rheta L.C. A WOMAN OF FIFTY. New York: Funk & Wagnalls, 1924. 451 p.

Feminist and journalist.

Douglass, Frederick

2277 Quarles, Benjamin. FREDERICK DOUGLASS. Studies in American Negro Life. New York: Atheneum Publishers, 1968. xvi, 378 p. Illus., biblio.

Black reformer and feminist.

Duncan, Isadora

2278 Duncan, Isadora. MY LIFE. New York: Boni Liveright, 1927. 359 p. Illus.

2279 MacDougall, Allan R. ISADORA: A REVOLUTIONARY IN ART AND LOVE. New York: T. Nelson, 1960. 296 p. Illus.

Dancer.

Dunham, Katherine

2280 Dunham, Katherine. A TOUCH OF INNOCENCE. New York: Harcourt, Brace, 1959. 312 p.

Dancer-anthropologist.

Duniway, Abigail S.

2281 Duniway, Abigail. PATH BREAKING: AN AUTOBIOGRAPHICAL HISTORY OF THE EQUAL SUFFRAGE MOVEMENT IN THE PACIFIC STATES. Portland, Oreg.: James, Kerns & Abbott, 1914. xvi, 297 p. Illus. Reprint. New York: Source Book Press, 1970; Millwood, N.Y.: Kraus; New York: Schocken Books, 1971.

Pioneer involved with suffrage and prohibition movements.

Earhart, Amelia

2282 Burke, John. WINGED LEGEND: THE STORY OF AMELIA EARHART. New York: G.P. Putnam's Sons, 1970. 255 p. Illus., biblio.

Aviator.

Eddy, Mary Baker

2283 Peel, Robert. MARY BAKER EDDY. New York: Holt, Rinehart & Winston, 1966. xi, 372 p.

Evangelist.

Enters, Angna

2284 Enters, Angna. ARTIST'S LIFE. New York: Coward McCann, 1958. 447 p. Illus.

Dancer, choreographer, mime, designer, and composer.

Farnham, Eliza W.B.

2285 Farnham, Eliza W.B. ELIZA WOODSON: OR, EARLY DAYS OF ONE OF THE WORLD'S WORKERS. A STORY OF AN AMERICAN LIFE. 2d ed. New York: A.J. Davis, 1864. xi, 425 p.

Frontiersperson, prison reformer, and feminist.

Fiske, Minnie Maddern

2286 Binns, Archie, and Kooken, Olive. MRS. FISKE AND THE AMERICAN THEATRE. New York: Crown Publishers, 1955. x, 436 p. Illus.

America's "greatest actress."

Fitzgerald, Zelda

2287 Milford, Nancy. ZELDA. New York: Harper & Row, 1970. xiv, 424 p. Illus. Paper.

Flynn, Elizabeth Gurley

2288 Flynn, Elizabeth G. THE ALDERSON STORY: MY LIFE AS A POLITICAL PRISONER. New York: International Publishers Co., 1963. 223 p.

American Communist. The appendix includes some poems.

2289 ______. I SPEAK MY PIECE: AUTOBIOGRAPHY OF A "REBEL GIRL." New York: Masses & Mainstream, 1955. 326 p. Reprinted as the REBEL GIRL, AN AUTOBIOGRAPHY: MY FIRST LIFE. New York: International Publishers Co., 1973. Paper.

Forten, Charlotte L.

2290 Billington, Ray A. THE JOURNAL OF CHARLOTTE L. FORTEN. New York: Collier; London: Collier-Macmillan, 1961. v, 286 p.

The black abolitionist, a relative of the Grimké sisters.

Fox Indian Woman

2291 Michelson, Truman, ed. "The Autobiography of a Fox Indian Woman." In U.S. AMERICAN ETHNOLOGY BUREAU ANNUAL REPORT NO. 40 (1918-1919), pp. 291-349. Translated by Horace Poweshiek. Washington, D.C.: Government Printing Office, 1925.

Bilingual Fox-English text.

Franklin, Rosalind

2292 Sayre, Anne. ROSALIND FRANKLIN & DNA. New York: W.W. Norton & Co., 1975. 221 p.

"Lost woman" in the major DNA research project.

Freeman, Mary E. Wilkins

2293 Foster, Edward. MARY E. WILKINS FREEMAN. New York: Hendricks House, 1956. 229 p.

Novelist and short story writer.

French, Alice [Thanet, Octave]

2294 McMichael, George L. JOURNEY TO OBSCURITY: THE LIFE OF OCTAVE THANET. Lincoln: University of Nebraska Press, 1965. v, 259 p. Illus., biblio.

Novelist.

FULLER MARGARET. see OSSOLI, MARGARET FULLER

Gale, Zona

2295 Derleth, August. STILL SMALL VOICE: THE BIOGRAPHY OF ZONA GALE. New York: D. Appleton-Century Co., 1940. 319 p. Illus.

Novelist.

Gardner, Isabella Stewart

2296 Tharp, Louise H. MRS. JACK: A BIOGRAPHY OF ISABELLA STEWART GARDNER. Boston: Little, Brown and Co., 1965. xii, 365 p. Illus., biblio.

Collector, and founder of Gardner Museum in Boston.

Garrison, William Lloyd

2297 WILLIAM L. GARRISON, 1805-1879: THE STORY OF HIS LIFE TOLD BY HIS CHILDREN. 4 vols. Boston: Houghton Mifflin Co., 1894.

Feminist-abolitionist. Note especially in volume 1, chapter 10, "Prudence Crandall"; in volume 2, passim, Garrison's meeting with the Grimkés; in volume 4, chapter 9, Garrison's writings as journalist on women's rights.

Gibson, Althea

2298 Gibson, Althea. I ALWAYS WANTED TO BE SOMEBODY. Edited by Ed Fitzgerald. New York: Harper, 1958. ix, 176 p. Illus.

Tennis star and golfer.

Gilman, Charlotte Perkins

2299 Gilman, Charlotte Perkins. THE LIVING OF CHARLOTTE PERKINS GILMAN. New York: Appleton-Century-Crofts, 1935. Illus. Reprint. American Women: Images and Realities series. New York: Arno Press, 1972.

Feminist and economic theorist.

Gilson, Mary B.

2300 Gilson, Mary B. WHAT'S PAST IS PROLOGUE: REFLECTIONS ON MY INDUSTRIAL EXPERIENCE. New York: Harper & Brothers, 1940. xii, 307 p.

Economist in industrial relations.

Giovanni, Nikki

2301 Giovanni, Nikki. GEMINI: AN EXTENDED AUTOBIOGRAPHICAL STATEMENT ON MY FIRST TWENTY-FIVE YEARS OF BEING A BLACK POET. New York: Viking Press, 1971. xii, 149 p.

Poet.

Glasgow, Ellen

2302 Glasgow, Ellen. THE WOMAN WITHIN. New York: Harcourt, Brace, 1934. xii, 307 p. Illus., biblio.

Writer.

Goldman, Emma

2303 Drinnon, Richard. REBEL IN PARADISE: A BIOGRAPHY OF EMMA GOLDMAN. Chicago: University of Chicago Press, 1961. Reprint. Boston: Beacon Press, 1970. xiii, 351 p. Illus., biblio.

Russian-born American radical labor leader and feminist.

2304 Goldman, Emma. LIVING MY LIFE. 2 vols. New York: Alfred A. Knopf, 1931. Reprint. New York: Dover Publications, 1970.

Goodrich, Annie W.

2305 Werninghaus, Esther A. ANNIE W. GOODRICH: HER JOURNEY TO YALE. New York: Macmillan Co., 1950. 104 p. Biblio.

Nurse-administrator.

Graham, Martha

2306 McDonagh, Don. MARTHA GRAHAM: A BIOGRAPHY. New York: Praeger Publishers, 1973. x, 341 p. Illus., biblio. Paper.

Dancer.

See also 1638.

Green, Hetty

2307 Sparkes, Boyden, and Moore, Samuel T. HETTY GREEN: A WOMAN WHO LOVED MONEY. Garden City, N.Y.: Doubleday & Co., 1930. Reprinted as THE WITCH OF WALL STREET: HETTY GREEN. Garden City, N.Y.: Doubleday, Doran, 1936. 338 p. Illus.

Financier.

Grimké, Sarah and Angelina

2308 Birney, Catherine H. THE GRIMKÉ SISTERS: SARAH AND ANGELINA GRIMKÉ, THE FIRST WOMEN ADVOCATES OF ABOLITION AND WOMEN'S RIGHTS. Boston: Lee & Shepard, 1885. 319 p. Reprint. Westport, Conn.: Greenwood Press, 1969.

2309 Lerner, Gerda. THE GRIMKÉ SISTERS FROM SOUTH CAROLINA: REBELS AGAINST SLAVERY. Boston: Houghton Mifflin Co., 1967. xiv, 479 p. Illus., biblio.

2310 Lumpkin, Katherine D. THE EMANCIPATION OF ANGLINA GRIMKÉ. Chapel Hill: University of North Carolina Press, 1974. xv, 265 p. Illus., biblio.

2311 Weld, Theodore, et al. LETTERS OF THEODORE DWIGHT WELD, ANGELINA GRIMKÉ WELD AND SARAH GRIMKÉ. 2 vols. Edited by Gilbert H. Barnes, and Dwight I. Dumond. The American Historical Association. New York: D. Appleton-Century, 1934.

Hale, Sarah Josepha

2312 Finley, Ruth E. THE LADY OF GODEY'S, SARAH JOSEPHA HALE. Philadelphia: J.B. Lippincott Co., 1931. 318 p. Illus.

Feminist editor and author.

Harriman, Florence J.

2313 Harriman, Florence J. FROM PINAFORES TO POLITICS. New York: Henry Holt and Co., 1923. 359 p.

Civilian World War I worker who became a member of the Federal Industrial Relations Commission.

2314 Haviland, Laura S. A WOMAN'S LIFE-WORK: LABOR AND EXPERIENCES. Chicago: C.V. Waite, 1887. Reprint. Miami, Fla.: Mnemoysne Publishing Co., 1969. 554 p.

Hedgman, Anna A.

2315 Hedgman, Anna A. THE TRUMPET SOUNDS: A MEMOIR OF NEGRO LEADERSHIP. New York: Holt, Rinehart & Winston, 1964. 202 p.

Activist in government, church and the Young Women's Christian Association (YWCA).

Hellman, Lillian

2316 Hellman, Lillian. AN UNFINISHED WOMAN: A MEMOIR. New York: Pegasus, 1972. xv, 372 p. Biblio.

2317 Moody, Richard. LILLIAN HELLMAN: PLAYWRIGHT. New York: Pegasus, 1972. xv, 372 p. Biblio.

Higginson, Thomas Wentworth

2318 Edelstein, Tilden G. STRANGE ENTHUSIASM: A LIFE OF THOMAS

WENTWORTH HIGGINSON. New Haven, Conn.: Yale University Press, 1968. ix, 425 p. Biblio.

Feminist who was also an abolitionist, antiimperialist, and editor and friend of Emily Dickinson.

Hoffman, Malvina

2319 Hoffman, Malvina. YESTERDAY IS TOMORROW: A PERSONAL HISTORY. New York: Crown Publishers, 1965. 378 p. Illus.

Sculptor.

Holiday, Billie

2320 Holiday, Billie, with Dufty, William. LADY SINGS THE BLUES. Garden City, N.Y.: Doubleday & Co., 1956. 250 p. Paper.

Singer.

Howe, Julia Ward

2321 Howe, Julia Ward. REMINISCENCES, 1819-1899. Boston: Houghton Mifflin Co., 1899. vi, 465 p. Illus.

Author and suffragist.

2322 Richards, Laura E., and Elliott, Maud H. JULIA WARD HOWE, 1819-1910. 2 vols. Boston: Houghton Mifflin Co., 1915. Illus.

Hunt, Harriot K.

2323 Hunt, Harriot K. GLANCES AND GLIMPSES; OR, FIFTY YEARS SOCIAL, INCLUDING TWENTY YEARS PROFESSIONAL LIFE. Boston: J.P. Jewett, 1856. 418 p. Reprint. New York: Source Book Press, 1970.

Doctor and friend of leading feminists.

Hurst, Fanny

2324 Hurst, Fanny. ANATOMY OF ME: A WANDERER IN SEARCH OF HERSELF. Garden City, N.Y.: Doubleday & Co., 1958. 367 p.

Author.

Hurston, Zora Neale

2325 Hemenway, Robert E. ZORA NEALE HURSTON. Urbana: University of Illinois Press, 1977. 432 p.

Author.

2326 Hurston, Zora Neale. DUST TRACKS ON A ROAD: AN AUTOBIOGRAPHY. Philadelphia: J.P. Lippincott Co., 1942. v, 294 p. Reprint. The American Negro: History and Literature series. New York: Arno Press, 1969.

Jackson, Helen H.

2327 Banning, Evelyn I. HELEN HUNT JACKSON. New York: Vanguard Press, 1973. 248 p.

Author of RAMONA, poet and friend of Dickinson.

Jackson, Mahalia

2328 Jackson, Mahalia. MOVIN' ON UP. New York: Hawthorn Books, 1966. 212 p. Illus.

Gospel singer.

Jacobs, Harriet [Brent]

2329 Jacobs, Harriet [Brent]. INCIDENTS IN THE LIFE OF A SLAVE GIRL, WRITTEN BY HERSELF. Edited by Maria L. Child. Boston: 1861. Reprint. Detroit: Negro History Press, n.d. 306 p. Paper.

Jemison, Mary

2330 Seaver, James E. A NARRATIVE OF THE LIFE OF MRS. MARY JEMISON: THE WHITE WOMAN OF THE GENESEE. Canandaigua, N.Y.: J.D. Bemis, 1824. 182 p. Illus. Reprint. New York: Corinth Books, 1961.

Captured white woman who lived with and married into the Iroquois tribe during the French and Indian War.

Jewett, Sarah Orne

2331 Matthiessen, Frances O. SARAH ORNE JEWETT. Boston: Houghton Mifflin Co., 1929. 159 p.

Writer.

2332 Weber, Clara C., and Weber, Carl J. A BIBLIOGRAPHY OF THE PUBLISHED WRITINGS OF SARAH ORNE JEWETT. Colby College

Monograph, no. 18. Waterville, Maine: Colby College, 1949. xi, 105 p.

JOHNSON, PAULINE. See Tekahion-Wake.

Jones, Mary H. [Mother Jones]

2333 Jones, Mary H. AUTOBIOGRAPHY OF MOTHER JONES. Chicago: Charles H. Kerr, 1925. Reprint. American Labor: From Conspiracy to Collective Bargaining series. New York: Arno Press, 1969. 242 p.

Mine organizer.

Joplin, Janis

2334 Caserta, Peggy, as told to Knapp, Don. GOING DOWN WITH JANIS. Secaucus, N.J.: Lyle Stuart, 1973. 298 p.

Pop singer.

Kaibah

2335 Bennett, Kay. KAIBAH: RECOLLECTIONS OF AN ARAPAHO GIRL-HOOD. Los Angeles: Westernlore, 1964. 253 p. Illus.

Kearney, Belle

2336 Kearney, Belle. A SLAVEHOLDER'S DAUGHTER. New York: Abby, 1900. Reprint. New York: Negro Universities Press, 1969. 269 p. Illus.

Teacher, suffragist, and international figure in the Women's Christian Temperance Union. Contains material on Mormon women.

Keckley, Elizabeth

2337 Keckley, Elizabeth. BEHIND THE SCENES, OR, THIRTY YEARS A SLAVE, AND FOUR YEARS IN THE WHITE HOUSE. New York: G.W. Carleton, 1868. xvi, 271 p. Reprint. Buffalo, N.Y.: Stansil Education Press, 1931. The American Negro: History and Literature series. New York: Arno Press, 1968.

Housekeeper who held sympathetic views of Mary Todd Lincoln.

Keller, Helen

2338 Keller, Helen A. THE STORY OF MY LIFE: WITH HER LETTERS (1887-1901) AND A SUPPLEMENTARY ACCOUNT OF HER EDUCATION, INCLUDING PASSAGES FROM THE REPORTS AND LETTERS OF HER TEACHER, ANNIE MANSFIELD SULLIVAN, BY JOHN MACY. Garden City, N.Y.: Doubleday & Co., 1954. 382 p. Illus.

Woman who was deaf and mute from birth.

Kelley, Florence

2339 Blumberg, Dorothy R. FLORENCE KELLEY: THE MAKING OF A SOCIAL PIONEER. New York: Augustus M. Kelley, 1966. xii, 194 p. Illus., biblio.

Quaker. Member of the National Consumers' League and the National Woman's Suffrage Association, and one of the founders of the National Association for the Advancement of Colored People.

2340 Goldmark, Josephine C. IMPATIENT CRUSADER: FLORENCE KELLEY'S LIFE STORY. Urbana: University of Illinois Press, 1953. Reprint. Westport, Conn.: Greenwood Press, 1976. xii, 217 p.

Kemble, Fanny

2341 Driver, Leota S. FANNY KEMBLE. Chapel Hill: University of North Carolina Press, 1933. xiv, 271 p. Illus., biblio. Reprint. New York: Negro Universities Press, 1969.

First great actress to perform in America.

2342 Kemble, Fanny. A JOURNAL OF A RESIDENCE ON A GEORGIAN PLANTATION IN 1838-1839. New York: Harper, 1863. lxi, 415 p. Reprint. Edited by John A. Scott. New York: Alfred A. Knopf, 1961.

Note especially chapter 19, "Women in Slavery."

Kimball, Nell

2343 Kimball, Nell. NELL KIMBALL: HER LIFE AS AN AMERICAN MADAM. Edited by Stephen Longstreet. New York: Macmillan Co., 1970. ix, 286 p.

King, Billie Jean

2344 King, Billie Jean, with Chapin, Kim. BILLIE JEAN. New York: Harper & Row, 1974. xi, 208 p. Illus.

Tennis champion.

King, Coretta S.

2345 King, Coretta S. MY LIFE WITH MARTIN LUTHER KING, JR. New York: Holt, Rinehart & Winston, 1969. 372 p. Illus.

Kitt, Eartha

2346 Kitt, Eartha. THURSDAY'S CHILD. New York: Duell, Sloan & Pearce, 1956. 250 p.

Actress and singer.

Kohut, Rebekah

2347 Kohut, Rebekah. MY PORTION (AN AUTOBIOGRAPHY). New York: Albert & Charles Boni, 1927. xiv, 301 p.

Hungarian-Jewish immigrant after Civil War.

La Flesche, Suzette

2348 Wilson, Dorothy C. BRIGHT EYES: THE STORY OF SUZETTE LA FLESCHE, AN OMAHA INDIAN. New York: McGraw-Hill Book Co., 1974. 396 p. Biblio.

Nineteenth-century fighter for native American rights.

Larcom, Lucy

2349 Larcom, Lucy. A NEW ENGLAND GIRLHOOD. Boston: Houghton Mifflin Co., 1889. Reprint. Williamsport, Mass.: Corner House, 1973. 274 p.

A Lowell mill girl who became a well-known poet.

Lathrop, Julia

2350 Addams, Jane. MY FRIEND JULIA LATHROP. New York: Macmillan Co., 1935. ix, 228 p.

First head of the Children's Bureau.

Lathrop, Rose

2351 Maynard, Theodore. A FIRE WAS LIGHTED: THE LIFE OF ROSE HAWTHORNE LATHROP. Milwaukee: Bruce, 1948. x, 443 p. Biblio.

Daughter of Nathaniel Hawthorne, who became nurse of terminal cancer patients.

Lazarus, Emma

2352 Jacob, Heinrich E. THE WORLD OF EMMA LAZARUS. New York: Schocken Books, 1949. 222 p. Illus.

Poet.

Lee, Mary Ann

2353 Moore, Lillian. "Mary Ann Lee: First American Giselle." DANCE INDEX 2 (May 1943): 60-71. Illus.

America's first great classical ballerina.

Lee, Mother Ann

2354 Blinn, Henry C. THE LIFE AND GOSPEL OF MOTHER ANN LEE. East Canterbury, N.H.: Shakers, 1901. 264 p.

Founder of the Shaker sect.

Le Gallienne, Eva

2355 Le Gallienne, Eva. WITH A QUIET HEART: AN AUTOBIOGRAPHY OF EVA LE GALLIENNE. New York: Viking Press, 1953. 311 p.

Founder of the Civic Repertory Theatre.

Leslie, Mrs. Frank

2356 Stern, Madeleine B. PURPLE PASSAGE: THE LIFE OF MRS. FRANK LESLIE. Norman: University of Oklahoma Press, 1953. 281 p. Illus., biblio.

Magazine editor and publisher.

Liliuokalani

2357 Liliuokalani. HAWAII'S STORY BY HAWAII'S QUEEN, LILUOKALANI. Boston: Lee & Shepard, 1898. viii, 409 p. Illus.

Lincoln, Salome

2358 Davis, Almond H. THE FEMALE PREACHER, OR MEMOIR OF SALOME LINCOLN, AFTERWARDS THE WIFE OF ELDER J.S. MOWRY. Providence, R.I.: Elder J.S. Mowry, 1843. viii, 162 p. Reprint. American Women: Images and Realities series. New York: Arno Press, 1972.

New England Free Will Baptist preacher.

Livermore, Mary

2359 Livermore, Mary. THE STORY OF MY LIFE, OR THE SUNSHINE AND SHADOWS OF SEVENTY YEARS. Hartford, Conn.: A.D. Worthington, 1899. xxxiv, 730 p. Illus.

Southern woman who became Sanitary Commissioner during the war, editor of WOMAN'S JOURNAL, and a suffragist. Volume includes lecture, "What Shall We Do with Our Daughters?" See also 1251.

Low, Juliette

2360 Schultz, Gladys D., and Lawrence, Daicy G. LADY FROM SAVANNAH: THE LIFE OF JULIETTE LOW. Philadelphia: J.B. Lippincott Co., 1958. 383 p. Illus.

Founder of the Girl Scouts.

Lowell, Amy

2361 Damon, Samuel F. AMY LOWELL, A CHRONICLE, WITH EXTRACTS FROM HER CORRESPONDENCE. Boston: Houghton Mifflin Co., 1935. xxi, 773 p. Biblio.

Poet.

Lowell, Josephine Alan

2362 Stewart, William R. THE PHILANTHROPIC WORK OF JOSEPHINE ALAN LOWELL. New York: Macmillan Co., 1911. xv, 584 p. Illus., biblio.

Organizer of the Women's Municipal League and social activist.

Luhan, Mabel G. Dodge

2363 Luhan, Mabel [G.] Dodge. INTIMATE MEMORIES. 4 vols. New York: Harcourt, Brace and Co., 1933-37. Reprint. 4 vols. in 2. Millwood, N.Y.: Kraus Reprint Co., 1971. Illus.

Radical feminist.

Lyon, Mary

2364 Hitchcock, Edward, et al., comps. THE POWER OF CHRISTIAN BENEVOLENCE, ILLUSTRATED IN THE LIFE AND LABORS OF MARY LYON. Northampton, Mass.: Bridgman & Childs; Philadelphia: Thomas, Cowperwaite, 1851. viii, 486 p. Illus.

Founder of Mount Holyoke College.

McCarthy, Abigail

2365 McCarthy, Abigail. PRIVATE FACES/PUBLIC PLACES. Garden City, N.Y.: Doubleday & Co., 1972. viii, 448 p. Illus.

The wife of the U.S. senator Eugene McCarthy.

McCarthy, Mary T.

2366 McCarthy, Mary. MEMORIES OF A CATHOLIC GIRLHOOD. New York: Harcourt, Brace, 1957. 245 p. Illus. Paper.

Writer.

McDowell, Mary

2367 Wilson, Howard E. MARY McDOWELL, NEIGHBOR. Chicago: University of Chicago Press, 1928. xv, 235 p.

Founder of artists' retreat.

McGuire, Judith W.

2368 McGuire, Judith W (A Lady of Virginia). DIARY OF A SOUTHERN REFUGEE, DURING THE WAR. 2d ed. New York: E.J. Hale, 1867. 360 p. Reprint. American Women: Images and Realities series. New York: Arno Press, 1972.

MacLane, Mary I.

2369 MacLane, Mary I. MARY MacLANE: A DIARY OF HUMAN DAYS. New York: Frederick A. Stokes, 1917. 317 p.

McPherson, Aimee Semple

2370 McLoughlin, William G. "Aimee Semple McPherson: 'Your Sister in the King's Glad Service.' " JOURNAL OF POPULAR CULTURE 1 (Winter 1967): 193-217.

Evangelist.

Madison, Dolly

2371 Anthony, Katherine. DOLLY MADISON, HER LIFE AND TIMES. Garden City, N.Y.: Doubleday & Co., 1949. x, 246 p. Biblio.

Mahoney, Mary E.

2372 Chayer, Mary E. "Mary E. Mahoney." AMERICAN JOURNAL OF NURSING 54 (April 1954): 429-31.

America's first black nurse.

Marlowe, Julia

2373 Russell, Charles K. JULIA MARLOWE, HER LIFE AND ART. New York: D. Appleton, 1926. xxvi, 582 p. Illus.

Actress.

Maywood, Augusta

2374 Winter, Marian. "Augusta Maywood." DANCE INDEX 2 (January-February 1943): 4-18. Illus.

Nineteenth-century ballerina.

Mead, Margaret

2375 Mead, Margaret. BLACKBERRY WINTER: MY EARLIER YEARS. New York: William Morrow & Co., 1972. 305 p. Illus. Paper.

Anthropologist.

Meyer, Agnes E.

2376 Meyer, Agnes E. OUT OF THESE ROOTS. Boston: Little, Brown and Co., 1953. x, 385 p.

"Self-centered American girl" who later devoted her life to political, educational, and public health activities.

Millay, Edna St. Vincent

2377 Brittin, Norman A. EDNA ST. VINCENT MILLAY. Twayne's United States Authors Series. New York: Twayne Publishers, 1967. 192 p. Biblio.

Poet.

2378 Gould, Jean. THE POET AND HER BOOK. New York: Thomas Y. Crowell Co., 1962. xii, 308 p. Illus. Biblio.

Millett, Kate

2379 Millett, Kate. FLYING. New York: Alfred A. Knopf, 1974. 546 p.

Feminist.

Miner, Myrtilla

2380 O'Connor, Ellen M. MYRTILLA MINER: A MEMOIR. Boston, New York: Houghton Mifflin Co., 1885. 129 p. Reprint. The American Negro: History and Literature series. New York: Arno Press, 1969.

Black woman who established teacher-preparing institutions for blacks after the Civil War.

Mitchell, Maria

2381 Mitchell, Maria. MARIA MITCHELL: LIFE, LETTERS, AND JOURNALS. Compiled by Phebe N. Kendall. Boston: Lee & Shepard, 1896. vi, 293 p.

Nineteenth-century astronomer.

2382 Wright, Helen. SWEEPER OF THE SKY: THE LIFE OF MARIA MITCHELL, FIRST WOMAN ASTRONOMER IN AMERICA. New York: Macmillan Co., 1949. vii, 253 p. Illus.

Includes useful bibliographical essay.

Molek, Mary

2383 Molek, Mary. IMMIGRANT WOMAN. Dover, Del.: 1976. vii, 167 p. Illus. Offset, paper.

Child of Slovene parents.

Monroe, Marilyn

2384 Mailer, Norman. MARILYN: A BIOGRAPHY . . . PICTURES BY THE WORLD'S FOREMOST PHOTOGRAPHERS. New York: Grosset & Dunlap, 1973. 270 p. Illus. Paper.

Screen actress.

2385 Zolotow, Maurice. MARILYN MONROE. New York: Harcourt, Brace, Jovanovich, 1960. 340 p. Illus.

Moody, Anne

2386 Moody, Anne. COMING OF AGE IN MISSISSIPPI. New York: Dial Press, 1968. 348 p.

Civil rights worker with Martin Luther King.

Moody, Harriet C.B.

2387 Dunbar, Olivia H. A HOUSE IN CHICAGO. Chicago: University of Chicago Press, 1947. viii, 287 p.

Wife of the poet William Vaughan Moody and friend of Rabindranath Tagore, Robert Frost, Vachel Lindsay, Edwin Arlington Robinson, John Masefield, Madame Curie, James Stephens, and many other writers.

Morgan, Robin

2388 Morgan, Robin. GOING TOO FAR: THE PERSONAL CHRONICLE OF A FEMINIST. New York: Random House, 1977. xiii, 333 p.

Contemporary feminist poet.

Morton, Rosalie Slaughter

2389 Morton, Rosalie S. A WOMAN SURGEON: THE LIFE AND WORK

OF ROSALIE SLAUGHTER MORTON. New York: Frederick A. Stokes, 1937. ix, 399 p.

Moses, Anna M.R.

2390 Moses, Anna M.R. GRANDMA MOSES: MY LIFE'S HISTORY. Edited by Otto Kallir. New York: Harpers, 1952. 148 p.

Artist.

Mott, Lucretia

2391 Cromwell, Otelia. LUCRETIA MOTT. Cambridge, Mass.: Harvard University Press, 1958. x, 241 p. Biblio.

Feminist.

2392 Hallowell, Anne D. JAMES AND LUCRETIA MOTT. Boston: Houghton Mifflin Co., 1884. vi, 566 p. Illus.

Mountain Wolf Woman

2393 Mountain Wolf Woman. MOUNTAIN WOLF WOMAN: SISTER OF CRASHING THUNDER--THE AUTOBIOGRAPHY OF A WINNEBAGO INDIAN. Edited by Nancy O. Lurie. Ann Arbor: University of Michigan Press, 1961. 142 p. Illus.

Transcribed from tape.

Mowatt, Anna Cora

2394 Barnes, Eric W. THE LADY OF FASHION: THE LIFE AND THEATRE OF ANNA CORA MOWATT. New York: Charles Scribner's Sons, 1954. xi, 308 p.

Actress who became Poe's "ideal of womanhood."

Murfree, Mary Noailles [Charles Egbert]

2395 Parks, Edd W. CHARLES EGBERT CRADDOCK (MARY NOAILLES MURFREE). Chapel Hill: University of North Carolina, 1941. Reprint. Port Washington, N.Y.: Kennikat Press, 1972. x, 258 p. Illus., biblio.

Nineteenth-century novelist.

Murray, Judith Sargent [Constantia]

2396 Field, Venna B. CONSTANTIA: A STUDY OF THE LIFE AND WORKS OF JUDITH SARGENT MURRAY. University of Maine Studies, 2d series, no. 17. Orono: University Press, 1930. 118 p. Biblio.

Nineteenth-century feminist author.

Negri, Pola

2397 Negri, Pola. MEMORIES OF A STAR. Garden City, N.Y.: Doubleday & Co., 1970. 543 p. Illus.

Polish-born screen actress.

Noyes, John Humphrey

2398 Parker, Robert A. A YANKEE SAINT: JOHN HUMPHREY NOYES AND THE ONEIDA COMMUNITY. New York: G.P. Putnam's Sons, 1935. 322 p. Illus., biblio.

Nineteenth-century feminist.

Nurse, Rebecca

2399 Tapley, Charles S. REBECCA NURSE. Boston: Marshall Jones, 1930. xiii, 105 p. Illus.

Reputed "witch."

Nutting, Mary Adelaide

2400 Marshall, Helen E. MARY ADELAIDE NUTTING: PIONEER OF MODERN NURSING. Baltimore: Johns Hopkins University Press, 1972. ix, 396 p. Biblio.

O'Keefe, Georgia

2401 Goodrich, Lloyd, and Bry, Doris. GEORGIA O'KEEFE. New York: Frederick A. Praeger, 1970. 195 p. Illus., biblio.

Artist.

Ossoli, Margaret Fuller

2402 Chevigny, Bell G. THE WOMAN AND THE MYTH: MARGARET

FULLER'S LIFE AND WRITINGS. Old Westbury, N.Y.: Feminist Press, 1976. 500 p. Paper.

Feminist writer and intellectual.

2403 Ossoli, Margaret Fuller. THE WRITINGS OF MARGARET FULLER. Edited by Mason Wade. New York: Viking Press, 1941. xi, 608 p. Biblio.

Reprints "Woman in the Nineteenth Century," pages 105-218.

2404 Wade, Mason. MARGARET FULLER: WHETSTONE OF GENIUS. New York: Viking Press, 1940. xvi, 304 p. Illus., biblio.

Owen, Robert Dale

2405 Pancoast, E., and Lincoln, Anne E. THE INCORRIGIBLE IDEALIST: ROBERT DALE OWEN IN AMERICA. Bloomington, Ind.: Principia, 1940. 150 p. Biblio.

Male feminist.

Parsons, Lucy

2406 Ashbaugh, Carolyn. LUCY PARSONS: AMERICAN REVOLUTIONARY. Chicago: Charles H. Kerr, for the Illinois Labor History Society, 1976. 288 p. Illus., biblio. Paper.

Chicago black labor leader of the 1880s.

Pinkham, Lydia

2407 Burton, Jean. LYDIA PINKHAM IS HER NAME. New York: Farrar, Straus, 1949. 279 p. Illus.

Businesswoman interested in abolition and temperance.

Plath, Sylvia

2408 Butscher, Edward, ed. SYLVIA PLATH: THE WOMAN AND THE WORK. New York: Dodd, Mead & Co., 1977. xiii, 242 p.

Poet.

Pocohantas

2409 Watson, Virginia C. THE PRINCESS POCOHANTAS. Philadelphia: Penn Publishing Co., 1916. viii, 306 p. Illus.

Pretty-Shield

2410 Linderman, Frank B. RED MOTHER. New York: John Day, 1932. 256 p. Reprinted as PRETTY-SHIELD: MEDICINE WOMAN OF THE CROWS. Bison Book. Lincoln: University of Nebraska Press, 1972.

Prince, Nancy

2411 Prince, Nancy. A NARRATIVE OF THE LIFE AND TRAVELS OF MRS. NANCY PRINCE. WRITTEN BY HERSELF. 2d ed. Boston: 1853. 89 p. Pamph.

Early nineteenth-century black businesswoman and teacher.

Repplier, Agnes S.

2412 Stokes, George S. AGNES REPPLIER, LADY OF LETTERS. Philadelphia: University of Pennsylvania Press; London: Oxford, 1949. xiii, 274 p. Biblio.

Essayist.

Richards, Ellen H.

2413 Hunt, Caroline L. THE LIFE OF ELLEN H. RICHARDS. Boston: Whitcomb & Barrows, 1912. 202 p. Illus. Reprint. Washington, D.C.: American Home Economics Association, 1958.

Founder of the American Home Economics Association.

Richards, Linda

2414 Richards, Linda. REMINISCENCES OF LINDA RICHARDS: AMERICA'S FIRST TRAINED NURSE. Boston: Whitcomb & Barrows, 1911. xvi, 121 p. Reprint. Philadelphia: J.B. Lippincott Co., 1949.

Robins, Margaret Dreier

2415 Dreier, Mary E. MARGARET DREIER ROBINS: HER LIFE, LETTERS, AND WORK. New York: Island Press Cooperative, 1905. xviii, 278 p. Illus.

Leader of the Women's Trade Union League.

Roosevelt, Eleanor

2416 Lash, Joseph P. ELEANOR: THE YEARS ALONE. New York: W.W. Norton & Co., 1972. 368 p. Illus.

2417 _____. ELEANOR AND FRANKLIN: THE STORY OF THEIR RELATIONSHIP, BASED ON ELEANOR ROOSEVELT'S PRIVATE PAPERS. New York: W.W. Norton & Co., 1971. xviii, 765 p. Illus., biblio.

2418 Roosevelt, Eleanor. AUTOBIOGRAPHY. New York: Harper and Brothers, 1958. xix, 454 p. Illus.

See also 1337.

Rose, Ernestine L.

2419 Suhl, Yuri. ERNESTINE L. ROSE, AND THE BATTLE FOR HUMAN RIGHTS. New York: Reynal & Co., 1959. ix, 310 p. Illus., biblio.

Little known Polish immigrant who worked with Elizabeth Cady Stanton, Lucy Stone, and Lucretia Mott.

Rowson, Susanna Haswell

2420 Vail, Robert W.G. "Susanna Haswell Rowson, The Author of Charlotte Temple; A Bibliographical Study." AMERICAN ANTIQUARIAN SOCIETY PROCEEDINGS, n.s. 42 (1933): 47-160.

Eighteenth-century novelist.

Royall, Anne

2421 James, Bessie R. ANNE ROYALL'S U.S.A. New Brunswick, N.J.: Rutgers University Press, 1972. 447 p. Illus.

Eighteenth-century journalist.

See also 1297.

Royce, Sarah

2422 Royce, Sarah. A FRONTIER LADY: RECOLLECTIONS OF THE GOLD RUSH AND EARLY CALIFORNIA. Edited by Ralph Gabriel. Lincoln: University of Nebraska Press, 1977. xvi, 144 p. Paper.

Sacajawea

2423 Howard, Harold P. SACAJAWEA. Norman: University of Oklahoma Press, 1971. xiii, 208 p. Biblio.

Shoshone woman who acted as guide to Lewis and Clark.

St. Denis, Ruth

2424 St. Denis, Ruth. AN UNFINISHED LIFE: AN AUTOBIOGRAPHY. New York: Harper & Brothers, 1929. x, 291 p. Illus.

Dancer.

Sampson, Deborah

2425 Mann, Herman (A Citizen of Massachusetts). THE FEMALE REVIEW: OR, LIFE OF DEBORAH SAMPSON, THE FEMALE SOLDIER IN THE WAR OF THE REVOLUTION. Boston: J.K. Wiggin & William Parsons, 1866. xxxii, 267 p. Reprint. American Women: Images and Realities series. New York: Arno Press, 1972.

Sanapia

2426 Jones, David E. SANAPIA: COMANCHE MEDICINE WOMAN. New York: Holt, Rinehart & Winston, 1968. xvii, 107 p. Illus., biblio.

Sanger, Margaret

2427 Douglas, Emily T. MARGARET SANGER: PIONEER OF THE FUTURE. New York: Holt, Rinehart & Winston, 1970. viii, 274 p. Illus., biblio.

Pioneer of birth control movement.

2428 Kennedy, Daniel M. BIRTH CONTROL IN AMERICA: THE CAREER OF MARGARET SANGER. Yale Publications in American Studies, no. 18. New Haven, Conn.: Yale University Press, 1970. xi, 320 p. Biblio.

Note especially chapter 5, "Margaret Sanger, Sexuality and Feminism."

Schneiderman, Rose

2429 Schneiderman, Rose, with Goldthwaite, Rose. ALL FOR ONE. New York: Paul S. Eriksson, 1967. viii, 264 p. Biblio.

Suffragist and labor leader active in the Women's Trade Union League.

Sedgwick, Catharine Maria

2430 Welsh, Sister Mary M. CATHARINE MARIA SEDGWICK, HER POSITION IN THE LITERATURE AND THOUGHT OF HER TIME UP TO 1860. Washington, D.C.: Catholic University of America Press, 1937. Reprint. Philadelphia: Richard West, 1973. ix, 168 p. Biblio.

Nineteenth-century novelist.

Shaw, Anna H.

2431 Shaw, Anna H. THE STORY OF A PIONEER. New York: Harpers, 1915. 338 p. Illus.

Minister and suffragist.

Sigourney, Lydia H.

2432 Haight, Gordon S. MRS. SIGOURNEY, SWEET SINGER OF HARTFORD. New Haven, Conn.: Yale University Press, 1930. x, 201 p. Illus.

Poet and journalist.

Slayden, Ellen M.

2433 Slayden, Ellen M. WASHINGTON WIFE: JOURNAL OF ELLEN MAURY SLAYDEN, 1897-1919. New York: Harper & Row, 1963. xxiv, 385 p. Illus.

Wife of a U.S. senator.

Smedley, Agnes

2434 Smedley, Agnes. DAUGHTER OF EARTH. New York: Coward McCann, 1929. 344 p. Reprint. Old Westbury, N.Y.: Feminist

Press, 1973. 429 p.

Journalist born in rural Missouri who became a major chronicler of the Chinese Revolution.

Smith, Amanda

2435 Smith, Amanda. AN AUTOBIOGRAPHY: THE STORY OF THE LORD'S DEALINGS WITH AMANDA SMITH, THE COLORED EVANGELIST, CONTAINING AN ACCOUNT OF HER LIFE WORK OF FAITH, AND HER TRAVELS IN AMERICA, ENGLAND, IRELAND, SCOTLAND, INDIA AND AFRICA, AS AN INDEPENDENT MISSIONARY. Chicago: Meyer & Brother, 1893. xvi, 506 p. Illus. Reprint. Noblesville, Ind.: Newby Book Room, 1972.

A slave who subsequently became preacher.

Smith, Gerritt

2436 Harlow, Ralph V. GERRITT SMITH, PHILANTHROPIST AND REFORMER. New York: Henry Holt, 1939. vi, 501 p.

Male feminist.

Smith, Margaret B.

2437 Smith, Margaret. THE FIRST FORTY YEARS OF WASHINGTON SOCIETY IN THE FAMILY LETTERS OF MARGARET BAYARD SMITH. Edited by Gaillard Hunt. New York: Charles Scribner's Sons, 1906. xii, 424 p. Reprint. American Classics Series. New York: Frederick Ungar Publishing Co., 1965.

Friend of Thomas Jefferson, Maria Sedgwick, Harriet Martineau, Sarah Hale, and others.

Smith, Margaret Chase

2438 Graham, Frank. MARGARET CHASE SMITH: A WOMAN OF COURAGE. New York: John Day, 1964. 188 p.

U.S. senator from Maine.

Southworth, Mrs. Emma D.E.N.

2439 Boyle, Regis L. MRS. E.D.E.N. SOUTHWORTH, NOVELIST. Washington, D.C.: Catholic University of America Press, 1939. vii, 171 p. Biblio.

"Most popular authoress in the annals of American publishing."

Spencer, Lily Martin

2440 Bolton-Smith, Robin, and Truettner, William H. LILY MARTIN SPENCER, 1822-1902: THE JOYS OF SENTIMENT. Washington, D.C.: Smithsonian Institution for the National Collection of Fine Arts, 1973. 253 p. Illus., biblio.

Painter of popular subjects.

Stanton, Elizabeth Cady

2441 Lutz, Alma. CREATED EQUAL: A BIOGRAPHY OF ELIZABETH CADY STANTON: 1815-1902. New York: John Day, 1940. xi, 345 p. Illus., biblio.

Feminist.

2442 Stanton, Elizabeth Cady. ELIZABETH CADY STANTON AS REVEALED IN HER LETTERS, DIARY AND REMINISCENCES. 2 vols. Edited by Theodore Stanton, and Harriot S. Blatch. New York: Harper, 1922. Illus. Reprint. New York: Arno Press, 1969.

Volume 1 contains a revised edition of Stanton's EIGHTY YEARS AND MORE (London: T. Fisher Unwin, 1898); volume 2 contains letters and diary selections.

Stein, Gertrude

2443 Hobhouse, Janet. EVERYBODY WHO WAS ANYBODY: A BIOGRAPHY OF GERTRUDE STEIN. New York: G.P. Putnam's Sons, 1975. 244 p.

Author.

2444 Stein, Gertrude. THE AUTOBIOGRAPHY OF ALICE B. TOKLAS. New York: Harcourt, Brace, 1933. vii, 310 p.

Author.

Stern, Elizabeth Gertrude Levin [Leah Morton]

2445 Stern, Mrs. Elizabeth Gertrude Levin [Morton, Leah]. I AM A WOMAN--AND A JEW. New York: J.H. Sears, 1926. 362 p. Reprint. American Immigration Collection series. New York: Arno Press, 1969.

Immigrant.

Stewart, Elinore P.

2446 Stewart, Elinore P. LETTERS OF A WOMAN HOMESTEADER. Boston: Houghton Mifflin Co., 1914. 292 p. Illus.

Early twentieth-century widow. Includes visit to Mormons.

Stone, Lucy

2447 Blackwell, Alice S. LUCY STONE: PIONEER WOMAN SUFFRAGIST. Boston: Little, Brown and Co., 1930. viii, 313 p. Illus.

2448 Hays, Elinor A. MORNINGSTAR: A BIOGRAPHY OF LUCY STONE, 1818-1893. New York: Harcourt, Brace & World, 1961. 339 p. Biblio.

Stowe, Harriet Beecher

2449 Adams, John R. HARRIET BEECHER STOWE. Twayne's United States Authors Series. New York: Twayne Publishers, 1963. 172 p. Biblio. Paper.

Writer.

2450 Hildreth, Maragret H. HARRIET BEECHER STOWE: A BIBLIOGRAPHY. Hamden, Conn.: Shoe String Press, Archon Books, 1976. 257 p.

2451 Stowe, Charles W., comp. LIFE OF HARRIET BEECHER STOWE: COMPILED FROM HER LETTERS AND JOURNALS. Boston: Houghton Mifflin Co., 1889. 530 p. Illus. Reprint. Gale Library of Lives and Letters, American Writers Series, no. 10. Detroit: Gale Research Co., 1967.

Written with the collaboration of Stowe.

2452 Wilson, Robert. CRUSADER IN CRINOLINE: THE LIFE OF HARRIET BEECHER STOWE. Philadelphia: J.B. Lippincott Co., 1941. 606 p. Illus., biblio.

Swisshelm, Jane G.

2453 Swisshelm, Jane G. HALF A CENTURY. 2d ed. Chicago: Jansen, McClurg, 1880. 363 p. Reprint. New York: Source Book, 1970.

Journalist, reformer, and Civil War nurse, who worked for legal rights for married women, and for abolition and for temperance causes. Portrays life in cities and on the Minnesota frontier.

Tarbell, Ida

2454 Tarbell, Ida. IN A DAY'S WORK: AN AUTOBIOGRAPHY. New York: Macmillan Co., 1939. 412 p. Illus.

Muckraker.

Taylor, Susie K.

2455 Taylor, Susie K. REMINISCENCES OF MY LIFE IN CAMP, WITH THE 33D UNITED STATES COLORED TROOPS, LATE 1ST S[OUTH] C[AROLINA] VOLUNTEERS. Boston: 1902. xii, 82 p. Illus. Reprint. The American Negro: History and Literature series. New York: Arno Press, 1968.

Black laundress who served with Colonel Thomas Wentworth Higginson's regiment (see 2318) on St. Simon's Island.

Teasdale, Sara

2456 Carpenter, Margaret H. SARA TEASDALE: A BIOGRAPHY. New York: Schulte, 1960. 377 p. Illus.

Poet.

Tekahion-Wake [Pauline Johnson]

2457 Foster, Anne [Mrs. D. Garland]. THE MOHAWK PRINCESS: BEING SOME ACCOUNT OF THE LIFE OF TEKAHION-WAKE (PAULINE JOHNSON). Vancouver, British Columbia: Lion's Gate Publishing Co., 1931. 216 p. Illus., biblio.

Terrell, Mary C.

2458 Terrell, Mary C. A COLORED WOMAN IN A WHITE WORLD. Washington, D.C.: Ransdell, 1940. 436 p.

Delegate to the International Peace Conference. Friend of Jane Addams, Frederick Douglass, and H.G. Wells.

Terry, Ellen

2459 Terry, Ellen. THE THIRD DOOR: THE AUTOBIOGRAPHY OF AN

AMERICAN NEGRO WOMAN. New York: David McKay Co., 1955. ix, 304 p.

Black woman who became a writer, teacher, and worker at Friendship House and at the USO.

THANET, OCTAVE. See FRENCH, ALICE.

Thaxter, Julia

2460 Thaxter, Julia. AMONG THE ISLES OF SHOALS. Boston: Houghton Mifflin Co., 1882. 184 p. Plates.

Nineteenth-century poet.

Thompson, Era B.

2461 Thompson, Era B. AMERICAN DAUGHTER. Chicago: University of Chicago, 1946. Midway Reprint Series. Chicago: University of Chicago Press, 1974. 301 p. Paper.

Black girl during the depression of the thirties.

Truth, Sojourner

2462 Pauli, Hertha. HER NAME WAS SOJOURNER TRUTH. New York: Appleton-Century-Crofts, 1962. 250 p. Biblio.

Abolitionist and reformer.

2463 Truth, Sojourner. NARRATIVE OF SOJOURNER TRUTH, A BONDSWOMAN OF OLDEN TIME, EMANCIPATED BY THE NEW YORK LEGISLATURE IN THE EARLY PART OF THE PRESENT CENTURY, WITH A HISTORY OF HER LABORS AND CORRESPONDENCE DRAWN FROM HER "BOOK OF LIFE." Battle Creek, Mich.: 1878. xv, 240 p. Reprint. The American Negro: History and Literature series. New York: Arno Press, 1968. Chicago: Johnson Publishing Co., 1970.

Tubman, Harriet

2464 Bradford, Sarah H. SCENES IN THE LIFE OF HARRIET TUBMAN. Auburn, N.Y.: W.J. Moses, 1869. 129 p. Reprint of 1886 ed. New York: Corinth Books, 1961.

"Essay on Woman-Whipping" discusses Southern women who wielded the whip in context of "southern chivalry."

2465 Conrad, Earl. HARRIET TUBMAN: NEGRO SOLDIER AND ABOLI-

TIONIST. Washington, D.C.: Associated Publishers, 1943. xiv, 248 p.

Tyler, Mary Palmer

2466 Tyler, Mary O. GRANDMOTHER TYLER'S BOOK: THE RECOLLECTIONS OF MARY PALMER TYLER. Edited by Frederick Tupper, and Helen T. Brown. New York: G.P. Putnam's Sons, 1925. xxv, 366 p. Illus.

Upper-class New England woman.

Velasquez, Loreta J.

2467 Velasquez, Loreta J. THE WOMAN IN BATTLE: A NARRATIVE OF THE EXPLOITS, ADVENTURES, AND TRAVELS OF MADAME LORETA JANETA VELASQUEZ, OTHERWISE KNOWN AS LIEUTENANT HARRY T. BUFORD, CONFEDERATE STATES ARMY. IN WHICH IS GIVEN A FULL DESCRIPTION OF THE NUMEROUS BATTLES IN WHICH SHE PARTICIPATED AS A CONFEDERATE OFFICER: OF HER PERILOUS PERFORMANCES AS A SPY, AS A BEARER OF DISPATCHES, AS A SECRET-SERVICE AGENT, AND AS A BLOCKADE-RUNNER: OF HER ADVENTURES BEHIND THE SCENES AT WASHINGTON, INCLUDING THE BOND SWINDLE; OR HER CAREER AS A COUNTY SUBSTITUTE BROKER IN NEW YORK: OF HER TRAVELS IN EUROPE AND SOUTH AMERICA: HER MINING ADVENTURES ON THE PACIFIC SLOPE: HER RESIDENCE AMONG THE MORMONS: HER LOVE AFFAIRS, COURTSHIPS, MARRIAGES, ETC. ETC. Richmond, Va.: Dustin & Gilman, 1876. 606 p. Illus. Reprint. American Women: Images and Realities series. New York: Arno Press, 1972.

Vorse, Mary M. Heaton

2468 [Vorse, Mary H.] AUTOBIOGRAPHY OF AN ELDERLY WOMAN. Boston: Houghton Mifflin Co., 1911. 269 p. Reprint. Women in America: From Colonial Times to the 20th Century series. New York: Arno Press, 1974.

Wald, Lillian

2469 Duffus, Robert L. LILLIAN WALD: NEIGHBOR AND CRUSADER. New York: Macmillan Co., 1938. xiii, 371 p. Illus.

Public health nurse and social worker.

2470 Epstein, Beryl W. LILLIAN WALD, ANGEL OF HENRY STREET. New York: Julian Messner, 1948. 216 p. Illus.

Walker, Maggie L.

2471 Dabney, Wendell P. MAGGIE L. WALKER: HER LIFE AND DEEDS. Cincinnati: Dabney Publishing Co., 1927. 137 p. Illus.

First black woman bank president.

Walker, Mary

2472 Snyder, Charles McC. DR. MARY WALKER: THE LITTLE LADY IN PANTS. New York: Vantage, 1962. 166 p. Illus.

Feminist-reformer.

Walker, Mary [Mrs. Elkanah Walker]

2473 Drury, Clifford. ELKANAH AND MARY WALKER: PIONEERS AMONG THE SPOKANES. Caldwell, Idaho: Caxton Printers, 1940. 283 p. Illus.

Congregational couple who served the Spokane tribe as missionaries from 1833 to 1890.

Ward, Elizabeth Stuart Phelps

2474 Ward, Elizabeth S.P. CHAPTERS FROM A LIFE. Boston: Houghton Mifflin Co., 1896. 278 p.

Nineteenth-century novelist.

Warren, Mercy Otis

2475 Anthony, Katherine. FIRST LADY OF THE REVOLUTION: THE LIFE OF MERCY OTIS WARREN. Garden City, N.Y.: Doubleday & Co., 1958. 258 p. Biblio. Reprint. Port Washington, N.Y.: Kennikat Press, 1972.

Poet, dramatist, and historian.

Waters, Ethel

2476 Waters, Ethel. TO ME IT'S WONDERFUL. New York: Harper & Row, 1972. ix, 162 p.

Singer and actress.

Wells, Ida B.

2477 Barnett, Ida B. Wells. CRUSADE FOR JUSTICE: THE AUTOBIOGRAPHY OF IDA B. WELLS. Edited by Alfreda M. Dusten. Negro American Biographies and Autobiographies Series. Chicago: University of Chicago Press, 1970. xxxii, 434 p. Biblio. Paper.

Founder of the National Association for the Advancement of Colored People and black women's clubs.

West, Jessamyn

2478 West, Jessamyn. THE WOMAN SAID YES: ENCOUNTERS WITH LIFE AND DEATH. MEMOIRS. New York: Harcourt Brace Jovanovich, 1976. 180 p.

Writer.

Wharton, Edith

2479 Lewis, R.W.B. EDITH WHARTON: A BIOGRAPHY. New York: Harper & Row, 1975. xiv, 592 p. Illus. Biblio.

Novelist.

Wheatley, Phillis

2480 Richmond, Merle A. BID THE VASSAL SOAR: INTERPRETIVE ESSAYS ON THE LIFE AND POETRY OF PHILLIS WHEATLEY. Washington, D.C.: Howard University Press, 1974. xiii, 216 p.

Poet.

2481 Robinson, William H. PHILLIS WHEATLEY IN THE BLACK AMERICAN BEGINNINGS. Detroit: Broadside Press, 1975. 195 p.

Wilcox, Ella Wheeler

2482 Ballou, Jenny. PERIOD PIECE: ELLA WHEELER WILCOX AND HER TIMES. Boston: Houghton Mifflin Co., 1940. xiii, 285 p. Illus.

Poet.

Wilkinson, Jemima

2483 Hudson, Daniel. MEMOIR OF JEMIMA WILKINSON, A PREACHER OF THE EIGHTEENTH CENTURY, CONTAINING AN AUTHENTIC

NARRATIVE OF HER LIFE AND CHARACTER, AND OF THE RISE, PROGRESS AND CONCLUSION OF HER MINISTRY. Bath, N.Y.: L. Underhill, 1844. vii, 288 p.

Willard, Emma

2484 Lutz, Alma. EMMA WILLARD: PIONEER EDUCATOR OF AMERICAN WOMEN. Boston: Beacon Press, 1964. viii, 143 p.

Willard, Frances

2485 Dillon, Mary E. FRANCES WILLARD: FROM PRAYERS TO POLITICS. Chicago: University of Chicago Press, 1944. x, 417 p. Illus., biblio.

Founder of Women's Christian Temperance Union.

2486 Gordon, Anna A. THE LIFE OF FRANCES E. WILLARD. Evanston, Ill.: National Woman's Christian Temperance Union, 1912. xiii, 357 p.

2487 Willard, Frances E. GLIMPSES OF FIFTY YEARS: THE AUTOBIOGRAPHY OF AN AMERICAN WOMAN. Chicago: H.J. Smith, 1889. xvi, 698 p. Illus.

Wilson, Augusta Evans

2488 Fidler, William P. AUGUSTA EVANS WILSON, 1835-1909: A BIOGRAPHY. University: University of Alabama Press, 1951. 251 p. Illus., biblio.

Novelist.

Winslow, Ann G.

2489 Winslow, Ann G. DIARY OF ANNE GREENE WINSLOW, A BOSTON SCHOOL GIRL OF 1771. Edited by Alice M. Earle. Boston: Houghton Mifflin Co., 1894. xxi, 121 p. Reprint. Williamstown, Mass.: Corner House, 1974.

Woodhull, Victoria Claflin

2490 Arling, Emanie S. THE TERRIBLE SIREN, VICTORIA WOODHULL (1838-1927). New York: Harper, 1928. Illus., biblio. Reprint. American Women: Images and Realities series. New York: Arno Press, 1972.

Journalist and presidential candidate.

2491 Johnston, Joanna. MRS. SATAN: THE INCREDIBLE SAGA OF VICTORIA C. WOODHULL. New York: G.P. Putnam's Sons, 1967. 319 p. Illus., biblio.

See also 2159.

Woolson, Constance Fenimore

2492 Moore, Rayburn S. CONSTANCE FENIMORE WOOLSON. Twayne's United States Authors Series. New York: Twayne Publishers, 1963. 173 p. Biblio.

Novelist.

WRIGHT, FRANCES. See D'ARUSMONT, FRANCES (WRIGHT)

Wright, Patience

2493 Sellers, Charles C. PATIENCE WRIGHT: AMERICAN ARTIST AND SPY IN GEORGE III'S LONDON. Middletown, Conn.: Wesleyan University Press, 1976. 288 p. Illus.

Feminist a generation before Mary Wollstonecraft.

Young, Ann E.

2494 Young, Ann E. WIFE NO. 19, OR THE STORY OF A LIFE IN BONDAGE, BEING A COMPLETE EXPOSE OF MORMONISM, AND REVEALING THE SORROWS, SACRIFICES AND SUFFERINGS OF WOMEN IN POLYGAMY BY . . . BRIGHAM YOUNG'S APOSTATE WIFE. Hartford, Conn.: Dustin, Gilman, 1875. 605 p. Illus. Reprint. American Women: Images and Realities series. New York: Arno Press, 1972.

Zakrewska, Marie E.

2495 Zakrewska, Marie E. A WOMAN'S QUEST: THE LIFE OF MARIE E. ZAKREWSKA, M.D. Edited by Agnes C. Victor. New York: D. Appleton, 1924. xviii, 514 p. Illus. Reprint. American Women: Images and Realities series. New York: Arno Press, 1972.

Polish-born American doctor.

See also chapter 3, section B.

Appendix A
CENTERS

For a listing of centers in addition to those given below, see entry 418.

Alverno College, Research Center on Women
3401 South 39th Street
Milwaukee, Wisconsin 53215

Barnard College Women's Center
606 West 120th Street
New York, New York 10027

The Center for A Woman's Own Name
261 Kimberly Street
Barrington, Illinois 60010

The Center for Educational Reform
2115 S Street, N.W.
Washington, D.C. 20008

The Center for Feminist Art Historical Studies
83330 Willis Avenue
Panorama City, California 91412

The Center for Law and Social Policy
Women's Rights Division
1751 R Street, N.W.
Washington, D.C. 20036

The Center for the American Woman and Politics
Eagleton Institute of Politics
Rutgers University
New Brunswick, New Jersey 08901

The Center for Women and Sport
Pennsylvania State University
University Park, Pennsylvania 16802

The Center for Women Policy Studies
Suite 508
2000 P Street, N.W.
Washington, D.C. 20036

The Center for Women's Studies and Services
908 F Street
California State University
San Diego, California 92101

Information Center on the Mature Woman
515 Madison Avenue
New York, New York 10022

National Center for Voluntary Action
1785 Massachusetts Avenue, N.W.
Washington, D.C. 20036

Centers

Resource Center on Sex Roles in Education
National Foundation for the Improvement of Education
1156 Fifteenth Street, N.W.
Washington, D.C. 20005

University of Minnesota
Immigration History Research Center
826 Berry Street
St. Paul, Minnesota 55114

Women's History Research Center
2325 Oak Street
Berkeley, California 94708

Women's Law Center
1414 Avenue of the Americas
New York, New York 10019

Appendix B
COLLECTIONS

For more extensive listings on collections see Hamer's A GUIDE TO ARCHIVES AND MANUSCRIPTS IN THE UNITED STATES and the NATIONAL UNION CATALOG OF MANUSCRIPT COLLECTIONS, page 3.

Alma Lutz Collection
Zion Research Library
120 Seaver Street
Brookline, Massachusetts 02142
(Women in the church)

American Association of University Women Educational Foundation Library
2401 Virginia Avenue, N.W.
Washington, D.C. 20036
(Higher education)

Amistad Research Center
Dillard University
New Orleans, Louisiana 70122
(Missionary work, education)

Arthur and Elizabeth Schlesinger Library on the History of Women in America
Radcliffe College
3 James Street
Cambridge, Massachusetts 02138
(Women's liberation, personal and organizational collections)

Bancroft Library
University of California
Berkeley, California 94720
(Oral history)

Bertha Van Riper Overbury Gift Collection
Barnard College Library
Columbia University
New York, New York 10027
(Rare editions by American women)

Business and Professional Women's Foundation Library
2012 Massachusetts Avenue, N.W.
Washington, D.C. 20036
(Working women)

Collection
Medical College of Pennsylvania
3300 Henry Avenue
Philadelphia, Pennsylvania 19129
(Women in medicine; medical education)

Costume Reference Library
Costume Institute
Metropolitan Museum of Art
Fifth Avenue at 82d Street
New York, New York 10028
(Dress)

Elizabeth Bass Collection
Rudolph Matas Medical Library
Tulane University
1430 Tulane Avenue
New Orleans, Louisiana 70112
(Personal papers of women physicians)

Ella Strong Dennison Library
Scripps College
Claremont, California 91711
(Status and accomplishments)

Friends Historical Library
Swarthmore College
Swarthmore, Pennsylvania 19081
(Quaker women leaders; peace; Lucretia Mott; Jane Addams)

Gerritsen Collection
University of Kansas Library
Lawrence, Kansas 66044
(Late nineteenth, early twentieth century)

Home Economics Library
Pennsylvania State University
University Park, Pennsylvania 16802
(Dress)

Ida R. MacPherson Collection
Scripps College Library
Scripps College
Claremont, California 91711

Library of Congress
Washington, D.C. 20540
(Extensive, varied; personal papers; periodicals)

MBA Library
University of Connecticut
39 Woodland Street
Hartford, Connecticut 06105
(Business and management)

National Board Library
Young Women's Christian Association
600 Lexington Avenue
New York, New York 10022
(Mostly twentieth century)

National Woman's Party Library
144 Constitution Avenue, N.E.
Washington, D.C. 20002

Research Center on Women
Alverno College Library
3401 South 39th Street
Milwaukee, Wisconsin 53215
(Contemporary status, role)

Sophia Smith Collection
Smith College
Northampton, Massachusetts 10160
(Intellectual and social history)

Special Collections
Alumni Memorial Library
Lowell Technical Institute
Lowell, Massachusetts 01854
(Lowell mill girls)

Special Collections
General Library
University of California
Davis, California 95616
(Political movements and women's liberation)

Special Collections
King Library
University of Kentucky
Lexington, Kentucky 40506
(Suffrage)

Special Collections
Northwestern University Library
Evanston, Illinois 60201
(Women's liberation)

Special Collections in the Research Libraries
New York Public Library
Fifth Avenue and 42d Street
New York, New York 10018
(All areas; also in branch libraries)

Thomas Wentworth Higginson Collection
("Galatea Collection")
Boston Public Library
Copley Square
Boston, Massachusetts 02117
(History; suffrage movement)

Walter Clinton Jackson Library
University of North Carolina at Greensboro
Greensboro, North Carolina 27412
(Mostly contemporary)

Western Historical Collections
University of Colorado Libraries
Boulder, Colorado 80302
(Peace)

Women's Collection
Women's College Library
University of North Carolina at Greensboro
Greensboro, North Carolina
(Nineteenth and twentieth centuries)

Women's History Library
2325 Oak Street
Berkeley, California 94708
(All aspects)

Zion Research Library
Brookline, Massachusetts 02146
(Church ministry)

Appendix C
FILM, AUDIOVISUAL SOURCES

For a fuller listing of film and audiovisual sources, see page 2.

Black Box
P.O. Box 4172
Washington, D.C 20015

Film Images
17 West 60th Street
New York, New York 10023

Greenwood Press, Inc.
51 Riverside Avenue
Port Washington, New York 11050

Herstory Films, Inc.
137 East 13th Street
New York, New York 10003

Multi Media Resource Center
1525 Franklin Street
San Francisco, California 94109

New Day Films
P.O. Box 315
Franklin Lakes, New Jersey 07417

Pacifica Tape Library
Pacifica Program Service
5316 Venice Boulevard
Los Angeles, California 90019

Regional Oral History Office
Bancroft Library
University of California at Berkeley
Berkeley, California 94720

Research Publications
12 Lunar Drive
Woodbridge, Connecticut 06525

Serious Business Company
1145 Mandana Boulevard
Oakland, California 94610

Tomato Productions
Box 1952
Evergreen, Colorado 80439

University Microfilms International
300 N. Zeeb Road
Ann Arbor, Michigan 48106

The Women's Audio Exchange
Department
Natalie Slohm Associates
49 West Main Street
Cambridge, New York 12816

Women's Film Co-op (Project)
200 Main Street
Northampton, Massachusetts 01060

Women's History Research Center
2325 Oak Street
Berkeley, California 94708

Appendix D
GOVERNMENT AGENCIES

Citizen's Advisory Council on the
Status of Women
Room 4211
U.S. Department of Labor
Washington, D.C. 20210

Commission on Civil Rights
1121 Vermont Avenue, N.W.
Washington, D.C. 20425

Director Office of Public Affairs
Equal Employment Opportunity
Commission
2401 E Street, N.W.
Washington, D.C. 20506

Equal Employment Opportunity
Commission
2401 E Street, N.W.
Washington, D.C. 20506

Federal Women's Program
U.S. Civil Service Commission
1900 E Street, N.W.
Washington, D.C. 20415

Interdepartmental Committee on the
Status of Women
New Department of Labor Building
Washington, D.C. 20210

National Center for Educational
Statistics
Office of the Assistant Secretary for
Education
400 Maryland Drive, S.W.
Washington, D.C. 20202

National Center for Health Statistics
Health Resources Administration
5600 Fisher's Lane
Rockville, Maryland 20852

National Commission on the
Observance of International
Women's Year
Department of State
Washington, D.C. 20520

National Institute on Aging
National Institutes of Health
Bethesda, Maryland 20014

National Labor Relations Board
1717 Pennsylvania Avenue, N.W.
Washington, D.C. 20570

Office for Federal Contract
Compliance
Employment Standards Administration
U.S. Department of Labor
200 Constitution Avenue, N.W.
Washington, D.C. 20210

Government Agencies

Office of Information, Publications and Reports
U.S. Bureau of Labor Statistics
Room S1032
200 Constitution Avenue, N.W.
Washington, D.C. 20210

Public Information Office
Bureau of the Census
Department of Commerce
Washington, D.C. 20233

Superintendent of Documents
U.S. Government Printing Office
Washington, D.C. 20402

The Women's Bureau
Employment Standards Administration
U.S. Department of Labor
200 Constitution Avenue, N.W.
Washington, D.C. 20210

Wage and Hour Division
Employment Standards Administration
U.S. Department of Labor
200 Constitution Avenue, N.W.
Washington, D.C. 20210

Appendix E

NEWS AND INFORMATION SERVICES AND DISTRIBUTORS

Cragsmoor Books
P.O. Box 55
Cragsmoor, New York 14240

ERIC (Educational Resources Information Center)
Document Reproduction Service
P.O. Box 190
Arlington, Virginia 22210

Family Planning and Information Service
300 Park Avenue South
New York, New York 10010

Feminist Book Service
2092 Linden Avenue
Long Beach, California 90806

Feminist Bookmart
162-11 9th Avenue
Beechhurst, New York 11368

First Things First
23 7th Street S.E.
Washington, D.C. 20003

KNOW News Service
KNOW, Inc.
P.O. Box 86031
Pittsburgh, Pennsylvania 15221

Ragwomen Distributors Company
74 Grove Street
New York, New York 10014

Today Publications & News Service
621 National Press Building
Washington, D.C. 20045

Women in Distribution, Inc.
P.O. Box 8858
Washington, D.C. 20003

Women Law Reporter
5141 Massachusetts Avenue
Washington, D.C. 20016

Appendix F
NEWSLETTERS

ADULT AND CONTINUING EDUCATION
Today Publications & News Service, Inc.
621 National Press Building
Washington, D.C. 20045

AFFIRMATIVE ACTION REGISTER
10 South Brentwood Boulevard
St. Louis, Missouri 63105

BREAKTHROUGH
Interstate Association of Commissions on the Status of Women
Room 204
District Building
14th and E Streets, N.W.
Washington, D.C. 20004

COMMENT
American Council on Education
Office of Women in Higher Education
1 Dupont Circle
Washington, D.C. 20036

DO IT NOW: MONTHLY NEWSLETTER OF THE NATIONAL ORGANIZATION FOR WOMEN
National Organization for Women
Suite 1615
5 South Wabash Street
Chicago, Illinois 60603

EQUAL OPPORTUNITY IN HIGHER EDUCATION
Capitol Publications, Inc.
Suite G-12K
2430 Pennsylvania Avenue N.W.
Washington, D.C. 20037

THE EXECUTIVE WOMAN
747 Third Avenue
New York, New York 10017

HEALTH RIGHT
Women's Health Forum
175 Fifth Avenue
New York, New York 10010

HRW NEWSLETTER
Human Rights for Woman
1128 National Press Building
Washington, D.C. 20045

MUSICA
Indy Allen
1668 A Great Highway
San Francisco, California 94122

NETWORK NEWSLETTER
National Women's Health Network
P.O. Box 24192
Washington, D.C.

9 TO 5
140 Clarendon Street
Boston, Massachusetts 02116

ON CAMPUS WITH WOMEN
Project on the Status and Education of Women
Association of American Colleges
1818 R Street, N.W.
Washington, D.C. 20009

PEER PERSPECTIVE
NOW Legal Defense and Education Fund
1522 Connecticut Avenue, N.W.
Washington, D.C. 20036

LA RAZON MASTIZA
c/o Concillio Mujeres
Room 237
2588 Mission Street
San Francisco, California 94110

THE SPOKESWOMAN
1957 East 73d Street
Chicago, Illinois 60649

UNION W.A.G.E.
Union Women's Alliance to Gain Equality
P.O. Box 462
Berkeley, California 94701

WEAL WASHINGTON REPORT
Women's Equity Action League
821 National Press Building
Washington, D.C. 20045

WOMEN IN PERFORMING ARTS
Theater Department
Northwestern University
Evanston, Illinois 60201

WOMEN SPEAK OUT
1376 Hollister Road
Cleveland Heights, Ohio 44118

WOMEN'S STUDIES NEWSLETTER
The Feminist Press
Box 334
State University of New York
College at Old Westbury
Old Westbury, New York 10009

WOMEN'S WORK
1111 20th Street N.W.
Washington, D.C. 20036

WOMEN TODAY
Today Publications & News Service
621 National Press Building
Washington, D.C. 20045

Appendix G
ORGANIZATIONS

For a fuller listing of organizations see entries 402, 403.

American Agri-Women
Joan Adams, National Coordinator
P.O. Box 424
Buffalo, Okalhoma 73834

American Association for Health, Physical Education and Recreation
1201 Sixteenth Street, N.W.
Washington, D.C. 20036

American Association of University Women
2401 Virginia Avenue, N.W.
Washington, D.C. 20037

American Medical Women's Association
1740 Broadway
New York, New York 10019

American Nurses Association
2420 Pershing Road
Kansas City, Missouri 64108

American Society of Women Accountants
327 South La Salle Street
Chicago, Illinois 60604

American Women in Radio and Television
1321 Connecticut Avenue, N.W.
Washington, D.C. 20036

Association for the Study of Abortion
120 West 57th Street
New York, New York 10019

Association of Intercollegiate Athletics for Women
1201 Sixteenth Street N.W.
Washington, D.C. 20036

Association of Women in Architecture
P.O. Box 1
Clayton, Missouri 63105

Association of Women in Psychology
7012 Western Avenue
Chevy Chase, Maryland 20015

Association of Women in Science
1818 R Street, N.W.
Washington, D.C. 20009

Boston Women's Collective
490 Beacon Street
Boston, Massachusetts 02115

Business and Professional Women's Foundation
2012 Massachusetts Avenue, N.W.
Washington, D.C. 20036

Call for Action
1625 Massachusetts Avenue, N.W.
Washington, D.C. 20036

Church Employed Women
830 Witherspoon Building
Philadelphia, Pennsylvania 19107

Clearinghouse on Women's Studies
The Feminist Press
Box 334
State University of New York
College at Old Westbury
Old Westbury, New York 10009

Coalition Task Force in Women and Religion
4759 Fifteenth Avenue, N.E.
Seattle, Washington 98105

Commission on the Continuing Education of Women
Adult Education Association
810 Eighteenth Street, N.W.
Washington, D.C. 20036

Commission on Voluntary Service and Action
Room 665
475 Riverside Drive
New York, New York 10027

Daughters of Bilitis
P.O. Box 62
Fanwood, New Jersey 07023

Daughters of the American Revolution
1776 D Street, N.W.
Washington, D.C. 20006

Day Care and Child Development Council of America
1012 Fourteenth Street, N.W.
Washington, D.C. 20005

Education Commission of the States
300 Lincoln Tower Building
1860 Lincoln Street
Denver, Colorado 80203

Emma Willard Task Force on Education
Box 14229
Minneapolis, Minnesota 55414

Federally Employed Women
1249 National Press Building
Washington, D.C. 20045

Federation of Organization for Professional Women
Room 1122
1346 Connecticut Avenue, N.W.
Washington, D.C. 20036

Feminists on Children's Media
Box 4315
Grand Central Station
New York, New York 10017

Florence Crittenden Association of America
Room 1216
201 North Wells Street
Chicago, Illinois 60606

General Federation of Women's Clubs
1734 N Street, N.W..
Washington, D.C. 20036

Gray Panthers
3700 Chestnut Street
Philadelphia, Pennsylvania 19118

Health Research Group
2000 P Street, N.W.
Washington, D.C. 20036

Health Right
175 Fifth Avenue
New York, New York 10010

Human Rights for Women
1128 National Press Building
Washington, D.C. 20054

Institute for Sex Education
18 South Michigan Avenue
Chicago, Illinois 60603

Intercollegiate Association of Women Students
Box 2
2401 Virginia Avenue, N.W.
Washington, D.C. 20037

International Association of Women Ministers
1464 West 101st Street
Cleveland, Ohio 44102

International Association of Women Police
6655 North Avondale Avenue
Chicago, Illinois 60631

International Federation of Women Lawyers
150 Nassau Street
New York, New York 10038

International Institute of Women's Studies
1346 Connecticut Avenue, N.W.
Washington, D.C. 20036

Interstate Association of Commissions on the Status of Women
204 District Building
14th and E Streets, N.W.
Washington, D.C. 20004

Joint Committee of Organizations Concerned about the Status of Women in the Catholic Church
1600 Sunset Avenue
Waukegan, Illinois 60085

League of Women Composers
5610 Holston Hills Road
Knoxville, Tennessee 37914

League of Women Voters of the United States
1730 M Street, N.W.
Washington, D.C. 20036

Lucy Stone League
133 East 58th Street
New York, New York 10022

Media Women
320 Central Park West
New York, New York 10025

MOMMA
Box 5759
Santa Monica, California 90405

National Assembly of Women Religious
25 West Chicago Avenue
Chicago, Illinois 60611

National Association of Bank Women
111 East Wacker Drive
Chicago, Illinois 60601

National Association of Female Executives
160 East 57th Street
New York, New York 10016

National Association of Negro Business and Professional Women's Clubs
2861 Urban Avenue
Columbus, Georgia 31907

National Association of Women Artists
156 Fifth Avenue
New York, New York 10010

National Association of Women Deans, Administrators and Counselors
1201 Sixteenth Street N.W.
Washington, D.C. 20036

National Association of Women in Construction
2800 West Lancaster Avenue
Fort Worth, Texas 76107

National Association of Women Lawyers
American Bar Center
1155 East 60th Street
Chicago, Illinois 60637

National Black Feminist Organization
285 Madison Avenue
New York, New York 10017

National Committee on Household Employment
Suite 300
8120 Fenton Street
Silver Spring, Maryland 20910

National Consumers League
1785 Massachusetts Avenue, N.W.
Washington, D.C. 20036

National Council of Administrative Women in Education
1815 Fort Myer Drive, N.
Arlington, Virginia 22209

National Council of Catholic Women
United States Catholic Conference
1312 Massachusetts Avenue, N.W.
Washington, D.C. 20005

National Council of Jewish Women
1 West 47th Street
New York, New York 10036

National Council of Negro Women
1346 Connecticut Avenue, N.W.
Washington, D.C. 20036

National Council of Women in the United States
345 East 64th Street
New York, New York 10017

National Council on the Aging
1828 L Street, N.W.
Washington, D.C. 22036

National Federation of Business and Professional Women's Clubs
2012 Massachusetts Avenue, N.W.
Washington, D.C. 20036

National Institute of Spanish-Speaking Women
Suite 1020
9841 Airport Boulevard
Los Angeles, California 90045

National League for Nursing
10 Columbus Circle
New York, New York 10019

National Organization for Women
Suite 1615
5 South Wabash Street
Chicago, Illinois 60603

National Welfare Rights Organization
1424 Sixteenth Street, N.W.
Washington, D.C. 20036

National Woman's Party
144 Constitution Avenue, N.E.
Washington, D.C. 20002

National Women's Political Caucus
1921 Pennsylvania Avenue, N.W.
Washington, D.C. 20006

National Women's Studies Association
University of Maryland
College Park, Maryland 20704

New Women Lawyers
c/o Mary Kelly
382 Central Park, W.
New York, New York 10025

North American Indian Women Association
Box 314
Isleta, New Mexico 87022

NOW Legal Defense and Education Fund
1522 Connecticut Avenue, N.W.
Washington, D.C. 20036

Organization for Women Office Workers
c/o Boston YWCA
140 Clarendon Street
Boston, Massachusetts 02116

Professional Women's Caucus
P.O. Box 1057
Radio City Station
New York, New York 10019

Project on the Status and Education of Women
Association of American Colleges
1818 R Street, N.W.
Washington, D.C. 20009

Redstockings
P.O. Box 413
New Paltz, New York 12561

Regional Oral History Office
Bancroft Library
University of California at Berkeley
Berkeley, California 94720

Scientific Manpower Commission
1776 Massachusetts Avenue, N.W.
Washington, D.C. 20036

Sense and Sensibility Collective
57 Ellery Street
Cambridge, Massachusetts 02138

Society of Women Engineers
United Engineering Center
345 East 47th Street
New York, New York 10017

Union Women's Alliance to Gain Equality
2137 Oregon Street
Berkeley, California 94705

Welfare Reform Information Service Community
1420 N Street, N.W.
Washington, D.C. 20005

Woman's Action Alliance
Room 313
370 Lexington Avenue
New York, New York 10017

Womanspace: Feminist Therapy Collective, Inc.
Suite 607
636 Beacon Street
Boston, Massachusetts 02215

Women and Health Roundtable
Suite 403
2000 P Street, N.W.
Washington, D.C. 20036

Women for Change
Zale Building
3000 Diamond Park
Dallas, Texas 75247

Women in Communications
8305-A Shoal Creek Boulevard
Austin, Texas 78758

Women in Transition
4634 Chester Avenue
Philadelphia, Pennsylvania 19143

Women Office Workers (WOW)
P.O. Box 439
Planetarium Station
New York, New York 10024

Women on Words and Images
P.O. Box 2163
Princeton, N.J. 08540

Women's Equity Action League
821 National Press Building
Washington, D.C. 20045

Women's International League for Peace and Freedom
1213 Race Street
Philadelphia, Pennsylvania 19107

Women's Law Project
Suite 1012
112 South Sixteenth Street
Philadelphia, Pennsylvania 19102

Women's Lobby
1345 G Street, S.E.
Washington, D.C. 20003

Women's Musical Collective
188 Second Avenue
New York, New York 10003

Women's National Press Club
National Press Building
Washington, D.C. 20004

Women's Rights Project
American Civil Liberty Union
22 East 40th Street
New York, New York 10016

Women's Sports Foundation
No. 266
1660 South Amphlett Boulevard
San Mateo, California 94402

Women Strike for Peace
No. 709
145 South Thirteenth Street
Philadelphia, Pennsylvania 19107

Women United
Crystal Plaza 1
Suite 805
20001 Jefferson Davis Highway
Arlington, Virginia 22202

Working Conference for Women in Theology
Church Women United
P.O. Box 134
Manhattanville Station
New York, New York 10027

Young Woman's Christian Association
600 Lexington Avenue
New York, New York 10022

Appendix H
PERIODICALS

For a fuller listing of periodicals see entry 1670.

AMAZON: A FEMINIST JOURNAL
2211 East Kenwood Boulevard
Milwaukee, Wisconsin 53211

APHRA: THE FEMINIST LITERARY MAGAZINE
Box 893
Ansonia Station
New York, New York 10023

BIG MAMA RAG: COLORADO WOMAN'S JOURNAL
1724 Gaylord Street
Denver, Colorado 80206

BLACK WOMAN'S LOG: AN INDEPENDENT MONTHLY FOR AND BY BLACK WOMEN
P.O. Box 398
Forest Park Street
Springfield, Massachusetts 01108

BOOTLEGGER
Bootlegger Press
555 29th Street
San Francisco, California 94131

CHRYSALIS: A MAGAZINE FOR WOMEN'S CULTURE
1727 North Spring Street
Los Angeles, California 90012

LA COSECHA: LITERATURA DE LA MUJER CHICANA
Pajarito Publications
2633 Granite, N.W.
Albuquerque, New Mexico 87104

COUNTRY WOMEN
P.O. Box 51
Allison, California 95410

DAUGHTERS OF SARAH
5104 North Christian Street
Chicago, Illinois 60625

ESSENCE: THE MAGAZINE FOR TODAY'S BLACK WOMAN
300 East 42d Street
New York, New York 10016

THE FEMINIST ART JOURNAL
41 Montgomery Place
Brooklyn, New York 11215

Periodicals

THE FEMINIST QUARTERLY JOURNAL
1520 New Hampshire Avenue, N.W.
Washington, D.C. 20036

FEMINIST STUDIES
Women's Studies Program
University of Maryland
College Park, Maryland 20742

FOCUS: A JOURNAL FOR GAY WOMEN
Room 323
419 Boylston Street
Boston, Massachusetts 02116

GRAVIDA
P.O. Box 76
Hartsdale, New York 10530

HERSELF: WOMEN'S COMMUNITY JOURNAL
Suite 200
222 East Liberty Street
Ann Arbor, Michigan 48108

THE LADDER
P.O. Box 5025
Washington Station
Reno, Nevada 89503

MAJORITY REPORT
74 Grove Street
New York, New York 10014

MS.
370 Lexington Avenue
New York, New York 10017

MS. ON SCENE
Alliance of Media Women
12310 Chandler Boulevard
North Hollywood, California 91607

THE NEW DEBORAH
c/o Jean A. Schneider
6914 Dartmouth Street
St. Louis, Missouri 63130

OFF OUR BACKS: A WOMEN'S NEWS JOURNAL
1724 Twentieth Street, N.W.
Washington, D.C. 20009

PAID MY DUES
P.O. Box 6517 #1
Chicago, Illinois 60680

EL POPE FEMINI
Chicana Studies Department
California State University
Berkeley, California 94704

PRIME TIME
264 Piermont Avenue
Piermont, New York 10968

SEX ROLES
Plenum Publishing Company
227 West 17th Street
New York, New York 10011

SIGNS: JOURNAL OF WOMEN IN CULTURE AND SOCIETY
The University of Chicago Press
11030 Langley Avenue
Chicago, Illinois 60628

SOJOURNER: A MAGAZINE OF WOMEN'S WRITING AND VISUAL ART
Sojourner Collective
549 West 52d Street
New York, New York 10019

SPEAKOUT
P.O. Box 6165
Albany, New York 12206

THE SPORTSWOMAN
5599 West Touhy Avenue
Skokie, Illinois 60076

13TH MOON
c/o Ellen Bissert and Kathleen Chodar
30 Seaman Avenue
New York, New York 10034

UP FROM UNDER
339 Lafayette Street
New York, New York 10012

THE VOCAL MAJORITY
Washington D.C. NOW
1424 Sixteenth Street, N.W.
Washington, D.C. 20033

THE WOMAN ACTIVIST
2310 Barbour Road
Falls Church, Virginia 22043

WOMAN BECOMING
6664 Woodwell Street
Pittsburgh, Pennsylvania 15102

WOMANSPACE JOURNAL
11007 Venice Boulevard
Los Angeles, California 90034

THE WOMAN'S PULPIT
3717 Third Street
Des Moines, Iowa 50313

WOMEN: A JOURNAL OF LIBERATION
3028 Greenmount Avenue
Baltimore, Maryland 21218

WOMEN AND ART: A NEWSPAPER QUARTERLY
89 East Broadway
New York, New York 10002

WOMEN AND FILM
P.O. Box 4501
Berkeley, California 94704

WOMEN AND HEALTH
Biological Services Program
State University of New York
College of Old Westbury
Westbury, New York 11568

WOMEN AND LITERATURE
Department of English
Douglass College
Rutgers University
New Brunswick, New Jersey 08903

WOMEN LAWYERS JOURNAL
1155 East 60th Street
Chicago, Illinois 60637

WOMEN'S JOURNAL OF THE ARTS
c/o Jan Oxenberg
School of Arts
California Institute of the Arts
24700 McBean Parkway
Valencia, California 91355

WOMEN'S LAW JOURNAL
P.O. Box 130
308 Westwood Plaza
Los Angeles, California 90024

WOMEN'S LOBBY QUARTERLY: AN ANALYSIS OF LEGISLATION AFFECTING WOMEN
Women's Lobby, Inc.
1345 G Street, S.E.
Washington, D.C. 20003

WOMEN'S RIGHTS LAW REPORTER
Rutgers Law School
180 University Avenue
Newark, New Jersey 07102

WOMEN'S SPORTS
314 Town & Country Village
Palo Alto, California 94301

WOMEN'S STUDIES: AN INTER-DISCIPLINARY JOURNAL
Gordon & Breach, Inc.
440 Park Avenue
New York, New York 10016

WOMEN'S STUDIES ABSTRACTS
P.O. Box 1
Rush, New York 14543

WOMEN'S WORK
Wider Opportunities for Women
1649 K Street, N.W.
Washington, D.C. 20006

WORKING WOMAN MAGAZINE
600 Madison Avenue
New York, New York 10022

Appendix I
PRESSES

For a fuller listing of presses see entry 1670.

Alice Jamesbooks
138 Mount Auburn Street
Cambridge, Massachusetts 02138

American Bibliographical Center--Clio Press
Box 4397
Riviera Campus, 2040 A.P.S.
Santa Barbara, California 93103

Bootlegger Press
555 29th Street
San Francisco, California 94131

Daughters
Plainfield, Vermont 05667

Diana Press
12 West 25th Street
Baltimore, Maryland 21218

Elizabeth Cady Stanton Publishing Co.
5857 Marbury Road
Bethesda, Maryland 20034

The Feminist Press
Box 334
State University of New York
College at Old Westbury
Old Westbury, New York 11590

Les Femmes
231 Adrian Road
Millbrae, California 94030

Glide Publications
330 Ellis Street
San Francisco, California 94102

Human Service Press
Suite 160
4301 Connecticut Avenue, N.W.
Washington, D.C. 20008

KNOW, Inc.
P.O. Box 86031
Pittsburgh, Pennsylvania 15221

Lavender Press
P.O. Box 60206
Chicago, Illinois 60660

Lollipop Power
P.O. Box 1171
Chapel Hill, North Carolina 27514

Mother Jones Press
19 Hawley Street
Northampton, Massachusetts 01060

Presses

New England Free Press
60 Union Square
Somerville, Massachusetts 02143

Pathfinder Press
410 West Street
New York, New York 10014

Scarecrow Press
52 Liberty Street
P.O. Box 656
Metuchen, New Jersey 08840

Sense and Sensibility Collective
57 Ellery Street
Cambridge, Massachusetts 02138

Shameless Hussy Press
P.O. Box 424
San Lorenzo, California 94580

The Violet Press
P.O. Box 398
New York, New York 10009

Times Change Press
62 West Fourteenth Street
New York, New York 10011

Today Publications & News Service
621 National Press Building
Washington, D.C. 20045

Wollstonecraft, Inc.
No. 815
6399 Wilshire Boulevard
Los Angeles, California 90048

Womanpress
Box 59330
Chicago, Illinois 60645

Woman's Soul Publishing
P.O. Box 11646
Milwaukee, Wisconsin 53211

Women's Press Collective
5251 Broadway
Oakland, California 94618

Appendix J
REPRINT HOUSES

AMS Press, Inc.
56 East Thirteenth Street
New York, New York 10003

Arno Press
330 Madison Avenue
New York, New York 10017

Books for Libraries, Inc.
1 Dupont Street
Plainview, New York 11803

Burt Franklin
Lenox Hill Publishing and
Distributing Co.
235 East 44th Street
New York, New York 10017

Corner House Publishers
Green River Road
Williamstown, Massachusetts 01267

Greenwood Press, Inc.
51 Riverside Avenue
Westport, Connecticut 06880

Hyperion Press
45 Riverside Avenue
Westport, Connecticut 16880

Kennikat Press
90 South Bayles Avenue
Port Washington, New York 11050

Kraus Reprint Company
Millwood, New York 10546

Octagon Books
19 Union Square, W.
New York, New York 10003

Source Book Press
185 Madison Avenue
New York, New York 10016

AUTHOR INDEX

This index includes all authors, editors, compilers, translators, and other contributors to the text. It is alphabetized letter by letter, and references are to entry numbers, except where the page is indicated.

A

B

C

D

G

H

I

J

K

L

M

O

P

Q

R

S

T

U

V

W

Y

Z

TITLE INDEX

This index lists all titles mentioned in the text in shortened form, except where the full title is necessary for clarity. The titles of articles, chapters of larger works, and special issues appear in quotation marks. In case of duplicate short titles, the names of the authors are parenthesized, as are the names of the subjects of biographies and autobiographies where the subject is not apparent in the short title. This index is alphabetized letter by letter, references are to entry numbers, except where a page number is indicated.

A

B

C

D

E

F

G

H

I

J

K

L

M

N

O

P

Q

R

S

T

U

V

W

Y

Z

SUBJECT INDEX

This index lists main areas of interest within the text. It is alphabetized letter by letter, and references are to entry numbers. "Av" indicates audiovisual sources.

A

B

D

G

N

O

P

Q

R

S

Y

Z